German Pioneers on the American Frontier

The Wagners in Texas and Illinois

by

Andreas V. Reichstein

University of North Texas Press
Denton, Texas

Printed in the United States of America.

10 9 8 7 6 5 4 3 2 1

Permissions:
University of North Texas Press
P.O. Box 311336
Denton, TX 76203-1336

The paper used in this book meets the minimum requirements of the American National Standard for Permanence of Paper for Printed Library Materials, z39.48.1984. Binding materials have been chosen for durability.

Library of Congress Cataloging-in-Publication Data

Reichstein, Andreas.

German pioneers on the American frontier : the Wagners in Texas and Illinois / Andreas V. Reichstein.

p. cm.

Includes bibliographical references and index.

ISBN 1-57441-134-9 (cloth : alk. paper)

1. Wagner, Wilhelm. 2. Wagner, Julius. 3. Wagner family. 4. German Americans—Biography. 5. Pioneers—Texas—Biography. 6. Texas—Biography. 7. Freeport (Ill.)—Biography. 8. United States—Emigration and immigration—History—19th century. 9. Baden (Germany)—Emigration and immigration—History—19th century. 10. Acculturation—United States—Case studies. I. Title.

E184.G3 R355 2001
304.8'73043'0922—dc21
[B] 2001046468

Design by Angela Schmitt
Cover illustrations of Wilhelm and Julius Wagner care of Wagner family descendants

In loving memory of

Hildegard Kattermann
Hans-Otto Soellner
Paul Guenzel

Contents

List of Illustrations following page 160

Acknowledgments

While writing *The Rise of the Lone Star* in 1981, I found a collection of letters written by various members of a German family, of whom some had moved to Austria and to the United States in the middle of the nineteenth century. I noticed that one of them, Julius Wagner, had emigrated to Texas in 1847. This alone would not have been enough for me to dig any deeper. A large number of Germans had immigrated to the United States during the nineteenth century. What aroused my curiosity, though, was the fact that this Julius Wagner obviously had travelled to Texas with a communistic group, as one letter from his wife Emilie indicated. At that time it was new to me that a communistic group had come to Texas to settle. The first colleagues I asked couldn't help me either. None of them seemed to have heard of such an endeavor. I was getting curious and began my research. It was a long and tedious process, very often interrupted for months, one time even for a few years, because of my job and family situation.

Although it is true for all books that every author is indebted to many people, this study would never have been possible without the continuous help and encouragement of many persons and institutions. The late historian Hildegard Kattermann had in many ways laid the foundation stone for this book by collecting and editing those letters that had survived the destruction of various archives and private homes in Germany in the hands of an Austrian member of the Wagner family during World War II. Dr. Kattermann helped me to establish contact with a relative of hers, Hans-Otto Soellner in Pforzheim, who had owned a jewellery manufacturing company there. For the last years of his life, he shared his knowledge about the Wagner family with me and provided me with various letters, documents, and addresses of descendants of Julius Wagner's brother Wilhelm, who had immigrated to the United States too. Yet, no one knew anything more about Julius Wagner than the fact that he had once been postmaster at Indianola, Texas. No one could tell me if he had any living descendants. This seemed to be the premature end of my study.

Then I contacted Brownson Malsch, whose book on Indianola I had read with great interest. Maybe he had come across the name of Julius Wagner and knew a little more about him. This was not the case but, in another way, this contact was most important. Whether it was simply luck or fate, two years earlier a descendant of Julius Wagner, Paul Guenzel from Chicago, had corresponded with Brownson Malsch. The latter gave me Paul's address and this proved to be the turning point for my study. With Paul's help, I was able to get in contact with this branch of the Wagner family that seemed to have been lost. All those people not only opened their doors to me but also their hearts and shared with me everything they had: old letters, photographs, and memories. Without their help I would never have been able to complete my study.

I am deeply thankful and greatly indebted to Bob and Billie Wagner in Cuero, Texas, to Bob's grand-aunt, the late Juanita Wagner-Dahme, to Harrison Wagner in Austin, Texas, to the brothers Wellford and Hermann Wilms in Topanga, California, and Overland Park, Kansas, who actually found the spot where Julius Wagner's farm once existed, to Paula Zurcher in Aspen, Colorado, who presented me with a few highly valuable letters of Julius' wife Emilie, which she wrote to her parents in Germany, to Mark M. Wagner in San Antonio, Texas, to Mark Wagner in Freeport, Illinois, who provided me with invaluable information on the Wagners and Gunds in Freeport, to his son Eric and the other children of Mark and Susan as well as Susan's sister Marita in Milwaukee, Wisconsin, to Mark's brother Fred in Clinton, Wisconsin, to Peter Kleinpell in Naples, Florida, to Pamela Ritter in Fairfield, Connecticut, to Karl W. Wagner in Bettendorf, Iowa, as well as his sister Edith L. Meier in Davenport, Iowa, to Carl A. Siebel in Düsseldorf, Germany, and to the sisters Alice Weber in Bad Homburg, Germany, Doris Fairweather in Harlow, England, and Ingrid Paterson on the Isle of Harris in Scotland.

Many other individuals helped me enormously gathering and sorting out all the additional information I needed. Most of all I want to thank Jean Andrews (Austin), Megaera Ausman (United States Postal Service, Washington, D.C.), Don E. Carleton (Director of the Center for American History at the University of Texas at Austin), Ralph Elder (assistant director of the Center for American History at the University of Texas at Austin), David Farmer (Director DeGolyer Library, SMU, Dallas), Walter D. Kamphoefner (A&M University, College Station, Texas), John Locascio (Director of the Freeport Public Library), W.M. Von Maszewski (German-Texan Heritage Society), Malcolm D. McLean and his wife Margaret (Georgetown, Texas), Sam Ratcliffe (Head of the Bywaters Special Collections, Hamon Arts Library, SMU, Dallas), William H. Richter (former archivist at the Center for American History at the University of Texas at Austin), Flora von Roeder (Houston), Ron Tyler (Director of the Texas State Historical Association Austin, Texas), Eric C. Welsh (Director of Learning Resources at Highland Community College, Freeport, Illinois), Jeanne R. Willson (Austin), Otto Kissel (Aglasterhausen), Hans-J. Kothe (Isenbüttel), Friedrich Wilhelm von Loewenstein zu Loewenstein (Jesberg), E.S. Schlange-Schöningen (Königswinter), Annelise Ries (Lörrach) as well as my German colleagues and professors Dirk Hoerder (Bremen), Antonius Holtmann (Oldenburg), Detlef Junker (Heidelberg), Andrea Mehrländer (Wittenberg), the late Günter Moltmann (Hamburg), Jörg Nagler (Jena), Ulrike Skorsetz (Jena), Michael Wala, (Erlangen-Nürnberg), and to Hartmut Heinemann from the Hessisches Hauptstaatsarchiv Wiesbaden, who sent me his most valuable article on the so-called Darmstädter group.

Without the most generous support of the following archives and institutions which provided me with precious information, my work would have been impossible to complete: Generallandesarchiv Karlsruhe, Hessisches Hauptstaatsarchiv Wiesbaden, Hessisches Staatsarchiv Darmstadt, Staatsarchiv Freiburg i. Br., Stadtarchiv Freiburg i. Br., Universitätsarchiv Freiburg i. Br., Universitätsarchiv Heidelberg, Fürstlich Leiningensche Verwaltung Amorbach / Odenwald, Archiv der Stadt Boxberg, Stadtverwaltung Bad Dürkheim, Ortsverwaltung Stadt Lörrach, Archiv der Stadt Schopfheim, Archiv der Hansestadt Lübeck, Archiv der Stadt Offenburg, Stadtverwaltung Stadt Oberkirch, Presseamt Landeshauptstadt Düsseldorf, Grund- und Hauptschule Gersbach, Hoffmann von Fallersleben-Gesellschaft e.V. at Wolfsburg, the Texas State Library at Austin, the Rosenberg Library at Galveston, the Newberry Library at Chicago, the Chicago Historical Society, the Illinois Regional Archives Depository at DeKalb (Northern Illinois University), and the Archives of Loyola University in Chicago.

Special thanks go to my friends Manfred Strack and L. Tuffly Ellis who patiently listened to my stories and always encouraged me to continue despite many setbacks. I am also greatly indebted to my friend Arthur Zapf who, on rather short notice, was able to help me out and produce the maps I needed for this book.

I am also highly indebted to Joetta Moltmann who took the time to read the first version of my manuscript and make invaluable suggestions on the form and contents of my study.

Of special importance to me was the generous and continuous help of Rüttger and Gisela Böker and the encouraging support of Renate Reichstein and my mother Barbara Reichstein. I owe all of them a lot and will never forget how much they helped me to finish my study. At this point I also want to appologize to my children Georg and Angelika. They showed great patience with me when I bothered (and bored!) them with all the various stories of my progress.

Last but not least I want to thank my editor Karen DeVinney from University of North Texas Press who was wonderful to work with and who had a vital part in improving the final text of my manuscript.

All these persons did their best in helping me. I can only hope that I forgot no one who needed to be mentioned and do apologise to those who do not find their names here. If there is any mistake in the book, the fault is entirely mine. Yet, I do hope that with this book I can give something back to all those who believed in me and my work.

Andreas Reichstein
Bremen, 2001

Introduction

IMMIGRATION TO THE UNITED STATES has become one of the major fields of study for American historians and sociologists since the 1920s. Numerous scholars on both sides of the Atlantic have covered this topic extensively and examined it from various points of view. Likewise, the immigration of Germans to the States has been the subject of an imposing array of scholarly works. One should not forget that the largest group of non-English speaking immigrants in the nineteenth century came from Germany. In 1847, more than 74,000 Germans reached the shores of the New World; and in 1850 there were nearly 79,000. The largest number came in 1882: 250,630 Germans migrated to the United States during that year. The approaches of social scientists, political scientists, and historians have mainly been either general or individual. The general studies have covered areas like immigration from various German regions and through the different European ports, the economic and social factors of immigration, and the impact of politics on all those who had decided to leave their homelands. The individual approaches have tried to trace the fate of single persons, families, and groups who migrated to the United States. For quite some time, studies about certain individuals concentrated on more or less famous people, persons who received national or even international recognition for what they had accomplished or represented. For the last twenty years, social historians have focused on European, Latin American, and Asian mass immigration to the United States by looking at the reasons for emigration, as well as assimilation in the New World and the incorporation of the various immigrants into the American economy and labor market. By editing and publishing immigrant correspondence, historians have also paid more and more attention to the so-called "ordinary" people. This correspondence generally illustrates the beginning and end of the migration process; it illustrates the hopes and expectations on one side and the realities found by the newcomers on the other.[1]

Looking at the individual who moved to the United States, scholars noted that the process of immigration became manifest either when the immigrant decided to stay permanently or at the moment the respective person gained the citizenship of the United States. According to the melting pot theory, immigrants found a new identity in their new homeland and merged into American society. First formulated by the Frenchman Michel Guillaume Jean de Crèvecoeur in his *Letters from an American Farmer* (published in Philadelphia in 1782), the term "melting pot" came into vogue after President Theodore Roosevelt's enthusiastic reaction to Israel Zangwill's play *The Melting Pot* in 1908. Despite heavy criticism for some years now, the melting pot theory has had and still has numerous adherents.[2] The first question to answer, though, should be when and how the immigrant became an American not in legal terms but in social and cultural ones. When did he or she gain the "feeling" of being an American? Was this a process of giving up one's heritage by blending into an established, dominant society or of bringing in one's cultural background and thus forming a new, different society? A "yes" to the first question would make American society a melting pot; a "yes" to the latter would make it a society in a continuous process of cultural change.

In recent years, social scientists as well as historians have more and more frequently started using the term "acculturation," coined by anthropologists and ethnographers, to describe the process of forming the American society. In general works examining this process they have focused on groups rather than individuals. It seems important, though, to add a detailed analysis of particular immigrants in order to clearly follow the specific process of becoming an American citizen, either by acculturation or assimilation.[3] This is a difficult task because of limited sources. The question of whether this process is confined to the generation of the immigrant or if it is a process spanning more than one generation makes this task even more critical. Very rarely do we have the chance to follow the fate of an immigrant family through several generations. The present volume wants to fill the gap by presenting a case study of two immigrant brothers who migrated to the United States in the first half of the nineteenth century.

In 1981, I came across a collection of transcribed and edited letters in a bound volume called *Familien-Briefe (Family Letters)*. This collection consists of 142 letters on 230 pages, written between 1811 and 1871 by various members of the different Wagner family branches, the Kleinpells, the Wagners, the Beckers, and the Baumanns. The letters had been compiled and edited by the late Wagner family historian, Dr. Hildegard Kattermann in 1977.[4] Two Wagner brothers, Wilhelm and Julius, emigrated to the United States in the first half of the nineteenth century from their German homestate Baden. Julius Wagner came to the United States in 1847 and his elder brother Wilhelm in 1851. While Julius arrived with a group of young idealists to establish Bettina, a communist community in Texas, Wilhelm fled from political oppression and founded the newspaper *Deutsche Zeitung* in Freeport, Illinois, praising the liberties of his new homeland.

Familien-Briefe alone would not have sufficed to recreate the lives of the various members of the Wagner family in the United States. In contrast to Wilhelm Wagner, who wrote many long letters describing the situation he lived in as well as his feelings and beliefs and who used his newspaper to express his political ideas, Julius Wagner wrote only very few and short letters. Only through his wife's very long letters as well as accounts of his fellow travellers who were often prominent enough to have their papers later kept in archives is it possible for us today to retrace his life. At the same time, a considerable number of letters by his relatives mention Julius and discuss his doings and decisions extensively. This—together with unpublished and published sources about the group he went to America with—made it possible to recreate his life. To get an impression of this family's history during the first half of the twentieth century, I had to rely mainly on interviews and pictures that lent authenticity to the stories I heard. The dangers of relying on personal accounts, oral interviews, and individual autobiographies, of course, are evident: the truth about these stories can often not be verified. Therefore, historians have usually criticized the use of private material, "but in these debates about truth and true art, critics overlook the intersection of personal and cultural identities expressed in each text and the contribution popular memories make to historical research."[5] In this context, the historical truth in personal recollections regarding certain dates or minor events is of less importance than the feeling these recollections convey. They tell us a lot about the people, their upbringing, their beliefs, and therefore about their part in each specific story.

The possibility of generalization and general conclusions about assimilation and acculturation is rather limited for this study, however, as the Wagners, being white Protestants, already fulfilled two criteria of the so-called dominant culture in the United States. The only issue which separated them was their language. Questions that arose in the 1960s about the ways gender, class, and race have influenced the process of Americanization can therefore be discussed only to a limited extent. Although class and gender are important issues in the history of the Wagners, race is not. Despite these shortcomings, certain things will become quite clear. The euphoric, oversimplifying approach of Crèvecoeur— "Here individuals of all nations are melted into a new race of men"—and his present-day "disciples" like Arthur M. Schlesinger Jr., who wrote, "The point of America was not to preserve old cultures, but to forge a new *American* culture," might apply to a number of individual immigrants but certainly not to all of them.[6] The simplistic explanation that the immigrants came to America to find a new identity and to merge with an existing society, is questionable because it does not consider the various motives for emigration as well as the social and ethnic conditions of the immigrants. Even a case study like this about a family over the generations might challenge this rather nationalistic approach. The opposition to Crèvecoeur is by no means homogeneous though. Since the 1980s two camps have evolved. Lawrence H. Fuchs and Werner Sollors, for instance, see the United States as a multicultural nation where each group can create its own identity and keep it. Others, like Gwendolyn Mink, Roy Rosenzweig, Lizabeth Cohen, and Irving Howe, emphasize the fact that class and gender have always hindered various individuals and groups from living up to a certain chosen identity.[7] Following this particular line I also want to point out that besides gender and race, the social environment of the immigrants is of equal importance. We will have to see how far the Wagners were influenced by their surroundings. The importance of this in regards to race is emphasized in recent scholarship by authors like Michael Rogin and David R. Roediger among others.[8] Most of these post-modern historians deal with immigration at the turn of the century and the twentieth century. At that time, the immigration pattern was changing as more and more people from eastern Europe, Central and South America and Asia were coming to the United States. The numbers of the "classical" immigrants of the eighteenth and nineteenth century from central and northern Europe were declining. Touching the issues of gender, race, and social environment in regards to German immigrants in the first half of the nineteenth century therefore is a new approach. More than that, the present study does not only and simply look at the immigrants but also explains their past in Germany as well as their motives for emigration and takes a closer look at their descendants and their development in the United States.

The present study follows the family histories of the two American Wagner family branches after the deaths of the immigrants up to the present day, and thus paints a historical panorama. It is not only a history of an immigrant family, though, but also touches on the history of the states of Texas and Illinois. Before writing this study, an important question for me was how to present my findings and conclusions. How far would I be able to draw general conclusions from looking at a single family? Would the tools of the "classical" historian suffice for such an undertaking? I saw myself drawn into the old controversy between the traditional historians of political history and the theorists of social history—a debate that is summed up by Heinrich Rickert, who made a clear distinction between the "cultural" and the natural sciences.[9] In deciding to use every tool and method available, in a way, I followed the ideas of Hobsbawn's "Grassroot History" by writing a sociohistorical study which, at the same time, tries to put the rather personal family events into a larger perspective. Thus I want to demonstrate their relevance for our understanding of the past and the present: "It is not simply to discover the past but to *explain* it, and in doing so to provide a link with the present. . . . What we want to know is *why*, as well as *what*," Hobsbawn wrote.[10]

Tilly once described this combination as a leap from a micro-historical to a macro-historical perspective. Motives, reasons, and conditions of the single actors should be embedded in a structure, a frame that makes the action of the individual possible and, at the same time, regulates it. As much as I apply this to the methods I use, I know that I am part of a cultural frame, too. This makes my perspective and choice of sources highly subjective. Arthur C. Danto has emphasized this in his discussions of the works of Carl G. Hempel. This means that I can try to see structures behind interdependent individual biographies and place them into a general context, yet, at the same time, I have to be aware that I am bound by a historical, sociocultural framework, too. Here again I follow Rickert who argues that the historian discerns patterns based on his own value judgments. This study therefore does not claim to present an objective truth—whatever that may be—but rather to give my interpretation of facts I discovered. As Hayden White pointed out too, I do believe that presenting a complex text in a narrative form implies moralizing judgment and yet, at the same time, I simply want to tell a story. This storytelling, combined with the effort to see structures behind the individual actions, gives this study its form. I believe that this way, the process of immigrants becoming Americans becomes easier to understand and more transparent.[11]

This family saga therefore is more than a colorful history of immigrant families. It demonstrates how ordinary people are connected with those events we all know from history books. In this way, it combines so-called "world history" with the lives of normal people, people who have not found their way into history books. Becoming aware of the fact that it was not only men and women like George Washington, Andrew Jackson, Abraham Lincoln, Jane Addams, Emily Greene Balch, Eleanor Roosevelt, Sam Houston, Stephen F. Austin, and Miriam A. Ferguson alone who contributed to the shaping of the United States, and of states like Texas and Illinois especially, but those men and women who worked hard all day long to make a living, this study is devoted to those unsung heroes and heroines who are the foundation of every society. It is also based on the presumption that every human being, like a small wheel in a gigantic machine, contributes to history in general. No individual leads an isolated life having no effect whatsoever on society. We might not realize the effects of a single life; but all these lives, like small wheels, form units that again influence other units until we have the history of a society. This influence stretches from the example we set for others with our lives to what we teach the next generation. Like Clarence the angel (played by Henry Travers) says in Frank Capra's movie *It's a Wonderful Life* (1946), "Each man's life touches so many other lives, and when he isn't around he leaves an awful hole, doesn't he?" History is created by and reflected in the everyday life of men and women who struggled hard to make a living and who, at the same time, with their influence on future generations, provide us with a fascinating view of a process that only a close look at more than one generation can reveal. Here I take the same approach as, for instance, Stephen Greenblatt, who wrote, "the intensely personal moment . . . is intertwined with the great public crises."[12] To take a look at this "machine" we have to use sociohistorical, cultural-historical and other methods and viewpoints from the various social sciences besides the classic historical approach described by Morton White.[13] Only then does the analysis of the various individual fates allow us a glimpse at a process which becomes visible by looking at more than one generation. For this reason, this study also dwells upon the lives of individuals other than the Wagners to exemplify the important social network and the social interdependence which influence the interaction of all individuals. It would be a gross misunderstanding to think that just a straightforward "family-history" of the Wagners could explain the integration process in American society. After we have seen how the various branches of the Wagner family developed in the United States, we might be able to answer the question of whether they assimilated in the society they found, or if they were part of an acculturation process.

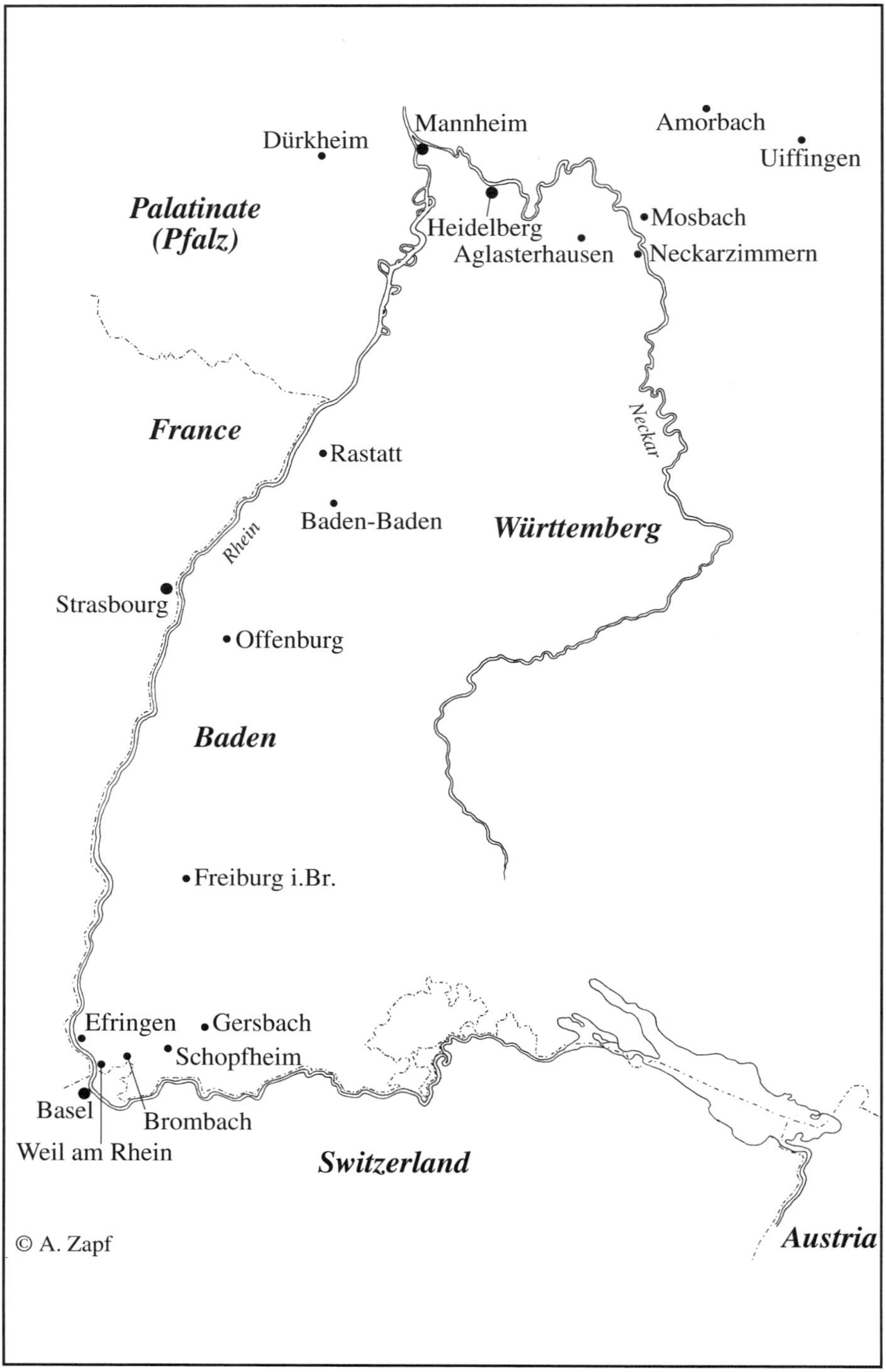
Mannheim
Amorbach
Dürkheim
Uiffingen
Palatinate
(Pfalz)
Heidelberg
Mosbach
Aglasterhausen
Neckarzimmern
France
Neckar
Rastatt
Baden-Baden
Württemberg
Rhein
Strasbourg
Offenburg
Baden
Freiburg i.Br.
Efringen
Gersbach
Schopfheim
Basel
Brombach
Weil am Rhein
Switzerland
© A. Zapf
Austria

1. The Beginning in Germany

JULIUS WAGNER'S FATHER PETER WAS a Protestant pastor, respected and loved by his family and community. Peter Wagner had been born on 26 April 1772, in Dürkheim, then a country town of 2,337 inhabitants. Situated to the west of the Rhine River, Dürkheim, which belongs to Rhein-Pfalz (Palatinate), with its nearly 400 houses, two churches, and the castle of the Dukes of Leiningen, was described as a narrow, angular town embedded in a romantic landscape. Although small and rural in character, it nevertheless was a residential city. Besides the typical business structure of this region, based on craftsmanship like glassworks, tar factories, mills, and rafting as well as agriculture (wheat, grapes, fruit) and stock farming, the prince's court attracted gold- and silversmiths, hatters, wig manufacturers, and small printers. In 1743, Peter Wagner's father Christoph (1719-1771) had moved to Dürkheim from Ruhla in Thüringen where the Wagners originated. They seemed to have been employees of the Protestant church from early times in one way or the other.[1] Peter Wagner attended the Latin school in Dürkheim, where his father had worked as a teacher, then studied theology and became a pastor in 1795. That year Prussia in the peace treaty of Basel conceded all German territory west of the Rhine River to the French emperor Napoleon I, and Dürkheim came under French jurisdiction. Besides being responsible for his parish at Herxheim, Peter Wagner also had to teach the twenty to thirty pupils of the Latin school or *Gymnasium* (the German equivalent of the high school) of Dürkheim—a common combination for a pastor. As the French revolutionary army sacked Dürkheim and forced the local inhabitants to care for its maintenance, the school was closed between 1796 and 1800 due to the lack of funds.

On 3 October 1802, at the age of thirty, Peter Wagner married twenty-one-year-old Luise Wilhelmine Kleinpell, the daughter of Georg Wilhelm Kleinpell, who was *Hofmusikdirektor* (musical director) and *fürstlicher Verwalter* (administrator/superintendent) at the court of the Duke of

Leiningen. The von Leiningens were very fond of music and theater and spent more money on these pastimes than they sometimes could afford. In 1791 for example, their indebtedness of 204,328 *Florin* surpassed their net receipts of 118,223 *Florin* (*Florin* is another word for *Gulden*, which at that time was the equivalent of one-half *Taler* or sixty *Kreuzer* or about forty cents in 1851).[2] The French revolutionary army had destroyed their castle in Dürkheim in 1792 and had forced them to move east of the Rhine River. To compensate them for their losses, Napoleon I granted them an area south of the Main River with 82,000 inhabitants, fifteen villages, and nearly 200 hamlets in 1803. Their residence became Amorbach. As they did not have a permanent residence between 1792 and 1803, most members of this princely household, like Georg Wilhelm Kleinpell and his son-in-law Peter Wagner, had to remain in Dürkheim during that period.

But Peter Wagner could not live and sustain a family on the small fee he received from his parish, and there were three persons to feed, for on 24 September 1803, Luise Wagner gave birth to their first child Wilhelm. Therefore, on 27 October 1803, he asked for his dismissal. This was granted, and he was given the position of a *fürstlicher Hofkaplan* (court chaplain) at Amorbach, which included the education of the local youth in Latin, Greek, and Hebrew at the elementary school. This new job was not any easier than the earlier one. For one thing the pay was not very high: Peter Wagner received 400 *Florin* as well as ten *Malter* of grain, ten *Malter* of spelt (*Malter* is an old German grain measurement that was the equivalent of 150 liters in Baden between 1810 and 1871) and five *Klafter* of wood annually (*Klafter* is a cord; one *Klafter* firewood was the equivalent of 2.97 cubic yards in Baden between 1810 and 1871). At those times it was customary to pay public officials in cash *and* natural products. The other problem was the locals. They had to provide these natural products as payment for Peter Wagner but were unreliable as far as the delivery of wood and grain was concerned.

The part of the Odenwald to which Amorbach belonged was a rather poor area, and the people did not have enough for themselves, let alone for the officials like Peter Wagner. Agriculture and craftsmanship were the main sources of sustenance for the 1,611 inhabitants. Amorbach was smaller than Dürkheim and consisted of 243 houses. Most men were craftsmen, not only working in Amorbach but also serving the many small hamlets nearby. The meadows, farmland, vineyards, and gardens belonging to Amorbach were too small to feed its inhabitants, though. Bad harvests and the war against France had increased the economic misery of this region. Not only did the citizens of Amorbach not have enough money, but many were highly indebted. Only the tanners could still be considered well-off. The rest were poor, and one-third of Amorbach was even destitute. The city itself had debts of 14,911 *Florin.* This situation improved between 1803 and 1806 when the court of the von Leiningens with its administrative body and its small army of more than 400 men moved into Amorbach, and the small village became a residential town. For three years Amorbach experienced a sort of economic boom. Streets were widened, and new, impressive buildings were erected. After the Duke of Leiningen lost his sovereignty in 1806, however, the economic situation again worsened. This is illustrated by the fact that Peter Wagner and his colleague, Professor Walter, desperately asked the Duke of Leiningen for firewood to heat the schoolrooms in December 1808, as well as for a room into which they could lock it. Otherwise the locals might steal this wood. This wish was granted.[3]

Here Wagner and his colleague were fortunate, as the duke had to cope with severe problems. After Napoleon's victory over Austria at Austerlitz on 2 December 1805, the Austrian Emperor Franz II not only lost his south German possessions, he also eventually abdicated as German Emperor on 6 August 1806. On 12 July 1806, Napoleon had created a new political order for the southwest of Germany by putting into effect the *Rheinbund* (Rhine Confederation) which he presided over as protector. Thus, Württemberg became an independent kingdom and Baden an independent Grand Duchy under Grand Duke Karl Friedrich von Baden. This meant that a number of formerly independent dukes and barons, like the Dukes of Fürstenberg, Hohenlohe, Thurn und Taxis, and Leiningen, lost their sovereignty. Especially powerful and important dukes like Fürstenberg and Leiningen did not get over their degradation easily. They not only lost political power and influence, they also lost many sources of considerable income.[4] All of this seemed to have put too much strain on the eighty-two-year-old Duke Karl Friedrich Wilhelm von Leiningen. He died on 9 January 1807.

On 30 April 1807, Peter Wagner asked the new Duke of Leiningen, Emich Karl, to be rewarded for his twelve years of service as a teacher. His wish was granted, and he was appointed second director of the Latin school at Amorbach in addition to his position as court chaplain. These years were hard on him as he had to teach religion, Latin, Greek, Hebrew, philosophy, mathematics, "popular" geometry, writing, arts, and natural history. Each week the five to ten pupils had to write two German and two Latin tests. In addition to this he had to give private lessons to the Duke's children and history lessons to the Duchess. Whenever he went to the castle he had to wear a powdered wig, breeches, and silk stockings. All of this became too much for Peter Wagner, and he asked to be transferred again. He wanted to be a simple pastor with a parish.[5] Thus, in 1810 he moved to Uiffingen, about twenty-five miles away from Amorbach.

Again, life proved to be hard. Uiffingen was a very small village. In 1815, only 498 inhabitants were counted: 419 of them Lutheran, seventy-one Catholic and eight Reformed Protestants. The Protestant church, *die alte Wehrkirche,* was in extremely bad condition and nearly falling apart. The main problem, though, was the lack of funds to build a new one. Peter Wagner asked the Count of Löwenstein-Wertheim for help, as he was partially responsible for Uiffingen. The count hesitated. In 1813, Peter Wagner complained about the highly dangerous condition of the church, and Mayor Hohnickel wrote that the church tower was deteriorating rapidly. One night in August 1813 some enraged citizens spontaneously tore down the tower. Since it was impossible now to hold services in the church, they were held in the council chamber of Uiffingen, although the room was much too small for this parish. In the winter of 1813-14 Peter Wagner wrote that no service was held without some members of his parish fainting. Being jammed in the crowd, they didn't get enough air. These persons had to be carried away. In the summer this situation would only worsen. The parties had to go to court, and it wasn't until 15 January 1817, that the verdict was pronounced: Count Wertheim had to pay for the choir, the tower, the pulpit, and the vestry. The parish had to raise the money for the rest of the building. But it wasn't until 1819 that the Protestants of Uiffingen consecrated their new church.[6] By that time though, Peter Wagner was moving again.

The church building did not pose the only problem Peter Wagner had to face in Uiffingen. The vicarage turned out to be dark and damp. Everyone knew that this place was not a healthy one. Besides, Peter Wagner had to share it with the Catholic teacher who also worked as the local registrar and in addition increased his small income by running a small store in the vicarage. Although the teacher eventually moved out, life was not any easier for the Wagners. The salary was less than in Amorbach, and the family had grown there: Karl was born on 12 August 1805, and Luise on 23 May 1808. Three more children were born in Uiffingen: Auguste on 3 March 1813, Julius on 30 December 1816, and Henriette on 6 April 1818. Peter Wagner's salary consisted of *accidenzien* (fees for his official duties like twenty *Kronen* for a baptism and a marriage, one *Florin* plus thirty *Kronen* for a funeral and one *Florin* for a marriage certificate[7]) and whatever the small meadows, vineyard, fields, and woods belonging to the poor parish yielded for him. As this was not enough to sustain a family with six children, he had to fall back upon the small inheritance he had received and kept for hard times.

None of this, however, affected Peter Wagner's positive outlook on life. Everyone praised him as an affectionate father and husband and as a devoted shepherd of his parish's flock. He was quite famous for smoking his beloved pipe while working in his study. Whenever a child was born, he stepped to the cradle and, with a twinkle in his eyes, produced a small smoke ring over the child's head to "make the baby fit for life," as he put it humorously. His wife Luise was an ideal partner for him. Not only did she work hard farming the vicarage's lands (a job Peter Wagner was not so fond of), she also showed great enthusiasm in running a house open to interesting and interested people. Not common in those days, she demonstrated a great interest in politics and was never afraid to speak openly. She detested *Junker* (country noblemen) and especially Otto von Bismarck in her later days. The ideals of enlightenment, liberty, justice, and equality for all as foundation stones for society (as the United States and France had put into practice only years before) had found their way into the Wagner household and replaced absolutism. The Wagners were loyal and law-abiding citizens; but they spoke out against injustice and encouraged those who fought for more democracy and rights for everybody. They lived in times that fostered hopes for a new, better, and more tolerant society. In 1783, Margrave Karl Friedrich of Baden (who was later to become Archduke) abolished bondage in his territories. His subjects loved him not only for that, but also because he believed in legal equality for everybody and in religious tolerance. Under his guidance, the union between the Lutheran and the Reformed Church was achieved on 28 October 1821. Thus, with the liberal constitution of Baden from 1818 and the Protestant Union (which is still valid today in Baden) in 1821, the southwest of Germany experienced a sort of political "spring" that was also nourished by the new consciousness of national unity in the Napoleonic era.[8]

In 1814 Peter Wagner asked for additional firewood and in 1817, for two additional *Malter* of spelt as they had nothing left from what the vicarage had yielded that year. The region of Uiffingen was a poor one. To add to this more or less miserable situation, the "hunger years" 1816 and 1817 lay heavily upon the residents of Uiffingen and upon many parts of the Odenwald. The summer of 1816 had been extremely wet, and the crops (potatoes, wheat, and turnips) had rotted in the fields. Hailstorms and early snow did the rest. This led to an enormous increase in prices. A loaf of bread weighing six pounds had cost twelve *Kreuzer* in February 1816, but before the year was out it cost thirty *Kreuzer*. By July 1817, the price had risen to fifty *Kreuzer*. Hunger was knocking on many doors. The government of Baden realized that not only crop failures were responsible for a general poverty but also the system of feudal dues which meant double taxation. It took many years, however, until this system was changed.[9] After 1817 the harvests were better, and the economic situation of this region improved. But between 1814 and 1817 it was still so difficult that both requests of Peter Wagner were denied to him; he was told that harvest had begun already, and prices were sinking for that reason. It had been nice to work only as a pastor for a parish, but raising a family under these conditions simply was asking too much from him. Therefore, he looked for a new position once again.

In 1818, he applied for the rich parish of Allmannsweier. He explained that the income from his parish and vicarage in Uiffingen had been extremely overrated officially during the past eight years. His family, therefore, had suffered from many deficiencies. He did not get the rich parish but the one in Aglasterhausen instead. It was not too far away from Amorbach, yet better off than the former parish because it was bigger. He was chosen for this job from among eight competitors, not only because his superiors thought well of him, but also because he was highly recommended by the Duchess of Kent, born Marie Luise Viktoria von

Sachsen-Coburg-Saalfeld and widow of the Duke Emich Karl von Leiningen (who had died on 4 July 1814, at the age of only fifty-one years). On 17 October 1819, Wagner was introduced to his two new parishes: Aglasterhausen and Bargen. The small village of Aglasterhausen with its 681 inhabitants in 1820[10] was located in a part of the hilly Odenwald which was blessed with fertile soil. Bargen was only a hamlet southeast from Aglasterhausen, and Peter Wagner used to get there on horseback in about two hours. This time he was more fortunate with the vicarage, built in 1756 by the Catholic monastery of St. Peter Wimpfen. Its roof and some barns had been renovated in 1804 and 1819. Before the Wagners moved in, 232 *Gulden* were invested to build five new pigsties and to repair the wash-house, among other things. In addition to the usual natural products he received as part of his income, he was entitled to 6,438 *Gläser* wine yearly (ten *Gläser* came to one *Mass* which was the equivalent to nearly two liters). All this wine was not meant for him and his family alone, however. The servants and hired hands serving on the farmland of the vicarage received their share, too. The wine also caused problems. It was not always delivered on time. Some years it was so sour the servants became literally ill and at other times Peter Wagner had to fetch it himself in places some miles away. Finally, he asked to receive money in compensation for the wine. This wish was granted to him in 1836. Although this new position did not prove to be heaven on earth, Peter Wagner managed to get along. He was able to afford a good education for his children. Thus his youngest son Julius was sent to the *Lyceum* (old expression for *Gymnasium*) in Mannheim. There they hoped the young boy would learn to face the demands of life and his responsibilities.

Through all the letters among the various family members and their friends, the loving care among the Wagners is conspicuous. They tried to see the good and positive in every member of the family and acted accordingly. But all of this could not hide the carelessness and the happy-go-lucky attitude that Julius Wagner showed occasionally from early times. He was drawn to the sunny side of life, to entertainment, to wealthy and influential people, to all kinds of enjoyment. He neglected his schoolwork.

By 1836, his family was worried, especially as Julius' behavior was in sharp contrast to that of the rest of the Wagners. Various *Visitationsberichte* (inspection reports) mention that Peter Wagner was opposed to card games, inebriation, luxury, and other worldly pleasures in his parish. He spoke out against too much pomp at weddings and baptisms and agitated for early closing hours in the local bars. The different confessions were living together in harmony, and his church was so clean, neat, and friendly that it was pleasant to be in it.[11] Julius' oldest brother Wilhelm had followed his father's footsteps and was already a devoted clergyman. The next brother, Karl, was beginning to make good money as *Bergrat* (counselor of mines) in Mariazell, Austria. His oldest sister Luise had married Friedrich Jakob Becker who was a Protestant pastor in Neckarzimmern. In addition to all that, Peter Wagner turned sixty-four in April 1836. Although he was still quite healthy, and praised by his superiors for his ardor and vigor, nobody could foresee how old he would become considering the hard rural life of the nineteenth century. Julius had two more years to go to school, and then it was decided that he would study at the university like his two brothers.

In 1834, Julius made the acquaintance of Carl Baumann who had been born on 22 March 1816, in Heidelberg, as the illegitimate son of the Benedictine monk, Adalbert Bachmann (born as Georg Adam Bachmann) and Maria Catharina Karr. Both boys attended the *Lyceum* in Mannheim. Soon they became close friends, and from time to time, Julius invited Carl to his family's home at Aglasterhausen over the weekend. The Wagners kept an open house for friends and welcomed the new face. Wilhelm especially took to Carl, who had already decided to become a schoolteacher. A favorite pastime of the boys was hiking through the woods of the Katzenbuckel, a mountain in the Odenwald. Nearly the same age, Carl was able to finish school three years ahead of Julius, who found it hard to concentrate and did not show the necessary perseverance in doing his homework. This worried the whole Wagner family, and Wilhelm urged his new friend Carl to help Julius and remind him of his obligations. Various family letters also indicate that despite his often irresponsible manners and his seemingly happy-go-lucky attitudes towards life, Julius seemed to harbor deep in his heart feelings of despair, and a lack of self-confidence. Wilhelm especially sensed this and asked Carl over and over again to look after his younger brother, and to lend him a hand whenever needed.[12]

The friends and fellow pupils of Julius did not see the gloomy side of his character, however. Judging by his health, his height (he was taller than his brothers) and strength, they gave him the nickname, "Icebear." On 7

November 1838, Julius Wagner matriculated as student No. 254 at the University of Heidelberg to study law.[13] He also joined the *Guestphalia* (also spelled as *Westfalen*) fraternity and soon became a respected member of this group. This fraternity was a *Corps* and thus not as nationalistic as the *Burschenschaften* fraternities. To identify each other easily in public, the members of each fraternity wore small ribbons with different colors. Those of the *Guestphalia* were green, black, and white and their motto was "gloria virtutis comes" ("fame is the companion of true manhood"). As is still customary today, each of the fraternities had its own house where the members could live and/or gather for social events. The one belonging to the *Guestphalia* in Heidelberg was located in the Hirschgasse, just below the castle. It was destroyed by a fire after World War II and is a modern hotel today. In this house the members of the fraternity had their *Kneipe* (in colloquial German this word means "inn," but in the language of the fraternities this word meant and still means "beer party"), their *Commers* (a festive form of beer party with many traditional fraternity songs that Julius Wagner was especially fond of) and their *Mensur* (fraternity duels with swords or sabers).[14] Julius spent a lot of time at that house in the Hirschgasse. The Perkeo became his favorite pub in downtown Heidelberg.

As a member of the *Guestphalia*, Julius became acquainted with members of the nobility and even achieved friendly terms with one or another, like the Baron von Berlichingen. Soon he climbed the social ladder in his *Corps*. On 10 August 1839, he became a *Corps-Bursch*, a full member of the fraternity and on 4 November 1840, he was appointed "X" or *Erst-Chargierte*, which meant he presided over the various social meetings, especially the *Kommers,* and represented the *Corps* officially in public. When Fritz Reuter came to Heidelberg in November 1840 to study law, he became *Con-Kneipant* (apprentice) of the *Guestphalia* under Julius Wagner. Wagner, Reuter, and von Berlichingen were known as inseparable friends who used to visit the Perkeo frequently.[15] Fritz Reuter, who later became one of the most prominent North German authors of his time, was a frequent guest at the Wagner house in Aglasterhausen. He even painted the only existing portrait of Julius Wagner. On 9 November 1841, Julius was made an honorary member for life of the *Guestphalia.*

Julius studied law for eight semesters and left the University of Heidelberg at the end of the 1842 summer term. He had finished his studies, but he had not taken his exams yet. In those days the state exam in law was administered in Karlsruhe only. After four years of study, most students were able to take their exams right away, but Julius had to work hard to prepare himself for the final exam in Karlsruhe. Not only had he not studied seriously in Heidelberg, he had heaped up quite a large amount of debt for which his family had to stand. At the end of his four years in Heidelberg, Julius' debts totaled 280 *Florin*. Considering the fact that his father Peter received 1,272 *Florin* and 44 *Kronen* in cash annually, one can imagine how much money Julius had spent to keep up with his noble friends! The family did not complain. On the contrary, they all tried to extenuate his conduct and to play down weak points in his character. In a letter to his son Karl in Austria, Peter Wagner wrote on 1 December 1842 that Julius had left the university and was preparing for his final exam. Peter wrote that Julius was loved and respected by his fellow students as well as by his teachers, that he was now a *Senior* in his fraternity and had a lot of contact with noblemen as well as rich people and worked with great zeal to make up for his earlier idleness: "if only he never has to regret the long term of four years and the great sacrifices we and his brothers and sisters had to make during this time."[16]

What Julius actually did between January 1843 and April 1846 is extremely difficult to ascertain today. Most private or official papers pertaining to those years are lost. On the one hand various family members, especially Henriette Wagner, pointed out in their letters that Julius was preparing hard for his law exam; on the other hand he does not seem to have been able to pull himself together to take the final step. Instead, he was in constant need of money. Henriette, who had fallen in love with Carl Bauman the first moment he came into their home in Aglasterhausen, had married the young schoolteacher on 26 April 1843. She tried to sustain her brother as best as she could by sending money whenever possible and paying for his clothes and other necessities. Julius moved from place to place. He spent some time in 1842-43 with his sister Luise and her husband, the pastor Friedrich Jacob Becker, in Neckarzimmern, later lived at the house of his sister Henriette in Offenburg, and met his future wife in Freiburg in 1844. In addition to his studies in Heidelberg, Julius, still determined to pass his exams, seemed to have studied law in Freiburg i. Br. in 1844-45. There he met Karl

Richard Schneider who studied law, too, and passed his exam in Karlsruhe on 14 June 1845, with distinction. Schneider was then enrolled as *Rechtspraktikant* (probationer)[17] and later became *Oberlandesgerichts-präsident*, a highly renowned judge. Karl introduced Julius to his older sister Emilie Marie who had been born on 6 May 1820, in Ettlingen. They fell in love right away, but they had to hide their feelings as Emilie had already been promised to a young physician. Her father, the physician and *Geheimer Hofrat* Dr. Peter Josef Schneider, strongly approved of the union between his daughter and his young colleague. Julius, therefore, only informed his brother Wilhelm and his friend and brother-in-law Carl Baumann about the woman he loved and wanted to marry.

Finally, in autumn of 1845, Julius must have plucked up all his courage and took the state law exams in Karlsruhe. Having studied hard, he was sure to pass his exams easily. After the tests, his examiners expressed satisfaction and Julius went to Offenburg, where Emilie still lived with her parents, to find himself a position as *Praktikant*. When the results finally came, and Julius learned that he had failed, he broke down and cried. His mother and father tried to comfort him and encouraged their son to take the exams again in 1846.[18] Julius spent the next months learning, most of the time at the home of his brother-in-law Friedrich Becker in Neckarzimmern where he hiked in the woods of the Odenwald and visited his friends in Heidelberg.

Very likely it was in Heidelberg that he first heard of the so-called *Adelsverein*, the *Verein zum Schutze deutscher Einwanderer in Texas* (Society for the Protection of German Immigrants in Texas). Julius might have also heard about the activities of this society during his time in Freiburg, when in 1845 Oberlieutenant Adolf von Göler had spoken with a lot of students and families and had convinced them to settle on the land of the *Adelsverein* in Texas.[19] Additionally, a variety of German newspapers had reported about the activities of the *Adelsverein* and run numerous ads to attract potential settlers between 1844 and 1846. The turning point in Julius Wagner's life, though, came in 1846 when Prince Solms-Braunfels inspired students and their friends in Heidelberg, Darmstadt, and Gießen with his enthusiastic speeches about life in Texas.

What exactly brought the *Adelsverein* together cannot be determined today. In April 1842, a number of German noblemen and officers met at the castle Biebrich near Mainz (which belonged to the reigning Archduke of Nassau) under the guidance of Count Carl von Castell to discuss how they could possibly provide a remedy for the social misery in various parts of Germany. This situation, brought about by increasing unemployment, rising prices, and only marginal wage raises became known as *Pauperismus*.[20] An additional reason for the existing misery seemed to be overpopulation. Therefore, the idea of forming a society to help emigration came naturally to them. Most likely they modeled their *Verein* after the English New Zealand Company. Texas seemed to be the ideal country for this enterprise not only because of the many inspiring books and articles on this part of the world, but also because the young Republic could offer much more favorable conditions to immigrants than the United States. Thus, on 20 April 1842, the twenty noblemen present founded the *Adelsverein*: "We, the undersigned, hereby make known that we have today constituted ourselves as a society for the purpose of purchasing lands in the Republic of Texas."[21] As true sons of Romanticism, these noblemen were guided not only by pure altruism and care for those they reigned over but also by the romantic goal of spreading German culture, strengthening the German element and the German way of life throughout the world. Besides four reigning dukes and princes, the family of the von Leiningens was represented twice in the *Adelsverein*: Duke Karl Friedrich Wilhelm Emich von Leiningen, the employer of Peter Wagner, and Count Viktor von Alt-Leiningen-Westerburg. After some ups and downs in April 1844 the Society named Prince Carl von Solms-Braunfels commissioner-general for the colonial establishment in Texas and established itself formally as a joint-stock company in Wiesbaden. It had proven to be highly difficult to get land on reasonable conditions for potential settlers in Texas on the one hand, and on the other to find enough financial and political support for their society in Germany. Additionally, the members of the society (who never numbered more than twenty-four) made numerous mistakes, as they were too credulous and had virtually no experience with colonization. Finally, in June 1844, Prince Solms-Braunfels was able to acquire an interest in the Fisher-Miller Land Grant, and on 30 December 1845, Fisher and Miller sold their rights in this grant to the *Adelsverein*.[22] Now they had land they could settle people on, but this land lay in the heart of Texas and was still Indian territory.

Thus they faced three problems: the land was not easily accessible, the Comanches living there were hostile towards the white man, and the *Adelsverein* had to settle this land with 600 families by 1849 or they would lose any right to it.

After Christmas of 1846, Julius Wagner made his decision: he stopped studying for his final law exam and joined the *Darmstädter* group that was determined to begin with their project of settling in the New World soon. But fearing discussions in his family, Julius kept his decision a secret. Nobody in his family knew what he was up to. Louis Reinhardt, a gardener from Darmstadt, remembered how he got involved in this enterprise:

> Prince Solms had been in Texas as early as 1844, and his accounts, as well as those of Spiess, in writings and speeches caused a sensation among the students of the universities of Giessen and Heidelberg. Solms also made a speech to the students of the industrial school (*Gewerbeschule*) in Darmstadt, where I was studying, and his extravagant descriptions made the students mad. He remarked that there was no demand in the old country for all the professional men whom the universities were turning out, and that they must find a new and developing country where their services would be in demand. He glowingly described Texas as a land of milk and honey, of perennial flowers, of crystal streams rich and fruitful beyond measure, where roamed myriads of deer and buffalo, while the primeval forests abounded in wild fowl of every kind.[23]

In what way Julius Wagner came to join the *Darmstädter* exactly can no longer be determined. It is highly possible, however, that he met with members through his fraternity activities and social life. Gustav Schleicher (a civil engineer who was born 1 November 1823, in Darmstadt), Dr. Ferdinand von Herff (already a famous physician), Hermann Spiess (a forester from Sprendlingen), Adam Vogt (a forester candidate from Lehrbach), August Lerch (an architect), Jakob Küchler (a forester from Schöllenbach), Wilhelm Friedrich (a forester from Griedel), and Theodor Schleuning (a law student from Darmstadt) were members of the Corps *Starkenburgia*. Like them, Julius Wagner was fond of duels and of singing.

Corps student von Herff fought twenty duels with cavalry blades and ordinary sabers and the police of Bonn had arrested him once during his student days for singing loudly in the early hours of the morning on the streets of that city.

Soon, five men emerged as the guiding spirits of this group: Gustav Schleicher, Ferdinand von Herff, Hermann Spiess, Friedrich Schenk (a forester from Darmstadt) and Julius Wagner.[24] Outwardly the *Darmstädter* (or *Gesellschaft der Vierziger*—Society of the Forty—as they were called sometimes, too, because of their number), were represented by Spiess and von Herff who had originally founded this group seven years earlier. Their first idea had been to establish a German colony in Wisconsin or Iowa, but contact with the *Adelsverein* made Spiess and von Herff change their plans. Von Herff and Spiess met the secretary of the *Adelsverein* as a result of the action of Dr. Heinrich Künzel. The editor of the highly popular magazine *Der deutsche Auswanderer* (The German Emigrant) Künzel had told Dr. Ernst Grosse, the secretary of the *Adelsverein,* about this group of promising young men and their plans of migration. One should not be astonished that Künzel knew about this group, as he was a teacher at the *Höhere Gewerbeschule* (industrial highschool) at Darmstadt, too. A great number of the *Darmstädter,* like Wilhelm Friedrich, Christian Hesse, Jakob Küchler, August Lerch, Louis Reinhardt, and Gustav Schleicher, had been students of this institution. Grosse had been a highly idealistic student once himself, having delivered a flaming speech on nationalistic ideals at the student gathering *Hambacher Fest* in 1832. He later became a journalist and was hired by the Count of Castell in March 1846, to fight against criticism in the press. He hastened to deliver a formal invitation to Spiess and von Herff from the Count of Castell to visit the latter in Wiesbaden. On 28 January 1847, the two young men met with the count in the presence of Dr. Künzel and Dr. Grosse. Soon the two *Darmstädter* were convinced to settle in Texas with the help of the *Adelsverein*. The first step had been taken. Now it was time for the second one: the other members of the Forty had to be convinced that Texas was a better place for immigration than Wisconsin. Dr. Grosse was especially nervous and excited during the heated discussions of the Forty on 2 February 1847. At the end of a long day, though, the members agreed to follow von Herff's and Spiess' recommendation and go to Texas, even though eight members were strongly opposed to this change of plans.[25] Once again, Spiess had proven that he was a born leader.

Born around 1818 in Offenbach (Hessen-Darmstadt), Hermann Spiess became acquainted with von Herff as a fellow pupil during their time at the *Gymnasium* of Darmstadt where they both took their *Abitur* (final exam) in 1838. Hermann's brother Adolf was a famous teacher in Switzerland with many contacts with liberals and had also been a tutor to the young Prince Solms-Braunfels. In 1842, having passed his exams in natural science at the University of Giessen, Hermann Spiess first spent some time in Paris and then entered the service for the woods and forests commission in Darmstadt. In the spring of 1845, Spiess took a leave of absence and traveled through the United States for nearly two years. From New York, via Milwaukee, New Orleans, and Galveston, he came to New Braunfels and encountered the efforts of the *Adelsverein* to settle Germans on Texas soil. Spiess returned to Germany in 1846. In his *Corps* he met with his old friend von Herff again. Ferdinand Karl von Herff was born in Darmstadt (Hessen) on 29 November 1820. His father, Christian Samuel von Herff, a judge at the Supreme Court of Hesse-Darmstadt, had married Eleonora Meusebach, the sister of Karl Hartwig Gregor von Meusebach, who, in turn, was the father of Ottfried Hans von Meusebach, one of the most prominent German colonizers in Texas.[26] After leaving school in 1838, von Herff attended the University of Bonn for two years and the University of Berlin for an additional two years. Fulfilling the requirements of the law at that time (which asked the student to take his final medical exams at his home university), he returned to Giessen and received his degree in medicine in March 1843. He was appointed surgeon in the Hessian army, and by 1846 he had already become known for his brilliant surgical work.

During his time in Bonn, he had met and befriended the illustrious naturalist, statesman, and explorer Alexander von Humboldt and had been introduced to Prince Albert, the future husband of Queen Victoria.[27] Like Meusebach, von Herff thus became part of a social circle of idealists. When Ottfried von Meusebach's father Karl had been transferred from Koblenz to Berlin to become *Geheimer Oberrevisionsrat* (president of the Court of Review) in 1819, the professors Jacob and Wilhelm Grimm became frequent guests of the house. The Grimm brothers, who published the great dictionary *Deutsches Wörterbuch* in 1854 and are remembered worldwide today for their collection of fairy tales, became close friends of the older Meusebach.[28] In 1838, Ottfried was appointed assistant judge in Berlin. In his father's home, he became acquainted with Bettina von Arnim, who had visited the famous German writer, poet, and statesman Johann Wolfgang von Goethe with her mother when she was a child. Later she had started a remarkable correspondence with Goethe that was published with the help of the older Meusebach in 1835.[29] Bettina von Arnim introduced Ottfried to this "Berlin Circle" that included men like Alexander and Wilhelm von Humboldt, the famous modern military tactician General Carl von Clausewitz, the philosopher Georg Friedrich Wilhelm Hegel, and the poets Adalbert von Chamisso and Hoffmann von Fallersleben.

The importance of this circle and others does not rest in the fact that some noble people and artists met socially, but in the ideas they discussed. These ideas became the the intellectual ground for the *Darmstädter* group. They spread and established the common basis for Meusebach, Herff, Spiess, Schenk, and Julius Wagner. They were the same ideas that were discussed in the Wagner household in Aglasterhausen. Napoleon I had liberated the various German peoples from the reign of the numerous autocratic dukes, barons, and earls as well as from the dominion of church rule by creating the German states that still exist today, such as Baden, Württemberg, Pfalz (the Palatinate), and the Saarland. In doing this, Napoleon had abolished most of the petty principalities of Germany that had prevented German unification and religious and political freedom. In the *Befreiungskriege* (wars of liberation) the Germans, especially the students (and mainly those organized in fraternities), put these new liberties to the test by fighting against Napoleon to gain liberty from his foreign domination. It was a political springtime for students and intellectuals who hoped for democratic political reforms. But all of this was ruined by the restoration brought about by the Vienna Congress in 1815 and the politics of Clemens Lothar Wenzel Duke of Metternich, the Austrian chancellor. He formed the so-called "Holy Alliance" between Austria, Prussia, and Russia. The main purpose of this alliance was to restore the monarchies and the old order. This, of course, was in opposition to the ideas of a united Germany, of democracy and of political freedom for all Germans. The German students started to rebel by first organizing themselves into the *Allgemeine Deutsche Burschenschaft* (General German Fraternity) in Jena in 1815. Then, after years of growing stronger and gaining more confidence, they demonstrated their refusal to accept a reinstitution of the old, undemocratic, authoritarian governments at the so-called "Hambacher Fest" on 27 May 1832, with 30,000 participants calling for unity and political freedom.[30] Political freedom bespoke liberty for all. Bettina von Arnim happily quoted one of her favorite authors, Alexis Charles Henri de Tocqueville: "Politics should be directed to the happiness of the little man."[31] The more these young people discussed the grievances of their times, the more radical they became. As the old political system became more and more despicable, they looked for new and better forms of society. The ideas of a young man named Karl Marx, who had begun to startle young European intellectuals with his philosophical writings, were discussed widely. In 1848 he would change the world by publishing the *Communist Manifesto* with his friend Friedrich Engels.

Von Herff, Spiess, Schenk, and Wagner belonged to these young "radicals" who loved to engage in endless discussions. Sooner or later though, they got tired of their conversations as they realized that talking alone would change nothing. They had talked so much about emigrating to the United States already and about the new society they wanted to help establish there, that now it was time for some action. They began to think about putting their ideas into practice. The idea of a classless society, where all property and all means of production were owned by the community without any interference by an authoritarian government, had appealed to people for a long time. Many utopias had been described in literature like Thomas More's *Utopia*. Julius Wagner and his friends were fond of a new French novel that expressed their desire for creating a better world in which to live. It is highly possible that Spiess brought the book with him after his first visit to Paris in 1842. The French author, Étienne Cabet, had published his philosophical novel *Voyage en Icarie, roman philosophique et social* in Paris in 1840. He described a communistic, philanthropical, idyllic community where all men were not only equal but also shared all possessions and owned nothing individually. He also called for a propaganda organization, "for an expedient and efficient distribution of the communistic ideas." In this context it is important to define the word "communistic."

"The term *communism* frightens people. Instead of connoting community sharing and happy cooperation, the word suggests terrorism, gulags, and Soviet activities designed to embarrass or damage the Western world."[32] Actually the idea of communism is much older than the Soviet Union and even Karl Marx. Two revolutions in Europe in the eighteenth century established this new idea of a better form of society: the French and the Industrial Revolution. The latter began in Britain around 1780 and the former nine years later. Child labor, bad living and working conditions, and the increasing poverty among the working class as results of the worst aspect of the Industrial Revolution brought about critics of the system who would become the fathers of socialism and communism. Robert Owen (1771-1858) had inherited a textile factory in Scotland in 1799 and had turned it into a model social institution. Later he founded a communistic settlement, "New Harmony," in the United States and became one of the most important British socialists.[33] His work had a lasting impact on Cabet, who had met Owen in 1834 after choosing exile in Great Britain instead of two years imprisonment because of his political activities. In the aftermath of the French Revolution, after the Jacobin Reign of Terror (1793-1794) had been followed by a conservative reaction, certain people wanted to complete the revolution by seizing all personal wealth and by generalizing equality. The leader of this group, which called itself the "Conspiracy of Equals," was François Noel Babeuf (1760-1797). Since Babeuf was the first one to advocate the abolition of private property rather than its fairer distribution he is generally considered the father of socialism and communism. His *Manifeste des plébéiens* published on 30 November 1795, had considerable influence on Cabet. Like all these men, Cabet used the word "communism" to describe their special form of socialism: they all wanted to abolish property and distribute all means of production to everybody by reforming society. As the word "communism" derives from the Latin word "communis," which can be translated "joint, common, together," these men can all be called communists by their standards. Yet Karl Marx and Friedrich Engels denounced all these socialists and early communists as dreamers and utopians. They argued vehemently that Owen, Cabet, Babeuf, Charles Fourier, and Henri de St. Simon did not see the inherent class antagonism between workers and the exploiting employers, who were the owners of all means of production. No reform could cure this impropriety, only revolution, Marx and Engels declared. Their way of defining communism led to our understanding of this philosophy. But

Étienne Cabet saw this class antagonism. He believed that only reforms and model societies, which he wanted to establish in America like his mentor Owen, could bring about a communistic society, not a bloody revolution. And he also believed in centralism: "Centralization is the principle, the foundation, the soul, the strength and the life of the Community. For Communists especially, this must be the ABC of all social doctrine and all propaganda."[34]

Cabet, who also expressed his idealistic ideas of a communistic society in his Sunday magazine *Le Populaire*, founded a group called "Communistes Icariens," and in 1847 published his intentions to migrate to Texas where he wanted to create an "icarien" colony on the banks of the Red River. His plans were known in Germany, too:

> The well-known communist Cabet in Paris is thinking about organizing a large-scale immigration to Texas. He wants to unite one million disciples of communism, to sail with them to America and establish his "Ikarien" in a remote area, "that hasn't been reached by civilization and the corruption of our times yet." He claims to have gathered over 100,000 participants already and wants to start his enterprise next spring. The question is, though, whether one million communists can be found in Europe and if they all would want to emigrate.[35]

America in general and Texas especially had inspired young German idealists for years. With his romantic description of Texas and the heroic deeds of the Texans in their struggle for independence, Charles Sealsfield (the pen name of Carl Magnus Postl) had pointed the way for those who were looking for a better place to live. His book, *Das Cajütenbuch oder nationale Charakteristiken* (The Cabin Book or National Characteristics) was first published anonymously in two volumes in Zürich in 1841. The novel was received with great enthusiasm. Prominent critics like Arnold Ruge (1803-1880) wrote:

> The German genius could not escape from liberties grown boggy and the historical lethargy brought about by political catholicism other than by migrating to the empire of freedom and struggles for

> liberty; and yearning we follow him with our eyes, being content and happy when he returns some times later from the far away land—liberated and enriched. This will be a definite sign that it was not his fault that our literature and poetry is falling behind those of the English and French but the fault of the suffocating atmosphere of our fatherland.[36]

Others had described Texas as a country overflowing with milk and honey; but Carl Magnus Postl, the son of a Bohemian farmer, writing as Charles Sealsfield, had pointed the way for idealists. He asked: "Why do we love America? Because she makes us love Freedom for the whole human race, and stands for the progress of all civilization."[37]

Alexander Büchner, the brother of the famous German author and playwright Georg Büchner, was in close contact with the *Darmstädter* group, as Darmstadt was his hometown. He accompanied them when they met at the newly opened hotel Köhler in the Rheinstrasse at the west end of Darmstadt nearly every evening, bent over maps and involved in heated discussions about the necessary supplies they believed they needed. In fact, they acquired some rifles and ammunition. In his memoirs, Büchner, who did not believe in the ideas and ideals of this group, described them rather ironically as a bunch of very naive young men, who spent most of their time at the *Trinkstube* (bar) of the hotel, consuming lots of *Grog* (a drink consisting of hot water, sugar and rum):

> What tasted even more like it [America] was Grog, which they drank every night with great zeal, as they thought they had to practice drinking. To be able to drink Grog seemed to be the primary requirement for living in the free West. The docility of our Texans in this matter was truly astounding but—although they made considerable progress—they remained in the bar of the hotel during nights quite often in a recumbent or prone position. They called this preparation for their life in the camp and that was it![38]

Julius Wagner and his friends knew , however, that their communistic "touch" would probably alienate the leading men of the *Adelsverein*. This was true, indeed, as the secretary of the *Adelsverein*, Dr. Ernst Grosse, had written to the Count von Castell in 1846: "the governments are afraid of the ghost of communism (which is growing alarmingly) . . . and as all governments are highly embarrassed by pauperism and emigration they are admittedly even more afraid of communism. . . ."[39] For this reason they did not use the word "communistic" to describe their projected settlement in public while they were still in Germany. They decided that Spiess and von Herff should carry their petition for land in Texas to Prince Solms-Braunfels as those two young men had the best public standing. After having stated their request for land in Texas and for help by the *Adelsverein* in letters to Count Carl von Castell, Spiess and von Herff met with Prince Solms-Braunfels in Darmstadt on 5 February 1847. They talked for over two hours and left a highly favorable impression with the Prince. Spiess, especially, impressed him. The Prince wrote that his "ideas about colonization are reasonable and correct."

Spiess asked the Prince to speed up their request for a contract with the Count von Castell. Solms-Braunfels had already checked the list of the proposed immigrants with his confidant, *Justizrath* (counselor) Dr. Winter from Darmstadt, and could report to the Count von Castell on 5 February 1847, that most of the young men were known for their respectability and were highly recommended for this enterprise. "There is nobody on the list who wants to leave because of any folly or other despicable deeds and most of them either own a good fortune or are expecting to inherit one."[40] This was an important remark, intended to soothe von Castell and his noble companions. Rich immigrants would not complain if they discovered that things were not adequately prepared for them in Texas. This had been the case in 1844 when the first 150 immigrants had followed the invitation of the *Adelsverein* and realized on their arrival in Texas that Prince Solms, as representative of the *Adelsverein,* could provide them neither with the promised tools for farming and construction nor with any means of transportation to their land on the Fisher-Miller grant. Nearly the same happened with the over 4,000 new settlers who came to Texas on thirty boats in the winter of 1845-46. As nothing had been prepared for them, more than 800 died of diseases in the severe winter of 1846. This left the *Adelsverein* with a bad reputation in Texas. In Germany, the press had watched the first steps of the *Adelsverein* more or less positively, but by now more and more critical reports and articles had appeared.[41]

Consequently, only very few people approached the society to migrate with its help after 1846. The *Adelsverein* was quite happy about the *Darmstädter* group. They needed the good publicity that they hoped to receive from the successful settlement by the Forty. They also hoped for the stimulating effect the Forty would have on the settlements of the *Adelsverein* already in Texas and eventually on other would-be emigrants. When Spiess presented the Count of Castell with an eight-page paper on the views and goals of his group a few days later in order to speed up procedures, the latter felt obliged to accept it.

Spiess was smart enough to use exactly the arrogant language of a messianic elite that the society of noblemen would understand, because they used it themselves all the time. He talked about setting an example for other emigrants. Therefore, their group consisted only of young men who had passed their exams and already proven themselves in life. This of course was a gross exaggeration as quite a few of them were still students. Their objective of keeping up the *Deutschthum* (German spirit/culture/tradition) by establishing their colony in Texas would prove to be of general historical importance one day, Spiess continued to write. And Texas provided enough space to grant asylum for the proletarian masses especially.[42] This was the only hint in Spiess' paper at the communistic ideas the group harbored. Some of those young men who appeared in those papers or on the list the Count von Castell had had checked, like the rich landowner and architect Carl Matheus Ducassé from Heppenheim and the pharmacist Alexander Schue from Biedenkopf, did not go to Texas with the Forty. Both belonged to the group that opposed the idea of going to Texas and had voted against it on the meeting on 5 February. Ducassé and Schue stuck to their original plan and moved to the northern part of the United States a little later.

The Count von Castell, Hermann Spiess, and Ferdinand von Herff signed a contract in Wiesbaden on 11 February 1847, which promised the group of up to fifty settlers free transport on ten two-wheel ox carts from Galveston (their port of arrival) to their land, free food until their first harvest, 320 acres of free land of their own choice on the grant of the *Adelsverein* for everyone and free tools and material for farming and construction for every settler. To guarantee every one of the *Darmstädter* a place for living in Texas, this group was given 500 acres of land on the grant land of the *Adelsverein*, wherever they choose, for free: either near the Pedernales

River, or the Nassau Farm, or New Braunfels. In case the settlement plans failed, another 500 acres would be given this group for free. As additional guarantee for the settlers, the society granted the *Darmstädter* group, represented by Spiess and von Herff, a credit of 30,000 *Florin*. Gustav Dresel from Geisenheim, then general agent or representative of the society in Texas, was to travel to Texas with Spiess and von Herff in advance of the settlers to prepare everything for the arrival of the rest of the *Darmstädters*. The *Adelsverein* paid the travel expenses for Herff and Spiess (though not for the rest of the group) and granted them free provisions, Spiess until the first harvest and von Herff for one year. Von Herff on the other hand agreed to provide free medical care for the settlers. Both men guaranteed to do all in their power to foster colonization on the land of the *Adelsverein*. The contract also stated in § 5 that the group of the Forty under the leadership of Spiess and von Herff was independent from the *Adelsverein* and therefore not under the control of the society's officials in Texas. The *Verein* only organized the immigration itself. The sole obligation towards the society was a report Spiess and von Herff had to write for the director of the *Adelsverein* in Wiesbaden every three months. In case of the deaths of Spiess and von Herff, Gustav Schleicher and Fritz Schenck would take their places. In its preamble, the contract stated that originally Spiess and von Herff had had the intention of establishing a German settlement with some fifty friends in Wisconsin or Iowa. The contract stated that after lengthy conversations with the Count von Castell, they had changed their plans and decided to form a settlement in Texas instead. Spiess and von Herff were not bound to the number of fifty members of their party, of course, but their number should be at least thirty. According to § 6, Spiess and von Herff were allowed to enlist other German immigrants to join them. Only a number of 600 settlers or more would constitute a right for the Forty to settle permanently on the land of the *Adelsverein* legally.[43]
This enterprise attracted attention among all classes of society in Hessen. For one thing, quite a few of the young men were sons of respected and well-known civil cervants in that German State, like Christian Hesse, whose father then was the *Präsident* (speaker) of the *2. Kammer* (a kind of House of Commons) in the parliament of the Grand Duchy of Hesse. And for another, the press covered the activities of the *Darmstädter* extensively. Some articles mentioned that this project might cast a favorable light on

the *Adelsverein*, which had been criticized in the past for appearing as an exclusive venture of the nobility with little popularity and little contact with the common man. It was also emphasized that the young men around Spiess and von Herff were giving up most promising careers and the safety of their families in order to "pick up the spade and show the world what German power and German culture are able to perform once they are freed from the bounds of Old Europe!"[44]

On 21 February 1847, the young men threw an *Abschieds-Kommers*, a *Corps* farewell party for Spiess, von Herff, and Dresel in the house of Dresel's father at Geisenheim, west of Mainz on the Rhine River. Besides Spiess, Gustav Dresel (1818-1848), a friend of Gustav Schleicher, was the only one who had considerable experience with living in the United States, and especially in Texas. In 1837 he had sailed to the United States and one year later arrived in Houston where he got himself a job as salesman and bookkeeper. He traveled through Texas extensively and kept a diary about his journeys that was published after his death. In 1842, he returned to Germany. At that time, his father, the highly respected wine merchant and liberal politician Karl Johann Dietrich Dresel, accommodated the famous German poet, professor, and vigorous revolutionary August Heinrich Hoffmann von Fallersleben who had already written poems about Texas and was at present wanted by the police for his highly critical political poems "Politische Lieder." His best known poem today is the German national anthem, "Deutschland, Deutschland über alles." Since he was such a prominent admirer of Texas, the *Adelsverein* desperately tried to enlist Fallersleben and on 6 November 1846, Dr. Grosse had presented him with a gift deed for 300 acres signed by the Count von Castell. Fallersleben actually thought about emigrating to Texas, but he had fallen in love with Elvira Détroit who successfully talked him out of this plan. Hoffmann von Fallersleben arrived at Dresel's house on January 5 and was present at the farewell party. Other guests included Schleicher, Schenk, and most of the other *Darmstädters*, as well as the general agent for Germany of the *Adelsverein*, Settegast von Bieberich, Eberhard Soherr von Bingen, and the painter Müller. All in all, there were thirty-seven persons present. On this occasion, Hoffmann von Fallersleben wrote a farewell song for those men of the Forty who were to leave the next day and dedicated it especially to Gustav Dresel:

Leb wohl! Leb wohl! zwar hielte gerne
Dich unsre Liebe hier zurück -
Du willst, und ziehest in die Ferne:
Des Menschen Will' ist auch sein Glück.

Du siehst dort viel, was hier uns fehlet;
Was wir erstreben, ist dort schon!
Was hier uns ängstet, drückt und quälet,
Ist dort gemildert, ist entfloh'n.

Wenn Dich umspielt der Freiheit Oden
Auf Texas blumigen Prärie'n,
Dann denk, daß wir auf unserm Boden
Der Freiheit Blume auch erzieh'n.

Wir wollen gleiche Recht' und Pflichten,
Wir wollen keinen Herrn und Knecht,
Auf Vorrecht, Stand und Rang verzichten,
Wir wollen Freiheit, Ehr' und Recht.

O denk an uns und unser Streben -
Schon strahlt der Zukunft Sonnenschein!
Frei ist auch unser Thun und Leben -
Es lohnt ein Deutscher noch zu sein!

Und wenn von Deutschland frohe Kunde
Einst dringt zu Dir nach Texas hin,
Dann ruf in dieser schönen Stunde:
"Wohl mir, daß ich ein Deutscher bin!

"Das sind die Rebenberge wieder!
Das ist des Rheines grüner Strand!
Heil dir, du Land der Freud' und Lieder!
Mein Vaterland, mein Heimatland!"

Farewell! Farewell! Although our love
would want to hold you here -
You want to move far away:
Men's will can be his fortune too.

There you see much which we here miss;
What we aspire to, is there already!
What frightens, tortures us here still,
Is better there, is even gone.

When you listen to the songs of freedom
On Texas' prairies full of flowers,
Remember please, that we on this our soil
Are cultivating freedom's blossoms too.

Equal rights and duties we want to see,
No master and no slave shall be,
We want to renounce privileges and classes,
We want freedom, honor and justice.

Oh think of us and our efforts -
the future's sun already shines on us!
Free are our actions and our lives -
It still is worthwhile being German!

And when one day the happy message
from Germany arrives in Texas,
Then cry out loud in this most happy hour:
"How wonderful, that I'm a German

"There are the vine hills all again!
And there the green shore of the Rhine!
Hail to you, you land of joy and songs!

"My fatherland, my homeland!" [trans. by author]

Spiess, von Herff, and Dresel left Geisenheim on 22 February on a steamboat for St. Goar. There they parted from their fellow members in tears and set off for London where they presented their credentials signed by Dr. Heinrich Künzel, one of the most prominent emigration experts of his times, to the Prussian ambassador in London, Carl Josias von Bunsen. Von Bunsen had not only shown considerable interest in creating a German colony on former Mexican territory but since 1840 had also undertaken several efforts to realize such plans. They finally arrived in New York in April 1847. They did not sail directly to Texas, however, because Spiess wanted to pay a visit to the bank of Schuchardt and Gebhardt first. This banking house had helped him by arranging for a place near Milwaukee, where the *Darmstädter* had wanted to settle originally. Spiess had been able to make this arrangement through Ludwig Schuchardt, the brother of the bank's owner and the husband of Spiess' sister, Marie. From New York they sailed to Galveston, with one stop in New Orleans. Von Herff then went to Indianola, Texas, to wait for the rest of the group, while Spiess traveled to New Braunfels to arrange everything necessary there. The latter carried with him two letters from Count von Castell to Ottfried von Meusebach, who since his arrival in Texas in May 1845 as Commissioner-General of the Society for the Protection of German Immigrants in Texas, had dropped his noble title of a baron and called himself John O. Meusebach. The first letter introduced Spiess, von Herff, and Dresel and described their plan to settle on the land of the *Adelsverein*. The second one was a sharp and highly critical reply to Meusebach's last two letters in which he had requested $80,000.[46]

Both letters clearly stated, however, that the settlement project of the *Darmstädter* group was of the highest importance for the German society. Running out of funds and credibility, the German noblemen were anxiously hoping and praying for the success of Spiess, von Herff and their friends. A successful *Darmstädter* settlement could turn the tide for the *Adelsverein*: "when their colony is successful, a stream of emigrants will undoubtedly flow into Texas which will make the price of our lands rise." It was not only speculation in land that guided Count von Castell, however. The *Adelsverein* feared the competition of another society that was about to constitute itself: the *Nationalverein für deutsche Auswanderung und Ansiedlung*. Although this new society was to meet on 3 March 1847, in the large hall of the hotel Darmstädter Hof to discuss its articles and to establish itself officially, it was already known some months before that Dr. Heinrich Künzel, editor of the magazine *Der Deutsche Auswanderer*, wanted to found a national society for German emigration and colonization together with some friends. It was obvious that this would not only be a rival organization to the *Adelsverein*, but most likely its final deathblow too. As Künzel was such a well-known and respected expert on questions of emigration, the society of noblemen had tried to embrace him and his organization for quite some time. Castell wrote to Meusebach:

> Mr. Spiess, Herff, and Dresel will tell you something about the prevailing opinion in Germany. There is a strong movement for emigration at the moment, and a national society has constituted itself that will join us, if we are successful with our settlement. Then we will have enough money, and everything will look magnificent. Therefore, it is of the utmost importance that the colonization project of Mr. Spiess be successful, because only then they will join us.[47]

The society desperately hoped for a successful colonization by the *Darmstädter* group. They needed it. That is why all members of the *Adelsverein* voted to accept the treaty with the Forty on their general assembly on 15 and 16 of June 1847, after a heated debate. A lot of shareholders complained about the credit of over 30,000 *Florin* the society had given the emigrants. They knew that the society's financial situation was desperate, but the Forty on the other hand presented the last chance for survival of the *Adelsverein*. This situation was also understood by the young emigrants. Public opinion equaling support, the group found it necessary to publish a declaration before their departure at the end of March. There, Wilhelm Friedrich, Fritz Schenck, and Gustav Schleicher, representing the whole group, told the readers of the *Der Deutsche Auswanderer* that they had chosen Texas because only there could they establish a community which would maintain Germany's national characteristics, its language, and customs. The *Adelsverein* had given them strong and unconditional support. Hermann Spiess had gained considerable knowledge about the land they wanted to settle in; and if former colonization projects had failed, it had been because of bad management and weak leadership. The *Darmstädter* group promised to inform the German public about their progress regularly and only asked for the blessing of their fellow countrymen.[48] Yet they did not convey their ideas by means of newspaper articles alone. In the beginning of 1847, Schenk wrote a poem, "Der Herr und seine Vögel" (The Master and His Birds). In the disguise of a fable about birds leaving their cages to fly over the ocean and settle in a new land, he described the political and social situation in Baden at that time and presented the goals of the Forty. These goals were also fixed in a paper the young men drew up before their departure. Unfortunately, this paper is lost. All we know today is that they committed themselves to five years of working together, that their project was of model character, and that the next group of friends, brides, and relatives should follow them as soon as the fall of 1847.[49] They were ready for an adventure; they were positive about its success.

Julius Wagner had told nobody in his family about his plans to go to Texas. In complete secrecy he left the state of Baden and went to Mainz. There he met with the others of the group. On Good Friday of 1847, which was 2 April, the Forty parted from their friends and families who shed many a tear, waved, and shouted "Hurrah!" from the quayside. They boarded the steamboat *Prinzessin von Preussen* in Mainz that took them down the Rhine River to Cologne. From there they took the train to Hamburg, where they arrived on 6 April, as their departure was scheduled for 8 April. At this north German port city they had to wait for several weeks, however, as their ship, the *St. Pauli*, had to discharge its old cargo first. Ships did not always run on schedule in those days, and the vessel that belonged to the shipping company of Schroeder und Co. was no exception. And it was not only the fault of the company. The Forty had their share in prolonging their stay in Hamburg too, as they did not travel lightly. It took awhile to load their luggage, which weighed 6,000 kilograms and also included all parts and tools to build a windmill. Every member of the group was equipped with three double-barreled guns, pistols, and other weapons to meet the challenges of the wilderness. They had a little trouble with the fifteen dogs they took on board too, as an additional fee had to be paid for the animals. The *Darmstädter* actually appeared to be more like a hunting party than a group of emigrants. On 26 April they set sail for their new homeland. At the beginning they did not have favorable winds. Instead of reaching the Channel between France and England in two days, it took them eight days to sail the North Sea. Reaching the channel, the *St. Pauli* encountered a fierce storm that forced them to cross between Dover and Calais several times. Even after the storm had settled down, the weather did not improve very much. Captain Boljahn therefore cast anchor at Deal, today a small port city north of Dover, but at that time the main harbor town of southeast England. Many ships that wanted to cross the channel or pass through it used to be provisioned there with fresh vegetables, meat, water, flour, and whatever else they needed for their voyage. On 28 May, the *St. Pauli* set sail again and began her voyage over the Atlantic Ocean. After thirty-eight days that passed by in the usual monotony and troublesomeness—only three passengers were spared the notorious seasickness—the German immigrants landed at the port of Galveston, Texas, on 4 July 1847. It was Independence Day, and the celebrations must have seemed like a very special welcome to the newly arrived. Julius Wagner and his friends had reached their destination. Full of hope and the best intentions, they faced an uncertain future.[50]

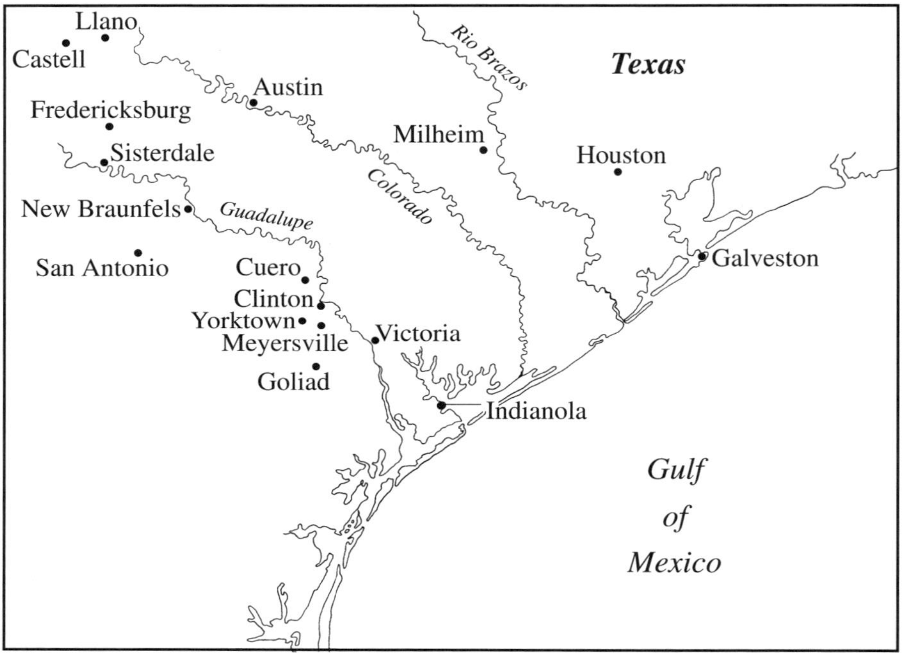
Llano
Castell
Fredericksburg
Sisterdale
New Braunfels
San Antonio
Austin
Rio Brazos
Texas
Milheim
Houston
Colorado
Guadalupe
Cuero
Clinton
Yorktown
Meyersville
Goliad
Victoria
Indianola
Galveston
Gulf
of
Mexico

2. Life on the Texas Frontier

THE *DARMSTÄDTER* GROUP WAS VERY happy to be on solid ground again. Von Herff had rented quarters at a small hotel, the William Tell, run by John Henry Coers, a Swiss immigrant. The William Tell on Market Street between 22nd and 23rd Streets was one of nine hotels Galveston had at that time. Whereas the most prominent one, the Tremont House, still exists (although in a different location), the William Tell went out of business at the end of the 1860s. Having been originally erected by Peter J. Menard, the first postmaster of Galveston in 1838 and brother of Galveston's founder Michael Menard, as the conspicuous Yellow House it soon became a hotel, was then changed into a store and in 1875 gave place to a substantial business house.

Now the young men from Germany waited for their schooner to be repaired. It would carry them to the harbor closest to their next destination, New Braunfels, where Spiess was supposed to have arranged everything for their journey. This harbor was Indian Point at Lavaca Bay, a small town consisting of about fifteen wooden houses. Whether Indian Point was the same place as Carlshafen (Carl's Harbor), as many Germans called this landing place, or another small settlement situated a few miles northwest from Carlshafen cannot be ascertained any more. Many people, including the *Adelsverein* itself, believed that Carlshafen and Indian Point were one and the same place, but other sources indicate that the two were separate establishments. In 1849, the name Indian Point was changed to Indianola.[1]

Many in Galveston looked sceptically upon the young Germans. Hardly one of them could speak English, and their enthusiasm seemed to be in sharp contrast with the experience of those Germans who had come before with the help of the *Adelsverein*. Had the *Darmstädters* only consisted of students and university graduates like Julius Wagner, this might well have been the case. Yet all kinds of professionals and craftsmen were members of this group, too. It is nearly impossible today to determine exactly who belonged to the *Darmstädters* originally. The earliest list, composed by Spiess and written about the time when he first thought of going to Texas, mentions twenty-one persons. Only eleven of them went to Texas: Backofen, Friedrich, von Herff, Küchler, Lerch, Louis, Müller, Schleicher, Schulz, Spiess, and Vogt. With the exception of von Herff and Spiess who had sailed in advance but are listed here nevertheless, those who had set out from Mainz for Hamburg, most likely included:

1) Ernst Otto Amelung an architect or lawyer from Darmstadt
2) Heinrich Backofen, maker of musical instruments from Darmstadt (1804–1872)
3) Peter Bub, farmer from Heppenheim
4) Adam Deichert (blacksmith from Kronau);
5) Christoph Flach, overseer of a foundry and mechanic in Michelstadt (b. 1826, d. after 1894)
6) Wilhelm Friedrich, lawyer from Griedel
7) Georg Gerlach, saddler from Darmstadt
8) Adolph Hahn, lieutenant of artillery from Darmstadt (b. circa 1825, d 1848)
9) Dr. Ferdinand von Herff, physician from Darmstadt (1820–1912)
10) Christian von Hesse, law student from Darmstadt (1825–1893)
11) Johannes Hörner, carpenter from Heppenheim (1829–1917)
12) Louis Kappelhof, ship carpenter from Hamburg
13) Adam Koeppel, chemist, pharmacist from Wörrstadt (1801–1849)
14) Jakob Küchler, forester from Schöffenbach (1823–1893)
15) Friedrich Louis, forester from Eulbach (d. 1860)
16) Christian Michel, cooper and brewer from Babenhausen
17) Franz Mördes, law student from Mannheim (1822–1866)
18) Eduard Müller, economist from Staaden (d. 1906)
19) Peter Neff, carpenter from Heppenheim
20) Philipp Neff, butcher from Heppenheim
21) Jakob Obert, farmer from Sulzbach
22) Louis Reinhardt, gardener from Darmstadt
23) Friedrich Schenk, forester from Darmstadt (1820–1875)
24) Gustav Schleicher, civil engineer from Darmstadt
25) Theodor Schleuning, law student from Darmstadt (1826–1894)

26) Leopold Schulz, bookseller from Darmstadt
27) Anton Schunk, maker of musical instruments from Heppenheim
28) Hermann Spiess, forester from Offenbach
29) August Strauss, mechanic from Darmstadt
30) Adam Vogt, forester from Lehrbach (b. circa 1822, d. 1883)
31) Julius Wagner, lawyer from Aglasterhausen
32) Karl Wundt, economist, lawyer from Laudenbach
33) Franz Zentner, tanner from Heppenheim
34) Philipp Zöller, carpenter, architect from Darmstadt

These were the names and professions given by the group itself to the magazine *Der Deutsche Auswanderer* on the day of their departure at Mainz. Exact passenger lists for Hamburg and Galveston do not exist for that time. In 1894, Adolf Paul Weber in his book *Deutsche Pioniere—zur Geschichte des Deutschthums in Texas* gives the names of thirty-three immigrants. He does not mention Gerlach, Mördes, and Schunk but adds Lerch and Kattmann. In 1899, Louis Reinhardt was interviewed by Rudolph Kleberg, who published the reminiscences of this member of the *Darmstädter* group in the *Quarterly of the Texas State Historical Association.* Reinhardt remembered all the names with the exception of Gerlach, Hörner, Kappel, Mördes, Obert, and Zentner but gives other names instead: Lerch, Fuchs, Herrman, Lindheimer, Ottmer, Mertins, and Rock.[2] As Gerlach is mentioned neither by Weber nor by Reinhardt and is not listed by Chester and Ethel Geue in their compilation of German immigrants coming to Texas between 1844-1847[3], the assumption seems to be justified that he probably never boarded the *St. Pauli* but stayed in Hamburg or maybe even returned home to Darmstadt. Rudolf Fuchs might have joined the group at Fredericksburg, but no details are known about him. He certainly did not come to Galveston from Hamburg with the others. Instead, a Miss Julie Herf from Baden (not related to Dr. von Herff) had joined the men in Hamburg. Although Reinhardt and Weber do not mention Anton Schunk and Franz Mördes, various letters prove they did come to Texas with the others.[4] The architect August Lerch from Darmstadt (who died in 1866) and the lawyer Dr. Heinrich Kattmann from Frankfurt (b. 1815, d. after 1875) arrived with the others on the *St. Pauli* in Galveston on 4 July 1847. They had either joined the Forty in Hamburg or boarded the ship later.

Four persons mentioned by Reinhardt could not be traced after checking all the available documents: Fuchs, Herrman, Ottmer, and Mertins. They might have come earlier or later to Texas, and Reinhardt probably mixed up the dates. Reinhardt might not have remembered the names of Mertins and Ottmer exactly, considering the fact that his interview with Kleberg took place more than fifty years after the events. The name of Ottmer might be Obert, not only because of the similar sound pattern but also because of the similarity in professions: Obert was a farmer and, according to Reinhardt, Ottmer was a miller. The same goes for Mertins who might have been Mördes. Mertins is listed by Reinhardt as a student of theology, whereas Mördes was a student of law. August Vogelsang, a former *Leibjäger* (a hunter, serving as a kind of personal bodyguard) of the King of Hannover, joined the Forty at Galveston; the Canadian, Rock, who ran into them at Victoria and Ferdinand Lindheimer, whom Reinhardt recollected belonged to their group, had nothing to do with them originally. He had already come to the United States in 1834 and had joined the Texan army in 1836.[5] The Austrian, Blaudeck, who had become a member of the Forty at Galveston, left them at New Braunfels. The group called the Forty that started out from Galveston, therefore, consisted most likely of: Amelung, Backofen, Bub, Deichert, Flach, Friedrich, Hahn, Herf, von Herff, Hesse, Hörner, Kappelhof, Kattmann, Koeppel, Küchler, Lerch, Louis, Michel, Mördes, Müller, the brothers Peter and Philipp Neff, Obert, Reinhardt, Rock, Schenk, Schleicher, Schleuning, Schulz, Schunk, Spiess, Strauss, Vogelsang, Vogt, Wagner, Wundt, Zentner, and Zöller, which makes thirty-eight members of the Forty or *Darmstädter.*

Most of the newcomers enjoyed their stay in Galveston:

> As far as Galveston is concerned, I must confess I had a wrong image of that town. I always thought it was a rotten hole. But this is not the case. In the short time of its existence Galveston has improved considerably. There are now nearly 6,000 inhabitants who live in considerable wealth. There are no beggars. Trade is flourishing, and would the harbor be suitable for big ships, this port would become as important as New Orleans. The only thing I don't like is that out of ten inhabitants nine possess two to four slaves, who have to do the hard work. One can see really beautiful

> farms; splendid houses situated in gardens where figs and other tropical fruits grow in abundance. Farming is most satisfactory; cattle is on the pasture night and day; many a farmer doesn't know even how much cattle he owns. Hogs roam around the streets in the hundreds and they multiply like sand at the sea.[6]

This description was not an exaggeration. Between 1836 and 1850, Galveston was the commercial, shipping, financial, and cultural center of Texas. During that time it was not only the largest port of Texas, but also its biggest city. Sources indicate that during 1847 alone, 8,000 Germans arrived there. Many of them settled in Galveston directly, making up a fourth to a half of the total population before the Civil War. The census of 1850 indicates that 1,088 persons out of a total population of 4,117 in Galveston were of German origin. Whereas the city with its several churches, schools, and warehouses, its avenues, residential homes, and gardens provided a pleasant sight, the surroundings of Galveston were not so appealing: "Grass grows in shabby abundance on heaps of shell dust. Several swamps spread evil odor. There are no wooded sections."[7]

Many of the Forty, like Eduard Müller, Theodor Schleuning, Friedrich Schenck, and Julius Wagner, wrote letters to their families in Germany from Galveston. Julius Wagner's letter must have been a big relief for his family and prompted his love Emilie to tell her parents about their relationship, which she had previously kept a secret:

> The news of Julius' arrival made all of us happy. Emilie Schneider, the fiancée of Julius, was here lately and felt reassured and happy by this news, too. Her relationship with Julius is known to her parents now; after a tough argument with her father, where her pure heart, the power of love and her just claim stood by her side, everything is fine now. Her father shows a tacit understanding, while her mother demonstrates consent and affection. Her description of this quarrel made us see clearly once more how well-advised our Julius will be to let Emilie move into his home.[8]

After two weeks, the group received notice that they could board their schooner *Lavinia*. As they were about to do so, however, the United States

Government requisitioned the ship to transport soldiers to Veracruz. In the war against Mexico a turning point had come early in 1846, when President James K. Polk decided to invade central Mexico and to march against Mexico City itself in order to defeat the Mexican President Santa Anna once and for all. In order to capture the Mexican capital, United States troops had to attack and conquer the city of Veracruz first, and thus capture its important harbor. On 5 March 1847, the attack on Veracruz started, and on 29 March the city surrendered. In July 1847, the march on Mexico City began.[9] Thus, the *Darmstädters* had no vessel anymore. They were compensated with one hundred dollars, but it took them several days and a lot of patience until they found another ship, the *Roma*, that would carry them to Indian Point. This ship, though, was in miserable condition and the whole crew, including the captain, in a state of continual drunkenness. On the morning of 18 July, they finally embarked for their last sea passage before reaching their destiny. The first day the immigrants had a swift voyage, though, and at the end of that day passed the west point of Galveston, heading for the open sea. They rested at the forward deck, some of them sound asleep already, when a sudden crash woke them. The ship had hit a sandbank: "We were stranded. Of the crew not one man was to be seen; the wheel, without steersman, was tied to a chest, the light was out and the compass had fallen over. Breaking waves sounded dully on a nearby shore, and wave after wave threatened to destroy the weak hull."[10]

The captain and his crew tried to get into the rowboat secretly in order to escape to the shore and leave the Germans behind. Von Herff, the only one who was able to understand and speak English sufficiently, drew a pistol and forced the captain and his drunken men to stay on board. Then the Forty held a council of war and decided that Louis Kappelhof, the ship carpenter from Hamburg, should be the new captain of this vessel as he was the only one with any nautical knowledge. Quickly he showed them the most important maneuvers to run a ship, and thus they sailed on. It was not to be the last incident of this trip, however. On 20 July, one day before their scheduled arrival at Indian Point, the *Roma* hit a sandbank again at Matagorda Bay, and planks went loose. The members of the Forty feared they would have to swim to the coast that was already so near. Fortunately, a sailor from Danzig named Schirmacher, who was not associated with them, helped Kappelhof patch up the new damage and gave them a hand in sailing to Indian Point where they arrived in the afternoon of 21 July. There, a Consul Lee paid the Forty a premium of $10,000 in gold for settling on the Fisher-Miller grant, according to Reinhardt's memories.[11]

After a few days in Indian Point, the Forty started out for New Braunfels on 26 July, using fourteen carts pulled by mules that had been provided for them by Spiess. Originally, John Meusebach, the general agent of the *Adelsverein*, had had to provide the group with ten ox carts as stipulated in the contract. Spiess, though, knew better what his friends would need and had taken care of the situation. Actually they even had to buy some additional wagons and oxen and mules, as they had not only brought with them an enormous amount of supplies but had also purchased a lot in Hamburg and Galveston, too: "We had supplies of every kind imaginable; for instance, complete machinery for a mill, a number of barrels of whiskey, and a great many dogs of whom Morro was the largest, being three feet high. We came prepared to conquer the world."[12] As July and August were the hottest months in Texas, the Germans traveled mostly by night. From the accounts of those young idealists one can clearly see how impressed they were by the vast prairie. It was not a trip through an untouched wilderness though, as they trod along a well-traveled road, passing farms every six to ten miles. Most of them enjoyed their trip and were generally in high spirits. Although they had to walk, the majority of them looked towards the future optimistically and kept singing their old German fraternity songs. This doesn't mean that the strain of the long walk did not get to them. Some of them became tired and took turns sitting on the wagons and taking a short ride. Heinrich Backofen, and a few others who could afford it (some had funds of 100,000 *Gulden*!), for instance, bought themselves horses as soon as the group reached Victoria on 28 July.

On 4 August, they arrived at Gonzales, three days later at Seguin, and finally at New Braunfels on 8 August where Spiess waited for them. There they had to stay for nearly an additional five weeks as Friedrich Schenck, Adam Koeppel, and Louis Reinhardt were struck with typhoid, Adam Deichert, having been thrown off a horse, had broken his leg, and provisions that were supposed to have been at New Braunfels had not come yet. They camped outside of the town on the construction site of the clubhouse of the *Adelsverein*, Sophienburg, which provided some shelter from sun and rain. As they did not want to waste any time, the Forty decided to establish a farm according to paragraph ten of the Castell-Spiess-Herff-treaty from 11 February. Still full of enthusiasm, they chose 500 acres of premium land about 2.5 miles away from New Braunfels and called this place *Darmstädter* Farm, or *Fürchtegott* (Fear God) as close friends nicknamed it.[13] Quickly they built a log cabin and laid out a vegetable garden. They even planted grapevines, which soon flourished. The Forty had arrived in New Braunfels early in August and left on 1 September.

From New Braunfels the main group moved on to Friedrichsburg, or Fredericksburg as it is called today. The Forty had divided responsibilities by then. The leader of the group who settled on the Llano was von Herff. The eight men who stayed behind to run the Darmstädter Farm were headed by Gustav Schleicher. Fritz Schenck had been chosen to keep up contact between the two groups. Hermann Spiess, as general commissioner of the *Adelsverein,* was responsible for general organization. The group that had started out for the Fisher-Miller lands near Fredericksburg with thirteen wagons was guided by the botanist Ferdinand J. Lindheimer and Baron Emil von Kriewitz, who had lived among the Indians and knew the country quite well. The Indians, especially the Comanches, posed no more threat for the German settlers, however.

Normally, the Comanches were feared by all settlers for their savagery. Horror stories about their conduct circulated widely. For this reason, John Meusebach decided to try to reach an agreement with this Indian tribe for peace with the coming Germans. He set out on an expedition into the Fisher-Miller Grant north of Fredericksburg, right into the Comanche territory. It took him several negotiations with Comanche Chief Santana in March 1847 until a peace treaty could be signed between the Germans and the Indians in Fredericksburg on 9 May 1847. It was a treaty that established a good relationship between the two peoples and allowed the new German settlers to pass through Comanche territory and settle on it. In regards to the numerous treaties that were made between Whites and Indians, this was one of the very few that worked and lasted.[14] It opened over 3,000,000 acres of the Fisher-Miller Grant to German settlement.

The main group of the Forty got along slowly, though, as they had to drive their newly acquired cattle northward on an increasingly difficult road. At the end of September, they finally reached the north bank of the Llano River at the point where Elm Creek flows into it, about thirty-five miles north of Fredericksburg (the equivalent of about fourteen hours travel at that time!). Originally they had wanted to settle further to the east where the Colorado flows into the Llano; Spiess had marked a spot for them there. But they had become tired of moving and were deeply touched by the beauty of the land that spread out in front of them: "The Llano is a magnificent little stream, incredibly rich with fish and with such crystal-clear water that one can distinguish the smallest details on the bottom, even where it is deeper than a man's height. The banks are like a thicket with heaven-high pecan and poplar trees, which, due to the impenetrable overgrowth of vines, and with giant cactus and palm-like bushes, create the impression of a primeval tropical forest. The climate is magnificent."[15] It took the group two days to find a ford were they could cross the river with their wagons and cattle. On 1 October they finally succeeded and after another two miles they settled down. Six months after they had left the south of Germany, they had reached their new home. "On the other side we came to a big live-oak; and here we camped. Putting our wagons in a circle, we constructed a big tent in the center, planted our cannon, and put out a guard. Feeling perfectly secure in our fortified camp, celebrated that night until 3 o'clock. A bowl of punch was prepared, and we sang our favorite songs, while those who could performed on musical instruments of which we had a whole chest. We gave: Lebe Hoch, United States! Lebe Hoch, Texas!"[16] Meusebach suggested calling this place Bettina, in honor of the woman who had impressed him so deeply in Berlin and who in some way had become one of the guiding spirits of the Forty: Bettina von Arnim.

Eager to put their ideals to the test, the Forty started working. From the end of 1847 on, they hardly found time to write any more letters. So far, all they had reported back home concurred with the existing literature on Texas—either as immigrant guides or travel accounts. Texas was described nearly as heaven on earth. As there lived an abundance of deer, one could survive simply by hunting; and as the climate was so mild, a simple log house sufficed for nearly all days of the year. This presumably easy way of living had been an important part of all narrations on Texas, and thus had inspired most of the romantic and idealistic immigrants:

> Nothing is simpler than Texan farming. There is hardly a land on earth which rewards more richly than Texas the least efforts ex-

> pended by the farmer. But certainly there is no population in any land that feels itself freer, more independent, and happier than the Texan farmer. His life-style is simple, for the most refined pleasures and luxuries of the Old World are for him of no concern—he knows them not. The rich earth and the excellent climate freely yield a rich harvest that frees one from nearly all refined needs.[17]

Soon the Forty had erected one large log building, forty feet long and twenty feet wide, with a grass roof, in which they all slept on camp beds. They also built an adobe house that they covered with shingles made from pecan wood. Reinhardt remembered Leopold Schulz producing an artistic weather vane that he planted on top of the roof. This adobe brick house had a large fireplace made out of rock by August Strauss and served as the kitchen. Several smaller huts were erected, too; fields were laid out and plowed, the windmill erected as planned and a ferry was built to cross the Llano River.

Besides Bettina, four other settlements were founded along the north bank of the Llano River on the land of the *Adelsverein* in 1847: Castell, Leiningen, Schoenburg, and Meerholz. The first two were named by the Count von Castell and the others by John Meusebach after members and founders of the *Adelsverein*. In mid-November of 1847, about eighty persons set out from Fredericksburg under the guidance of Peter Bickel from Wiesbaden and established the Castell settlement. Six weeks later, Leiningen was founded, and Schoenburg at the end of January 1848. Castell was the only one to survive, however, as it was supported by the settlers of Fredericksburg. Like the other settlements, Bettina got into trouble. Everything had appeared very promising.

The Comanches kept their word and established a peaceful relationship with the Forty. They traded with the Germans, brought them pecans and meat, and even tried to learn German. Reinhardt described a visit of this Indian tribe: "I saw a big crowd of savages riding up, and as they drew nearer, I recognized the chief, Santana. Upon my asking him if he were not the chief, he seemed greatly surprised that I should know him. He was very much puzzled, too, because I had no beard; for all our party wore them. I told him with my fingers that I was only seventeen."[18] The Comanches and Lipan Apaches were especially fond of von Herff who, as a doctor, was able to cure them when they came and asked for help. The

Indians received not only medical treatment but also German hospitality. They never left Bettina without having received their share of corn meal, bacon, and whiskey. And although the descendants of these two cultures never fully understood each other, they practiced a form of tolerant togetherness and acceptance that was nearly unparalleled in the history of the United States. One of the stories told about the special relationship of the Indians and Germans is that about Lena Spiess, the second wife of Hermann Spiess. Von Herff had successfully conducted an eye operation on a Comanche warrior, and the grateful Indian promised to present von Herff with a girl. All the witnesses of this scene are said to have laughed and not taken this promise seriously. However, six months later, the Indian returned and brought a little Mexican girl named Lena with him. She stayed with the Germans and was taken care of by Miss Julie Herf, the cook. Later Lena married Spiess.[19] In contrast to some old reports, it was not the Indians who posed a threat to this German settlement; it was internal discord.

From the beginning, the Forty had divided the work according to the various skills of every member. Jakob Küchler and Fritz Schenck, for instance, had taken on the duty of providing the group with meat. They went on hunting trips. Whenever they could not kill a bear or deer, they brought home wild pigs, rabbits, turkeys, geese, some fish, or even armadillos. Other members cut trees, mended the house, washed the dishes, and worked in the fields. In the first year, about 200 bushels of corn were raised. Everybody giving firsthand accounts of Bettina reported, however, that not every one of the Forty joined in the necessary work:

> After one year of hard work—in which not everyone participated in the same way, as quite a lot preferred to lead an idle life, to dream about bygone *Burschen-Herrlichkeit* [the splendor of fraternity life] in the shade of live oak trees and to wait for dinnertime according to the convenient principle "ede, bibe, post mortem nulla voluptas" ["eat and drink, for after death there is no joy"]—this form of communism went to pieces, for the reasons mentioned above and other things.[20]

Reinhardt gives the same reason for the failure of Bettina, adding, that "most of the professional men wanted to do the directing and ordering, while the mechanics and laborers were to carry out their plans. Of course, the latter failed to see the justice of this ruling, and so no one did anything." Wilhelm Hermes remembered to have found an organization of mostly highly educated men who naturally were unaccustomed to manual labor and understood little about farming but loved the hunt, and classic lectures. . . .The Bettina organization was of communistic form. The cooking chores here like in Castell were the first source of discord. For me it was interesting and instructive to see communism tried practically. At classical school in Hamburg I attended Professor Wurm's lectures on communism and socialism and had learned there the beautiful reform-ideals of Fourier and Louis Blanz. But here, experience taught me, that an organization of communism requires a capable organizer and leader and that the old adage: "many heads, many-sidedness" still holds true.[21]

Yet there seems to have been more reasons why the communistic experiment failed. From all accounts mentioned so far, everything went well more or less for one year. This cannot be true, however. Even as Fritz Schenk was writing to his mother from Bettina on 4 December 1847: "We all live in agreement, are perfectly healthy and more content than ever," nearly half of the group had already left the settlement.[22]

On 17 November 1847, Dr. Heinrich Kattmann wrote back home:

> I am no longer a member of this society, because I did not want to dance to the tune of Dr. Herff and Spiess any longer. I could not accept their interpretation of communism after which I would have had to work for the society all my life, eat and drink but would have to give up my free will. Everything one acquires belongs to the society. No thanks—everything I earn and possess I want to have at my disposal. . . Schunk and Backofen have left too.[23]

They had not been the first ones, however. Two members had been expelled while the Forty stayed at Galveston. It cannot be determined exactly any more who those two were. Possibly Anton Schunk was one of them as he had declared at Galveston that he wanted to move onward to Havana. The other one may have been one of the Neff brothers. In Galveston he had declared one night at an inn that he would not bet five cents any more on the whole project, having heard of the disaster German immigrants had met the previous year. When von Herff heard what the one Neff brother had said, he had the man expelled immediately. A similar occurrence took place at Indian Point on 25 July 1847, one day before the group set out for New Braunfels. This time Louis Kappelhoff, Franz Mördes, and the other Neff brother were expelled. A so-called court of honor consisting of von Herff, Kattmann, and others had found them guilty of unbecoming conduct. The next one to leave the group obviously was Kattmann himself.

Heated discussions in New Braunfels about how strongly communism should prevail in the new settlement they wanted to establish at the Llano made certain members turn their back on their comrades. As far as the most radical members of the Forty were concerned, all property (including the land) should be common and not individual, and everything that was produced should be for the benefit of all, and the whole community should profit from it. This was too much for Kattmann, Backofen, Koeppel, and many others, especially as the radical members had fixed their terms in a contract they wanted the others to sign. This contract, written in English (which offended many of them), should be valid forever and not only for five years as they had agreed upon before their departure. Even the compromise that was reached later, specifying that half of the land each member was entitled to (160 acres) would be owned by this person privately and that each one of the Forty was entitled to a certain part of the crop and the profits, did not soothe those who had enough of this communistic experiment.

For Heinrich Backofen, the discussion about the best way to execute a communistic form of life was the last drop in a overflowing barrel. Being forty-three years old, he always felt uneasy among men who were mostly much younger than he. He complained about the disorder, the lack of discipline, and the carelessness with which his fellow immigrants treated each other's property. This had already begun during their voyage to America: "As many had noticed by now, that I wouldn't behave like them and kept my belongings tidy, I soon became the target of their scorn. They ridiculed me so strongly that I told Schenck I'd leave the society as soon as we'd reach Galveston if this behavior wouldn't stop—which it did then." As Backofen had been quite a prominent member of their group, his withdrawal was a great loss for the Forty. He accompanied the main group to the Llano but soon left there. Being a decent man, he did not just leave by night but asked the others for permission to return to New Braunfels and work on the Darmstädter Farm, which was granted to him. Life and work there disappointed him too though, and the disillusioned instrument maker left New Braunfels on 4 January 1848. Spiess tried very hard to persuade Backofen to stay and even granted him the right to return any time and get his land and all rights therein back, as he assured him that he held Backofen in the highest esteem. Actually, the forty-three-year old instrument maker was one of the richest of the Forty and had lent money to Spiess and the society on various occasions. It was the goose that laid golden eggs whom Spiess wanted to prevent from leaving the nest. But Backofen insisted and returned to his hometown Darmstadt in summer of 1848 for good where he became quite a well-known photographer.[24] Maybe even more had left by the end of 1847, but no other names are given in the various documents and letters.

Lieutenant a.D. Ludwig Bene, who had been in the Prussian military service, was one of the two officials of the *Adelsverein* supporting the colonial director and became the last commissioner general of the *Adelsverein* in Texas after Spiess left this office.[25] He reported to Count von Castell on 9 January 1848, that Castell consisted of thirty families, Bettina of thirty-five persons, Leiningen of twelve families, and Schoenburg of ten families. Everything appeared prosperous and well, especially for the *Adelsverein*. The figure of thirty-five persons Bene gives for Bettina needs some analyzing though. We know of five members having been expelled, and of at least three who had left the group deliberately. About eight stayed behind at the Darmstädter Farm near New Braunfels, which means that only about twenty-two of the thirty-eight so-called "original" members mentioned earlier in this chapter could have left for the final settlement at the Llano. The discrepancy between the number twenty-two and the number thirty-five that Bene gives, might be explained by something quite customary at that time. Whenever groups of new settlers moved through a town or village on or close to the frontier, they were frequently joined by others who had lived in that village and wanted to move onward or by newly arrived immigrants who had come on their own and felt more comfortable by joining such a group now. This had already happened to the Forty in the cases of Vogelsang and Rock, for example. Ferdinand Lindheimer stayed at Bettina for one month. Somewhere along their way, the physician Rudolf Fuchs from Giessen had joined the Forty, too. Obviously others, whose names we do not have, had done so too , either already at Galveston or at any other village through which the group had passed. Settlers from Fredericksburg had been attracted to join the Forty, as the equipment and provisions of this group were better than those of most other German immigrants. Adam Koeppel even mentioned thirty families from that town who came to Bettina but mostly returned after a short time. Therefore, the number of thirty-five that Bene gives in his report is likely to be correct, although only twenty-two of our original Forty probably belonged to the settlers of Bettina. Two weeks later, Bene, in a report to the *Adelsverein* directly, even gives the number of forty-five *Darmstädter* at Bettina. Either he was exaggerating enormously to create an optimistic picture of the development of Bettina for the *Adelsverein*, or newcomers were pouring into Bettina constantly at that time.

Yet things looked different at the end of February 1848. Whereas the settlements of Castell with its seventeen log-cabins, Leiningen with six log cabins and Schoenburg with its couple of huts were prospering and still growing, Bettina had fallen behind in its development. According to Bene, sixteen members of the Forty had left the group altogether, and only eight members of this communistic society remained at Bettina to farm the forty acres they had turned into fertile ground. The rest of about eleven to twenty-one persons had moved to New Braunfels, either to work on the Darmstädter Farm or to establish a new one on the 500 acres that were surveyed for the *Adelsverein* there. Adam Koeppel had been one of those who had left the Forty in January 1848. In his letter to his father and siblings dated April 1848, he stated that nearly half of the old members and most of the newcomers were fed up with the "communistic" rules set up by Spiess and von Herff and thus had left too. Nearly one month later, he complained to his brother Gottlieb about their first weeks on the Llano: "Our food consisted of raw bacon, rotten biscuit [Zwieback] and coffee! . . . Then we had to spend the winter in miserable reed huts. The tissue of lies, doctor Herf [sic] had spun in Galveston—that ten negroes had gone to the Llano in advance to build blockhouses and plough the land, that thousands of sheep and other cattle had been bought and had been transported there—was soon torn apart." In August of that year, Eberhard Ihrig from Esbach in the Odenwald visited Bettina on the Llano. According to his account, fifteen men still lived there, among them Jakob Küchler, Christoph Flach, and Friedrich Louis. This small band seemed to live there quite happily but soon moved to the Darmstädter Farm near New Braunfels too. In his special report to the *Adelsverein* Bene had stated at the end of March 1848: "This society has been reduced by eighteen members, because the resigning members—who did not belong to the most unqualified—believed their principles of life to be incompatible with the communistic principles of this society." Therefore, Spiess as general commissioner of the *Adelsverein* had officially asked for the reduction or even dissolution of the administration and thus of the society itself. The property of the *Darmstädter* society was to be sold by the end of January 1849. Bene complained that Spiess tried to out-maneuver him in order to get hold of the land and property of the society. He accused Spiess of being head of this communistic "conspiracy" and even threatened to step down as Colonial Director. The lawyer Dr. Ludwig Martin from Freiburg i.Br. even wrote to the Duke of Nassau about his activities in Texas since 1848 saying that Spiess and Schleicher acted together. Spiess tried to get all authority from Meusebach after the latter retired as general commissioner, and Schleicher tried the same with Dresel's power as representative of the *Adelsverein*, Martin wrote. He accused Spiess also of having disposed of all property of the *Darmstädter* society, such as ox carts, horses, mules, tents, oxen, forging tools, mill inventories, and all other items belonging to this society. In 1847 the whole inventory of the society was valued at $37,000, which Spiess was supposed to have put in his own pocket by 1852.[26]

All of this could be just one-sided propaganda as the *Adelsverein*, of course, never was and never could have been a friend of a communistic society. When one reads articles in favor of the Forty like Ferdinand Lindheimer's, published in the German paper *Wöchentlicher Anzeiger des Westens* from St. Louis, Missouri, in March 1848, praising the young men because they worked in their fields instead of defending themselves in newspapers, it indicates that accusations and criticism had spread in Texas and beyond. A group of New Braunfels' settlers complained to the *Adelsverein* at Wiesbaden in a 20 March 1848 letter that the Forty with all their communistic ideals and ideas had been unfairly favored. And even further north in the United States, this communistic experiment of the

Darmstädters was being watched with scepticism and criticism. In the same paper *Wöchentlicher Anzeiger des Westens* where Lindheimer published his article in favor of the Forty, an article was printed on 4 August 1849, which commented scornfully on the decline of the Bettina settlement. This criticism undoubtedly must have had its effect on the remaining members of the Forty, or at least on those who had identified with the communistic ideals until the bitter end. This can been seen, for instance, by an article Hermann Spiess wrote in 1853 in answer to a Mr. "K" that was published in the *Neu Braunfelser Zeitung*. Obviously Mr. "K," like Dr. Martin, had accused Spiess of having embezzled the entire funds and property of the Forty with some devious communistic tricks. It is very likely that this Mr. "K" was Heinrich Kattmann, as he had expressed strong resentment against Spiess earlier. The accused reacted furiously:

> You talk about a dissolved communistic society. I have never known a communistic society in Texas with the exception of a few men who tried to establish one. I only know that a group arrived once which declared that some of its members had been accused of roguеries in Germany. Whether "Herr K" had a communistic relationship with these men, I cannot tell. . . . I received a letter from the Llano, where "Herr K" lived at that time too. . . . This letter mentions the society, "Herr K" is talking about. This society was divided into three classes then. The lowest class was sweet-soundingly referred to as the *Stinker* [lazybone skunks]. It is further said about these amiable members that not only they did not receive a dividend but also have to face a deduction as they haven't earned the bread they mostly ate with extreme appetite. . . . The report continues: "Other amusing things happened too. Sugar was eaten on the sly in such quantities that its reduction became obvious. The last cans of whiskey were secretly tapped and drunk, the flour barrel showed distinct signs of being tampered with and other items like shoes, tobacco, etc. were stolen. Every day saw new eatings on the sly; one day it was 'K' who came nibbling from the sugar barrel, the other 'Herr K' performed in the egg cupboard like a weasel and later 'Herr K' had licked up the cream from the milk; in short: one thought to be in a kindergarten."

Spiess ended his article by asking this Mr. "K" to have a serious discussion with him about a possible guarantee of success for such an idealistic experiment that puts to test the character of average men. He further asked how many men show enough courage to admit the truth—even if this makes them look unfavorable—and how to judge men who defend certain principles, use them against others but cry out loud if these principles are turned against them.[27]

This article clearly shows that Spiess had indeed been one of the founders of the idealistic communistic emigration group called the Forty, that this group broke up because of internal quarrels and that each side later accused the other of being guilty of this failure. Spiess and the other most idealistic members accused the rest of having been idle and lazy, and this faction responded by blaming Spiess and his friends of establishing a communistic dictatorship in order to get hold of all the money, land, and possessions of the Forty. The lawsuits concerning these questions dragged on for decades.[28] Another reason for the failure of Bettina might have been that the majority of the Forty were single—young, unmarried men without any responsibility for a family. They had to care for nobody but themselves. When they did not want to work, no wife and no children would complain. Life on the frontier was not easy at all and they only had their dreams and their ideals. When these dreams did not come true, there was no sense in staying together.

It was not only that some were idle and others had to work harder, however. Even the craftsmen who were used to hard manual labor complained, like the instrument maker Heinrich Backofen shortly before he left Bettina: "All human beings who have some sense for the beautiful and the noble will feel a desire for these sooner or later and will eventually loathe the close contact with bulls and donkeys. This is a dull, insipid life."[29] Most of them had not come to Texas because they had no future in the Old World; they had emigrated to the United States to try out a new form of living and working together. As this idea did not work out, the only reason for remaining together in Bettina had vanished. Actually, it could not have worked out, because everyday life together showed that a lot of them had different and often even dissenting conceptions about how to set their common idea into practice. The older, and through experience more realistic, professionals of their group like Backofen and Koeppel soon became discontented with the lack of discipline showed by their younger partners, especially the students. Little things added to these more general reasons. A lot of small items needed for the everyday life, like kitchenware, were not available even in nearby Fredericksburg, but had to be brought in from New Braunfels. The land they tried to cultivate proved not to be as fertile as the land of the Darmstädter Farm near New Braunfels, and the isolation on this sparcely populated frontier bore heavily upon them, as even von Herff had to admit.[30] Therefore, it is only natural that the various letters and descriptions about Texas during the first weeks of the Forty in their new homeland differ greatly. The disappointed emphasized the problems that really existed, whereas men like von Herff—who wanted to encourage further immigration—as well as the youngest members and the most determined, described the new land as heaven on earth. Thus, they mixed fact with the hope of how it should be one day. Whatever the truth really might have been, the fact was that Bettina had ceased to exist; the communistic experiment of the Forty had failed. It was, however, not the only one.

About 130 idealistic, utopian communities of all types were established in the United States between 1663 and 1860. Most of these communities were located in the Ohio and the Upper Mississippi Valleys, the Great Lakes Region and the Middle Atlantic Seaboard. Bettina was the 124th and the first one in Texas. One year later, in 1848, about seventy members of Étienne Cabet's group, "Communistes Icariens" left France on 3 February. They landed in New Orleans, moved on to Texas and settled on land that was part of the Peter's Colony grant near present-day Justin in southwest Denton County. They called their settlement of thirty or forty log houses "Icaria" and elected Cabet "dictator" for ten years in absentia, since he had stayed behind in France. He came to Texas at the end of 1848 only to see that his colony had failed; fever, malaria, and bad harvests had ruined this communistic experiment. In February 1849, Cabet moved with his remaining followers to the town of Nauvoo in Hancock County in western Illinois, which had been abandoned by the Mormons. And in 1855, followers of the communist Charles Fourier established Réunion three or four miles west of Dallas across the Trinity River. Like the other two, this experiment failed.[31]

With Bettina ceasing to exist when a settler of nearby Leiningen bought the rest of the colony in the fall of 1848, the remaining members of the Forty spread in all directions, some of them even returning to Germany.

Two of them became prominent Texan citizens: Dr. Ferdinand von Herff and Gustav Schleicher. From Bettina, von Herff first went back to Germany, too, but mainly to marry his bride Mathilde Klingelhöffer from Giessen. The other reason was to promote further emigration to Texas as had been planned by the Forty, together with the *Adelsverein,* before their departure from Germany. The letters of the leading members, like those from Schenk, had been designed to create a positive image of Texas and to conceal the more negative aspects of their journey. This way, they wanted to foster further migration into the lands of the *Adelsverein*. For the same reason, von Herff also wrote a book which was published with the help of the *Adelsverein*: *Die geregelte Auswanderung des deutschen Proletariats mit besonderer Beziehung auf Texas* (The Regulated Emigration of the German Proletariat With Special Reference to Texas). Like authors before him who wrote with a purpose, von Herff describes Texas as a utopian heaven on earth:

> The great ease with which the necessities of life are obtained from a small quantity of land. . . . The slight amount of work required of the colonists and the shorter time between their arrival and their first harvest. . . . Texas has up to now been the only region where a grandiose colonizing undertaking has been accomplished and has succeeded at least to the extent that large districts have been cultivated, towns founded in the wilderness, and thousands of Germans guided to an independent and happy station in life.[32]

The society of noblemen obviously was so pleased with the praise of Texas, which they could not know was highly exaggerated, that they even paid 200 *Gulden* to publisher Franz Varrentrapp at Frankfurt/Main who published this little booklet in 1850. After having delivered his report to the executive committee of the *Adelsverein* in person on 7 August 1849, von Herff and his wife returned to Texas in September, moved to New Braunfels first and then to San Antonio where he became an eminent physician and surgeon. At his death in 1912, Ferdinand von Herff was one of the most prominent and distinguished citizens of San Antonio.

After working as a farmer for some time, Gustav Schleicher moved to San Antonio too, where he practised law, worked as surveyor, and tried his hand at publishing a German newspaper. He represented San Antonio in the Legislature in Austin in 1859, became a member of the Texas Senate in 1861, and was elected to the United States Congress in Washington, D.C., in 1875, where he served for three terms. He died in Washington during his third term in January 1879. In honor of his service to the State of Texas, Schleicher County in west Texas was named for him.

Friedrich Schenck stayed in Texas until he went back to Germany in 1850. There he married Caroline Luise Friedericke Lorenz (1827-1916) and returned with his wife to Texas in 1851. The Schencks settled down in Austin where Friedrich worked in the General Land Office. A respected and well-known citizen of Austin, Schenck died in 1875.

Hermann Spiess had succeeded John O. Meusebach, when the latter had resigned as commissioner general of the *Adelsverein* on 20 July 1847. While his friends and comrades tried to form Bettina into an ideal community, Spiess had some trouble at hand. Ill advisedly, he believed he was representing the interests of the *Adelsverein* when he tried to remove a Dr. Schubbert (whose real name was Friedrich Armand Strubberg) from the Nassau Farm by force. This Strubberg had been colonial director of Fredericksburg until July 1847, and then moved to Nassau Farm, a 5,000-acre plantation in Fayette County owned by the *Adelsverein* for which he had a valid lease. Not knowing this, Spiess attacked the farm with some men in the early morning hours of 28 October 1847. The ensuing skirmish cost two lives, for which the State of Texas subsequently tried Spiess and some of his men on murder charges. Spiess was lucky to be acquitted on the grounds of self-defense, but this trial cost the *Adelsverein* a good deal. At the beginning of the 1850s, the settlements of the *Adelsverein* faced better times, largely due to the recognition of the various land titles by the Texan Congress on 11 February 1850. The enormous debts that the *Adelsverein* had piled up during the past years forced the society to end its activities in February 1852, however, and finally to dissolve its business by 1 October 1861. The settlement of all debts lasted well over thirty years.

In Texas, Spiess tried his best to keep the various settlements of the *Adelsverein* going. Together with some other men, Spiess founded the Guadalupe River Bridge Company in 1850 in order to build a bridge over the river in New Braunfels. He was not very successful as a farmer and businessman though, as many in Texas distrusted him because of his role as general commissioner for the *Adelsverein*. He participated in various social and business activities of New Braunfels, and in 1852 married Lena, the Mexican girl who had been presented to von Herff in Bettina. As his health deteriorated after the Civil War, he sold all of his properties in Texas in 1867 and moved north to Warrensburg, Missouri, where he died some time after 1873.[33]

After leaving Bettina, Jacob Küchler and a few others of the Forty moved to the *Darmstädter* Farm. At the end of 1848 they were joined by some friends from Darmstadt, who had arrived in Galveston on 20 November, under the leadership of Ernst Dosch on board the *Louis* from Antwerpen. Besides Dosch, there were Ernst and Ludwig von Lichtenberg, Baron von Rotsmann, Hermann Schenck, and Carl Keller. At the end of 1849, this group also broke up. As in Bettina, Küchler had mainly made himself useful as hunter for the settlers at the Darmstädter Farm. After he had left the farm, he worked as a ranger at the Mexican border for a while before he joined the colonists of the newly formed settlement Sisterdale. Sisterdale belonged to the so-called "Latin Colonies" or "Latin Settlements." Sisterdale was actually founded in 1847 by Nikolas Zink and later attracted educated and illustrious persons from Germany like the scientist Alexander von Humboldt and Ottmar von Behr, son of the prime minister of Anhalt-Köthen. Both were acquainted with Bettina von Arnim. The name "Latin Settlements" applies to about five communities in Texas that were established during the late 1840s. The most prominent were Millheim in Austin County, Latium in Washington County, Bettina, and Sisterdale and Tusculum in Kendall County. The word "Latin" was chosen to describe those German settlements that showed a high intellectual standard. Often living in rude cabins, the settlers conducted weekly meetings in Latin and frequently had more to read than to eat:

> In spite of his troublesome pioneer-life, the educated settler has neither sunk beneath the cultural and intellectual level of his fatherland, nor has he become completely practical. On the contrary—he has carried the living seeds of German spiritual life deeply into Indian territory. I have been to various remote valleys where the German settlers have founded magazine-clubs and reading-circles. They were absolutely familiar with the newest literary publica-

> tions. In the most shabby log cabins you will often find the works of our great poets and don't have to look long for the latest economic science-, history-, and philosophy-authors.[34]

Jacob Küchler married in Sisterdale and rose to some wealth. Having been surveyor since 1856, he was elected County Surveyor in and for the County of Gillespie on 2 August 1858. He was elected captain of a German company of Union volunteers at the beginning of the Civil War. After a battle with Confederate forces at the Nueces River in August 1862, he had to flee to Mexico together with the surviving members of his group. He returned to Texas in 1868 and was appointed Deputy Collector of Customs and Storekeeper of the Bonded Warehouse at the Port of San Antonio on 25 June 1869. On 6 April 1870, Küchler was appointed manager of the Texas State Lunatic Asylum by Governor E. Davis and on 31 August 1878, he was appointed principal land surveyor of the Texas & Pacific Railway Company. Jacob Küchler died in Austin on 3 April 1893.

Little is known about the other members of the Forty. At least two of them died in 1848: Peter Bub of yellow fever on 21 August and Adolf Hahn of typhoid fever on 17 October. Adam Koeppel was struck by a similar fate. The oldest son of a physician, the forty-seven-year-old pharmacist wanted to establish a new life in his old trade when he joined the Forty rather late, on 14 March 1847, nearly a month before the group left Germany. His hopes were not fulfilled, however. After leaving the Forty, he wanted to change his securities into cash in Fredericksburg in order to travel to the northern states. He only received promissory notes drawn on the *Adelsverein*, however, as the people in Fredericksburg also lacked cash. Therefore Koeppel only went to New Braunfels where he rented a small cottage with a garden. There he planted beans, lettuce, radishes, sweet potatoes, and cucumbers. At the end of 1848 he acquired a piece of farmland and planted additional potatoes, cucumbers, melons, squash, beans, and corn. Having realized that it was impossible for him to make a living as a pharmacist, because even doctors could hand out medicine and not many people became ill in the first place, he familiarized himself with the idea of becoming a farmer for good. He even dreamt of making enough money this way to buy cattle and becoming a rancher one day. Yet, in the summer of 1849 he caught biliary fever and died on 16 August.[35]

Philipp Zoeller, Adam Vogt, Wilhelm Friedrich, Leopold Schulz, and Christoph Flach founded another communistic and "Latin" settlement, which they called Tusculum after the name of the Roman philosopher and author Cicero's country house.[36] This "Latin" colony survived two years. Christoph Flach moved to New Braunfels and from there to Boerne in 1852. There he joined Captain Connor's company of U.S. Mounted Volunteer Rangers. After being honorably discharged in 1853, he settled in Sisterdale at the Guadalupe River. There he met and married Antonie Kapp, the eldest daughter of Ernst Kapp (1808–1896). This highly renowned historian, geographer, and philosopher was one of the most prominent settlers of Sisterdale. Flach was one of the first citizens of Comfort. Together with Johann Hörner, who was 1st Sergeant, he became a member of the German Union militia of Comfort Precinct No. 2 in 1862. Both men took part in the battle of the Nueces on 10 August 1862, under the command of 1st Lieutenant Ernst Schwethelm. In 1871, Christoph Flach formed a business partnership with Otto Brinkmann. In 1881, they sold their mercantile business to August Faltin.

The German schoolmaster W. Steinert travelled through Texas from 22 May to 5 June 1849. On 23 May he met Christian Michel at Meyer's Hotel in Galveston and remarked, "He had just returned from the Society's land grant area where he, being one of forty men called 'the Forty' or 'the Darmstädters,' had wanted to establish a colony. Their plan failed, and he valued his 320 acres of land situated there so highly that he wanted to sell them for a bottle of wine worth one-half dollar."[37] Theodor Schleuning was a dealer in groceries, crockery, woodware, Rhine wines, liquors, and tobacco in San Antonio from the 1860s until shortly before his death in the early 1890s. Ernst Otto Amelung was listed in Comal County in 1849 but later moved to Arizona with his family where all of them were murdered by Indians. Wilhelm Friedrich lived in Mason County in 1859 but was blown up with his gunpowder factory in San Antonio during the Civil War; Christian Hesse ran a liquor store near Fredericksburg in June 1849; Heinrich Kattmann was listed in Guadalupe County in 1850; Friedrich Louis lived in Kendall County in 1850 but was shot by a drunken Irishman in Fredericksburg some years later; Jakob Obert was registered as single in Comal County in 1850 and 1860; and Leopold Schulz lived in Kendall County in 1849. In 1894, Philipp Zoeller still lived in Boerne, Christoph

Flach in Comfort, Jakob Obert in New Braunfels, Louis Reinhardt in Arneckeville (De Witt County) and probably Edward Müller somewhere, as Adolf Paul Weber discovered. He also mentioned Julius Wagner, living in Chicago in 1894.[38] But what had happened to him?

Julius Wagner had left the Forty rather early, like Schunck, Backofen, Koeppel, and Kattmann, only a little later, probably in February of 1848. Very likely, Karl Wundt accompanied him. They settled down in the southeast of Texas between Meyersville, founded by Adolph Meyer in 1849, and the community that became Steiner's Settlement, about ten miles west of Victoria. Carl Steiner, born on 22 February 1812, in Prussia, became an American citizen in Victoria County on 8 September 1855, after having lived in Texas for five years. This sets the founding of his settlement around 1850. Besides Julius Wagner, one of the early settlers in this area was Georg Witting from Morschen near Kassel (Hesse) who had settled there in 1847. He had left the German port of Bremen on board the *Neptune* on 10 October 1846, and had arrived at Galveston on 23 December the same year. Georg Witting was a neighbor of Julius Wagner, and they soon became close friends. The reasons Julius had left the communistic *Darmstädter* group with whom he had come to Texas, can no longer be determined exactly. It seems, though, that he was distressed with other members of the Forty—either with those who did not share in the work or with those who were outspoken communists. The first years were not easy at any rate, and Julius had to work hard: "At the beginning I faced very bad and hard times in America, but it got better later."[39] When he thought he had established himself in a way that would support a family, he returned to Germany to marry his bride Emilie Schneider and bring her to his farm at Twelve-Mile-Coleto Creek, also called just "the Coleto."

In April 1849, Julius Wagner surprised his fiancée Emilie Schneider when he arrived at her parents' home in Offenburg (Baden) to ask her to marry him and join him in Texas. Nobody had expected his return at that moment. On 10 July, they were married. Her father had blessed the young couple, although it was not easy at all for the Schneiders to see their beloved daughter move away over the ocean to a distant shore where she faced an uncertain future. Although Julius described his new home and life in Texas as pleasant, he nevertheless emphasized that quite a lot of strain, hardship, and privation might await Emilie and him—not only on their voyage to the United States but also in the first years of their life together at the Coleto. They would have to work hard and lead a frugal life at first. All of this could not shock Emilie: "We'll have to overcome some hardship naturally and will have to endure privation but my deep and wholehearted love for Julius will make things easy for me. If we had more funds, we could have it much more comfortable; yet—we only have enough for our long and expensive journey but, with GOD's help we'll be able to make it." Thus she already expressed one of her most important traits: a desire to fulfill her duties and obligations towards her husband and her family. She was determined to go with Julius and help him as best as she could, but she did not go lightly. Could she have chosen freely, she would have stayed in Germany. Going to America for her was going into an uncertain, uneasy exile.[40]

Given the political situation in Germany at this time, however, quite a few were attracted by Julius' descriptions of his life in Texas. How many persons accompanied him and his wife cannot be determined anymore, but one of them was twenty-year-old Hermann Henkenius, the son of the local chemist, who himself considered following his son to Texas later.[41] Julius' stories about his life at the Coleto must have been so tempting that his parents came close to emigrating too, if only they had had 1000 *Florin* to cover their expenses. A "family-colony" at the banks of Coleto Creek, a peaceful and independent life in the heart of nature, seemed most attractive to all the Wagners in Germany. A wealthy friend of Carl Baumann even tried to sell all his property in order to get enough money to buy land in Missouri for a "Wagner-family-colony." Not only old Peter Wagner and his wife, but also Julius and Emilie declared that in this case they would join the rest and follow Carl and his friend to Missouri.[42] But, nothing came out of this plan, and so Julius Wagner and his wife Emilie left their families in Baden and boarded the ship *Franziska* at Bremen on 15 September. They reached Galveston on 2 December and before the end of the year, they arrived at their farm at the Dry Branch Creek between the Twelve-Mile Coleto Creek and the Five-Mile Coleto Creek. Now their life in Texas really began. Julius was thirty-two years old and Emilie three years younger.

The Texas they had chosen to spend their lives in had become independent from Mexico in 1836. Nearly ten years later, Texas was admitted to the Union as the twenty-eighth state of the Union. After the war with Mexico

1846-48, the young state faced two major problems: the boundary question and enormous debts. After the Mexican War, Texas once again had announced its claim to the Rio Grande as boundary line which would include Santa Fe. President Zachary Taylor, who held an old dislike towards Texas, encouraged New Mexico to petition for statehood, in order to give them the Santa Fe area. This controversy dragged on well into the year 1850. It was strongly connected with the issue of the Texas debt that amounted to more than twelve million dollars. In the compromise of 1850, Texas "sold" its claim to parts of New Mexico for the takeover of its debts by the United States Treasury.

The year 1849 saw more immigrants to the United States than any year before: 297,024 persons. A lot of them were lured to the States by the beginning of the gold rush and Texas found itself on the route of many gold and fortune seekers bound for California. Nearly twenty percent of the total white population of Texas (which was about 154,000 in 1850) was of German origin. Most of the Germans settled in East Texas.[43] Steiner's Settlement in Victoria County at the border of Goliad County, as well as Meyersville, were in an area that had a German population of thirty to forty percent in 1850. Thus it was only natural that the Wagners were mainly surrounded by Germans. Besides Steiner, Wundt, and Georg Witting, there were Baron Eduard von Lochhausen, who had come as a bachelor at the age of twenty-five to New Braunfels in 1845 and had moved on to the Twelve-Mile Coleto. The Wagners' neighbors also included the unmarried former Prussian officers von Hoyer and Adolph von Zobel, a Dr. Wolff, Julius Schorre and family, Robert Kleberg, and the brothers Albrecht and Wilhelm von Roeder.

The Roeders were the sons of former Lieutenant Ludwig Sigismund Anton von Roeder (1775-1847) and his wife Caroline Louise Sack (1782-1865). They had eleven children: seven sons and four daughters. The von Roeders had followed the call of Friedrich Ernst's letter. In this 1831 letter to his friend Schwarz, published in German newspapers, Ernst—the first prominent German settler in Texas—had described Texas as heaven on earth. This was especially appealing to the von Roeders as their economic situation at home had become worse and worse. Lower grain prices had led to a decline in land value. Taxes and other financial burdens on their land ate up more money than came in. It was at last too difficult to raise eleven children according to the values of their class. As the story is told in the family, the decision to emigrate in a way was also forced upon them as one of the von Roeder boys obviously had to go to prison and had brought disgrace to his family.[44] Before they could set out on their voyage, the oldest von Roeder boy died after a long illness. The first ones to sail to Texas at the end of March 1834, in order to find a place where the whole family could settle down, were Ludwig von Roeder's sons Ludwig (Louis), Albrecht, and Joachim as well as his daughter Valeska. Nearly six months later, on 31 September 1834, the day they embarked for Texas, Ludwig von Roeder's daughter Rosalie—called Rosa—(1813-1906) married Robert Justus Kleberg (1803-1888).

Robert Kleberg was the son of the prominent and successful merchant Lucas Kleberg and his wife Veronica Meier. He had studied law at Göttingen were he had met and socialized with the von Roeder brothers. Having received his Ph.D. in law he became *Oberlandesgerichtsreferendar* (junior barrister at the high court) at the *Oberlandesgericht* (high court) at Paderborn. After having read Fritz Ernst's descriptions of Texas and hearing about his friend's decision to migrate there, he made up his mind to go: "I want to live under a republican form of government, with unlimited personal, religious and political liberties. . . . I was and always have been a enthusiastic admirer of republican institutions and I expect to find my most ardent hopes fulfilled in Texas of all countries." Some forty years later he remembered: "At the time we left, hardly anything was known of Texas, except that my ideas and those of my party were formed by the above mentioned letter, [the famous one by Friedrich Ernst from Oldenburg, the founder of Industry] in which Texas was described as a beautiful country, with enchanting scenery and delightful climate, similar to that of Italy, the most fruitful soil and republican government, with unbounded personal and political liberty, free from so many disadvantages and evils of old countries."[45] The emigration group to which Robert Kleberg and his newlywed wife Rosa belonged consisted of Rosa's parents Ludwig and Caroline, their sons Otto, Wilhelm, and Rudolf, their daughters Luise and Caroline, as well as the sisters Antoinette and Pauline von Donop, (who were engaged to Rudolph and Otto von Roeder respectively) and Robert Kleberg's brother Louis. By the time this second von Roeder group arrived in Texas, Joachim and Valeska von Roeder had already died of a vicious fever. Robert and Louis Kleberg as well as Robert's five brothers-in-law Louis, Otto, Ludwig, Rudolph, and Wilhelm von Roeder joined the Texan forces in their war for independence against Mexico in 1835-36. While the men were serving in the army and their families were on the "runaway scrape," their homes in Cat Springs were ravaged.[46] On 22 February 1850, Otto von Roeder bought the Nassau Farm for $14,000 from Spiess' successor Bene, but his creditors filed suit. The Nassau Farm was then sold at a public auction to James A. Chandler of Massachusetts for $177.76.[47]

In 1847, Robert J. Kleberg, Sr., Albrecht (b. 31 July 1811), and Wilhelm von Roeder (b. 18 May 1821), as well as their families settled down at the Twelve-Mile-Coleto Creek, between Steiner's Settlement and Meyersville. Many years later, Robert Justus Kleberg, Jr., would become head of the famous King Ranch. That was in the distant future in the 1850s when Albrecht von Roeder, Robert Kleberg, Sr., and Julius Wagner were not only close neighbors but also close friends. Julius had leased his nearly ninety-three acres of land from Albrecht von Roeder. Situated directly on Dry Branch Creek and about a half-hour walk from the Twelve-Mile-Coleto Creek, Julius and Emilie Wagners' house stood on a slight hill, about 570 yards away from the von Roeders' home that lay on a hill even higher than the Wagners'. Kleberg lived in a house about 400 yards apart from the von Roeders', which means that the von Roeders were living right between the Wagners and the Klebergs. The children of Albrecht von Roeder, above all Ludwig, Hermann, Sigismund, and young Rosa, loved Emilie Wagner, visited her often and could hardly wait to get the toys Emilie had asked her parents to ship over from Germany. One day, waiting for the toys to arrive, little Ludwig asked Emilie: "Tell me, Madam Wagner, are those soldiers you promised me real people, or can I take them into my hands?" When the toys finally arrived for Christmas of 1851, the children were overwhelmed with joy; there were dolls for the girls and tin soldiers and picture books for the boys. Emilie quite often baked cakes using traditional German recipes, of which the children were especially fond.

In one of her first letters to her parents and siblings in Germany in 1851, Emilie describes the relationshship of Julius and Albrecht von Roeder quite vividly:

> As I wrote to you earlier, Julius is loved and respected by everybody; he is most welcome everywhere, but especially Albrecht von Roeder, our closest neighbor, loves him like a brother. This Albrecht von Roeder is an extraordinary man, witty, educated, bright, and highly sensitive. He might show rugged manners, but he can still turn into a German nobleman if he wishes. Yet most of the time he mocks at such foolishness. The life he has been leading here for nearly fifteen years has been as wild and rough as the nature is here, and this has made him develop certain weaknesses. Thus it can happen occasionally that he gets drunk, which is not very difficult as the men drink "Schnaps" mainly. Yet he always knows what he is doing, and the next day he shows his wife and children that he is a repentant sinner. His wife is a marvelous woman and their marriage life—like all of their family life—is a very happy one. We have spent many happy days together already, and when something special is happening at the house of the Roeders they want us to be present too or at least send us a message. In such moments, when Roeder has something on his mind, he talks about how dear Julius is to him and how much he thinks of him. He proves this all the time too. When Julius for example expresses his wish to have one or two more nice horses and Roeder is present, the latter immediately says: "I will give you this or that horse." When Julius then answers, "Well, I don't want it now as I cannot pay for it at the moment," Roeder replies: "Have I ever asked you for money? Aren't you the Wagner?" A short time ago, Julius said, "I wish I had some two to four cows more in addition to the six old ones I have." Whereupon Roeder said: "Drive up some from my herd!" Julius has to be careful not to utter wishes like these aloud, as he is not immodest. A short time ago Julius rode out to watch after Roeder's hogs a few times. Roeder presented him with two healthy sows and many piglets. Often Loess [another neighbor] is very envious of Roeder's friendship to Julius. He even said once: "I'd love to have such a neighborhood too."

Von Roeder was not only obviously fond of the Wagners, he also liked the house Julius had built and Emilie had furnished and decorated. Stopping by with strangers, Albrecht von Roeder used to say: "Well, what do you say to the tidiness of the Wagner's house? Is not this house as neat and dainty as only homes in Germany are?" What impressed him obviously was the great care Emilie had taken in decorating the place and making it as homey as possible. It was a normal log house with two rooms. The wooden floor of the living room was about a half foot above the ground. Three wooden stairs led to the main door which was at the southern side. Another door inside the house led from the living room to the kitchen that stretched itself along the northern side of the house. A third door led from the kitchen to the backyard. This was especially pleasant for Emilie, who could create some air circulation in summer by opening all three doors. The living room had one window facing west. On the short wall to the east they had a fireplace, and Emilie loved to keep the fire burning all night and sat there during the cool hours of the morning and the evening. On the northern wall of the living room, which separated that room from the kitchen, stood both their beds. Julius had put a portrait of his father Peter above his bed along with a picture of Martin Luther. Next to the kitchen door hung his double-barrelled gun and the usual hunting implements. Paintings of friends and relatives hung over Emilie's bed together with Julius' guitar. Above the kitchen door they had placed the family medicine chest. On the other side, above the entrance door, the Wagners had hung a large picture of Emilie's beloved hometown Offenburg. On the chest of drawers to the right they had put some glasses and china. Every piece meant something special to them, like the two cups from Julius' student days and the small vase Emilie had once received from her sister Sophie for her birthday. Above the chest of drawers hung a large old clock, on both sides of it portraits of Emilie's parents and beneath it smaller pictures of Julius' family. A small rug covered the trunk on the left side of the entrance door. More family portraits above that trunk kept the strong bonds between the immigrants and their families and friends back home in Germany alive. Corner cupboards held the clothes of Julius and Emilie and the small collection of books they possessed. On both sides of the fireplace they had hung various hats and caps and the deck of cards on the mantelpiece showed signs of frequent use. Opposite the fireplace, to the right of the window facing west, stood a small table where Emilie used to work. Curtains in the German style gave the window a homey appearance, and the pictures on that wall showed various scenes of Offenburg. The center of the room was dominated by a big, beautiful table covered with fine cloth. The four chairs matching it stood at the bedsides when nobody was sitting at the table. As the kitchen was on ground level, one had to take two steps down when entering it. It was not until winter of 1851 that Julius was able to cover the kitchen floor with the white clay that could be found at the Dry Branch Creek. This made the ground drier and warmer.

A friend of the Schneider family, a man named Loess, who had come to Texas in December of 1850, lived with the Wagners for some months and slept in the kitchen. It was a pretty crowded room with another table in the center, the cooking oven, the many boxes, trunks, and cupboards where Emilie kept her kitchenware and supplies like coffee, sugar, and flour and the small cot where visitors like Loess used to sleep. The kitchen actually was a rather hot place, and a few years later they built a porch where guests could sleep during the summer months. Not counting the work of Julius and the others who helped build it, the house had cost them seventy-five dollars. In front of the house a huge live oak tree cast its most welcome shade over it. In the mid-fifties Emilie enriched the view of the entrance by planting acacia trees close to the porch. Other, smaller live oaks stood in the back where the Wagners had built a barn first and later a stable and a smokehouse.

In 1851, the Wagners had fifteen head of cattle, and Emilie dreamed of buying some additional twenty cows and calves, which would have cost them $200. They also had a couple of chickens and Emilie had been able to raise sixty chicks in the spring of that year. The year before, she had had to butcher all their poultry in the winter as Julius was fed up with the hens ruining his new garden. Emilie planned to sell as many chickens as possible—in 1851 there were about fifty—at twenty cents each. She also had a couple of ducks, but only for their feathers, as she wrote. Other livestock promised higher profits:

> The beginner has to concentrate on raising cattle which is recommended, especially for those who are not used to hard manual labor. Cattle guarantees high profits without having to work too hard for it, although it takes quite a few years to make a lot of money that way . . . There are schemes to get rich faster, however, and the

> one on top of the list is raising sheep. To start this, though, you need some 800 to 2000 *Gulden*. Julius mentioned once that sheep yield a good profit, and he often says: "If we could only keep sheep" because then we could return to Germany in about ten years for good. . . . The countryside here is ideal for raising sheep, as the pasture is excellent. Very soon A. von Roeder will buy himself an additional flock of sheep from the profits he got out of his cattle breeding.

At the time Emilie wrote her letter, Albrecht von Roeder owned a little more than 200 head of cattle and about 400 hogs. One ox would sell for $180 cash in hand in San Antonio at the beginning of the 1850s, which meant a profit of nearly sixty to seventy percent, Emilie Wagner figured. Von Roeder also had some twenty horses, each one worth nearly one hundred dollars. In October 1850 he had sold Julius Wagner a three-year-old grey horse for sixty-five dollars.

Whereas von Roeder had settled down as a rancher, Robert Kleberg had established himself mainly as a farmer, raising mostly potatoes and corn. To get all the work done, he even had employed a hired hand for twenty-five *Gulden* a month, which was equivalent to about twelve dollars then. In the summer of 1850 he had sold potatoes in the market of San Antonio for nearly $190. Julius did not know yet on what he should concentrate—on farming or ranching. He tried his hand at everything. Besides the poultry and the few cattle the Wagners had, Julius planted potatoes, corn, lettuce, cabbage, beans, radishes, some sweet potatoes, and some cotton. During the summer, when there was not much to do in the field, Julius even began earning additional money in the freight transport business. In the spring of 1851, Julius had bought himself a brown gelding for twenty dollars, in addition to the yellow mare he had acquired for thirty dollars some time earlier and the mule they had. Transporting goods from the Coleto to Indian Point and others from there to San Antonio was a good way for small farmers to make good additional money as long as they did not want to or could not yet sell any of their cattle or other products. Many on the Coleto, like Albrecht von Roeder, did this. It was not only civilian goods, however, as the United States Army depended on this supply line that led far onto the frontier and into Indian territory. Goods worth millions of dollar were thus transported every year. The German settlers were not the first and only ones to grasp at this opportunity, however. The Mexicans actually held a monopoly over this lucrative freight hauling business first, and competition between these two groups soon ran high. In 1857, the German and Mexican teamsters clashed in what became known as the "Cart War." Many men died during this campaign. One of the first was Albrecht von Roeder on 11 June 1857.[48] Another one who had tried to make money in that business was Julius Schorre.

Julius August Christian Schorre (1825-1880) came to Texas from Kassel, Germany, on board the ship *Friedrich* that had left Bremen on 13 August 1846, with 129 immigrants and had reached Galveston on 24 October that year. He belonged to a group coming to the States with the help of the *Adelsverein*. Realizing that nothing was prepared for the immigrants, he quickly abandoned the group he had come with and moved on to Victoria and from there to the Coleto, where he purchased land north of the Five-Mile Coleto Creek. After having settled down there, he returned to Germany in 1849 to marry Sophia Catherine Wilhelmina Baldewin (1826-1892). The couple returned to the log house Julius Schorre had built. On 29 April 1852, Julius Schorre, Charles (Karl) Wundt, and Julius Wagner became citizens of the United States. With the money Julius Schorre's wife Sophia had received from her rather rich parents they could acquire more land until they had accumulated 670 acres by 1872. The Schorres were fairly successful farmers and ranchers.[49]

Wilhelm von Roeder had to sell his farm in 1851, as he had turned mad according to Emilie Wagner. His life had not been a happy one. When he turned twenty in 1841, he had already lost four brothers. In 1845 he married Elizabeth Stephenson and was already divorced two years later after his young wife had been found guilty of adultery by the court at Austin. Seventeen days after his divorce, Wilhelm married again on 22 April 1847. His bride Louisa, called Lulu, was the daughter of the Pastor Adolphus Fuchs who had come to Texas in 1845. "My oldest sister, Lulu, as dear and lovely a young girl as one can imagine, had married Wilhelm von Roeder, the youngest son of that family, when she was but seventeen years old, only to die after two months from an acute fever, fatal to so many of the immigrants of that time." This time it took Wilhelm three and a half years to overcome this shock before he married a third time. On 12 October

1850, he was wed to his cousin, Theodore Henriette Sack. After living in a happy and joyous marriage for half a year, Wilhelm suddenly became pathologically jealous, and accused his wife of trying to poison him, as Emilie Wagner wrote. On 2 December 1852, Wilhelm von Roeder died suddenly.[50] Julius Wagner wanted to buy his farm when it was for sale but did not succeed.

At the age of twenty-one, Georg Witting's brother Friedrich came from Bremen on board the *Solon* and arrived at Galveston on 29 November 1850. In 1853, Eduard Froböse, who had been born on 23 July 1834, at Wanfried, Hessen-Nassau, worked for Georg Witting for one year. Froböse had come to Texas on 3 December 1852, after a stormy sea voyage from Bremen on board the *Bremen*. He had been lured to Texas by the stories Georg Witting had told him when the latter had visited his family in Morschen in 1852. Later Froböse joined the Texas Rangers, then worked in the freight hauling business which he led to considerable success and profit. In 1884 he was elected county treasurer.

It is difficult to say when the name "Steiner's Settlement" was changed into Coletoville. Some sources say that this was done when the post office was established there, but this was no earlier than 1875. On the other hand, reports and letters from this settlement written in the 1850s don't speak of Steiner's Settlement but simply of "Coletto."[51]

In the winter of 1853, Julius Schütze settled down at the Coleto with his mother and sister. Born at Dessau (Sachsen-Anhalt) on 29 March 1835, he came to Texas with his family on 2 November 1852, and later become a prominent German in Texas, publishing, together with O. H. Dietzel, the well-known *Texas Vorwärts*, a German-language newspaper. In 1853 he rented a small farm from Jacob Schiewitz, who had moved to Victoria. This farm was located at Coleto Creek at the foot of a hill where Georg and Friedrich (Fritz) Witting had build the first windmill in Texas. Schütze liked his neighbors very much:

> They were kind, good and joyful people who lived at the Coletto at that time. About two or three miles above the "windmill" there lived the highly educated Kleberg- and Roeder families, Julius Wagner and others. At the "crossing" of the roads from Victoria to Yorktown and San Antonio, Mr. von Hoyer and von Zobel, former

> officers from Germany, ran a highly frequented country store. With them stayed William Westhoff—then thirty years younger of course [Schütze wrote his account in 1884]—who was a quite handsome, quick and cheerful young man. Already at that time he was a busy and hardworking salesman, and quite often I transported bundles of cattle- and deerhides for him to Indianola when I went there to fetch some cargo. Further down the creek lived the brothers Witting, Baron von Lochhausen, with whom I did a lot of trips hauling freight, Dr. Wolff who had moved up here only recently after having lived some miles south of Victoria on the road to Indianola and some other people.[52]

On his farm, Schütze planted potatoes, wheat, and cotton. The white Irish potato had become very popular with the German farmers as it grew very well in the light soil of this region and could be harvested twice a year. Whereas the white potato and wheat grew successfully, cotton did not become very popular with the Germans at the Coleto settlements. The German farmers at the Coleto Creek were especially fond of growing and cultivating grapes for wine. They were acknowledged as the leading winegrowers of the state, making wine from wild grapes. Carl Steiner alone produced 2,000 gallons from the local Mustang grapes in 1860.[53]

Von Hoyer and von Zobel, whom Julius Schütze mentioned, had come to Texas in 1845. According to his wife Emilie, Julius Wagner had met them soon after his arrival in Texas, and the three men had become good friends. Very often they came to the Wagners' house to enjoy the hospitality of Emilie and Julius. They were especially fond of Emilie's art of cooking. Every now and then Emilie treated them with a special dinner, like the one she prepared on 2 June 1851: potato soup, a three-chicken casserole with noodles, plum cake, chocolates, rolls from white flour, fresh butter and cheese, and finally coffee with sweet and sour milk. Hoyer and Zobel loved the coffee they got at the Wagners' house and envied Emilie for her coffee grinder she had brought with her from Germany. As she wanted to do Julius' two friends a favor she asked her parents to send her another grinder that she could give the two young men.[54]

Julius' friend Karl Wundt married Louisa Caroline von Roeder on 18 March 1856. She was the daughter of Carl Ludwig Socrates von Roeder

(1806-1840) and his wife Caroline, who later married Albrecht von Roeder. The justice of the peace who celebrated the marriage rites was Ernst Kleberg, a Notary Public in Austin County and a brother of Rudolph Kleberg.[55] In 1857, their first son Carl Julius was born and one year later, Karl and his family left their friends at the Coleto and moved to Mexico to raise rice. He became ill in 1861, however, and died on 11 November of that year.

On Sunday, 7 April 1854, the Coleto *Gesangsverein* (singing society) was established at Witting's mill by ten persons living at the Twelve-Mile Coleto, among them Julius Wagner who had always been fond of singing. They made Julius Schütze, who was only nineteen years old then, their conductor and director. He was deeply honored by their confidence. "Sitting in shirt-sleeves on crude wooden benches in the shade of a live oak tree—our favorite meeting place—on Sundays, talking and disputing, smoking their inseparable pipes, these people showed the good fashion and manners of men who had moved around in the best and highest circles in Germany and someone like me could learn a lot from them."[56] They had no public building at the Coleto where they could meet, only their farmhouses. But spirits were high, and they decided to send a delegation of singers to the big German-Texan *Sängerfest* (singers festival) in San Antonio on 13 May 1854. It was the second official singer's festival in Texas. Celebrating the Fourth of July in 1853, the singing society *Germania* from New Braunfels (established on 2 March 1850) had invited other singers from San Antonio.

> In the open area where the present singer's hall was later built, a round dancing floor was cleared, its lime surface compacted and roofed over with wagon canvas that had been borrowed from some teamsters for the purpose. Cedar posts formed the columns of this open pavilion. Next to it in a long shelter covered with green branches, roughly made tables and benches were set up for the guests. The single, narrow sliding window in the log cabin served as a dispensing counter where one could get three bottles of good French wine from the society for a dollar. Mrs. Krentz supplied good coffee in demitasses that resembled eggshells. Mr. Louis Korn also had a booth where all kinds of pastries were to be had. Light was given by the moon that shone as bright as day and by the

> society's oil lamps that L. Henne had made and Ernst Blum lit and tended.

The music was provided by the members of the *Germania*. This joyful gathering inspired those present to establish a tradition and form a *Sängerbund* (a singers' league). The first official *Sängerfest* thus was held that same year, on 15 and 16 October, with the singers' societies of San Antonio and Austin joining the *Germania*. The second one at San Antonio, which Julius Wagner and his friends also attended, lasted from 14 May to 16 May 1854 and was held at a hall built of wood especially for this purpose. There, the *Germania* from New Braunfels was present with eighty members and was praised for their performance of the song "Gebet der Erde." Besides the *Germania* and the *Coleto Gesangsverein*, the singing societies from Sisterdale, La Grange and Victoria were present. This *Sängerfest* was a tremendous success and loved by participants as well as listeners alike. There were more than songs, though. On the third day, the members of the Sisterdale choral society had invited all to a meeting at the "Vauxhall Garden" on Alamo Street. It was a political gathering where those "Latin" farmers present from Sisterdale tried to register their fellow Germans against slavery and form an unanimous protest against the "peculiar institution." The director of Sisterdale's choral society was the local schoolteacher, August Siemering (1828-1883) who—as an outspoken liberal—had to flee from Germany during the revolution of 1848-49 and had sailed from Hamburg to Galveston in October 1851. Being so outspoken against slavery, he became more prominent during the Civil War and gained a reputation later as editor of San Antonio's German newspaper *Freie Presse für Texas*. Thus, the gatherings of German singers took on political implications that in some ways were inseparable from the rest of these singing societies. This shall be discussed, however, in a later chapter. At this meeting in 1854, the singers also decided to establish a state-wide singing society: the *Deutsch Texanischer Sängerbund*.[57]

Life at the Coleto was not just singing for Julius Wagner, however. Means of transportation were by no means satisfactory, and most of their farming products could not be taken to bigger marketplaces like Indianola, Victoria, or even San Antonio. Very often they only had enough to survive. And in the beginning they were also harassed by roaming bands of

Comanches.[58] The first child of Julius and Emilie Wagner, a girl, died in infancy in May 1851. Although a Dr. Plockville had been present, the lack of instruments and medicine had caused the baby to die. Emilie had not been alone with this doctor though. All the women in the neighborhood helped when a baby was expected. At the beginning of May 1851, Emilie had spent nearly a week with Sophie Schorre, who finally gave birth to her first child, a healthy son. Twelve days later, Emilie cared for Caroline Ernst von Roeder, the wife of Albrecht (daughter of Friedrich Ernst and widow of Albrecht's brother Ludwig who had died in 1840), when she delivered her eighth baby, a daughter. "How powerfully I was reminded of my own ill luck during both cases and my dear, sweet Sophie Schorre—whom I do not begrudge her happiness wholeheartedly—could hardly calm and comfort me."[59] Finally, on 29 December 1851, Julius' and Emilie's first son, Sigmund, was born. He was followed by Wilhelm, Sophie, Paula, Carolina, and Karl Friedrich Richard. All the children were born on the farm. Newspaper articles would later refer to documents stating that the Wagner children had been born in Clinton. This was due to the fact that Clinton was the county seat of DeWitt County from 1850—after it had been removed from Cameron to Clinton—until 1876 when the county seat was moved to Cuero. Clinton was laid out as a town in the summer of 1846 and started to prosper in the 1850s. The Civil War and Reconstruction brought about lawlessness and decline. When the railroad passed Clinton by and was led through Cuero instead, not only the county seat was removed, the whole town began dying. In the times before the Civil War though, Clinton was the closest city for the Wagners with a post office. This was housed in the General Dry Goods and Grocery Store run by Sam J. Webb. For this reason, Julius Wagner often went to Clinton to fetch his mail.[60]

Considering the fact that Julius Wagner never was much of a letter writer, with all his work he had not even found the time to write his family in Germany on the death of his father Peter Wagner, who had passed away on 6 November 1853, in Mannheim. His family was irritated but in good old Wagner fashion and knowing Julius, they waited without judgment about his conduct until they heard from him again. Whether he wrote any earlier cannot be determined, but the next letter of Julius Wagner to his relatives in Germany we possess is from May 1858. After detailed excuses for not having written for so long, he explains his situation: "Our financial situation has been very critical until recently, lots of debts, no harvests and merely no chance of earning some money. For one year now we are nearly free of debts and have managed to move ahead despite the bad years, whereas many neighbors have lost a lot. Even though my wife and I have lived through much trouble together, which we had never thought of when single, it has had no effect on our mutual love; I even think we love each other more than ever." He then lists the children they had in the meantime and describes them all as rascals who eat well and prosper accordingly. At that time they had not yet been baptized.[61] Julius Wagner had given this letter to his friend Georg Witting for the latter to deliver it to the Wagner family. Georg Witting was on a trip to Germany to visit his brother, who was director of mines at Borbeck near Düsseldorf, to pay his respects to the Wagner family, and to find himself a wife. Witting supposedly came to Germany in autumn of 1858 and left in spring of 1859. Julius described his friend as rather shy but highly respected, quite wealthy and hard working and asked his family to receive him warmly. Maybe they knew a girl, probably one of the daughters of his sister Luise Becker even, who would want to marry the young man from Texas. The whole family was amused to hear that Julius now tried his hands as a matchmaker. Very likely Georg Witting found a bride. At least he sent engagement cards.[62] It can not be verified, though, who his wife was.

Julius Wagner had pointed out in his letters to his family that life was not at all easy for his wife Emilie. The sentences of old Noah Smithwick about Texas at the end of the 1820s in most ways still rang true for the pioneer life of the 1840s and 1850s: "Men talked hopefully of the future; children reveled in the novelty of the present; but the women—ah, there was where the situation bore heaviest. As one old lady remarked, Texas was 'a heaven for men and dogs, but a hell for women and oxen.' They—the women—talked sadly of the old homes and friends left behind, so very far behind it seemed then, of the hardships and bitter privations they were undergoing and the dangers that surrounded them."[63] The German women were unaccustomed and unprepared for the life that waited for them in Texas: few roads, great distances, few towns, little amusement, hard work. And there was more—something most settlers were not even aware of conciously and most travelers are not today either—something men might not have even recognized as much as women, as they were out during daytime and too distracted from their daily work to realize it in the nights: the sounds and smells of Texas are different from those in central Europe. The concert of the birds and insects at night in Texas is much louder and completely different from that in Germany. The smell of the plants and the earth is different. Although that did not cause a direct problem for anyone, it made it much more difficult for many women who stayed at home all day and night to feel at home. Mary Crownover Rabb remembered: "How many tryels and trubbles have we past threw to gether in texas."[64] Emilie Wagner wrote back home: "It is true, when I described the situation of a woman who had belonged to the educated class in Germany as being unpleasant—especially during the beginning—as far as her daily work, her sphere of influence and her family life are concerned. This remains true as long as the financial situation is deplorable." And Friedrich Schlecht who had come to Texas in 1848 and met a number of German settlers on his trips through East- and Central-Texas recalled: "A farmer who has settled in the wilderness, built a house, made fences, and cultivated land is to be respected for this very reason, since it takes great energy and endurance to surmount the hardships and difficulties such a colonization entails."[65]

It wouldn't be true, however, to say that all German women in Texas suffered and had to endure hard times. Quite a number of the women with a higher education or from families with a higher cultural background and standard tried to cultivate the arts and maintain a certain standard of living in the wilderness. The story of Valeska von Roeder who had her piano brought to Texas is just one example. Although she died before the piano arrived, her sister Rosa took it and used to play it on various festive occasions. Another was Agnes von Beust who sang opera arias. Her husband, Dr. Adolf Douai, accompanied her on the piano in concerts they gave together with other German musicians, like the violinist Listich and the violoncellist von Scheliche in New Braunfels.[66] And even those who indeed faced hard times tried to keep their good spirits and their optimism. Only a few could not really cope with the situation on the frontier and suffered. Emilie Wagner was one of those.

Although she managed to get along, raise her children, and be a loyal and faithful wife to her husband, she always felt homesick and never came to like her life in Texas. In the long letter she wrote her parents in the spring of 1851 one can read between the lines how difficult life on the frontier was for her. Housework alone proved to be a difficult task:

> Washing is my hardest business, and I have to do it once a week because it's impossible to do when I let it pile up over a longer period of time. Normally my washing day is Friday and I generally have fifteen to thirty pieces to do. When I strip the beds it's much more of course; on Saturdays I do the ironing and clean the house and the kitchen. Everything has to be neat and shining and I work the whole day even if I cannot move a limb in the evening for exhaustion. There is so much to do in and around the house. . . . Everyone can see how much I love to keep everything in order. Even Julius, who does not care so much about tidiness himself, is pleased at how nice and clean our house is. I could make him get rid of some of his bad habits even. Still he does not understand why he should not be allowed to spit in his Texan blockhouse, yet I do not like it at all as I try to keep the floor of our house as clean as possible.

It was not only the hard labor with which Emilie had to cope. The lack of money and many goods she was used to from Germany bore hard on her. Her parents had sent the young couple a check for over 200 *Gulden*. It was neither the first nor the last subsidy they received. The horse Julius had bought from Roeder was not paid cash on hand either; and although buying on credit was common on the frontier, it was not easy for Emilie to accept this. Along with the money and the toys for the children mentioned earlier, Emilie's parents sent her numerous things that were hard to obtain or too expensive for the Wagners then, like clothes, cloth, medicine, china, wine, dried fruit, wicks, sewing silk, and guitar strings. These things were not difficult to get for the Wagners only. From Galveston Alwin Sörgel wrote back home to Germany in 1846: "A few iron pots and pans, china plates and cups, as cheap here as in Germany, an ax, a saw and auger—though expensive they are superior to the German counterpart—will complete a fully equipped household. Linens, clothes, and shoes are the only items that you should bring along and, if possible, money, the more the better."[67] Emilie tried to soothe her parents, thus revealing how much she had complained before: "How on earth was it possible that my letters have made such a horrible impression on you, as they have obviously?! Did I really paint everything black in black or does this impression derive from the fact that you all—at least the major part of you—lead a rich life full of sensual enjoyments (I'm thinking of your laden tables)? I think that's why my reports about the various privations we suffer in this country have frightened you, as much as they have frightened me in the beginning because I have been a spoilt child of Europe."[68] During the first years in Texas she tried to make the best out of the situation, but as Julius did not succeed as much as they had hoped, she longed for her beloved home country more and more.

Fortunately she never conveyed these feelings to her children who remembered their parents differently:

> One must think of the difficulties of all sorts with which they had to struggle, coming as they did from an orderly way of life and transplanted to an inhospitable and lawless country. But both were naturally happy and optimistic, and so they were able to overcome all dangers and hardships. They lived in Colettoville for fifteen years and made friends there with some German families, who like them had come from Beautiful Germany to find a new home here. These friendships stood the test in all situations and held firm until fate or death brought them to an end.[69]

One of these friendships had been to Albrecht von Roeder and his family, as already mentioned. Even after Albrecht's early death, Julius helped his family. As he had been quite successful, he was able to buy the land they lived on from Albrecht's widow Caroline von Roeder on 19 April 1858 for ninety-two dollars. Together with Albrecht's nephew Joachim, Julius also appraised the forty-eight horses, the 150 head of cattle, the seventy-eight hogs and the one yoke of oxen that Albrecht's widow Caroline had to sell in order to pay her debts. In 1860, Julius bought five heads of cattle from the von Roeder estate for fifty-four dollars and the next year another four for thirty-seven dollars. His friend William Westhoff bought eight horses from Caroline von Roeder for $390. One cannot say anymore if Julius Wagner bought this beef to increase his stock or simply for butchering, because in the census of 1860 he was listed as butcher. His real estate value in the 1860 census is given at $450 and his personal property value at $1,210. Obviously things were not going badly for him. [70]A cæsura in the life of Julius and Emilie Wagner which brought an end to some friendships was the outbreak of the Civil War in 1861. It brought an end to their life on the Coleto and cut Julius off from his brother Wilhelm, who by that time was living in the United States too, but in the northern States, in Illinois.

3. A "Revolutionary" Emigrant

THE STRONG, BEARDED MAN OF medium height is said to have attended the court's session in disguise at the Mannheimer *Obergerichtshof* (high court) in November 1850. He could not believe that this court of appeal would uphold the sentence of the *Hofgericht* (court) at Freiburg i.Br. from June 8, 1850. But when the judges came and announced their verdict, Wilhelm Wagner was stunned. The *Obergerichtshof* confirmed the sentence: "Pastor Wagner is guilty of high treason, and therefore sentenced to one and a half years of *Arbeitshaus* [workhouse, a slightly milder form of hard labor], to pay damages and to take over all costs of the proceedings. That is the sentence of the whole court." As fast as he could, Wilhelm Wagner left the building and hastened down Kurpfalz Street straight towards the impressive castle. There he turned left in the direction of the railway station, which he reached after about twenty minutes. He took the next train to Efringen, close to the Swiss border.[1]

Wilhelm Wagner had been born on 24 September 1803, the first son of Peter Wagner and his wife Luise. At that time, Peter Wagner was a pastor and schoolteacher at Dürkheim. When the family moved to Amorbach and Wilhelm had reached the proper age, he went to elementary school where he was taught by his father too. After he finished elementary school, his father took over his education completely and tutored him at home, giving his son lessons in Greek and Latin. The Napoleonic wars left a deep impression on young Wilhelm. In later years he would never get tired of telling his children how the various armies—first the French, then the Saxons, the Prussians, Austrians, Bavarians and later even the Russians—had marched through Amorbach and Uiffingen, even taking up quarters there. The wars of liberation against Napoleon had led to an era of nationalism. Sentiments were especially high among Germans students. Wilhelm Wagner was no exception here.[2]

In 1819, the Wagners moved to Aglasterhausen and from 1820 to 1822 Wilhelm attended the final three classes of the Lyceum in Heidelberg. He stayed in Heidelberg to study theology and history. In contrast to his brother Julius, he gave private lessons to ease the financial burden his education caused his father. His favorite professors were the celebrated theologian Heinrich Eberhard Gottlob Paulus (1761-1851) and the historian Friedrich Christoph Schlosser (1776-1861). Like the rest of his family, including his father, Wilhelm was a true son of enlightenment and an ardent fighter against religious and political intolerance. This spiritual basis was further strengthened by the lectures and writings of Schlosser and Paulus. The latter had first been professor of oriental languages at the University of Jena and had been on friendly terms with such famous German authors as Goethe, Schiller, Herder, and Fichte. In 1810 Paulus was appointed professor of theology and philosophy at the University of Heidelberg and received the title *Geheimer Kirchenrath* (special member of the church consistory). He was one of the leading advocates of religious rationalism. Psychology and pragmatism to him were the only valid means of interpretation of the Bible, especially the miracles. Schlosser had studied theology originally before he was chosen as Wilken's successor for a history chair at the University of Heidelberg in 1817. Being forty-one at that time, Schlosser was already rather old when he received this appointment. During his first years in Heidelberg he wrote volume one of his most famous work, the *History of the Eighteenth and Nineteenth Centuries* in six volumes. Being the first historian to study the significance of literature as historical source, he made the moralistic principles of enlightenment the basis for his judgment of history. This way, he formed the conception of history of the German liberal middle class.[3] Paulus' rationalism and Schlosser's moral principles intensified the spiritual education Wilhelm Wagner had received from his father. In one of his final exams Wilhelm wrote: "Reason is the ability of our mind to imagine perfection. Those who believe in reason only keep that in mind which they realize as being concordant with the ideas of perfection, shown by reason."[4] In 1826, Wilhelm passed his theological exams. He had become a member of a fraternity like his brother Julius would, but he strictly avoided drinking and did not care that many fellow students ridiculed him for that. Although his father was a heavy smoker, Wilhelm never smoked. Even as a student, he already led a rather ascetic life.

After his exams, Wilhelm did not find a suitable position right away. At first he helped his father Peter as vicar in Bargen until he accepted the position of a private tutor at the home of forester Wetzel at the Zwingenberg castle close to the Neckar River. During the summer holidays, Wilhelm took the two Wetzel boys on a number of hiking tours. In 1833, after a tour to Baden-Baden, Wilhelm realized one morning in Karlsruhe that he had run out of money. As it was a sunny and warm September day, he and the boys started walking home. In Dühren, near Sinsheim, he stopped by the local vicarage to ask the pastor there for a small loan. This pastor was Jakob Christian Odenwald (1779-1838) who was married to Charlotte Wucherer (1793-1838). They had eight children: seven daughters and one son, Karl who had been born in 1822. Odenwald's oldest daughter Friederike, who was then twenty-one, immediately caught the eye of Wilhelm and they both fell in love right away. The expenses for Karl's going to the *Lyceum* in Heidelberg were so high that Jakob Odenwald asked for the richer parish of Ansbach. He got this position, and the Odenwalds moved there on 25 October 1834, with the help of Wilhelm Wagner. In November, Wilhelm and Friederike officially announced their engagement.

After eight years of waiting, Wilhelm Wagner finally received his first parish in Gersbach near Schopfheim in 1835. "He wanted this pastorate especially, because he was a great admirer of the poet Johann Peter Hebel. He wanted to live in these parts, where Hebel had lived in order to get better acquainted with the country and the people there and to be able to understand his poetic works more fully."[5] Wilhelm's fiancée had to stay at home because her father was seriously ill at that time. On June 19, 1836, Wilhelm and Friederike were married at the church in Ansbach. After their wedding the young couple travelled back to Gersbach, a small village with nearly 580 inhabitants in the Black Forest. It was a poor community living off the forest, the raising of sheep, and a few cattle. Life was not easy for the young pastor and his wife. As this area of the Black Forest was covered with woods and small meadows on thin soil, farming, which could have eased the economic situation of the Wagners, was not possible. Quite a lot of the daily necessities had to be brought from the next town at some expense. For breakfast the Wagners had a thick bean soup; for lunch Friederike served vegetables, potatoes, and starchy food like pancakes and noodles.

Only twice a week was she able to put roast meat on the table. Milk, white cheese, and fruit were their normal supper. Coffee, tea, cocoa, wine, or beer were only served to a visitor. Wilhelm was very proud of having introduced buckwheat to this remote region of the Black Forest. He also planted the first black cherry tree in Gersbach and it bore plenty of fruit. Having some sheep, Wilhelm dressed in a dark cloth made out of sheep wool. He only wore linen shirts and a cap with a peak. Getting up early, Wilhelm Wagner went to bed with the sunset. As Gersbach was such a remote place in the Black Forest, snowfall in winter cut the Wagners off from civilization. In 1841 Wilhelm complained: "During the hard winter which often lasts for eight months, it is very often impossible to get medical care. The next doctor is about three hours away. Already we have to mourn the loss of two of our children, and we cannot free ourselves from the painful thoughts that these, our loved ones, could still be alive if only a doctor could have come to us in the turbulent days of their illnesses."[6]

The two children whom Wilhelm Wagner mentioned were Friederike's and his first child, Karl, and their third child, the first girl, Luise who did not live long after her birth in 1840. These were not the only losses the Wagners had to mourn during their years in Gersbach. Friederike's parents had been seriously ill in 1837 and did not recover. After a severe winter, her father Jakob died in February 1838 and her mother only two months later. Suddenly Friederike had lost both her parents. It was especially hard for her as her father had died before she could see him once again. And while she rushed to Ansbach to comfort her mother, her firstborn child Karl died of diphtheria. Together with her mother-in-law Louise, she hurried back home but was not allowed to see her dead little boy who had been buried quickly in order to prevent the dangerous disease from spreading. Being orphans now, her brother Karl stayed in Heidelberg and her eighteen-year-old sister Karoline was taken up by Wilhelm's parents in Aglasterhausen. Wilhelm and Friederike gave a home to the four youngest Odenwald girls (between five and ten years old). To help her oldest sister, twenty-year-old Sophie Odenwald accompanied the little ones to Gersbach.[7]

Considering the many people he had to feed now, the pay of Wilhelm Wagner was extremely bad. He only received 478 *Gulden* and 43 *Kreuzer*. Only twice was he granted a special bonus of 100 *Gulden*. In thirteen petitions between 1838 and 1844, he asked for a new position or for another parish. He received no answer although he was recommended highly by his superiors. They attested that he was a perfect pastor; he was preaching by heart and always caring for others. When the local teacher fell ill, he taught the children. When someone in his flock was struck with an illness, even at night he would walk to the next doctor, three hours away. After the two Sunday services, he used to walk to the woods with the local youth, singing and merrymaking, even occasionally lighting homemade fireworks. All this was possible because Wilhelm Wagner was not only a kind and Christian man, but also a person with an iron physical constitution, incredible strength, and enormous willpower. Yet, there was more to him. Although never active in party politics, Wilhelm Wagner was a *homo politicus*, an outspoken liberal. As a young vicar he had been enthusiastic about the Greeks and their war of independence against the Turks from 1821 to 1829, and voiced his solidarity with the Polish people in their war of 1815 against Russia.

In 1839, his friend and future brother-in-law Carl Baumann, who also was the godfather of Wilhelm's first son Karl, was in a dilemma since he was Catholic and his fiancée Henriette Wagner, Protestant. In Cologne, the Catholic Archbishop Clemens August von Droste zu Vischering vigorously fought for the Catholic doctrine, that "mixed" marriages were only acceptable to the church when the couple solemnly swore to raise their children in the Catholic faith. His predecessor, Archbishop Count August Ferdinand von Spiegel, had reached a secret understanding with the Prussian authorities to tolerate "mixed" marriages without asking for such an oath, so the government asked Droste to stick to the agreement made with Spiegel, which Droste vehemently refused. This ongoing quarrel, known as the *kölnische Wirren,* reached its peak with the arrest of Droste in 1837. He was imprisoned in the *Festung* (special form of prison) Minden. The curia in Rome responded by declaring Droste's opinion the only valid one. The Prussian government had to give in. This situation led Wilhelm to write to Carl Baumann: "Whose reason in politics doesn't develop any further than feudalism won't make any progress in religious and church matters either. Let everyone gain full acumen and spread the light of reason and knowledge everywhere! Then pastors, demagogues, and aristocrats can do no more harm. Give freedom of education and teaching, constitutions to the people, freedom of the press and not just words! It will get better!" Wilhelm did not want to confide more of his thoughts in writing so he ended his political statement by pointing out that he would say more about this once they met again.[8]

As often as his time permitted, he walked down the mountains of the Black Forest, marching the whole night through, and crossed the nearby border to Switzerland. There he met with many liberals. He was fond of the *Schützenfest* (shooting match festivities) in Aarau where he would listen to the patriotic speeches of like-minded compatriots. On one of his visits to Aarau (a major city in the canton Aargau, between Basel and Zürich) in July 1841 he became acquainted with Franz Waller and Augustin Keller. Waller (1803-1879) had studied law in Jena, was *Großrat* (representative) for the canton Aargau from 1837 to 1846 and director of the Rhine saltworks between 1849 and 1875. Holding many other official positions too, he completed the civil law code of Aargau between 1847 and 1855 and wrote the inheritance law for his canton in 1856. Together with Frey-Hérosé and Wieland he was responsible for the official politics of the canton Aargau during his lifetime. Wilhelm Wagner did not converse with him on matters of law but about religious issues. Besides being an expert in civil law, Waller was a radical Protestant. Here he had the same opinion as Augustin Keller (1805-1883). Having studied philosophy and history in Munich, Breslau, and Berlin, Keller became a teacher in 1831 at the *Gymnasium* in Luzern. Between 1834 and 1842 he was *Großrat* like Waller. As a liberal Catholic he fought for the emancipation of the Jews and fiercely against the Jesuits. Rejecting the Catholic dogma of papal infallibility he was one of the founders of the "Old Catholic" movement—a special group of Catholics who rejected the authority of the Pope and who lived mainly in Germany, England, and Switzerland.

With their radical liberal ideas and religious beliefs, Waller and Keller were the right match for Wilhelm Wagner. He praised the day he had met them and saw them as heroes in their common fight against Catholics and Pietists. To be able to talk with them he did not mind his night-long walks to Aarau.[9]

After eight years of service in Gersbach, Wilhelm was finally transferred to Brombach in the Wiesental near Lörrach in 1844. In 1840, Brombach had 753 inhabitants and in 1850 there were already 1,000. Brombach was prospering in a way because of the industrialization of the

Wiesental which began around 1830, mainly with textile industries promoted by Swiss investors. Three of the five children born in Gersbach had survived: Karl F. in 1839, Wilhelm H. in 1841, and Luise in 1843. It was quite customary at the time to give subsequent children the same names as children who had died. As he had done in Gersbach, Wilhelm founded a reading club in Brombach at the Wilden Mann Inn in 1847 to read to his flock, thus making them familiar with German literature. His joy was great when a farmer called Rösch once stepped up to him and told him: "Pastor, you have made a human being out of me, because only since I read and have learned to think, I feel like a human being."[10] He also established a singing society together with his close friend Wenck, who was the local teacher. The next four years were happy years for Wilhelm Wagner. Two more children were born: Hermann Ludwig in 1845 and Julius in 1848. Wilhelm was loved and respected by most citizens of Brombach.

The years 1848 and 1849 changed all this. These years became known as the German Revolution of 1848-1849. The roots basically lay in the restoration policy of Clemens Lothar Wenzel Duke of Metternich, the Austrian chancellor. Baden had become the hope for German liberalism, for unity and freedom. Those Germans who were interested in politics watched the development in the southwest of Germany. The parliament of Baden, the *Landtag,* was faced with five difficult questions that it had to solve: the new *Gemeinde-Ordnung* (local codes), the emancipation of the Jews, the discharge of the feudal taxes and duties, new industrial legislation, and the relationship of church and state. Parliamentary elections in the spring of 1831 brought a liberal majority to the house. Metternich's influence was so strong, however, that censorship had to be reestablished in Baden. After the liberal foreign minister of Baden, von Türkheim, was replaced with a confidant of Metternich, the highly despised and feared Freiherr Friedrich Landolin Karl von Blittersdorff, as a result of the secret Vienna conferences of 1834, liberalism was at stake again in Baden. At the same time, the dissonant and dissenting opposition in the parliament of Baden was united by Blittersdorff's outward rejection of any form of liberal constitution or liberalism in general. He fought hard, especially against the liberal tendencies in the *2. Kammer* (a kind of House of Commons) of the *Landtag* and the high officials who, as a special class in Baden, were very liberal. After the election of 1842, the liberal opposition returned to the *Landtag* stronger than ever. One year later, in November 1843, Blittersdorff resigned. Having failed with his restorative, conservative policy, his resignation nevertheless did not help to improve the situation. The Grand Duke of Baden simply was too hesitant to bring about the necessary reforms. After the election in 1846 that culminated in another sweeping victory for the liberals, the Grand Duke appointed the somewhat liberal president of parliament Johann Batist Bekk as secretary of the interior and head of the government. Yet, the situation got worse, the tension heightened. The public did not believe in the ability and the will of the government anymore to carry out the reforms, especially the much wanted and needed agrarian constitution.

Between 1815 and 1846 the population in Baden had risen about thirty-five percent—from 1,015,000 to 1,367,486. In 1849 most of these people still lived in the country. Only 322,558 out of 1,361,800 persons were citizens of the various towns of Baden, towns that still had the character of small country villages. Even Mannheim and Karlsruhe, the biggest cities of Baden, had just 24,000 inhabitants. Only twelve cities had more than 5,000 inhabitants. Industrialization was comparatively low still; merely 17,105 workers and 17,654 day laborers were counted in 1849. The so-called working class only made up about 2.5 percent of the total population. The rest, and among them most of the really poor people, were living in and off the country. And all these people were waiting for reforms that would lift the financial burdens of the old feudal rights. Although some steps had been taken to ease this burden, the nobility not only still possessed most of the farmland in Baden, they continued to exercise their old rights, such as the jurisdiction in their territories, the supervision of schools, churches, and medical care. The rise of the population figures and the lack of work led to a growing unrest among the impoverished rural Badeners. The so called "hunger-year" of 1847 with its bad harvests only aggravated this situation.[11]

Finally, the radical liberals called for a meeting on September 12, 1847, at the inn Zum Salmen in Offenburg. At this meeting they did not use the word "republic" but they demanded liberty and justice for all, freedom of the press as well as of education, and juries in court. The two leaders of this meeting had become quite prominent and popular already: the *Obergerichtsadvokat* (lawyer) Friedrich Hecker from Mannheim and the lawyer Gustav von Struve from the same city.

Friedrich Hecker (1811-1881) became one of the most prominent leaders of the radical liberals. After studying law in Munich and Heidelberg, Hecker received his Ph.D. in law in June 1834. He became a respected and well-known lawyer at the Mannheimer *Hofgericht*. In 1842 Hecker was elected to the second *Landtag* of Baden. Very soon he was recognized for his passionate speeches on social issues.[12] Gustav von Struve (1805-1870) was an inspiring leader like Hecker. He had studied law in Göttingen and Heidelberg, practiced law in Mannheim and was also editor of two outspoken liberal papers: the *Deutscher Zuschauer* and the *Mannheimer Journal*. He had been in prison for his articles many times and was fighting against censorship, social grievances, and for liberty and freedom for the common man.

The same questions that occupied the minds of all liberals in Germany also inflamed the students, workers, and members of the National Guard in France. With his interdiction of a reform debate in parliament, the French Prime Minister François-Pierre-Guillaume Guizot caused the French revolution of February 22 and 24, 1848. Barricade fights and his hesitation to dismiss the unpopular Guizot forced King Louis Philippe to resign. The French revolutionary forces proclaimed France's Second Republic. This revolutionary spirit soon spread all over Europe. When the first news from France reached Baden on 27 February, a big crowd gathered spontaneously in Mannheim. The so-called "radicals" soon controlled this gathering and issued a petition to parliament asking for absolute freedom of the press, the establishing of jury courts and a public militia as well as an immediate calling of a free and independent parliament. The same demands were put forward during a public gathering in Offenburg on 19 March 1848, which had been called by Gustav von Struve and Fritz Hecker. At the same time, the first militias were formed. Workers from Mannheim, professors and students from Heidelberg, and farmers from the Odenwald organized themselves. The same situation prevailed in the rest of the German states: new members of government were called into office, reforms were started, compromises were sought and radical agitators gathered followers and even militias at the same time. The revolutionary spirit which had spread from Paris did not confine itself to the German states but forced the much hated Austrian chancellor Metternich to resign on 13 March. Six days later, the Prussian King Friedrich Wilhelm, who had tried to suppress his citizen's uprisings by force of arms, had to give in and accept the rule of the people of Berlin. On April 12, 1848, Hecker and Struve proclaimed the Republic in Konstanz and called for a public uprising. The German revolution seemed to have won.

In a somewhat typical German manner, however, this revolution lost its impetus and eventually failed. The first national assembly constituted itself at the Paulskirche in Frankfurt on 18 May 1848. The delegates drew up a constitution for the whole of Germany. But instead of going all the way to make the united German State a republic, the delegates hesitated and turned to the conservative monarchs again by offering the Prussian King Friedrich Wilhelm IV the emperor's crown for this new German empire. Friedrich Wilhelm, like his fellow monarchs sensing that the liberal movement was losing its momentum, turned down this crown. The new constitution had failed before it ever went into real practice. During the following months the national assembly in Frankfurt dissolved, the reigning monarchs in the German states found their old strength again and marched against the radical liberals with armed forces. Grand Duke Leopold of Baden even called Prussian troops for help to crush the various liberal uprisings in his state. Not only the leading agitators like Hecker and Struve were pursued with all means—Hecker escaped to Switzerland and Struve was imprisoned—everybody who had shown sympathy with the so-called rebels had to fear criminal prosecution.[13] Slander for revenge and envy became a common practice those days. Wilhelm Wagner and even his old father Peter became victims of this practice too.

At the elections to the new *Landtag* in 1846, Wilhelm had become an elector. Many wanted him to go as a representative to this new parliament, but Wilhelm declined such requests. He saw his obligations to the common people by serving among them and not in representing them in a legislative body. He was no man for active political work.[14] When the revolution began though, he welcomed it wholeheartedly and supported it with his sermons. Loved and respected by most of his parishioners at Gersbach and Brombach he nevertheless made quite a few enemies, especially among his superiors, by being an outspoken liberal. He wished for a united, republican Germany. When Gustav von Struve raised a militia in Lörrach in September of 1848 and the *Brombacher Volkswehr* (the people's militia of Brombach) started their march to Lörrach in order to join him, Wilhelm let his ten-year-old son Karl accompany this group as drummer boy. In June 1849 Wilhelm gave a farewell sermon to the *Brombacher Volkswehr* when it followed the call of the provisional republican government of Baden to fight against the combined troops of the Grand Duke and the Prussians. Wilhelm addressed those men in his church officially as their pastor and praised the ideas of freedom and unity for Germany. He never made a secret out of his solidarity with Hecker, Struve, and their cause.

Thus, when the revolution was crushed, Wilhelm faced severe accusations of disloyalty towards the Grand Duke and even criminal charges for high treason. The first of the Wagner family to feel the wrath of the victorious old government was the seventy-seven-year-old Peter Wagner. He was arrested on 20 August 1849, on the accusation of having shown open sympathy with the rebellious liberals. Peter Wagner reportedly refused to have a seat in the back seat of the carriage at his arrest, as this place was not suitable for a prisoner. The local policeman is said to have replied that it was not correct for the pastor to sit on the box beside him either. Wagner was not only arrested, he was suspended from office and the payment of his salary was stopped effective July 23.[15] He spent fourteen days in the prison of Mosbach. Although he was acquitted nearly one year later, on Friday, 28 June 1850, he had lost his position. His superiors, the *Oberkirchenrat* (High Consistory) had actually thought of suspending him for quite a while. Assuring him that his conduct was above all criticism, he nevertheless was accused of having had a negative influence on his parish by following a liberal religious course and praising political freedom. His attendance at the memorial service for Robert Blum was especially held against him. Robert Blum (1807-1848) was a founder of the German-Catholic movement at Leipzig in 1845, became vice president of the provisional Austrian parliament in 1848, and was representative to the first national assembly in Frankfurt and in Vienna, to which he was elected on a leftist ticket. He agreed to the revolution. After its failure, he was shot, together with other leaders of this revolution, in Vienna. The authorities accused Peter Wagner of having used strong words, like "fighting against tyranny" and "draining every drop of blood out of the poor" in his sermon.

Most citizens of Aglasterhausen, together with the local council, wrote a letter to the church officials on 11 April 1850, asking for the reinstatement of Peter Wagner to his office. They declared their full confidence in

Wagner, that he had never spoken of "fighting against tyranny" and never called for revenge. He had been a devoted pastor, a true friend, counsellor and trusted adviser in hard times they wrote. Even the Catholic citizens wrote that they held Peter Wagner in the highest respect.[16] The die was cast, however; Peter Wagner never returned to his office. After his release from prison, he and his wife moved to Mannheim where they rented an apartment across the street from Carl Baumann and his family. There Peter Wagner died on November 6, 1853.

Wilhelm Wagner faced the same fate as his father Peter. Like the older Wagner he had become too liberal for most of his superiors and his religious beliefs aroused much criticism especially among the Pietists who were quite numerous in that area. Even his brother-in-law Karl Odenwald later wrote in his family chronicle that Wilhelm favored the poor, the helpless and all workers and deeply mistrusted the nobility, the military, and all officials: "This prejudice was based on his complete misunderstanding of the GOD-given order of all classes and the GOD-given existence of rich and poor. This wrong moral attitude led him to believe in democratic principles."[17] Wilhelm knew that he antagonized many people with his ideas. In August 1849 he met with his brother Julius, when the latter had come to Germany to marry Emilie Schneider in Offenburg. The two brothers talked for a couple of hours. Although Wilhelm appeared to be happy and in high spirits as ever, Julius nevertheless offered him to come to Texas and stay with them in case Wilhelm would suddenly need to go into exile. Wilhelm was still optimistic though that he would be able to stay aloof during the approaching political turmoil.

Three weeks after the revolution in Baden had been crushed by military force in August 1849, the *Oberkirchenrat* (High Consistory) asked the civil district officials for an investigation into Wilhelm Wagner's conduct during the upheaval. Having read the report by *Amtmann* Winter, the High Consistory then suspended Wilhelm temporarily from all his duties on 9 November that year and sent his files to the *Hofgericht* (court) at Freiburg im Breisgau. As was the custom then, this court came to a decision simply by reading the files and not calling for any witnesses. On 8 June 1850, the court came to the decision that Wilhelm Wagner was guilty of high treason. Immediately Wilhelm asked a lawyer, a Mr. Gräfle from Schopfheim, to represent him and to appeal against this verdict to the *Oberhofgericht* (high court). Wilhelm was not arrested and did not have to give bail, but all his means and property were confiscated. Wilhelm denied having accumulated much wealth, but over the years he had been able to buy land as a kind of security for his children. All in all he figured his wealth to be about 3,000 *Gulden*. All of this was in great danger now. Outwardly Wilhelm showed great confidence in the justice of the high court and expressed sound optimism. He confessed to his brother Karl in Austria at the end of July 1850 though, that he had secretly written Julius and asked him under what conditions Julius could take him and his family in. In this letter to Karl, Wilhelm also mentioned that another plan existed which involved their brother-in-law Carl Baumann. A friend of the latter wanted to sell all his property in order to establish a colony with all members of the Wagner family in Missouri. The problem was that all the 60,000 *Florin* this friend possessed had been confiscated for the same reasons Wilhelm's property had been seized. In case this friend of Carl's could regain some of the money, he still planned to buy land in America in April 1851. Whatever happened, one thing seemed to be sure though for Wilhelm: "We will not stay here any longer, that is, on this side of the ocean; we belong to another soil than the German one! And without doubt our children will live happier on a fertile farm than in the so called civilized Germany. My decision is not based upon the present political situation but on a thought that I have secretly harbored for some time now and that is bearing fruit these days." Wilhelm continued writing about his five children: Karl (age eleven), Wilhelm (age nine), Luise (age seven), Hermann (age five) and Julius (age two). Hoping that his children could stay healthy, Wilhelm dreamt of a life in the North American prairie, hunting buffalo and bears and creating a prosperous colony together with friends and others of the family he hoped would follow him soon.[18]

One month earlier he had already hinted about these plans in a note and a letter he had sent to his brother-in-law Carl Baumann. He also told Carl that he had not learned English yet but wanted to follow Carl's advice and do it now with great zeal. In these notes, which he had delivered personally and secretly by his sister-in-law Karoline (a sister of his wife), Wilhelm again mentioned his fantasies about hunting in the prairie. More realistically, he also emphazised that he and his wife Rike (nickname for Friederike) were practicing their farming abilities and raising cauliflower and cabbage with great success—vegetables they hoped to plant in the New World too.[19] Having more or less made up his mind to migrate to the United States, he most likely had hoped to set the date after his own choosing. Needless to say, he wanted to take his family and his money with him in order to give them a good start. Therefore, he hoped for a repeal of his verdict by the *Oberhofgericht* in Mannheim. Staying with his parents at Mannheim, Wilhelm waited for the decision of the court. When this high court upheld the sentence of the court at Freiburg, Wilhelm knew that he had to flee to the United States with nothing but his clothes.

After having heard the sentence of the high court on 25 November 1850, Wilhelm took the train to Efringen (a small village nearly three walking hours north of Basel) near Weil at the Rhine River where he could rest at the home of the Lenz family. A Protestant pastor himself, old Lenz was a friend of the Baumann family and glad to help Wilhelm. The same night, he arranged with a trustworthy ferryman to take Wilhelm by night to the other side of the Rhine to the French department of Alsace. This trip did not go unnoticed, and German frontier guards fired a few shots at the rowboat. The boatman made Wilhelm crouch in the bottom of the boat, and they made it safely to the French side of the river. From there Wilhelm went to Basel in Switzerland, where he took a room at Bertrand's Hotel in Klein-Basel ("lower"-Basel—a special part of the city). Here he not only communicated with his wife and friends by mail, he also received numerous visitors.

Wilhelm's fate had attracted wide attention. Even former political opponents voiced their sympathy and regretted that a man who had done so much good in his parish had suddenly become a victim of the political turbulence of his times. Many friends and members of his former parish collected money to help him. When some of his former parishioners visited him one day, he had just received notice that he could ask the Grand Duke for clemency and that this petition would most likely be granted. Chances were high his punishment would then be annulled. Wilhelm asked his visitors what to do. Among them was the farmer Rösch, who had praised Wilhelm for having introduced him to German literature. Now this simple man stepped forward and said: "Pastor, you once read Schiller's poem 'The Song of Joy' to us. There it says: 'men's pride comes before kings' thrones'— and more I cannot say." Deeply moved, Wilhelm started to cry and grabbed the farmer's hand: "You're right, Rösch, I will never ask for clemeny!"[20] It was after this meeting that Wilhelm Wagner definitely decided to emigrate to the United States as soon as possible, as soon as he had enough money to make the trip.

First, however, he had to move again, as the government of Baden formally complained to the Swiss government about the many German political refugees living in Basel. Wilhelm found shelter at the home of the chemist Sommer in Langenthal, canton Bern, to whom he had been recommended by a mutual friend. There he received an invitation from his brother Julius to come to Texas, where Julius offered him half of his seventy-five acres of land. Wilhelm knew from Julius' earlier descriptions though, that life in Texas was not easy. Especially in the region where Julius lived in, food was scarce and transportation as well as schools not highly developed. Therefore, he decided soon to go to one of the northern states. To be prepared as best as he could, Wilhelm not only learned English as fast as he could but also the cooper trade. He was excited about going to America now, although the news from back home was rather sad.

As soon as his flight became known to the authorities, Wilhelm's estate was confiscated and his household items were sold by auction. It was most bitter for Wilhelm that his beloved library was put up for auction too. In order to help him, his friends tried to buy back as many books as possible for him. His books not only had sentimental value for Wilhelm, but they were also part of his political belief system. This library, therefore, was also an issue in Wilhelm's legal dispute with the authorities. Point four of the official accusations of the *Hofgericht* at Freiburg i.Br. mentioned his reading club in which Wilhelm was said to have read books and articles that fostered the revolutionary spirit. In his lengthy statement of defence, Wilhelm scrupulously explained the articles and literature he had read with the members of his club and strictly denied any revolutionary tendencies of this circle. He nevertheless wrote: "With all the often expressed hopes for an improvement of our living conditions, I have always pointed out that without an individual improvement of our spirit and personal way of living no such change to a better society would be possible and durable. 'Should it get better, we have to get better first!' has always been my motto."[21]

Not only had the authorities stopped all financial support for the Wagner family, they also asked for the immediate payment of all law costs. On January 14, 1851, Wilhelm was officially dismissed from his office by decree of the Grand Duke's *Staatsministerium* (chancellory). At the beginning of 1851, Friederike and her children had to move out of the parsonage to make room for Wilhelm's successor, a staunch Pietist. This was especially hard for Friederike as she was pregnant. In February she asked the local authorities for financial aid as her situation was desperate. Her petition was viewed favorably and she received 100 *Gulden*. This was not so bad, considering that the average wages for skilled workers in the textile manufacturing industry was about one-half *Gulden* a day (working thirteen hours a day, but only for men as women earned just half that money), for skilled workers in the jewelry industry one and a half *Gulden* daily. The price of twenty pounds of wheat was a little over two *Gulden*. The argumentation of the local church committee sheds some light on the attitude of the authorities at that time:

> Although we have to admit regretfully that the wife of pastor Wagner has spoken about the political situation of the years 1848 and 1849 in the same spirit as her husband, we have to attest her nevertheless truthfully that we hold her irresponsible for her husband. We attest her that his influence, as well as that of other fakes who always crept into the parsonage, have made her crazy in a way that made her believe her husband's doings were correct.[22]

She also asked for permission to emigrate to the United States and follow her husband. This wish was granted. On March 17, 1851, she gave birth to their sixth child, a daughter named Friederike. The two oldest sons, Karl and Wilhelm, stayed with their Wagner grandparents at Mannheim. Together with her three youngest children, Hermann, Julius, and the baby Friederike, Wilhelm's wife found a home with the widow of the merchant Sturm at Steinen, a small town slightly northeast of Basel. Friederike had chosen that place because she wanted to be as close as possible to her husband. Their eight-year-old daughter Luise was given a home by the family of the businessman Strübe at Schopfheim. Wilhelm's family was now scattered and only hoped that he would find a place for them in the United States soon.

Wilhelm Wagner was, of course, not the only person who was driven out of Germany to the United States for political reasons. Between 1847 and 1853, 632,223 Germans emigrated in the United States, but the exact number of those who fled for political reasons during or after the revolution of 1848-1849 is nearly impossible to determine. This is even more difficult as they went individually and not in one or more groups. Historians have agreed to a number between three and four thousand "Forty-eighters," as this group is commonly called, who sought a new home in the United States. Many of them, like Wilhelm Wagner, first fled to Switzerland before they began their voyage to the New World. And most of them were not able to work in the same profession as they had done in Germany. The *Obergerichtsadvocat* (special lawyer) Lorenz Brentano who had been sentenced to life-long imprisonment *in absentia* ran a farm in Michigan, founded a German paper and as president of the Chicago City Council initiated the teaching of German at public schools. The lawyer Franz Heinrich Zitz from Mainz and colonel of the local militia who had been sentenced to death also had to earn his living as a farmer in the States and the *Hofgerichtsrat* Richter from Achern in Baden became a well-known saloon-keeper serving German beer in New York.[23]

Friedrich Hecker, Carl Schurz, Friedrich Kapp, Theodor Olshausen, and Emil Preetorius were immigrants who took an active part in United States politics and had considerable influence on labor and domestic politics there. Many of the Forty-eighters first joined the Democratic Party in the hope President Franklin Pierce would intervene in Germany to help the revolution win. When it was clear, though, that the revolutionary forces would not win, the Forty-eighters turned to another field of political activity. Many of them joined Abraham Lincoln and the Republican Party in their fight against slavery. Lincoln saw the American Germans as an important group of voters and thus held close contact with men like Carl Schurz, Theodor Canasius, and Friedrich Hecker. As many of the Forty-eighters were gifted orators and journalists, their influence on the German immigrants was considerable.[24]

The biggest problem for Wilhelm was money. Being deprived of all his funds, he depended on his friends to raise enough cash for his trip to the States and a start in the New World. In March of 1851, his brother-in-law Carl Baumann was able to send him 650 *Florin*, a sum that had been collected by friends, but how much Wilhelm received altogether is impossible to tell today. In his letter, Carl Baumann mentioned that a rich man from Basel, who held Wilhelm in the highest esteem, had provided him with a rather large sum of money for a fresh start in New York.[25] In the summer, Wilhelm must have collected enough to begin his voyage. Before he left, he had printed in the local paper a poem he had written as a form of "thanks" and "goodbye."

Ein Wagner, der kein Rad zu machen
Im Stande ist, werd ich geheissen
und wollt' als solcher , - s' ist zum Lachen -
Selbst nach Amerika reisen.
Wie würd' es mir ergangen sein,
Dort, wo die Freiheit nicht allein,
nein, auch die Arbeit thronet?

Da hat, als ich hier angekommen,
- Es war vor etwa sieben Wochen -
mein Freund sich meiner angenommen
Und ernstlich bald zu mir gesprochen:
"Ein Handwerk gold' nen Boden hat!
Befolgen Sie nun meinen Rat
Und lernen Sie ein Handwerk.

Des Freundes Rat hat mir gefallen,
Ich mußte es mir selber sagen:
Befolg' ich ihn, so wird in allen
Den kommenden wohl ernsten Tagen
Die Lehre mir von Nutzen sein;
Ich will der Küferei mich weih' n
In Mummenthalers Werkstatt!

Da fand ich einen braven Meister,
Der kann geschickt die Jungen lehren;
Und auch ein alter vielgereister
Geselle kann dort leicht vermehren

Noch seine Kunstgeschicklichkeit,
Wenn er zum Lernen nur bereit
Bei einem klugen Küfer.

Doch jetzt wird meine Lehrzeit leider
Hier allzu frühe unterbrochen.
Ich ziehe schon als Lehrling weiter
Und bilde mir nach wenig Wochen
Dort über'm Meere freudig ein,
Ein Küfermeister schon zu sein
In meinem kleinen Blockhaus.

Mich locket die Hoffnung zur eiligen Reise,
Doch schmerzt es mich wahrlich nicht minder,
Schon scheiden zu müssen aus häuslichem Kreise
Des freundlichen "Sommers" im Winter,
Und daß ich dem redlichen, biederen Mann
Ach, nimmer im Leben erwiedern kann
Die herzliche Liebe und Freundschaft!

Es möge der Vater im Himmel Dich lohnen
Mit seinen gesegneten Gaben!
Er lasse zur Seite die Gattin noch wohnen
Recht lange dem ehrlichen Schwaben!
Noch weiß ich die Pfade der Zukunft nicht
Für mich, doch die Stimme des Herzen spricht:
Euch bleib' ich zum Danke verpflichtet.

Hier hab' ich in traulichen Kreisen gefunden
Beim Gläschen am friedlichen Abend
So viele gar schöne erfreuliche Stunden,
Die waren erhebend und labend.
Darum dank ich Euch herzlich jetzt allzumal,
Ihr Freunde, im lieblichen Langenthal,
Ich werde Euch nimmer vergessen!

Und Du, Du herrliches Vaterland
Des Zwingli, Winkelried und Tell!
Wo stets die Freiheit Retter fand,
Es strahlet ungetrübt und hell
Dein Ruhm in alle Ewigkeit,
Wie zu der edlen Väter Zeit,
Du Schweizerland, leb wohl![26]

A cartwright (the English word for Wagner)
who can make no wheel, I'm called
and wanted to go – it's laughable—
to America as such.
How could I have lived there
where not only freedom
but also the ethics of work reign?

Therefore, as I arrived here,
about seven weeks ago
a friend took me aside
and spoke to me in earnest words:
"A craft is a sold foundation!
Follow my advice
and learn a craft."

I liked his words
and had to admit:
If I'd follow his advice,
an apprenticeship might come in handy
in future, tougher days.
I will learn the cooper trade
in Mummenthaler's factory!

There I met a good, old master,
who skillfully taught all the young;
But, even an old and much-travelled
apprentice can easily

enhance all his skills
if only he's prepared to learn
from a wise cooper.

Alas, my time of learning
is ending much too soon.
As an apprentice I move on
and happily imagine after
a few weeks there across the ocean
to be a full-fledged cooper
in my tiny log-cabin.

My hopes make me depart so early,
yet, at the same time I feel pain,
to leave this cosy home already,
"Sommer" (summer) provided me in winter,
and that I'll never be able to thank
this honest, simple man in all my life
for all his love and friendship!

Our father in heaven shall remunerate
you for your blessed gifts!
May HE keep the faithful wife
at the side of the honest Swabian!
I don't know the paths of the future yet
but the voice of my heart clearly says:
I will always be grateful to you.

Here at our intimate gatherings
I spent many wonderful hours
with a glass of wine in peaceful evenings
which were uplifting and refreshing.
For all of this I want to thank you all,
my dearest friends in lovely Langenthal,
I will never forget you!

And you, you wonderful fatherland
of Zwingli, Winkelried, and Tell!
Where freedom always found a savior,
your fame shines bright and clear
in all eternity, like in the times
of your noble forefathers
You, Switzerland, farewell! (trans. by author)

Together with newly found friends, pastor Johann Benedict Früh (1806-1866) and his wife Anna (1820-1901) from Baden, Wilhelm Wagner travelled to the French port of Le Havre via Basel, Strasbourg, and Paris. On board the vessel *Zürich*, they left Le Havre at the end of March 1851 and arrived in New York on 24 April together with their 288 fellow passengers after an uneventful, swift voyage.[27]

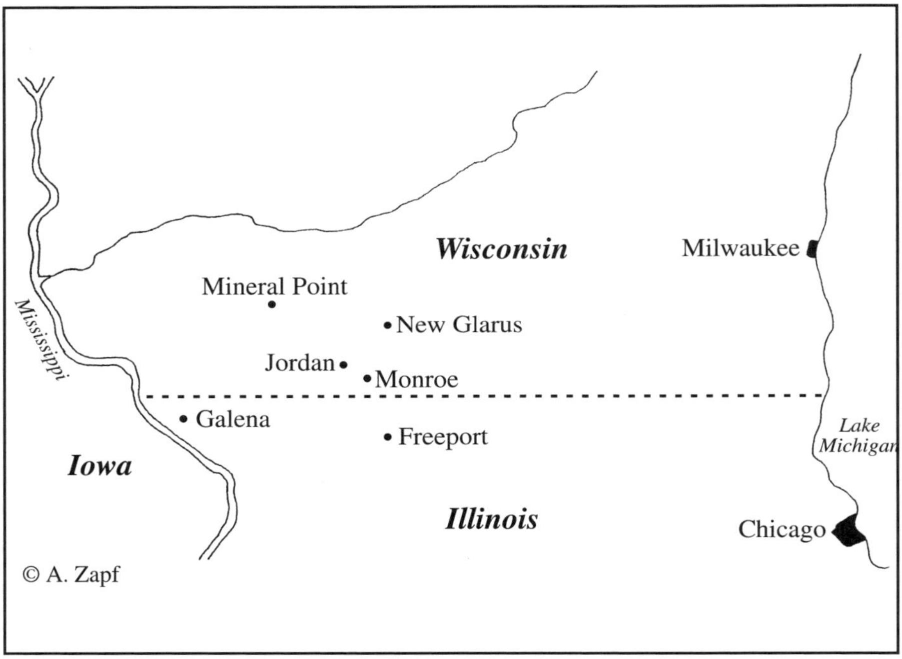
Wisconsin
Milwaukee
Mineral Point
New Glarus
Mississippi
Jordan
Monroe
Galena
Freeport
Lake Michigan
Iowa
Illinois
Chicago
© A. Zapf

4. A New Home in Illinois

ARRIVING AT THE PORT OF New York in the nineteenth century was very often not just the end of a long and tedious voyage for the hopeful immigrants, but the beginning of a difficult and sometimes dangerous undertaking: the start of a new life. New York in the 1850s was not yet the giant immigrant city of the end of the twentieth century with its slums and ethnic quarters, but with 515,547 inhabitants in 1850 and 813,669 in 1860, it was already the largest city in the United States. Whereas most of the Irish stayed in the cities, many of the Scandinavians and Germans moved towards the North and West. Still, the German element in New York City was strong. In 1850, 10.9 percent of all New Yorkers were born in Germany (making 23.9 percent of all immigrants) and in 1860 this figure had risen to 14.7 percent (making 31.3 percent of all immigrants), forming the second largest group of immigrants after the Irish. Although the Germans very often had difficulties with the English language, their skills made them an economically important group. Thus they constituted more than one-half of New York's shoemakers, tailors, bakers, and woodworkers in 1855.[1] In the first half of the nineteenth century, immigration and immigrants became a profitable business for many New Yorkers. The transportation of immigrants to the United States and further on to their various destinations soon proved to be a gold mine for numerous companies. The first one to realize this was the merchant Francis Thompson, who established his "Old Established Emigrant Office" in 1829. Many ships that carried goods to Europe were refurnished to bring back immigrants. Once the Europeans had reached New York harbor, they fell into the hands of agents who claimed to be helpful in finding lodging, work, and transportation. An American journalist wrote in 1853: "Everyone in the great City, who can make a living from the arriving immigrants, is here: Runners, sharpers, peddlers, agents of boarding houses, of forwarding offices and worst of all, of the houses where many a simple emigrant girl, far from friends and home, comes to a sad end."[2] Especially the runners were a curse for many of the newly arrived. It was their job to lure the helpless to a boarding house or transportation agency, making money out of the ignorance of the newcomers.

This was the situation Wilhelm Wagner found on his arrival. It was a confusing reception for the arriving immigrants, and the shouting of the runners to attract their attention made it even more so: "The swearing and fighting of these runners, the shouts of the passengers, the crying of the women and children, make as great a confusion as ever was heard at Babel," William Brown wrote upon his arrival in 1845.[3] Wilhelm Wagner and his friends, the Früh couple, were among the many who fell into the hands of a runner who brought them to the infamous German-American company Rischmüller & Wolf, later Rischmüller & Löscher.[4] On the advice of Rischmüller, Wilhelm and his companions set out for Milwaukee, Wisconsin.

Nearly three years earlier, on 29 May 1848, Wisconsin had become a state of the Union after having been a territory for twelve years. In his first message to the new legislature, Governor Nelson Dewey envisioned the new state becoming "one of the most populous and prosperous States of the American Union."[5] To fulfill this pledge, the state put up for sale fourteen million acres of its thirty-five million acres between 1849 and 1857 after having first sold about five million acres during the territorial period. Nearly 150 speculators acquired land in excess of 1,250,000 acres that they tried to sell to the newcomers. There were also landowners who hoped to make good profit by selling the land they had bought during the 1830s. And there was public land for $1.25 an acre. Thus, the immigrant had a variety from which he could choose. It was not only cheap land that attracted Europeans, however. Wisconsin could boast of providing the farmer with good soil, an abundance of water and forests, and—not to be underestimated—a climate very similar to middle and northern Europe. The state was not densely populated yet; the census for the year 1850 gives the population at 305,390 inhabitants. And there were the many letters new settlers had written home, as well as the numerous German publications that praised the new state, publications Wilhelm Wagner might have heard of or even read in Germany already. All of this bore fruit. The census of 1860 revealed that Wisconsin not only had the highest proportion of foreign-born inhabitants next to California, but also that the biggest group of them had come from Germany. Nearly sixteen percent of Wisconsin's population was German. Wilhelm might have also heard of the Swiss colony, New Glarus in Green County, while living in Switzerland. This at least is one story that is told in the Wagner family today. As Monroe lies only sixteen miles south of New Glarus, this might have been a reason, too, why he and his friend Früh set out for Monroe from Milwaukee.[6] For this trip, Richmüller had charged them eleven dollars per person. It was only some time later that Wilhelm found out they could have made that trip for $9.50 each if they had bought tickets from station to station.

Their trip was quite a long and boring one. From New York they went to Williamsville, New York, where they rested at the home of a Dr. Storch. On the evening of 2 May, they travelled to Buffalo, New York, and took the steamboat *May-Flower* to Detroit. There they had to wait for one day until they could board the train to New Buffalo, Michigan, on Lake Michigan. This train ride was very unpleasant as they were put in a freight car. This arrangement had been made by Richmüller. From New Buffalo they moved on by steamboat again to Milwaukee. This city on Lake Michigan had about 20,000 inhabitants in 1850, mostly European immigrants. Two-thirds had been born in Europe and two-thirds of these in Germany. Most revealing is a Milwaukee school census taken in August 1851 which shows that of all the 5914 pupils (between four and twenty years of age), 2577 were of German origin and only 1668 of American. Then came the Irish with 1286, the English with 294, the French with thirty-five, the Scots with twenty-nine, the Welsh with twelve, the Poles with eleven and finally the Danes with two children. Milwaukee probably was the most German city of the United States. More than forty percent of the population was German. Together with Saint Louis and Cincinnati it formed the German triangle—the most German region in the United States. Milwaukee had become a city in 1846. Two years later, the German Forty-eighters started pouring into this city and making it their own. They founded hotels, schools, newspapers, and theaters. The importance and influence of the German element in Milwaukee is demonstrated by the anecdote about two neighbors bragging about their ancestors: "So you got a Pilgrim father in your family tree? Listen, I got something better. My old man was an Acht und Vierziger [Forty-eighter]."[7]

Arriving in Milwaukee by boat in 1851, Wilhelm Wagner and his friends saw a prosperous city with wide open spaces, nice stores, and houses mostly built out of cream-colored brick. As soon as they had left the steamboat, they were taken to Market Square on East Water Street, at that time one of the most important public squares of Milwaukee and the center of the German commercial district.

> In 1848 Market Square was a wood market, and sometimes fifty teams could be counted on the square, with loads of wood. Not one horse would be seen, for the farmers brought their grain and wood to the city with oxen. . . . Market Square originally was nothing but a marsh, and "Father" Stein could shoot all the ducks he wanted from the door of his gunshop.[8]

The neighbor and friend of this gunshop owner Matthias Stein was the German Theodore Wettstein, who had opened his hotel Gasthof zum Deutschen Hause (Hotel to the German House) in 1850. It was at this hotel where Wilhelm Wagner and the Früh couple took up their residence. They felt right at home from the very beginning. No wonder, as the stout and spectacled owner was a fascinating character and a man of similar ideas as theirs. Wettstein's hotel was considered to be one of Milwaukee's best hotels of its time. Its fame even reached Europe and between 1851 and 1855 it saw such illustrious guests as the famous African explorer Dr. Moritz Wagner, the Duke of Neuwied, the Prinz of Nassau, Prinz Paul of Württemberg, and Charlotte Pfeiffer, the celebrated traveler and naturalist. In 1850, Wettstein had written and published a book in Germany, *Der Nordamerikanische Freistaat Wisconsin* in which he praised this state: "Of all states in America, Wisconsin has a climate best suited to Europeans, and particularly to Germans."[9]

After his long and tedious journey, Wilhelm Wagner felt right at home at Wettstein's hotel for the first time. Complaining about the American food he found to be very bad—no soup on the table, only miserable coffee without warm milk, mostly bad bread, meat served nearly raw, barely any fresh vegetables, only dried fruit and bad-tasting pastry—Wilhelm was delighted to be served German meals at the Gasthof zum Deutschen Hause. This food on the other hand, irritated Anglo-American guests who tended to sneer about it.[10]

Leaving Pastor Früh's wife Anna and all their money behind at Wettstein's house, Wilhelm and his friend Früh one day walked about hundred miles west-south-west to the farm of the German Alfred Wriesberg in Green County, about six miles (two hours walk) northwest of Monroe. Where they had heard about Wriesberg and farmland being available in Green County can no longer be ascertained. Maybe they had just followed a recommendation from someone at Wettstein's hotel. Wriesberg (who rose to some prominence in the small town Clarno and later served as lieutenant colonel in the 9th Regiment of the Union Army during the Civil War) had just bought a farm from George Blunt on 20 March 1851, himself.[11] There they arrived on 19 May. Wriesberg welcomed them wholeheartedly and already the next day they visited several farms that were for sale.

Soon Wilhelm and his friend found a farm they liked. For $300 they bought 150 acres on Skinner Creek (close to Wriesberg's farm and between the townships of Jordan and Monroe) from Cadwallader C. Washburn. Wilhelm was overwhelmed by the price of two dollars an acre, which he found to be very cheap compared to the prices in Germany. Most likely it was a little overpriced, however, as Cadwallader Washburn was a well-known and successful land speculator whose holdings were valued at half a million dollars in 1856. He became a major general during the Civil War and the eleventh Governor of Wisconsin from 1872 to 1874.[12] Unforeseen, Wilhelm Wagner and his friend had bought a farm from the future Governor of Wisconsin. Ten acres of this farm were cleared already. The rest of this land was covered with oaks, ash trees, elm trees, wild apple and cherry trees, and wild grapes, strawberries, gooseberries, and currants. The soil was black and rich and two freshwater springs gave enough water to run a sawmill and a cornmill. It is not very surprising that Wilhelm and his friend liked that land from the beginning. In contrast to southern Texas, where Julius and Emilie struggled to make a living, northern Illinois and southern Wisconsin closely resembled the German landscape as it can be found in Baden, the Palatine, Hesse, and Wuerttemberg. The rolling hills, the woods, the green meadows, the running streams, and the climate immediately gave the settlers from Germany the feeling that they were at home. Many of them praised the abundance of game and nature's resources which made this land appear to them like a better Germany—a Germany how it should be.[13]

According to Wilhelm's report, the blockhouse needed a little repair. It consisted of only one room, seven feet long and six feet wide, that also served as kitchen. The only window faced the entrance door. Another door led to a small annex, six to four feet in size, with two small windows. The roof was leaky, which made rainy nights very uncomfortable. Although Wilhelm admitted in his letter that this cabin was pretty poor by German standards, he nevertheless might have played the situation down in order not to worry his wife too much. In the short sketch of his father's life, Wilhelm's son William described the situation a little differently: "The cabin was in a very dilapidated condition. Windows and doors could not be properly closed and every time it rained they had to open the umbrellas over the beds. If it was windy everything rattled."[14]

However bad the living conditions might have really been, Wilhelm Wagner and his friend did not lose their optimistic attitude. As soon as Anna Früh had joined them, they started to mend the field and cultivate the land. With the rest of the little money they had left from Germany they bought two white horses and a wagon for $190, two cows with two calves for twenty-seven dollars, and a couple of chickens for forty cents in Milwaukee. They also planned to buy a hog together with six piglets as soon as they could. The cows obviously were in a rather poor condition and one of them ran away on their journey back to their farm and it took them a day to find it in the woods. The first thing they did after acquiring their livestock was to plant potatoes, summer barley, and corn. First they only had their boxes and trunks for tables and chairs, but they built themselves furniture, extended the building, dug up a cellar, and erected a stable. As the road to their farm did not deserve that name and was impassable during bad weather, they planned to improve it with limestone and brownstone that could be found in abundance in that area.

Despite their progress, Wilhelm experienced a hard time. On the one hand, he never got tired of praising his new homeland, the land of liberty and justice for all. To him, the contrast between Germany and the New World was striking. He especially lauded the constitution of the State of Wisconsin as the most liberal of the United States and the most favorable for immigrants and new settlers. On the other hand, however, he was very homesick during the first months. During eight days in May 1851 that he had to spend alone on their new farm because Benedict Früh had business to do in Milwaukee, he nearly scraped together all the money he had left to travel back to New York and from there home to Germany. Even in his weakest hour he never thought of asking for clemency, but he contemplated the idea of serving his term in prison only to be near his wife and children. Reviewing his present situation, he enjoyed the liberties of his new homeland, speaking about the land of freedom without bureaucracy, nobility, and the reign of the military and the police; on the other hand though he missed German *Gemütlichkeit*, the warmth of a cosy home with his family and friends. They were on good terms with their neighbors who helped them when necessary, but these other farmers were scattered and they did not meet very often. During those days in May, Wilhelm wrote to his brother Julius in Texas telling him the reasons that prevented him from visiting him in Texas, and at the same time asking him to move up north and settle close to his own farm. The colder climate would be much healthier for Julius than the hot humidity down in Texas, Wilhelm wrote.[15] Wilhelm felt lonely also because he had to tell his wife that due to the uncomfortable condition the farm was still in, he would not be able to come to Germany and fetch her and the children in autumn of 1851 as he had originally planned, but in the next spring. For him this meant nearly another year without his loved ones. In at least two pages of his first letter to his family in Germany, Wilhelm dreamt about the time his wife Friederike and his children would be with him. He envisioned his wife riding in their horse cart together with Hermann, Julius, and the little Rike, the boys riding the horses, eating wild strawberries and grapes, playing with lambs, watching the birds, and picking beautiful flowers—in short an earthly paradise and the dreams of a lonely man. And lonely he was indeed, when one compares the spiritually rich parish life in Baden (even the last months in Switzerland) to the rather monotonous life in near solitude. Wilhelm had been used to living in rural villages—however small they might have been—and now the nearest town, Monroe, lay about six miles away.

When William and his friend arrived in that area, Monroe was a fairly new community with about 500 to 600 inhabitants. It already had its first newspaper, *The Green County Union*, four hotels, two taverns, and a couple of stores. One of the most important events in the early history of Monroe was the arrival of the railroad, which led to its increasing growth in the second half of the 1850s. Construction had begun in 1853 and was finished in January 1858. Closer to Wilhelm's farm was the small village of Jordan, organized in April 1849, after the first white settler, Robert Brazel, had arrived in 1837.[16] Although it was only a little more than five miles to Jordan from the farm, Wilhelm and his friends preferred going to Monroe if they needed anything.

Despite their optimism and their ardor, Wilhelm Wagner and his friend Benedict Früh had to realize sooner or later that they were no natural born farmers. In the long run, they would get nowhere with farming alone. The question was, what other job could they get? One day in late fall of 1851, the wagon maker Michael Kachelhoffer came over from Yellow Creek, a few miles southeast of Freeport, Illinois, to get wood supplies he needed for his craft.[17] Coming up the road to the farm on Skinner Creek, he saw Wilhelm Wagner trotting behind his plow, singing a German folk song. He walked over to Wilhelm, and the men started a conversation that lasted for some time. Here Wilhelm told his visitor the story of his life.

When Kachelhoffer returned home he told his friends about the German pastor he had met. They listened with great interest as they were looking for a pastor. In May 1848, with the arrival of Ernest Beine from Germany, they had founded a German Protestant congregation called St. John. Beine served as the local preacher, and meetings were held in a schoolhouse until 1851 when they built their first church. Now they were in search of a pastor. Therefore, they invited Wilhelm Wagner over to Yellow Creek to visit them and give a sermon. It was his first sermon in the United States and not his last. After hearing his second sermon, the members of St. John asked Wilhelm to become their pastor. Wilhelm was overwhelmed with joy but had to ask them to wait until May next year, as he wanted to bring his family to the United States first. The congregation agreed upon his request and declared they would wait for his return from Germany in May of 1852.

When Wilhelm had taken care of everything at Skinner Creek, he said farewell to his friends and set out for Germany again in February of 1852 to finally join his family. He travelled the same route back he had come nearly one year ago. His journey from New York to Le Havre lasted twenty-seven days. Not being able to enter Germany, as the warrant for his arrest was still out, Wilhelm took residence in Basel, Switzerland, and began with the necessary arrangements to bring his wife and children over to the

United States. As all of this took some time, it was not until Easter Monday, 12 April 1852, that Wilhelm Wagner, his wife Friederike and their six children Karl, Wilhelm, Luise, Hermann Ludwig, Julius, and Friederike could start out for their journey from Basel. In Strasbourg they were joined by Friederike's sister Ernestine (who later married a Mr. Ziegler in the United States) who helped her older sister with the children. On 19 April, they left the French port of Le Havre on board the ship *Mercury* bound for New York.

After twenty-nine days they arrived at New York on 18 May. The family of Wilhelm Wagner had finally reached their new homeland. They had to stay in New York for a week as one of the children had become ill. From there they travelled to Buffalo where they visited some friends for several days. Then they took the steamboat across Lake Erie to Detroit and from there the railroad to New Buffalo on Lake Michigan. Another steamboat brought them across the lake to Chicago, where they arrived on 30 May 1852. The following day, they continued their journey by railroad. They got off at Cherry Valley, as the Galena and Chicago Union Railroad did not go any further at that time. The rest of the line to Galena, which was the center of the lead mining district, had not been built and was actually completed in 1854.

The Illinois where the Wagners had arrived was still a pioneer state. Settlers had begun moving into southern Illinois at the beginning of the nineteenth century. In April 1818, Illinois became the twenty-first state of the Union. Up to the 1850s, Galena was the commercial center of the north. Since 1845 it was the richest town of Illinois with miners streaming into the lead capital on the banks of the Mississippi since the beginning of the century and steamboats carrying the precious lead ore down the river. People slowly settled around Galena and the Chicago area. After the end of the infamous Black Hawk War in August 1832, and the subsequent removal of all Indians out of Illinois, settlers arrived in northern Illinois in growing numbers. Although mining was still going strong, it mainly was a state for the small farmer, in contrast to the southern plantations, and the trader. With the coming of the railroad at the beginning of the 1850s, Chicago took the lead as Illinois' most important city and became a gateway to the west.[18] Wilhelm Wagner belonged to the wave of German immigrants that made Illinois one of the the centers of German-American culture.

On the evening of 31 May, the eight Wagners and Friederike's sister Ernestine boarded a big covered wagon, which was to carry them to their new home. Near Winnebago, a few miles southwest of Rockford, they had to spend the night at a lonely inn in the prairie. The next day they set out again. Wilhelm's second son William, then eleven years old, remembered that part of the trip vividly:

> June 1, 1852, was a clear, beautiful day but in the afternoon it got terribly hot. About several miles from Freeport a terrific storm broke loose, coming from the north. A storm like they had never experienced in Germany. Continually the lightning crossed the sky from all directions at once. Our driver hurried to reach the destination before it would break loose in full force. Unfortunately the bridge over the Yellow Creek near the brewery was in bad condition and we had to go back for a stretch and drive across the Creek. In doing so one of the trunks broke loose and fell in the water. It had to be fished out and reloaded, and so half an hour passed. We had just reached the high near where Mr. Bergmann's house now stands, then a farm belonging to Mr. M. Doll, when the storm broke. The terrific wind swept the entire big wagon cover off. The rain came down in torrents, and everybody got drenched to the skin. We arrived at 9 o'clock at the City Hotel in Freeport, where the State Bank is now located, as wet as having been pulled out of the water. Thus was our arrival in Freeport. All the unfortunate incidents were soon forgotten over a good meal and knowing to have finally arrived we went to bed happily.[19]

The Mr. Doll whom William Wagner mentions in his account of their voyage, was Michael Doll from Baden, Germany, who had arrived at Silver Creek Township with his wife Mary and their children just a short time before the Wagners passed by. The Dolls were not completely settled and as he was anxious to get to his congregation, Wilhelm did not wait at Doll's farm till the storm had calmed down but pressed on for Freeport. The Wagners stayed at the City Hotel for a couple of days. At that time the hotel was managed by Frederick P. Koehler (1817-1896), a businessman who at the age of sixteen had come to the United States as a butcher from

Bavaria in 1833. In 1850, two years before Wilhelm Wagner and his family arrived, the town of Freeport only had 1,420 inhabitants. It had been founded in December of 1835 by William "Tutty" Baker from Kentucky, who established a trading post and a tavern that formed the nucleus of what was to become Freeport. Primarily a farmers' trading center, Freeport was incorporated as a city in 1855. By then, Wilhelm Wagner and his family were well established in the community.[20]

After a couple of days at Koehler's hotel, the Wagners found a small brick house in Spring Street where they could finally move with their belongings. When Wilhelm Wagner came to the St. John congregation to begin with his work as pastor, he met with a big disappointment. The position that had been promised to him had been given to a G. H. von Snell who had graduated from the mission school St. Chrischona at Basel, Switzerland. This young man suited the more conservative members of St. John's parish better than the rationalistic Wilhelm Wagner. The argument the orthodox members used against Wilhelm, however, was that he had not arrived on time in May as promised. Several other members of the congregation, like Philip H. Altemeier of Freeport and Heinrich Burckhardt of Town Silver Creek, spoke up for Wagner, but the conservative majority stood firmly against him. Wagner thanked those who had spoken in favor of him, but he declined their offer. Altemeier, Burckhardt, and Wagner remained friends but the latter did not want to be the cause for dissension within this congregation. For a few years he served as pastor for the Zion Reformed Church. The St. John's congregation soon grew dissatisfied with von Snell, as he seemed insensible to the needs of his parish, and got rid of him. Old church records indicate that the congregation asked Wilhelm Wagner once again, and he became their pastor (at least their preacher) until 1854 when they dismissed him for good. Whether it had something to do with Philip Altemeier's untimely death at the age of forty-seven on 27 February 1854, (as he had been one of the strongest advocates for Wilhelm Wagner) or with the unification of St. John's with the German Evangelical Synod—then the Evangelical Church Association of the West—can no longer be ascertained. Whatever the real cause might have been, on 13 March 1854, the Evangelical German United Lutheran & German Reformed Congregation informed the Reverend Wilhelm Wagner in writing about its resolution to prohibit him from preaching in its church and that the Reverend John Zimmermann was acknowledged as its regular minister.[21]

Another chance came up. Heinrich Burckhardt became so angry about the disloyalty of his old congregation towards Wilhelm Wagner that he, together with P. Hermann and Jakob Höbel as elders, formed a Unitarian congregation with members from Town Silver Creek and Ridott, two to three miles east of Freeport. Whereas the township of Ridott was founded nearly the same time as Freeport with the settlement of the brothers Jefferson and Andrew Jackson Niles in March 1836, Silver Creek Township was a little older. Thomas Crane (sometimes spelled Crain), who had worked with Oliver W. Kellog at Galena, built a tavern on the spot that was to become Town Silver Creek in 1829. Many Presbyterians from England and Scottland came to Ridott a few years later and the Protestant German farmers had been looking for some time to find a pastor until Wilhelm Wagner came their way. The first services were held in the old courthouse of Freeport and in the old schoolhouse of Ridott until 1870, when a real church could be built. Wilhelm decided to be pastor for this parish. The few members of these parishes were mainly German farmers coming from the Bodensee area, the Palatinate, and the Alsace. Wilhelm served these congregations until his death in 1877.

Wilhelm made good friends among his parish, like the farmers Adam Burckhardt, Joseph Rapple, Jakob Höbel, and Johann Adam Rippberger, whose son Adam married Philippina Molter by the blessing hand of Wilhelm on 27 May1874. In 1857, Burckart, Rapple, and Rippberger even visited Wilhelm's brother-in-law Carl Baumann and his family at Mannheim, carrying with them precious daguerreotypes of the American Wagner family for the loved ones back home. Wilhelm had advised them to bring back pictures of friends and the family in Baden likewise. The three farmers, who came from Ketsch near Schwetzingen originally and had to attend to some legal business there, also had the obligation to tell the Wagners in Germany how life was for Wilhelm and his family. Jakob Höbel did the same good offices for Wilhelm on his voyage to Germany in 1869. Wilhelm Wagner would have loved to do all this himself and travel to Baden once again, but for one thing his wife did not want to undertake such a long sea voyage in her lifetime and for another he simply did not have the means to make such a trip.[22] During the first months in Freeport, his income as pastor was so small that he could not live on it, let alone support his family. It was clear to him soon that he had to look for some additional means to make a living. Farming, he knew, was out of the question. The craft he had learned in Switzerland did not help him either, as there was no need for a cooper in Freeport. Then, suddenly, a chance came that changed his life.

German friends of his told him in the winter of 1852-1853 that a German newspaper had closed down in Galena. At first, he hesitated to go into the publishing business as he knew nothing about it, but finally he decided to try it. These friends and others collected ninety dollars to help Wilhelm buy the inventory of that press in the summer of 1853. The contributions were made by citizens like F. Bues, C. H. Rosenstiel, Dr. Minges, Matthias Hettinger, Phil. Fleischmann, Carl Baumgarten (the father of Freeport's genial mayor Albert Baumgarten), F. P. Köhler, and others and ranged from twenty-five cents to ten dollars. The start of this new business was by no means easy. The first issues of the *Deutscher Anzeiger* were printed at the press of the *Freeport Bulletin* (founded as the *Prairie Democrat* in November 1847) on the third floor of the Wright building and consisted of four pages with five columns. Only six issues were published during the first eleven weeks from mid-October 1853 until the end of December that year by the four men who were the publishing team of this new newspaper: Wilhelm Wagner himself who had undergone the ordeal of learning the craft of typesetting as best as he could, his son William (the oldest son Karl only helped from time to time as he was an apprentice to a lawyer), the schoolteacher Knecht, and his oldest son Philipp. William, who had attended the public school of Freeport after their arrival for the eight months necessary to finish his basic education, had to help his father by looking for a job in order to provide for his own support and maybe even contribute a little bit to the budget of the Wagner family. For a time he was employed at a harness shop, and after that he was able to get a clerkship at a cigar store where he worked until his father asked him to help them with the paper. Five issues had to be omitted as the unexperienced team was unable to get the copies ready for printing in time. Starting with a small readership, this German paper steadily grew until it was enlarged to seven columns a page in 1863 and changed to a quarto in January 1868. In the beginning, the paper had to be subscribed to, cost \$1.50 a year for fifty-two issues, and had to be paid in advance. The first page always contained two columns of ads, mostly of German businesspeople, and then something entertaining, such as short stories, fairy tales, and even novels often published in sequels. The second page contained news from the United States and the world, the third one presented local news in two columns and additional ads in the remaining sections and the fourth page contained some general and miscellaneous information (like new school laws) and some ads.

In January 1854, Wilhelm Wagner rented a couple of rooms at 8 South Galena Avenue, the first of six rented offices the *Anzeiger* used over the years until Wilhelm was in the position to build his own two-story press building at Chicago Street in the spring of 1874, twenty years after the paper had been founded. When they moved into their first office in 1854, Wilhelm was not only able to buy rather cheaply a small Washington handpress the *Bulletin* did not use anymore, he also hired a typesetter. Louis Crusius, a relative of F. P. Köhler from the Palatinate, was not only very industrious but also worked for only a nominal wage and thus secured the regular publication of the *Anzeiger* in an edition of at least 300. The future of the paper was still uncertain, however, for quite some time. The first customers very often had low morale as far as paying their bills was concerned, and Wilhelm Wagner's humorous and friendly payment reminders were often neglected. He had to cut costs whenever possible. Sometimes the Wagners only survived because members of his small parish presented them with potatoes, eggs, butter, and other food. Cash was not readily available for Wilhelm Wagner. He still owned his share of the land he had bought with his friend Früh, and it was not easy at all to find a buyer. Like Wilhelm, Johann Benedict Früh had quickly realized that he was not suited for the life of a farmer. On 11 November 1854, he therefore sold his share of a little more than fifty-three acres for $240 to Johann Haesely by help of Alfred Wriesberg. This money helped Früh to buy the grocery store of Philip H. Altemeier's widow on North Galena Avenue. Most likely Wilhelm had helped his friend make that deal. In mid-January 1855, Benedict Früh announced the opening of the new store in Wagner's paper, asking the old customers for their confidence. His Groceries and Provisions Store was situated right beside Damian Franz's inn Gasthaus zur Stadt Strassburg which also advertised its German food in the *Deutscher Anzeiger*. On 29 May 1855, Wilhelm Wagner was able to sell a little more than twelve acres of his share on the Wisconsin farm for a nominal fee of five dollars to Miner and Samuel Taylor and Daniel H. Morgan from Jordan, Green County, Wisconsin. It was not until 19 November 1868, that Wilhelm could finally sell the rest of the farm, nearly ninety-five acres, to Andrew Hansen from Green County, Wisconsin, for seventy-five dollars.[23] Until then he faced dire straits quite often, especially as his family had grown.

On 25 November 1853, Wilhelm's youngest son Friedrich (Fred) was born. The Wagners had to raise seven children now: five boys (Karl, William H. [he was baptized as Wilhelm but called himself William in order not to be confused with his father], Hermann Ludwig, Julius, and Friedrich) and two daughters (Luise and Friederike). Karl, the oldest son, was nearly fifteen then and could help his father already, but mainly it was Wilhelm's second son William who learned the printing trade from the start. With a lot of debts, Wilhelm had to cut down expenses wherever he could. In order to save the costs of fifty to sixty cents for the transportation of the paper for the *Anzeiger* from Chicago for instance, Wilhelm used to take the train personally to Chicago, as he had a free travel pass. He left Freeport at ten o'clock in the evening, arriving at Chicago at three o'clock the next morning. There he picked up the two paper bales that would last for about six weeks, weighing nearly hundred pounds, and took the train back at ten o'clock in the evening, arriving at Freeport again at three o'clock the next morning, carrying the bales to the press himself . After a short rest, he would resume his work at the press at seven o'clock in the morning. During his trips to Chicago and back he only ate a piece of bread and some cheese. It might well be that Wilhelm Wagner met with another Forty-eighter in Chicago who was in the newspaper business and became prominent later: Caspar Butz. Whether it was on these trips or later through the actual publication of the *Deutscher Anzeiger*, Caspar Butz and Wilhelm Wagner became friends.

Butz (1825- 1885) who had been an editor of radical journals in Germany before his escape to the United States in 1849, did not only belong to the editorial staff of the *Illinois Staatszeitung* and other papers but also published the *Monatshefte*, a journal in radical opposition to Abraham Lincoln. He served a term in the Illinois legislature, was in the Chicago hardware and building business, and was a clerk of the Superior Court of

Chicago at one time. Wagner and Butz were not the only Germans who worked in the newspaper business. Actually a lot of the Forty-eighters either turned to journalism in their new homeland or had been well-known writers in Germany already. The list of those Forty-eighters who established, owned, and/or edited a paper or simply wrote for one is very long. Approximately forty German papers existed in the United States in 1840, and by 1852 this number had nearly doubled. The Forty-eighters as a group of politically active and outspoken people were accustomed to use their editorial desk as "an effective sounding board for reform.... Especially intellectuals who were university trained, took up journalism as a source of revenue during their first difficult months in the United States and remained in the profession the rest of their lives."[24] Therefore, Wilhelm Wagner was no exception, but fit into the pattern of the intellectual Forty-eighter, using the newspaper as a medium to spread his ideas. Only, he did not choose this profession or means of political expression deliberately like most of the others. For him it was just a chance to make a living that came up when nothing else was in sight. And it had even been his friends who had pushed him in the direction of buying the old press and publishing a German newspaper. He had written a couple of poems in the past, mainly unpolitical in the first place, and was not a determined revolutionary as was, for instance, the teacher Dr. Adolf Douai (1819-1888). He came to Texas in 1852, after having spent a prison term for revolutionary activities, and edited the abolitionist paper *San Antonio Zeitung* between 1853 and 1856. He was on friendly terms and had a couple of whiskeys every now and then with like-minded anti-slavery German immigrants like Herman Spiess, Gustav Schleicher, von Herff, Adam Vogt, and Fritz Schenk, the old comrades of Wilhelm's brother Julius Wagner. Douai might have even met Julius when both attended the German-Texan *Sängerfest* at San Antonio in 1854. There, Douai was one of the political leaders agitating against slavery. After severe threats against his life, Douai fled north where he became one of the leading German socialist journalists after the Civil War in New York.[25] Starting out as editor of a simple local paper, Wilhelm Wagner nevertheless became involved in national politics during the Lincoln-Douglas debates and took sides like the other Forty-eighters. Besides writing editorials, he had also expressed his political beliefs a few years earlier.

On 15 December 1855, Wagner founded the *Freeporter Sängerbund* (singers society) that gave its first public concert on Easter Monday, 24 March 1856. Soon after that he was one of the organizers of the *Freeporter Turnverein* (athletic organization). The membership lists of these societies grew rapidly and after awhile nearly every influential citizen of Freeport belonged to one of these societies or even both. It does not seem to be evident today why the founding of such societies was an expression of political opinion. To understand this, one must again turn to the political situation of the various states that constitute Germany today in the first half of the nineteenth century. As explained in earlier chapters, the beginning of this century saw the rise and formation of a nationalistic, democratic movement in the aftermath of Napoleon's reign. It was a movement mainly carried on by the students and the middle class. As laws prohibiting public meetings were a common political instrument for the various German monarchies and duchies, the founding of societies at that time became a clear political expression of a democratic, nationalistic opinion. The prevailing idea among liberals and revolutionaries alike was that Germans in a united country should have the liberty of public meeting. The students organized themselves in corps and fraternities and the common citizens in all kinds of societies. Whereas the singing societies were political mainly in the act of their foundation, others like the *Schützenvereine* (shooting societies) and the *Turnvereine* were also used quite often to train the members militarily and thus even form militias. These became important in the revolution of 1848-1849.[26]

When the Forty-eighters came to the United States, they founded societies there, too. Even if these were "only" singing clubs without any political program, they nevertheless were a political act to that extent that the founders and members of these groups thus expressed their belief in a democratic system in contrast to the royalistic class society of old. Therefore, these German societies were based on something more than just the German "spirit of good fellowship" which Rudolph Biesele recognized. One cannot attribute the founding of the *Sängerbünde* to the German fondness for songs and merry gatherings alone. When Julius Wagner and Albrecht von Roeder were members of one and the same club this was not only because both were merry men, but because both had consciously cast aside their old undemocratic class order with which they had grown up.

All of this would have been impossible in Germany a century earlier. At the same time, these clubs served the purpose of preserving a little bit of the old world, of helping immigrants feel less alien in an Anglo-American society. Preserving parts of German culture and language strengthened the group of German immigrants but on the other hand isolated them even more in certain regards. The nationalistic strain and the desire for democracy, in addition to religious and romantic motives, become evident in quite a number of poems and songs these societies recited and sang. Fritz Goldbeck, who had come to Texas from Bremen as a young boy on board the vessel *Johann Dethardt*, arriving at Galveston on 23 November 1844, wrote a rather typical poem, "Ein Germane bin ich." The first verse already is symptomatic of the attitude of many German immigrants coming to the United States between 1820 and 1870:

> *Fort mit dem trügerischen Schein,*
> *Ein Deutscher bin ich, will es sein!*
> *Ob ich auch englisch reden kann,*
> *Bin ich darum kein and'rer Mann.*
>
> Away with deceiving appearances:
> I am and want to be a German. Even though
> I can speak English, I'm not
> someone else because of that.

All of these songs and poems speak of being "German" and "Germany" rather than Bavaria, Prussia, or other German states. Because Germany as a state did not exist until 1871, this constant reference to Germany implies the idealistic and nationalistic image of a united, democratic Germany, probably best expressed by Hoffman von Fallersleben in his "Auswanderungslied" (Song of the Emigrant):

> *Deutsche Freiheit lebet nur im Liede,*
> *Deutsches Recht, es ist ein Märchen nur.*
> *Deutsche Wohlfahrt ist ein langer Friede -*
> *Voll von lauter Willkür und Zensur.*

Darum ziehen wir aus dem Vaterlande,
Kehren nun und nimmermehr zurück,
Suchen Freiheit uns am fremden Strande -
Freiheit ist nur Leben, ist nur Glück.

German freedom lives but in the song,
German justice, a fairy tale at best.
On Germany's trip of peace you take along
Censorship and despotism, nothing less.

Thus we go forth from the fatherland,
Turn back not now or evermore,
Seek freedom in the foreign land -
Freedom is life and fortune, nothing more.

This spirit lived in Wilhelm Wagner too. In 1858, commemorating the death of the revolutionary Robert Blum ten years before, he published in his paper *Deutscher Anzeiger* the poem "Zur Erinnerung an Robert Blum," which he had written. Describing the sound of many church bells ringing, Wilhelm wrote:

Nein, nicht gilt es einer Krone,
Nicht der Höfe Lug und Trug,
Sondern Deutschlands frei'stem Sohne,
Den die Despotie erschlug.

Einem Mann aus niedrer Sphäre,
In der Hütte still gezeugt,
Aber an der Brust der Ehre
Groß und frei und stark gesäugt.

Robert Blum gilt's, ihm, dem Freien,
Ihm, dem Feind der Despotie;
Robert Blum gilt's, ihm, dem treuen
Freiheitskämpfer spät und früh.

No, it doesn't ring for a crown
and for courtly lies and deceit,
but for Germany's freest son,
whom despotism murdered.

A man from lower classes,
begotten in the secrecy of a hut,
but at honor's bosom nurtured
to become great and free.

They sound for Robert Blum, the free man,
for him, the enemy of despotism
They sound for Robert Blum, the faithful
fighter for freedom, all day long.[27]

The *Turnverein* of Freeport was not organized as a militia, and yet the *Turner* societies in the United States played an active role in politics. The first one was founded in Cincinnati in November 1848 under the influence and guiding spirit of the newly arrived German revolutionary Friedrich Hecker. Although many saw the *Turner* in a rather poetical and romantic light, reminding them of the bygone glorious days of student life in Germany, the *Turnvereine* nevertheless also embodied within them the idea of being an efficient striking force if necessary. This can be seen already in the description of the purposes of Cincinnati's *Turnverein*: "Cultivation of rational training, both intellectual and physical, in order that the members may become energetic, patriotic citizens of the Republic, who could and would represent and protect common human liberty by word and deed." Due to their willingness to fight for democracy and their new fatherland if necessary, the *Turner* played an essential part in forming some of the important regiments of the Union during the Civil War. After that war the *Turner* societies flourished more than ever. With their many educational programs and activities for all members of the family, they also had a great influence on the founding of the Y.M.C.A.[28]

On many occasions, Wilhelm Wagner was asked to be a candidate for a public office. He always declined. He did not care for public honors and appearances. In the *Deutscher Anzeiger* though, he clearly expressed his political opinions and always advertised for the one party he felt at home with: the Democratic Party. Until 1858, up to sixty-five percent of the Germans in the United States belonged to or voted for the Democrats. The son of Theodore Wettstein, Carl, described this attitude clearly:

> The Germans in our city [Milwaukee] all belonged at first to the Democratic party. For one of that nationality to ally himself with any other than the Democratic party was regarded as an impossibility, if not a crime. It was natural. The word Democrat had a different meaning for the Germans than for others amid the conditions of those times. In Germany—or, to speak more precisely, in Prussia, for there was no Germany then—Democrats were those who stood in opposition to tyranny, monarchy and aristocracy—upholding everything that was free and good and noble. Most of the emigrants from Germany in 1847 and 1848 were revolutionists. They left the fatherland because they were obliged to or because they were disgusted with its political outlook. When they arrived here and found a Democratic party, they joined it because they had been Democrats at home, and they supposed that word meant the same thing here as there.

When Wilhelm Wagner had arrived in the United States, the rupture between the North and the South had been postponed only by various compromises like the Missouri Compromise of 1820 and the Omnibus Bill of 1850. It was only a matter of time, however, until the two sides would clash, and everybody would have to take sides. One man who had made his position clear from the beginning was the Republican nominee for the Illinois Senate seat in the 1858 election: Abraham Lincoln. At the close of the Republican State Convention at Springfield, Illinois, on 17 June 1858, he gave special weight to a phrase that had been used before but since then is connected insolubly with his political beliefs: "'A house divided against itself cannot stand.' I believe this government cannot endure permanently half slave and half free. I do not expect the Union to be dissolved; I do not expect the house to fall; but I do expect it will cease to be divided." With this clear political statement, Lincoln entered into what would become the "hottest, the closest, the most momentous senatorial campaign in decades," as Allan Nevins called it.[30] Lincoln's opponent for this seat was the incumbent senator Stephen A. Douglas. For this election, the two men agreed on something completely new: a series of joint debates in public. These seven debates seized the attention of the whole nation. The second debate was to be held at Freeport, Illinois, on Friday, 27 August 1858. Nobody could foresee that on this cloudy and cool day this debate would become the most momentous of all the debates, would win Douglas the seat in the Senate and Lincoln the presidency two years later.[31]

Wilhelm Wagner among many others present did not fully realize the significance of this debate. The crowd that had gathered to hear the two contestants was enormous; estimates range from 10,000 to 20,000 spectators who had arrived from all over Stephenson County and even from Chicago, Galena, and Beloit. A platform had been built two blocks north of the new hotel Brewster House (where Douglas also stayed) and northeast of the intersection of Douglas and State (then Mechanic) streets on open land with a small grove of trees. Senator Douglas had already arrived at Freeport, then a town of nearly 6,000 inhabitants, on Thursday evening. Freeport, with its Democratic majority, gave him an enthusiastic welcome. Wilhelm Wagner, the Democrat, wrote about it in his paper accordingly:

> Already at the previous evening, August 26, Mr. Stephen A. Douglas, main leader of the Democratic Party, arrived by train from Galena and was welcomed by hundreds of his friends with much jubilation at the station. The local German music band and nearly 200 torch bearers—whose torches weren't manufactured properly though—accompanied the beloved defender of unconditional democracy to his lodgings, the Brewster House where he was greeted with a short speech in the name of the Democrats of Stephenson County by Mr. James Mitchell.

Two further paragraphs on the evening with Douglas emphazise how partisan Wilhelm Wagner was. Lincoln's arrival the next morning is described in one simple sentence later in this article. In the consecutive article one week later, Wilhelm Wagner went even further:

> From beginning to end, Douglas stood firm to the highest principles of democracy, that all peoples have to regulate their own affairs and have to create their own laws. Thus he is standing on the Cincinnati platform with both his feet and this has to secure him the vote of every true Democrat. Lincoln in contrast does not declare himself for this platform anymore, which has been agreed upon by his party a few years ago. This is why a lot of his followers even were not satisfied with the remarks he made at Freeport.[32]

Two things about the Freeport debate had been important: with his answer to Lincoln's question that free-soil settlers could refuse to admit slavery in the territories, Douglas alienated the South which would lead to a split of the Democratic Party in 1860; and Lincoln had shown in this debate that he could stand up against the then more popular and better known Douglas. In the end therefore, Lincoln had won. Marvin Trask Grattan, who as a boy was witness to this historical debate, remembered the political essence of that day remarkably clearly seventy years later:

> Uncle Orlando early secured a good position near the speakers and kept me with him as a reward for my enthusiastic Douglas Democracy. The judge spoke second, a magnetic, eloquent orator who swayed a sympathetic audience to his will and views, for Republicans in that great gathering were largely in the minority. . . . What did he say? What was his argument? I don't know. I simply knew that I was for him, just as the other boys and young men were who later volunteered when he held Lincoln's hat on inauguration day and declared for the Union.
>
> I can remember more of what Lincoln said than what Judge Douglas said. It did not matter what the judge said, he was our man anyway, but we were curious about the black Republican abolitionist, and hostile. And then he disarmed us completely. Rising to his great height slowly he lifted both hands, saying distinctly: "What a great orator Judge Douglas is!" This tribute to our idol won him respect if not actual liking. And then those puzzling questions that lost him the senatorship and won him the presidency. He was so frank, so honest, so sincere that we felt sorry for his certain

> defeat not realizing that in his wisdom, as harmless as the dove, he had the wisdom of the serpent as events demonstrated.[33]

Wilhelm Wagner remained a staunch Democrat throughout his life, even when quite a number of his fellow Forty-eighters changed their minds during the course of the years. In the presidential election of 1860, he vigorously campaigned for the Democratic candidate, Senator Stephen A. Douglas, again. Passionately to an extent one might even call polemic or crude, Wilhelm vehemently denounced all criticism of Douglas, bitterly opposing his colleagues who wrote in favor of Lincoln: "Go on, the more you rage against Douglas, the higher the admiration of the people will be for this much abused and persecuted little giant!" And in doing what he accused the others of, he even lashed out against Lincoln by citing another paper, the *Macomb Eagle*, that had published an alleged Lincoln speech on Thomas Jefferson from 1844:

> Lincoln said then: "Mr. Jefferson is a statesman, whose praise is never sung by the Democratic Party. . . . Jefferson's character is repulsive. Always whining about freedom, equality and the dishonorable course of slavery, he had his own children put up for sale and made money with his excesses. . . ." That is how Lincoln spoke about one founder of the Union, the author of the declaration of independence and great statesman Thomas Jefferson, whose fame spans the globe.

While the majority of the Forty-eighters had been on the side of the Democratic Party until 1858, this had started to change in 1859, when the consequences and effects of the Fugitive Slave Law and the Kansas Nebraska Act became noticeable around the country. Slowly the Germans in the Midwest began to turn to the Republican Party. In 1860 the Forty-eighters were divided, not only into Republicans and Democrats, but the Democrats into followers of Douglas and supporters of Davis and the Republicans into those who still favored Lincoln and those who promoted the presidential candidacy of Edward Bates. Wilhelm Wagner's friend Caspar Butz from Chicago and Adolph Douai from Boston played a prominent part in the heated discusions of the Germans at the Republican Convention of 1860. At the end, those who supported Lincoln prevailed with a considerable majority; and Carl Schurz later never got tired in emphazising how important the German vote had been for Lincoln. Four years later, the movement for Fremont would split the Forty-eighters again.[34]

With his decisive stand for the Democratic Party, Wilhelm Wagner was even accused of being a "copperhead" after the Civil War. This nickname was coined by the New York *Tribune* on July 20, 1861, for those northern Democrats who were in opposition to the war policy of the Union. This did not affect Wilhelm Wagner, however. He knew that he had always been loyal to the Union and even contributed in his own, personal way to the war effort of the northern states. He also knew that any accusation was brought forward only by a few fanatics and not from Freeport's majority. Wilhelm Wagner had become very popular with his fellow citizens. People paid attention to what he wrote in his paper and enjoyed his company. Although he was respected and loved by a great many people, he had some enemies nevertheless, especially among the orthodox Protestants who believed it was not correct to have any festivities on Sundays. Keeping in mind the lines of the famous German poet Johann Wolfgang von Goethe: "Tages Arbeit, abends Gäste! Saure Wochen, frohe Feste!" ("After a day's work, guests in the evening, after hard weeks, happy festivals" from Goethe's 1797 ballad, *Der Schatzgräber*), Wilhelm frequently organized picnics and other festivities for and with the other Germans of Freeport. For these occasions, he usually wrote one or more songs or poems. Later he had them printed in his newspaper. The people used to sing his songs to well-known German folk song melodies. According to his suggestion, the German community always celebrated the Fourth of July with a special party which was attended by many Germans from the whole county. Wilhelm Wagner was deeply moved when the men's choir of Davenport made him an honorary member on one of his visits there. He loved the social events that the *Turnverein* and the *Sängerbund* organized, and took active part by reciting a poem or giving a speech. After Wilhelm Wagner's death, these two societies united and became the *Germania Verein*, as the members of the two had worked together for many years.

In addition to the *Turnverein* and the *Sängerbund*, Wilhelm Wagner belonged to the founding fathers of the German Firefighting Company and the German Odd Fellow Lodge. From the moment he had arrived in the

United States, Wilhelm was interested in founding a German-American school. In this, he was a typical Forty-eighter again. Many of those who had fled to the United States after the failure of the German revolution had been schoolteachers, like Adolph Douai for instance. They had very definite ideas about how children should be taught and trained to become good democrats. In many ways they did not consider the American public school system suitable for educating children to become critical and independent citizens, essential for a living democratic and even republican society. For this reason, they joined with other liberal-minded Germans, who had arrived earlier, to establish their own schools. Here, their guiding principles were bilingualism, practical orientation, and secularism. Together with other German citizens, Wilhelm Wagner finally succeeded in establishing such a school in 1856. In 1860 it had eighty students and was respected as one of the better private institutions in the county.[35] When it had to be closed in 1870, Wilhelm was very sad. He had had such great hopes in it. The schoolhouse had to be sold. For himself though, things had gradually improved financially.

Wilhelm Wagner had been smart enough not to base his economic future solely on publishing a newspaper. He used his machines by advertising in his own paper that he also did book and job printing (business cards, pamphlets, notes, auction leaflets, catalogs, circulars, and letterhead stationery). Thus he laid the foundation stone for what would become the Wagner Printing Company. On 19 March 1857, Wilhelm was finally able to buy a little house for the family on Washington Street. One and a half stories high, it had four rooms, a cellar with brick walls, a cistern, and a small garden. Although it was worth about $800 (the equivalent of nearly 2,000 *Gulden/Florin*) it had cost him only $650. Three hundred dollars were granted him on respite with a ten percent interest rate until 1 April 1858; fifty dollars he paid in cash when signing the contract and the sum of one hundred dollars he wanted to pay in the following days after he collected outstanding debts. This was not enough though, and Wagner had to ask the bank for a loan of over $200. He had to pay the bank the usual interest of three percent a month. After a few months, the wagon maker Heinrich Schrenkler heard about this deal and offered to lend him the money at an interest of twelve percent a year. This was a big relief for Wilhelm, and he always remembered Schrenkler for what he had done for him in a time of need. They planned to move into their new home at the beginning of April that year, and Wilhelm was extremely happy about this:

> It looks like, you will say, as if the old prophecy is finally coming true, and Wilhelm is getting rich. None of you has so far become the owner of a house, even if he hasn't paid for it yet . . . . *One* thing is for certain though: as a political fugitive, I would not have been able to establish a livelihood in Germany as easy as I was able to do here—thanks to GOD and to liberty! Our future here looks brighter and friendlier from day to day, and there is no idea of us ever returning to the old homeland.[36]

Two years later they had dug a well and built a stable. In 1860, Wilhelm wrote back home that he might return, but only on certain conditions. What seems at first sight to be a contradiction to his statement cited above actually only confirms Wilhelm's opinion. Having heard from his German friends back home in Baden that an amnesty had been granted to the escaped revolutionaries, he had answered them that he would only return to Germany on certain conditions and then only for a couple of years. His conditions were first, the Grand Duke had to apologize to him in person; second, he had to receive all back wages since 9 November 1849, including interest; third, he wanted to be exempted from church rule and the supervision by his superiors and be able to hold his sermons as he pleased; fourth, he wanted to bring his printing business to Germany and publish his *Deutscher Anzeiger* free from any censorship; fifth, his sons had to be exempted from any military duties; and sixth he wanted to keep his American citizenship and never again have to swear obedience to any German duke.[37] All these conditions would never have been granted to him, and Wilhelm undoubtedly knew this. Proclaiming these conditions, Wilhelm thus manifested his political beliefs which made him a true citizen of the United States. He had left Germany behind in more than one way.

As his taste was very plain, he never wanted to have carpets on the floors or curtains at the windows. The whole family slept on straw mattresses. It was not until the last years of his life that his children could talk him into acquiring at least simple rugs and window drapes for the front rooms. His daily routine always saw him busy. At dawn, or earlier during the winter months, he got up, lit a fire in the stove, put a kettle of water on for the morning coffee, and fetched a bucket of water from the well. Then he fed the cattle and chopped some wood. Having done this, he woke the children. By that time, his wife had already prepared breakfast for them. Immediately after breakfast, he went to the printing office, doing whatever was necessary: writing, typesetting, or printing. He only allowed himself a half-hour lunch break before he resumed his work again. When dusk was settling in, he hurried home for dinner. His working day was normally not over yet. After the meal, he rushed back to the office to work until ten or sometimes even later. If his presence was not necessary at the printing office, he would stay at home, reading the latest news from other papers. He regularly attended the meetings of the various societies that he had helped to found. Wilhelm Wagner was very happy that he could serve his congregation as a pastor, and at the same time work as a newspaper editor and printer full-time. This, as he never grew tired of emphasizing, would have been impossible in the Germany he had left. To him, this was just another example of the freedom the common man had in the United States.

He was especially proud of his children. His oldest son, Karl, had turned twenty-one on 30 January 1860, and was thus entitled to vote, which he did the first time on 2 April the same year. He had studied law, was an associate of the local justice of the peace beginning in fall of 1859, and passed his final law exams in Chicago in spring 1860. In March 1860, his father Wilhelm wrote that Karl was paying his parents two dollars a week for board and food as he was already earning some money as advocate. Wilhelm was proud that the legal advice of his son was quite sought after in Freeport, but thought Karl could be more industrious and more mannerly. His second son, William, was already foreman in the printing house and responsible for the technical operations of the company. His father never ceased to praise his skills and his ability to work under pressure. With William in charge of the printing process, the help of Louis Crusius was no longer needed, and he was dismissed. In October 1863, William was officially made a partner of his father. At the same time, Wilhelm took on his brother-in-law, Oskar Ziegler (the husband of his wife's sister Ernestine) as partner. Business did not flourish as expected, however, and they had to part with Oskar Ziegler two years later. It was father and son again running the show. Wilhelm was also very proud of the musical talent of his second son. William not only played the piano, the violin, the cello, the guitar, and the trumpet, he also sang with the *Freeporter Sängerbund*. He was so good, in fact, that this singing club made him their president in 1860 although William was the youngest member at that time. Each day he practiced the piano on the instrument the *Sängerbund* had bought for $300; and his father even considered the idea of buying him one as soon as their debts could be reduced. Luise, who had turned seventeen in January 1860, was already taller than her mother and a very good seamstress too. Being especially fond of books and magazines, though, she often had to be reminded of her duties at home. Hermann, fifteen years old in 1860, and Julius, twelve years old that year, were both attending the German-American school of which their father was so proud. Seven-year-old Friedrich went to that school, too, and was the best in his class. In all his letters, Wilhelm clearly expressed how happy he was in the land of liberty and freedom and how proud he was of all his children.[38] What made him happy, too, was, that at least one branch of the family had followed his call and had also immigrated to the United States: Heinrich Kleinpell, the youngest brother of Wilhelm's mother Luise, who had been born in 1801, had emigrated to the United States with his wife Nannette and their seven children in 1857. Heinrich Kleinpell's oldest son Heinrich Wilhelm (1833-1885) actually did the same as his cousin Wilhelm at Freeport: he published a newspaper in Wisconsin. He favored the Republican Party, which did not shatter his friendship with his cousin, though. To keep the ties with the family in Germany strong and alive, Wilhelm not only wrote long letters whenever his time permitted but since the beginning of 1857 also started to send them the *Deutscher Anzeiger*, regularly. Sometimes Wilhelm published letters he received from the relatives in Germany when he thought them to be interesting for the general public. This was very important for both sides, and kept the feeling alive that they were very close as a family, although thousands of miles apart. Despite all the happiness and joy that Wilhelm received from his family and work, there were times of anxiety and worry too.

With the outbreak of the Civil War in April 1861, war fever spread through Freeport. When the surrender of Fort Sumter on Sunday, 14 April, and Lincoln's call for troops the next day became known at Freeport, an enormous crowd of people, Republicans and Democrats alike, followed a call, issued at noon of Thursday, 18 April, to assemble at Plymouth Hall that evening. Many heroic speeches were made in favor of the Union and condemning the South. Wilhelm Wagner, speaking in German, was one of those who "aroused the patriotic enthusiasm to fever heat." Many resolutions were adopted, all declaring the love for the Union by Freeport's citizens. The next day, recruiting began. On Saturday, 20 April, the first company enlisted in the county was formed under the command of Captain S. D. Atkins. Inflammatory speeches were not the only contributions of the Wagners to the war for the Union, however. Soon after Captain Atkins' company had left Freeport, Wilhelm Wagner saw his oldest son Karl become a sergeant together with Jacob Hoebel in Freeport's second company under the command of Captain W. J. McKim. His second son William played the trumpet in the Freeport Union Band, when the company marched into war. William himself joined the 142nd Infantry Illinois Volunteers that was organized by Colonel Rollin V. Ankeney on 18 June 1864, and served for one hundred days, guarding White's Station on the Memphis & Charleston Railroad, eleven miles from Memphis. On 1 January 1864, Hermann joined company C of the 46th Illinois Infantry in which he served until 20 January 1866. He participated in the skirmish at Benton, Mississippi, on 13 May 1864, at the battle near Jackson, Mississippi, on 7 July that year and took part in the capture of Fort Blakely and Mobile, Alabama, 9-12 April 1865. He had enlisted as a recruit, and was a private until 7 November 1865, when he was appointed Corporal by order of Lt. Col. Jones.

During the war between France and Germany in 1870-1871, Wilhelm Wagner wrote his sister Henriette in Germany sending her his best wishes for the safe return of her two sons Adalbert and Karl. He tried to console her by saying that he and Friederike knew from past experience how she must feel now:

> My beloved Rike still vividly remembers the long time (nearly three years), our Hermann faced the fierce enemy on many a battlefield. At that time, my dear wife asked me nearly every night: "How can you sleep? I have to think of Hermann all the time." And on February 2, 1866, we were overjoyed to welcome him back home, well and in one piece. I will never forget how I travelled thirty-five

> miles to meet him, how I searched for him in the more than ten stock cars, our more than one thousand emaciated soldiers, stiff from cold, were transported back home in and how I finally found him. But he came back well and unwounded, and we wish you too, that Adalbert and Karl will come back soon![39]

His greatest joy in later years were his grandchildren, growing in number steadily. He loved to take six or eight of them out to festivities or to visit a circus. One day he took some of his grandchildren to the start of a balloon in front of a circus tent. He did not realize that somebody stole his purse and all his money. When he discovered the loss he was not angry or sad, because he had had a wonderful time with his grandchildren. One of the things that made Wilhelm unhappy, though, was that he lost contact with his brother Julius whom he wrote frequently but from whom he never received an answer.[40] Another event that plagued him was the receipt of a summons to stand testimony in a lawsuit against himself. An article had appeared in the *Deutscher Anzeiger* on 26 March 1873, accusing August F. Broad, who was a member of the grand jury, of being biased against saloon-owners as he was a teetotaller and not the free-minded liberal he claimed to be. Broad foamed with rage and sued Wilhelm Wagner for slander. The legal procedures went on for some time. During the end of the trial in 1875, Wilhelm discovered that even in the land of the free it was not simply a matter of speaking the truth but of being able to prove it. Wilhelm's article had been based on the testimony of other members of the grand jury. Those men were not permitted to testify in another court, though, as the proceedings of a grand jury are not to be made public. Broad and his well-known attorney U. D. Meacham (who had settled in Freeport in 1852, was elected state attorney for the fourteenth judicial district and mayor of Freeport in 1862) had been smart enough to ask for a removal of the case as the old Wagner was too well-known and prominent in Freeport. At the final trial in December 1875, the jury at the court of Oregon, Ogle County, found Wilhelm Wagner guilty of slander and sentenced him to pay $263 in compensation to Broad. This lawsuit overshadowed the completion of the first *Deutscher Anzeiger* building that the Wagners had constructed in 1874. After the trial, Wilhelm Wagner was never really his old self again. The simple truth that in the land of utmost freedom he could not print what he thought was correct but had to be able to prove every statement in court if necessary, made Wilhelm Wagner see the United States in a different light. The Wagners actually had to pay $303.66 (including court fees) and at first did not know how to raise so much money. The German community of Freeport organized a benefit concert for Wagner on 9 March 1876, that yielded a net profit of $278.75. In addition, the members of his Ridott-Silver Creek congregation collected $109. All this was to the highest satisfaction of Wilhelm Wagner and moved him, but those who knew him very well sensed that the lawsuit had affected him greatly and that he had lost his strength and indomitable will.

In June of 1877 the eighth *Sängerfest* of the northwestern *Sängerbund* was held at Freeport and this revived Wilhelm Wagner for a last time. This festival lasted from Tuesday, 19 June to Friday, 22 June, and was a tremendous success. Thirteen societies of the twenty-five that constituted this *Sängerbund* had come to Freeport. The festival (the musical scores, the printing costs, postage and packing) had cost the *Sängerbund* $224.50. At their official meeting, the members elected Wilhelm Wagner vice president and a member of the committee of three that was to prepare the next festival to be held at Milwaukee. Everyone was full of praise for Wilhelm Wagner and the arrangements he made for the Freeport festival. Wilhelm was especially proud that his son William sang two arias and that these performances were loudly applauded. These were the last four days that Wilhelm Wagner enjoyed to the fullest.[41]

Being such a well-liked pastor, he had to perform numerous baptisms, weddings, and funerals, not only at Freeport but also in the vicinity. In October 1877, he was thus called to perform a baptism at Jefferson Township, in the southwest corner of Stephenson County. Riding in an open wagon on his way home he was drenched by a steady rain. He caught a cold, complications set in, and after being sick for about four weeks, Wilhelm Wagner died in the evening of 26 November 1877, at seventy-four years of age. He was buried in the Freeport City cemetery. The first of the immigrating Wagner brothers had died. His death was mourned by numerous people. Most of the German papers in the west published orbituaries, like the *Freie Presse* from Chicago, *Der Stern* from Belleville, Illinois, the *Iowa Staats-Anzeiger* from Des Moines, and the *Nord Iowa Herold* from Elkader, Iowa. They all sang his praise, emphasizing his good and amiable character, his courage, his humor, and his noble heart. But, there was more to Wilhelm Wagner's life and work. In working hard on the one hand and being able to enjoy festivities on the other, he strengthened the image of the good, industrious, amiable German who could contribute quite a lot to his new homeland. And there was more still, probably the most important factor in evaluating his life historically. Through his paper *Deutscher Anzeiger*, he had a considerable influence on his fellow Germans, especially those who weren't fluent yet in English.

> But able management has conquered success, and the sheet, which at first was weak, has continually grown in favor among the German population of Stephenson and adjoining counties, until it has become the leading German paper in the northwestern portion of Illinois, having a circulation of 1,300 copies, to which additions are made weekly. . . . Politically, as already stated, the paper is Democratic, locally a valuable source of domestic intelligence, and, in other respects, an enterprise deserving of the liberal support extended.[42]

Wilhelm Wagner's influence on the Germans of his area should not be underestimated. For many who had come to the States but weren't fluent in the English language yet, his newspaper was the only means of information about national and international affairs. And he used his influence as we have seen. In doing this, he also demonstrated clearly that he was a typical Forty-eighter with the strong desire to reform people wherever it seemed necessary to him. All he had wanted originally had been reforms in Baden, but the political situation had forced him to emigrate. One might see it as an ironic footnote in history that nearly 120 years after Wilhelm Wagner was forced to leave his home at Brombach, Baden, that community named a street after him (formerly named Friedrichstrasse), and today praises Wilhelm Wagner as one of their most prominent sons. No street is named after Wilhelm's brother Julius, however, who still lived in Texas when his oldest brother died in 1877.

5. Turbulent Times in Texas

AS WITH MANY OTHER AMERICANS, the Civil War completely changed the lives of Julius Wagner and his family. Not only did it sever whole families and friendships; it also had a calamitous effect on the Germans in Texas as a group. In contrast to the Germans living in the northern states, those in Texas and the other states of the Confederacy had to choose between loyalty towards the Union they had once chosen as their new homeland or towards the state where they were living. This was a difficult and sometimes even an acrimonious choice for many, especially since the overwhelming majority of Texans (at a rate of three to one) had voted for secession. It boiled down to the question: could one live with the "peculiar institution" or was one's opposition to slavery so vehement that one had to take sides against the Confederacy? It is impossible to say exactly how many German-Texans dissented against the Confederacy. Whereas authors like Robert W. Shook and Ella Lonn argue that the overall majority of Germans were loyal to the Confederacy, James Marten and Glen E. Lich claim that the majority of Germans opposed slavery and resisted secession. Rena M. Andrews differentiates between those Germans coming to Texas before the 1840s and those who arrived afterwards. Those arriving prior to 1840 tended to support the South in general, whereas antisecession and antislavery sentiments prevailed in the later group.

The pattern is a little more complicated when details are considered. The reasons for joining one or the other side might not have had something to do with the question of slavery at all but with other facts. Those Germans for instance who lived on the west Texas frontier and voted against secession were either indifferent to the issue because they saw it as a conflict between the eastern states or were afraid of a war that would eventually draw away the troops that were stationed along the frontier to protect them. They feared a war would leave them unprotected. In addition, only very few of them owned slaves.[1] Even those Germans who lived in the east, which was much more suited for plantations, and who could have afforded to own slaves, did so only at a much smaller proportion than their Anglo-American neighbors. There are hints that the German middle class, especially, saw slavery in a more positive light and owned as many slaves as they could afford. Thus Otto von Roeder could boast of owning twenty-nine slaves in 1851.[2] A lot of newer evidence seems to indicate that quite a large number of those German-Texans who supported the Confederacy in one way or another did this rather reluctantly and not out of absolute and pure conviction. Even the infamous advice of the editor of the *Neu Braunfelser Zeitung*, Ferdinand Lindheimer, to vote for secession did not spring out of Lindheimer's alleged sympathy for the Confederates and the "peculiar institution" but out of a very rational analysis of the political situation. He foresaw quite correctly that Texas would vote for secession, despite his countrymen's beliefs, and that life for the Germans in Comal County would then be much safer if they followed the mainstream.[3]

As we have seen, it was not simply a question of being for or against slavery. In many, if not most, cases of Germans voting for secession, the crucial, decisive factor was the neighborhood and the social and political environment in which the settlers lived. They generally followed the opinion of a person, a specific individual they believed in, trusted, and admired the most. This was and is the most common phenomenon of political opportunism. Those settlers who had already lived in Texas for some time wanted to be accepted by their Anglo-American neighbors as true Texans.[4] The significance of this lies in the conclusion that the Germans in Texas, as a group, were divided. The results of this were twofold: for one thing, the relationship between the Germans and the Anglo-Americans suffered considerably as the latter saw the former as traitors; and for the other, Reconstruction became the chance of a lifetime for many a Unionist-German, propelling him into a successful business or political career. In a way, Julius Wagner was one of them.

In their reminiscences some sixty years later, Julius Wagner's daughters Sophie and Lina give only a meager account of those years:

> Outbreak of the Civil War in 1861; at the end of 1863, flight to Mexico of our father and some other men who, like him, did not want to fight against the emancipation of the slaves. They would

> have lost their lives if they had not fled "in night and fog" ["bei Nacht und Nebel" is a common German idiom, not to be taken literally: it means to leave in darkness and secrecy] without being able to say goodbye to their families. Only much later were they able to send for their wives and children.[5]

The Wagners had lived happily on their farm close to Coletoville for fifteen years. In 1858 they had finally been able to pay off their debts and were facing better times. They began to look to the future full of hope. Then the Civil War struck them like lightning out of the blue. The old ties and friendships between the settlers along the Coleto broke up. One of Julius Wagner's neighbors, Robert Kleberg, although opposed to slavery, nevertheless felt obliged to raise a company for the Confederate army in which his two sons Otto and Rudolph as well as his foster child Joachim von Roeder served during the war. Kleberg's son-in-law Heinrich Hillebrand moved to California with his family at the outbreak of the Civil War because of his strong antislavery convictions. Two of the late Albrecht von Roeder's sons, Hermann (1846-1926) and Ludwig (1844-1864), served in the Confederate army as privates. The latter was the first von Roeder in two generations to die in combat. His brother wrote home on 16 April 1864: "Dear Mother, I have some very sad news to share with you: my brother fell in battle on the twelfth of this month. Wood's regiment had to make an attack on a gunboat, in which Loui was shot right through the heart. Besides him fourteen others were killed and thirty-four were wounded. Ever since his death I have had very sorrowful times. I arrived there just after he had been buried. He was buried in an old field near the bank of the Red River. I haven't even been able to go to his grave. It makes me very sad indeed that he had to give up his life in the first fight. He fell as a brave soldier."[6] Julius August Schorre, another friend of the Wagners, also sided with the Confederates by enlisting as a private in the Coleto Guards Reserve Company of DeWitt County under the command of Captain Robert Kleberg. Julius Schütze and Georg Witting on the other hand were vehemently opposed to slavery and secession. In the same way, the remaining members of the Forty were divided. Whereas Gustav Schleicher joined the Confederates and served in the Corps of Engineers as captain from 24 April 1861, until the company's surrender on 4 August 1865, and

Ferdinand Herff served as brigade surgeon of the Confederate Militia, Julius Wagner's friend Jacob Küchler as a Unionist barely survived the war.

Küchler had always been very outspoken against slavery and was among the Germans in Texas who formed the "Union Loyal League" in June 1861. For self-protection they formed three companies, and Küchler became captain of the Gillespie County Company. When the Union League received word of Confederate troops advancing, they decided to escape to Mexico. The group of Unionists—the figures vary between sixty and one hundred men—were not marching with great haste when they were attacked by a Confederate force under the command of Lt. C. D. McRae. This event became known as the Battle of the Nueces or the Massacre on the Nueces. About thirty Germans died during that ambush and about twenty were wounded. The surviviors, Küchler among them, fled across the Rio Grande.[7] In Mexico, Küchler was fortunate that the governor of Nuevo Leon and Coahuila, Señor Bidauri, was looking for a surveyor and with the intercession of wealthy and influential German businessmen from Monterey, Küchler got the job and was later even appointed civil engineer for both states. Thus, Küchler was able to stay there until the end of the Civil War.

More than one year later, Julius Wagner fled to Mexico. Unfortunately, no known source gives a reason why he took sides with the Unionists, whether it was because of his friends Schütze, Witting, and Küchler or because his political and ethical beliefs were stronger than his ties with his neighbors like Kleberg and Schorre and his usual desire to lead a pleasant life. In addition we have no source that tells us why he fled to Mexico. He might have become afraid of the stories about atrocities committed against Germans loyal to the Union. We do not know either with whom he fled or if he travelled by himself. In any case, one can probably assume that his escape to Mexico will have been very much like the story Charles Nagel tells about his and his father's flight in his memoirs. Nagel was fourteen and a half years old, when he and his father, the physician Hermann Nagel, left their home at Millheim, Austin County, on 3 November 1863, just around the same time Julius Wagner parted from his loved ones. The reasons for going alone, and the actual departure scene might well have been the same in both cases for the Wagners and the Nagels:

> and this finally brought them to the desperate decision to have father and me attempt the escape even at the risk of leaving mother and brother and sister to await the end of the war, with no one to look to but mother's courage and our faith in the South's traditional protection for a woman. . . . I had no look of farewell for Rossa or dogs, or any other animal or thing dear to me. Life had been sweet there. Really no one had been cruel to us, but now mother and sister and brother were to be left alone. We went by an unusual road leaving our pasture garden and field on one side and the forest on the other. . . . [8]

The Civil War period unfortunately presents more questions than answers as far as Julius Wagner and his family are concerned. We do not know when the family joined Julius, or where and how they lived. Since the last letters of Julius before the Civil War told us that they were nearly free of debts, he might have taken up a mortgage on the land or even have sold it or parts of it. Living in Mexico was cheap. Individual letters from Germans in Mexico give us a couple of names of those German-Texans who stayed there during the Civil War. How many they were cannot be determined although this group was not very large. Some others went to the North or even back to Germany. The letters Jacob Küchler wrote to his wife from Parras indicate that Mexico at that time was a good place to make money by trading with the Union or the Confederacy.[9] There was considerable traffic close to the border between Brownsville and Matamoros. Interestingly enough, it did not matter a great deal for some on which side they were. And even though Germans served in Confederate regiments, others in Union ones, some traded Southern cotton from Mexico to help the Confederate cause; others did business with the North. Many of them continually maintained some sort of contact, and information about one's fate was spread among the German community. If Julius Wagner pursued any kind of business, we have no proof of it. We do know, however, that at the end of 1863 or in 1864, the Wagners sent their oldest son Sigmund, at the age of thirteen, from Mexico to Emilie's parents, the Schneiders, in Offenburg, Germany. He attended the local *Volksschule* there until he was seventeen and then went to the *Polytechnicum* (technical college) in Karlsruhe, where he was trained as an engineer.

After the war, the Wagners returned to Texas and settled down at Indianola, the major port in the south of Texas. The small settlement Indian Point at Matagorda Bay was renamed Indianola in February of 1849. In 1867 it had around 2,200 inhabitants. When President Andrew Johnson had lifted the blockade of Matagorda Bay on 24 June 1865, Indianola quickly recovered its old commercial strength. It was the port where all government supplies for west Texas and the New Mexico and Arizona Territories were shipped in and unloaded. Family letters indicate that Julius Wagner had first established himself in some kind of commercial business in Indianola. On 9 March of that year he had even been able to sell his old farm at the Twelve-Mile Coleto to Charles Lang for $250. Then, suddenly, the coastal town was hit by disaster. In June of 1867, a small vessel coming from Vera Cruz not only brought secondhand blankets but also yellow fever to Indianola. Many suspected later that the contagious mosquitos were hidden in the blankets.

> The first death occurred on the 24th of June, and in less than a week the whole business part of the town was struck down, as by lightning, there being no less than 125 to 150 cases taken during that time out of a population of less than a thousand [Note: in the business section of Lower Indianola]. . . . In this place, with about 2,000 inhabitants, no less than 550 to 600 persons must have been sick, although no certain data can be given, owing to the sudden outbreak and spread. Of six physicians then here, four were taken sick, all recovered. The number of deaths from the epidemic may be estimated at from seventy-five to eighty-five.

In a letter dated 8 October 1867, Julius reported back home to Germany that they had had yellow fever too, especially he and his wife Emilie to a high degree, but that they had recovered, although their business had suffered greatly.[10]

Now it paid off for Julius Wagner that he had been loyal to the Union, as it did for many Germans in Texas after the Civil War when governors like A. J. Hamilton and E. J. Davis remembered those who had remained loyal to the Union under highly dangerous conditions. On 5 April 1869, President Ulysses S. Grant appointed Julius Wagner postmaster of Indianola, which was immediately confirmed by the Senate. Julius Wagner held this office for fourteen years until he left Indianola at the beginning of 1883. It would be misleading though to see the appointment of Julius Wagner as an isolated act and not recognize the network of help the old and new friends had established. A good example is the appointment on 25 June 1869 of Jacob Küchler as deputy collector of customs and storekeeper of the bonded warehouse at the port of San Antonio. Julius Wagner and his friend William Westhoff, who had been clerk at the store of von Hoyer and von Zobel in Colettoville and now was one of the richest wholesale and retail lumber dealers in Indianola, had strongly recommended Küchler to the Collector of Customs, James K. McCreary, who had a high regard for these two men. McCreary in return sent an official request for the appointment of Küchler to the secretary of the treasury, and Küchler was offered the job.[11]

Life was not meant to run smoothly for Julius Wagner, however. On 14 January 1871 his friend and brother-in-law Carl Baumann died suddenly at the age of fifty-four and then his father-in-law Peter J. Schneider died at the age of nearly eighty on 22 June. The deaths of these two men especially affected Julius' wife Emilie, as they had been very close to her. Carl Baumann's death also had the negative effect that Emilie's oldest son Sigmund, who apparently took after his father, had lost the guardian and mentor his uncle Carl had been to him. Emilie's father, still alive at that time, clearly saw the danger: "Now your son is mainly on his own, missing Baumann's protecting, organizing, and directing hand. He is in danger of degenerating, of giving in too easily to the temptations of a frivolous life as there are quite a lot of opportunities for that and as Sigmund tends to take on the habits of the rich polytechnicians." At the same time, Peter Schneider tried to ensure his daughter of the good character of her son Sigmund, of his diligence and perseverance in his studies. Yet, he not only writes that Sigmund looked very much like his father physically, he also mentions in his letter that he had to lend Sigmund sixty-six *Gulden* the last time he saw him. Sigmund had told his grandfather some threadbare stories about the impossibility of cashing a check from his parents, and how he needed money immediately to pay his rent.[12] Peter Schneider most certainly was not aware how much Sigmund's lifestyle, attitudes, and conduct resembled those of Sigmund's father Julius during his student days. Probably that was the last letter Peter Schneider wrote his daughter.

His death came suddenly for her and probably intensified her feelings of homesickness and despair. She had been weak throughout the summer of 1871 due to heavy dysentery. Emilie wrote to her nephew Karl, the third child of Carl Baumann and Henriette Wagner, in order to maintain contact with the Baumann family and to ask Karl to continue his father's "work" for and with Sigmund. In detail, Emilie apologizes for Julius' misconduct: he had not written his sister and sent her his condolences. She emphasizes the fact that the negligence of her husband as far as corresponding was concerned was widely known:

> Yet I have to excuse him because he is swamped with work at his post office —mainly writing—and thus hardly finds any time to write any private letters. . . . Last spring, our second son Wilhelm turned seventeen. He is a clerk to his father at the post office and earns twenty-five dollars a month, a rather bad salary. This job leaves him ample time though to broaden his knowledge. Wilhelm feels a strong yearning for Germany, and if it is GOD's will we can help him fulfill this dream as soon as Sigmund has finished his studies there. He can hardly wait to meet his cousins and all the rest of the family. After Wilhelm, there are our three girls, Sophie, Pauline and Lina who grow up to our full satisfaction. The latter is a little lady already. Richard, eight years old, is a real Texan boy and mighty spoiled. . . . In around eight days they'll open the railroad for a length of nearly twenty hours travel. The opinion of the consequences of this event are twofold. Whatever will be though, it will always be Texas and this Texas is and always will be a sad country and the burning desire for our beloved Germany will only die with us.[13]

In 1874, after ten years of education in Germany, Sigmund returned to his parents in Texas. Sources indicate that he then worked as a schoolteacher at Indianola.[14] But before Wilhelm could go to Germany, fate struck another blow. It was 15 September 1875. Nothing foretold what was to come. Sophie, the Wagner's oldest daughter, later wrote down what had happened that day and the following days when she had been just twenty years old. She wrote it down twenty years later but her story captures the atmosphere and the excitement:

It was the year 1875. The moon rose in full splendor over the small Texas town of Indianola, lying on Matagorda Bay, an arm of the Gulf of Mexico. A hot day, as are frequent in Texas during September, was followed by a lovely evening, bringing with it pleasant cooling.

My brother and sisters and I walked out to our garden with a few schoolmates, to accompany them to their buggy which was waiting in front of the house. Having arrived outside, we could admire the rise of the moon much better than from inside; it seemed to climb from the water and spilled a few beams of its silver light over the bay lying there so peacefully.

At the same time, however, we noticed that a rather strong wind was arising from an east-northeasterly direction. Nevertheless, this observation did not cause any feeling of anxiety among us children. From stories, as well as from personal experience, we knew that Indianola was usually flooded in part each autumn at the time of the equinox. Up to the present, such flooding had not been dangerous to the town and its inhabitants, as the storms were never strong enough to drive the water over the place in a destructive way.

This time, however, was to be different. The sea soon grew wild. The wind rose from hour to hour; the night passed uneasily and the following day brought a lead grey sky with rain. Had we considered Indianola's location, there was already reason enough to fear that danger was present.

The town was built on the flat shore, which was almost level with the water and was overgrown with cedar bushes; it exposed its broad side to the sea, and, when one came by steamer from Galveston, the largest port in Texas, gave the impression that it lay in the water. To the west, southwest and northwest, we were tied to the mainland, so that the piece of earth on which Indianola lay formed a half island.

The following night, from the 15th to the 16th, the wind had grown into a storm, so that by the next morning a substantial volume of water had already washed over the town. By noon, the outlook was very alarming, and it seemed as though the released, raging elements, which were continually gaining strength, would really drag us unfortunate people down in the roaring storm.

Under these circumstances, my eldest brother made an attempt to reach the business district, lying in the southeast section of the town, where my father, fearing the worst, had as Indianola's postmaster, gone early in the morning on the 16th to save money, valuables and documents. However, it was no longer possible for my brother to reach it; after working his way for two blocks, he was thrown to the ground, and swimming with all his might and energy, fighting against the storm and waves, reached our house again. Therefore, we were forced to leave our father to his fate.

The awful scene that presented itself to the eye now continually assumed an even more frightful aspect.

During the afternoon, a number of people from the neighborhood had fled to our sturdy house, which was constructed on stilts on top of a small rise, and truly, just in time, as when evening came, many different small houses, carrying everything that was within them, floated by our house like light boats, out to the sea and death!

And now came the night, the dreadful night for all Indianolans, the one that was to be the most horrifying and, of all, eternally unforgettable!

Among those who sought refuge in our house from destruction was a ship captain, who now stood watching wind and sea from a window on the second floor, where we had had to flee to, as the first floor had begun to fill with water during the afternoon. The moon spread a feeble light. The night seemed an eternity to us! The indescribable roar of the storm and the pounding of waves and rain against the windows almost drove us mad. Expecting death at any time, we children clung to our mother, who suffered twice and thrice as much out of fear for her husband. How often she spoke her wish: "Oh, if only this night would end, one way or the other!"

At midnight, the storm reached its climax; the wind was reported at 150 miles per hour. Soon after midnight, from the 16th to the 17th, there was an abrupt turn. Our captain spoke: "The wind is changing to the opposite direction, but the danger to us is that much greater!" Suddenly, our house began to move—we thought our last hour had come—and was driven a short distance, whereupon it lodged, still standing, against a tree and cedar bushes with a terrific jolt. We considered ourselves fortunate, because, if the house had been carried further by the storm, it most likely would have offered no more resistance, and we would have been either buried in the ruins or washed out into the endless sea. Yes, this period, from the change of direction of the storm to the grey morning, sealed the fate of many, many people of Indianola. The water, which now, with great strength and furious speed, roared back whence it had come, undermined nearly all the wooden stilt-houses, and carried away many as piles of rubbish or intact, if they had not been saved, as ours, by lucky accident.

It is easier to imagine than to describe the heart-rending scenes that took place during the night in the town that had been left to a cruel fate.

As the sun rose in the east over the still very rough bay, spilling a ghastly light through the heavy, leaden sky hanging over the destroyed town, a pitiful, indescribable scene greeted the eyes! Despairing, weeping, often only half-clothed, those who had escaped death wandered aimlessly. And the town itself was no longer recognizable; storm and water had completed a mighty work of destruction. One saw isolated houses, hardly recognizable as such; some totally ruined, others about to collapse and still others, that had been driven or flung from their previous site to another. The earth had been torn, full of deep gouges. Through the former town, it could now hardly make claim to such a name, flowed many canals, on which barge traffic had been established. There was no drinking water, because the cisterns, such as there were at that time in Indianola, were filled with salt water. After a few days, we also ran out of food, but we were soon supplied by Victoria and Cuero, two small towns lying on the mainland, and particularly, by Galveston. From the first towns through their generous people, supplies were brought by wagon, as the rail line had been totally destroyed. From Galveston, they brought beside food, also clothing, however, by sailing ship, on which the people risked their lives, as the Gulf of Mexico, which is known to be wild, was at this time especially dangerous to cross.

Yes, help was brought to us in great quantities! News of the great natural phenomenon which had befallen Indianola became known far and wide, and wonderful gifts, even money, was sent from afar to the needy homeless. And yet all this love and kindness could not heal all the wounds. Those who lost goods or possessions could conceivably replace them. Yet, the loss of one's relatives was irreplaceable. And many among the poorest, mourned the death of a loved one. How fortunate we were, not to have lost any member of our family; a kind fate brought our husband and father back to us. With heavy heart he set out on his way to come to us, which he succeeded in doing after overcoming many obstacles. Like many household heads, he had spent the night in the business district of the town and was counted one of the fortunate, the rescued!

On the 17th, it was ascertained that the great natural phenomenon had taken 317 lives; truly no small number when one considers that Indianola had hardly more than 3,000 inhabitants. Some of our dear schoolmates were among the unlucky ones. From the heartfelt feelings with which this news seized us, we could somewhat judge how those grieved who had lost loved-ones forever!

Words fail me as I sketch this picture for the honorable reader in portraying what occurred, yes, probably any language falls short in that respect.

For a few years, Indianola remained as it was after that night of horror. Then, however, the town began to disappear entirely. Many left the sad place right away and moved either as beggars or with a small remnant of their former possessions out into the world. Many a man still suffers from the blow of fate which struck him there and not only those who lost loved-ones, but also those whose lives were ruined and from whom all had been taken that they once had achieved in the flourishing town.[15]

When Sophie Wagner wrote the last lines she must have had her father in mind too. His house, valued at $500 in 1870, had been as severely damaged as the post office. Julius' friend William Westhoff had a damaged office building and had also lost all his lumber. Julius Wagner was facing another problem too: he simply was now too old to start all over again. When the hurricane hit Indianola, Julius was nearly fifty-nine years old. His youngest son Carl Friedrich Richard was still going to school. And his three daughters were still unmarried. Maybe these facts, along with the partial destruction of Indianola, gave Julius second thoughts about his future. For these reasons, and others we don't know of, Julius invested in land. On 22 November 1877, he bought nearly 500 acres on the east bank of Coleto Creek from Robert R. Barrow for $499.40. As Julius did not have the money, he signed a promissory note for the whole amount, due in twelve months at ten percent interest, thus placing a mortgage on the land.[16] Then, on 27 July 1878, Julius' twenty-one-year-old daughter Paula married the enterprising young German businessman Hermann Ludwig August Paepcke.

On 6 February 1883, after he turned sixty-six, Julius Wagner retired from his position as postmaster of Indianola. The reason for his retirement was not his age, as there was no mandatory retirement age for postmasters at that time. Although we do not have any letter or other document telling us the exact reason for his resigning as postmaster, we can guess with high probability that his salary had dropped so much that he was looking for another reliable source of income. Between 1864 and 1877, postmasters were divided into five classes, based on the average compensation of the postmaster for the two preceding years. After 1877, only four classes of post offices and postmasters existed. The post office at Indianola was a third class office, and Julius Wagner received an annual salary assigned in even hundreds of dollar, based on his preceding four quarterly financial returns. His salary also included the fees he received for renting out boxes in the post office as well as a percentage of other postal revenues. In 1871, he had earned $1,500, in 1873 it had been $1,800, in 1875 it was $1,700, in 1877 it had dropped to $1,400, in 1879 to $1,200 and in 1881 it was a meager $1,000. With business declining at Indianola, the revenues of the post office were going down rapidly too, and on 29 September 1882, the Indianola post office was discontinued as a third class office and reopened the next day as a fourth class office. As a natural consequence, Julius' income dropped too.[17] He simply needed another job. His son Wilhelm, who called himself William now, had his own business by now, Paula was married, and Lina had accompanied her sister Paula to Chicago, but Sigmund, Richard, and Sophie still lived with their parents. Although Julius had paid off his mortgage on the land he had bought from Robert R. Barrow in 1877, he still was not a wealthy man. Whether it was on the suggestion of his old friend Jacob Küchler, or his old neighbor from the Coleto, Edward (originally Eduard) Froböse (who had a very successful freight hauling business with his partner August Santleben in San Antonio at 15 N. Flores), or some other reason, Julius decided to move to San Antonio. Indianola was a dying place and the future for the city did not look very promising. Actually, Julius Wagner's successor as postmaster, John Mahon, closed the doors of the Indianola post office on 4 October 1887, forever. That meant that Indianola had officially ceased to exist.

In order to make a living at San Antonio, though, Julius first borrowed $1,185 on his land at the Coleto Creek from D. Sullivan from Bexar County on February 1, 1883. Then, in April of 1883, Julius Wagner and his family, with the exception of William who stayed at Indianola, moved to San Antonio. They moved into a house on 202 Blum Street at the corner of Bonham Street where Julius opened a grocery store. With his sons Sigmund and Richard working in his store as clerks, this business proved to be quite profitable. One thing has to be pointed out here, though: Julius Wagner had dearly paid for the laziness of his student days and had become a hard working citizen. On 26 March 1888, he was finally able to pay back his debts to D. Sullivan. According to his tax reports, he owned two carriages and two horses in 1890 and the total value of all his possessions came to $1205.[18]

Life might not have been that easy financially for Julius, but he kept his good spirits and never lost his joy of life. He had joined a singing society once again. This time it was the *San Antonio Deutscher Männerchor* (the men's choir of San Antonio). Julius' tenor voice proved to be a valuable asset for this choir, and they soon appointed him their secretary. It was almost like the good old times. Julius participated at the *18. Sängerfest des Deutsch-Texanischen Sängerbundes* (Eighteenth singing contest of the German-Texan singing society) which was held at Galveston from 14-17 April 1891. Julius Schütze, whom Julius Wagner and his neighbors had made conductor and director of the newly established Coleto *Gesangsverein* thirty-seven years earlier, came from Austin with his singing society and was president of this contest. W. Marx conducted the *San Antonio Deutscher Männerchor,* which consisted of eight first tenors (including Julius), six second tenors, six first bass and five second bass. Their performance of the *Ständchen* (serenade) by the German composer Franz Abt (1819-1885) won general acclaim.[19]

One year after this singing contest, Julius Wagner, his wife Emilie and their children Sigmund and Sophie moved to Chicago where Paula and Hermann Paepcke had lived since 1881. Carl Friedrich Richard stayed behind in Texas and moved in with his brother William. Again, we don't have actual proof for the reasons why Julius Wagner uprooted his family once again. He was seventy-five years old and Emilie seventy-two. He was free of debts and probably had made enough money to spend the rest of his life peacefully in retirement. Emilie had never loved Texas. And Paula, very likely, had urged her old parents to come and live with them in Chicago where her rich husband Hermann could support his parents-in-law in times of need. Together with their unmarried daughters, the old Wagners very likely took up residence on Eugenie Street near Lincoln Park, just a couple of blocks north from the Paepcke residence on 140 East Pearson Street.

Only four years after they had settled at their new home, on 7 October 1896, Emilie Wagner died in Chicago and was buried at Graceland cemetery two days later. Although she had longed for it, she had never seen her beloved native country, Germany, again. A friend of the family, Dr. Carl Pietsch, spoke at her grave. His words are revealing. Praising her performance of duty as wife and mother, her pure soul, her love and affection for her husband, children and grandchildren, he nevertheless had to concede: "Living for her was suffering. There was no place, no time, where she wouldn't encounter sorrow. Commanding that to stop only sleep could do, dreamless and eternal, like the one our dear beloved dead is embraced by now. Don't let us disturb her rest, which for her is redemption from grave sorrow!"[20]

Julius Wagner lived for another seven years.

> Our father, of whom our mother often jokingly said that he had never quite ceased to be a Korpsstudent (fraternity member) loved

> sociability and above all singing, right up to extreme old age; he had a fine voice himself. On his eightieth birthday the local (i.e., Chicago) association of Korpsstudents arranged a celebration. It was attended by the then German Ambassador in Washington, Mr. von Holleben, who was himself also a Heidelberg Guestphalian. On 16th February 1903, our father died, after only a short illness, aged eighty-six years and two months. As he had decided years earlier, he was cremated and his ashes placed in an urn in our mother's grave.

Actually, Alexander von Holleben belonged to the *Vandalia* corps and not to the *Guestphalen*, as Sophie Wagner meant, but much deep friendship existed between various members of the two corps.[21]

Now the other immigrant brother was dead, too, having outlived his older brother by twenty-six years. He had been reckless and irresponsible as a young student, a big spender who lived beyond his means and made his family pay for his livestyle. When he failed his exams, and was thus suddenly faced with the realities of life, he fell only too easily for the utopian ideas of an adventurous, communistic life on the Texas frontier. Like many other German emigrants he was also lured to Texas by the exaggerated, fantastic German literature that existed about this state in the nineteenth century. This literature and many of the letters, like those from Fritz Schenck, belong to the era and style of Romanticism with its deep longing for freedom, its lyrical love for nature and the inherent harmony between the human being and nature.

Some authors have classified German immigration in the first half of the nineteenth century as an expression of the *Biedermeier* epoch, between 1819 and 1848. Although the time frame seems to be absolutely fitting, this assumption is wrong. The *Biedermeier* as a reaction to the changing world (in political, social, and economic terms) resulted in the retreat of the middle-class citizen into the private world. In the arts one focused on the little, modest things, the items close to one's own experience. As an epoch, it was the classical example of personal retreat combined with the passive acceptance of the world. This alone shows the contradiction between a *Biedermeier* attitude and the German immigrants of the middle-class. In leaving their homeland, they were quite active, demonstrating they were not ready to accept the change passively by staying at home and taking refuge in some inner world of peace. That they continued to play music in their log cabins, read aloud to each other in the light of a lamp, had pictures of their hometown on the walls, and curtains at the windows showed their middle-class attitude of expressing themselves through their possessions and rituals copied from the aristocracy. For another it simply was a way of feeling at home in a strange land—as many non-English speaking groups of first generation immigrants did, like the Italians and the Chinese with their very special way of decorating homes and using certain rooms of the apartment or house for a specific purpose. German-Texas artists like Friedrich Richard Petri (1824-1857), Carl G. von Iwonski (1830-1912), and Hermann Lungkwitz (1813-1891) are good examples of the romantic immigrant too. Having studied at Dresden's Academy of Fine Arts under instructors like Ludwig Richter and the "Nazarene" painter Julius Hübner, Petri created paintings that show all the signs of Romanticism and not really *Biedermeier* (although an influence of *Biedermeier* traditions cannot be denied in his work).

Like Richter and the other painters of Romanticism he very often placed well-dressed craftsmen and middle-class people in wild and untamed landscapes. The well-dressed Germans in the Texas paintings of Petri, as well as the home furnishings and interior designs of those Germans, do not reflect the *Biedermeier* attitude of home-seeking and the urge for political stability but rather the desire of the *Bürgertum*, the Forty-eighters as well as the Latin settlers, to maintain a certain standard of living in the wilderness. Like the old English joke: "what proves that a man is a gentleman? When he uses sugar tongs to take his sugar for tea, even when he's alone in a desert." To decorate their homes as properly and nicely as possible and to dress well was an important factor for those middle-class Germans who wanted to keep up their class standards on the frontier. As Petri and Lungkwitz had been Forty-eighters in a way, too, having fought at the Dresden barricades in 1849, and living among former middle-class Germans in Texas, they portrayed their class and consciously or unconsciously emphasized in their paintings that those German settlers were able to maintain a certain standard of living and had not sunk to a shabby life.[22] Julius Wagner and his friends also liked, loved, and were closer to writers, scholars, and poets of Romanticism like Achim and Bettina von Arnim, Clemens

Brentano, the brothers Grimm and Hoffmann von Fallersleben than to poets and writers of the *Biedermeier* like Franz Grillparzer, Jeremias Gotthelf, and Adalbert Stifter.[23] Texas especially appealed to those Romantic Germans, as it had been described in an extremely romantic way. Texas is and surely was a fascinating country, but in the middle of the nineteenth century it also was no earthly paradise as depicted by German authors, many of them writing to lure other Germans over to Texas.[24] One had to work hard to make a living, and one could even make a fortune but it did not fall into one's lap. Julius Wagner found that out for himself too, the hard way. He turned into a hard working man who found recreation and amusement at gathering with friends and singing in choirs. It was not all that easy for his wife Emilie; she only had her memories, the hope she might see her beloved fatherland once again, corresponding regularly with her family in Germany, and her children to whom she gave all her love. With all he had experienced in life, Julius bequeathed his children two things (besides a few items like a clock and a sofa): you have to work hard to gain something in life, and you have to have a good education. The former he had learned to do, the latter he had gambled away. In a way, Julius Wagner represents the classic image of the German "Latin" immigrant of the nineteenth century.

Bad Dürkheim (Rhein-Pfalz) at the time the Wagners lived there (1790s). Lith. by Aust. v. J. Rheinberger. Courtesy Stadtverwaltung Bad Dürkheim.

Peter Wagner (1772–1853) pastor and father of Wilhelm and Julius, first decade of the nineteenth century. Courtesy Wagner family descendants.

Luise Wagner, born Kleinpell (1781–1865), wife of Peter Wagner, first decade of the nineteenth century. Courtesy Wagner family descendants.

Julius Wagner (1816–1903) as corps-student at Heidelberg. Courtesy Wagner family descendants.

Heidelberger Mensur (duel) at the house of the *Guestphalia* fraternity in the Hirschgasse at Heidelberg in the 1840s. By v. L. Blum. Courtesy Wagner family descendants.

Emilie Marie Wagner, born Schneider (1820–1896), 1840s. Courtesy Wagner family descendants.

Julius Wagner (1816–1903), drawing by his friend Fritz Reuter, Heidelberg, 1840s. Courtesy Wagner family descendants.

The farm of Julius and Emilie Wagner at the Twelve-Mile Coleto Creek (between Steiner's Settlement, Clinton and Meyersville, DeWitt County, Texas), where Julius and his wife settled at the end of the 1840s. Picture taken in 1996. Courtesy Wagner family descendants.

The farm that Wilhelm Wagner and the Frühs bought from C. C. Washburn in 1851 at Skinner Creek, Green County, Wisconsin, near Monroe. Photo by the author in 1995.

Wilhelm Wagner (1803–1877), 1850s. Courtesy Wagner family descendants.

Wilhelm Wagner in his sixties. Courtesy Wagner family descendants.

Emilie Wagner, born Schneider, during her years at Indianola, 1870s. Courtesy Wagner family descendants.

Erstes Anzeiger-Gebäude (1874).

The first building of Wilhelm Wagner's German paper *Deutscher Anzeiger* on Chicago Street, Freeport, Illinois, in 1874. Courtesy Wagner family descendants.

Wilhelm "William" Wagner (1841–1910), second son of Wilhelm Wagner and second owner of Wagner Printing. Courtesy Wagner family descendants.

Paula Paepcke, born Wagner (1857–1909), second daughter of Julius Wagner, shortly after her marriage to Hermann Paepcke in 1878. Courtesy Wagner family descendants.

Hermann Ludwig August Paepcke (1850–1922) in Chicago. Courtesy Wagner family descendants.

Wilhelm "William" Wagner (1854–1926), Julius Wagner's second son, with his sons August Wilhelm (1888–1978), right, and Richard Julius "Dick" (1886–1939), left, with cigarette. Courtesy Wagner family descendants.

The house of Wilhelm "William" Wagner (Julius Wagner's son) and his family on Hunt Street, Cuero, Texas, at the beginning of the twentieth century. From left to right: young Juanita Sophie (1897–1993), her mother Julie Wagner, born Schorre (1861–1922), her sisters Anna Julie (1883–1977) and Emma Marie (1884–1946). Courtesy Wagner family descendants.

Printing room of Wagner Printing Company, Freeport, Illinois, around 1930. Courtesy Wagner family descendants.

Emma Wagner, born Gund (1873–1961), who ran Wagner Printing during World War II. Courtesy Wagner family descendants.

The Wagner Printing Company building (the third in the company's history) on East Spring Street, Freeport, Illinois in 1995. Photo by the author.

Mark W. Wagner (b. 1937), present president of Wagner Printing at his office in 1995. Photo by the author.

Walter "Bully" Wagner (1903–1957), on the far right with tie, and his employees at his store at Brayton Flying Field, Cuero, Texas, during World War II. Courtesy Wagner family descendants.

The old Bates hardware store that "Bully" Wagner bought after the war on North Esplanade, Cuero, Texas. Courtesy Wagner family descendants.

The Wagner Hardware Company at North Esplanade, Cuero, Texas, in 1995. Photo by the author.

“Bully” Wagner’s son Robert “Bob” Wagner (b. 1930) in the office of Wagner Hardware Company in 1995 with his son Robert Reed (b. 1954) who runs the company today. Photo by the author.

6. The Legacy of the Immigrants

THERE WERE NOT AS MANY obituaries for Julius Wagner as for his brother Wilhelm, but they were not only confined to German papers in Texas. Articles appeared in German papers of Chicago and one in the *Freeport Deutscher Anzeiger*. William Wagner, the second son of Julius' brother Wilhelm, wrote half a column about his uncle.[1]

After Wilhelm's death in 1877, William had become the sole owner of the *Deutscher Anzeiger* and the printing company. In 1879, the printing company kept pace with progress and moved from printing with a small handpress to the use of a steam-powered printing machine. In 1886 the first building of the Wagner Printing Company proved to be too small, and the company was transplanted into a larger building on the corner of Chicago and Galena Streets. In 1902, they had to move a third time and have stayed ever since in the large building on the corner of Chicago and Spring Streets. At that time, the company had about fifty employees. It was not only buildings and machinery that changed and expanded over the years; William followed the example his father had set in many ways. On 14 May 1861, William married Wilhelmina Seyfarth. Together with her parents, Andreas and Rosine (Glaser) Seyfarth, she had come to the United States in 1851. Both her parents died very early. William and Wilhelmina had seven children: all sons and an adopted girl Rose. On 1 July 1891, William took in his sons Albert and Oscar as partners, naming the company William H. Wagner & Sons. William's second son Otto had learned the bookbinding trade with the bookbinder and blank bookmaker William Massenburg. Together with his brother Paul, Otto opened his own business Wagner Brothers, bookbinders and blank book manufacturers, in 1885 (later called The Otto Wagner Store). The youngest sons of William—Frederic and William, Jr.—worked for their father too: Frederic as his father's assistant in the editorial department and William in the pressroom. They not only published the *Deutscher Anzeiger* but also the church paper

Der Sonntags Gast. In 1901 Frederic (whom his father and family used to call Fritz) joined the management as partner too.

William was not the only child of Wilhelm who worked in the printing and publishing business. Wilhelm's third son Hermann Ludwig had moved to Davenport, Iowa, and established a printing company of his own: Wagners Printers, Inc. The fourth son, Julius, worked as a foreman for the *Deutscher Anzeiger* at Freeport and his son Julius, Jr., followed in his father's footsteps and became a compositer in his uncle's company. The youngest daughter, Friederike, married Carl Reineke, the publisher of the *Nord Iowa Herold* at Elkader, Iowa.

William did not confine himself to the printing business alone. He was one of the founders of the German Insurance Company, which went under in the big San Francisco earthquake and fire of 1906, after prospering for forty years. And, like his father, he used his paper to express his ideas: "Through the columns of his paper he has exerted a wide influence for the benefit of Freeport and the county at large, for his journal has ever been an advocate of reform, improvement and advancement."[2] He also took part in the social life of Freeport. With the musical talent his father was so proud of, William became musical director of the male chorus of the *Freeport Sängerbund* and held this position for thirty-three years. Being a member of the Germania Society, he held several of the important offices, including that of president. More than his father though, William was also active in politics. Elected city treasurer in 1871 and assistant supervisor in 1876-1877, he represented the third ward in the city council in 1881-1882 and was even chosen president of the board of education for one year. At one time he even was a Democratic candidate for Congress, Ninth Congressional District. In whatever he did, he was a true son of his father, continuing what Wilhelm Wagner had once begun. He had a rich life and belonged to the most respected citizens of Freeport. With his death in 1910 though, things slowly began to change.

When William Wagner died at the age of sixty-nine, the three sons who had been in management together with their father, began running the company with Albert F. as president. It must have been shortly after that though, that Frederic had a nervous breakdown and moved out of Wagner Printing. Twelve years later, in 1922, Albert stepped down as president because of ill health, and the two older brothers made their former partner and second youngest son of William, Frederic, president of the company. Maybe they wanted to help him by giving him a task that would challenge the best in him. Oscar belonged to the managment until his death seven years later, and Albert stayed on as vice president until his death in 1938. The decision to make Frederic president proved to have been unwise, although his brothers thought it to be the best decision. Maybe they thought that his three years training at the University of Wisconsin made Frederic the best suited for the tasks ahead. He had been one of the first students from Freeport there. Yet, Frederic did not show as much interest in business as was necessary. He liked to enjoy the pleasant sides of life more as he hated pressure; he was a dreamer, a musician. This was a dangerous attitude, as he was made president when fundamental changes loomed on the horizon. In 1912, the company was incorporated as Wagner Printing Co. On 6 April 1917, the United States declared war against Germany after that country had announced the resumption of unrestricted submarine warfare which already had cost many American lives. The war against Germany was not only fought in the field but was also accompanied by a vigorous propaganda campaign, which depicted all Germans as evil Huns, monsters, and threats against any civilized society (in contrast to the propaganda during World War II which aimed at the evil Nazi only, not the Germans as a whole nation).[3] Because of this massive anti-German sentiment during World War I, the paper *Deutscher Anzeiger* with which it had all begun went out of business in 1918.

The *Anzeiger* had not been the only German weekly paper in the area. Papers like the *Freeport Banner*, founded by H.W. Frick in 1879, had numerous subscribers too.[4] All of them, however, had a short life span and used other material from outside the city. The *Anzeiger* was the most prominent, and the only one written, printed, and issued from its own office in Freeport. From 1918 onwards, the Wagners concentrated completely on commercial printing. When Frederic Wagner died at the age of fifty-seven, ten years after the *Anzeiger* had ceased to exist, the local papers placed his obituary on their front page. He did not, however, make the headlines because someone of higher prominence had died just a few hours after Frederic: the English commander-in-chief of the British armies in France during World War I, Field Marshall Sir Douglas Haig.[5] The first American-born heir to the business which the immigrant Wilhelm Wagner had founded, had died.

The industrious German attitude lived on in other family members. As already mentioned, Hermann Wagner at the age of twenty-four moved to Davenport, Iowa, and founded his company Wagners Printers, Inc. there. He had married Maria M. Waldecker on 18 July 1867. His bride actually had been born at Schopfheim, which was pretty close to Brombach in the Wiesental where he had been born. In the beginning, his was not an incorporated company. Hermann started his business as a one-man shop in the 200 block of West Third Street, Davenport. He began with a single case of lead types and a hand press of limited capability. However, since he was industrious the business prospered. In 1889, Hermann Wagner already grossed the grand total of $2,959.04. Although the company grew, it was still mainly a family business with four to five employees. When Hermann died at only fifty-six, his sons Wilhelm Frederick and Reinhart Jacob as well as his daughter Ida Theresa Fredericke took over. At that time, they only did job printing, business or window cards, and letterheads. It was still a small local firm until it expanded after World War I.

In a way they all lived up to the ideals and standards Wilhelm had set with his life. Only one thing had changed fundamentally—the family ties that had been so important for Wilhelm throughout his life had loosened, especially those to Germany. The knowledge that the Wagners in Ilinois, Iowa, and Wisconsin had cousins in Texas, and that Wilhelm had had a brother, had actually been lost by most of the Wilhelm Wagner descendants over the generations. This is astounding, especially since Wilhelm's oldest son Karl had been the reason for Julius Wagner's daughter Paula and her husband Hermann Paepcke to move to Chicago and settle there.

Hermann Ludwig August Paepcke was born in Teterow, Grand Duchy Mecklenburg-Schwerin, Germany, on 12 February 1851, to the merchant August Wilhelm Bernhard Paepcke (1808-1866) and his wife Johanna Luisa Maria Hanck (1816-1886). He went to school in his hometown and served his business apprenticeship in Wismar and Magdeburg. He was drafted for military training and served in the Franco-Prussian War of 1870-71. For his courage at the siege of Paris where he is said to have saved the life of his wounded captain under fire, he was decorated with the Iron Cross. In 1872 Hermann went to Texas. What made him travel to the United States in the first place and why he chose Texas can no longer be determined today. One thing is clear, though, from his letters to his many relatives back home: he had embarked to the shores of the New World to make good money. In addition, the following explanation is handed down from family historians: "After the war he became discontented about his prospects and dissatisfied with political and social conditions in Germany. On leaving the army he had not been welcomed back to the family granary business at Teterow by his older brother; and he resented the fact that some people looked down on him and his family because the business was considerably small and inelegant."[6] He landed at Indianola, moved on to Victoria and became a clerk to one of the biggest merchant companies of that area, Heyck & Brother, Commission Merchants & Shipping Agents. In August of 1873, August and Valentine Heyck (1832-1876) sent the young and eager man to their new branch and a newly-founded community: Cuero.

Charles W. Morgan, influential businessman from New York, had nearly established a monopoly on transportation in the western part of the Gulf of Mexico. His steamship company Harris & Morgan was run by his second son Henry R. Morgan and his son-in-law Israel C. Harris and controlled virtually all traffic between New Orleans, Galveston, and Indianola. In fact, Morgan's visionary business manner was a decisive factor in establishing Indianola as the main port for western Texas. With the increase of commerce and trade, railroads had become the most important element of speedy delivery. As competitors of Morgan had already started building railroads from the north and east in the direction of San Antonio, in May 1870, the clever businessman announced the founding of the Gulf, Western Texas, and Pacific Railroad Company that was to connect Indianola with San Antonio. Actually, Morgan had bought the old Indianola Railroad that had been chartered in 1858 and had not seen any major construction so far as well as the San Antonio and Mexican Gulf Railway which was not complete either, had combined and renamed them. As it was not possible to construct this new line in one piece, and as no major city lay between, the engineer and surveyor of the G.W.T.&P. Gustav Schleicher, the old comrade of Julius Wagner, had a brilliant idea: to turn the small settlement of Cuero into a city with a major railroad terminal. In May 1846, a post office had been established at Daniel Boone Friar's store where the town had been surveyed in 1842. Now, on 25 December 1871, Col. Schleicher, together with John C. French, Charles M. Terrell and Fletcher S. Stockdale, formed the Cuero Land and Immigration Company. On

8 February 1872, the company bought 4,128 acres from the J. O. Wheeler estate for $10,320 in gold. This became the foundation stone of the city of Cuero: "Day and night the sound of the saw and hammer was heard, and soon the original city of Cuero emerged from the groves of native trees and the barren prairie land."[7] Among the first ones to purchase land after the railroad had finally reached this new prospering city on 4 March 1873, were Gustav Schleicher, a Mr. R. Fromme, and August Heyck, the employer of young Hermann Paepcke.

At the beginning of May 1873, Hermann moved from Victoria to Cuero. Life in this new town had its challenging aspects, as he soon found out after having recovered from a high fever he had caught at the beginning of summer of 1873:

> And at just this time when I was beaten down physically and morally, this campaign for which they recruited even me, had to take place. "Campaign," you will say, "yes, campaign," I reply to you, "a real campaign." I don't know whether I have told you in my earlier letters about the disorderly conditions that prevail particularly in this country. This desperate state of affairs has not improved with time, but on the contrary has gotten twice as bad particularly on account of a law passed by the last democratic legislature, which abolishes the state police, the so-called militia, and, thereby allows robbers, murderers, and other riffraff free play. There exist around here at this time several well organized bands of robbers who by their murderous activities make the roads and trails unsafe and even threaten the property of the quiet urban citizen. Just very recently, one of these bands attacked a farmer, a certain Thamilton, on his farm, and, since he defended himself courageously, tried to force his surrender by starving him out. In his utmost distress, Thamilton succeeded in sending on a secret trail a messenger to the courthouse of the town of Clinton, with a request for protection. This was the signal to a general rise. The judge, who happened to be in a court session, dispatched his sheriff to cities and villages to call up the whole county. This is how on this particular day the news of a general mobilization spread like wildfire through our town and caused everybody to take to flight im-

mediately (to avoid being recruited). I, unfortunately, could not escape my fate; as I inquired into the reasons for the uproar, the sheriff stood already in front of me: "I want your name, Sir". I made reference to the German consulate and to my poor health, but to no avail. I was given just enough time to change clothes and to hand Hugo Timm (who had succeeded in saving himself by running away and who now came to me disguised as an old man) my testament, my earthly possessions and a few lines to you. Then the steed was mounted and we were off. We Cueroans were about sixty strong, men of just every nationality. I rode with mixed feelings; should I let myself be shot to death or even be massacred for a completely foreign nation?

A first sheriff took overall command. We were well armed. Two revolvers each and a so-called Winchester, a terrible murder weapon with eighteen rounds. But we were lacking, of course, patriotism, discipline, and most of all organization. The warriors from the various towns were supposed to have joined forces at a particular location, but in the great hurry it had been forgotten to determine such a location, so that everybody marched directly to the battleground. Now, I don't know whether it was our good fortune or our irresolute riding that caused us not to be the first warriors on the battlefield. Anyway, the city of Yorktown had beat us to it and had saved the honor of the day with her blood. We did not begrudge them this honor and collected enough glory ourselves anyway. Just as once upon a time Pappenheim with his cuirassiers changed the course of the battle of Luetzen [in 1632 one of the most decisive battles of the Thirty Years War in which the Swedish King Gustav Adolf fell as well as the imperial general Count Gottfried Heinrich von Pappenheim; comment by the author], so did our sheriff with us Cueroans at Yorktown, i.e. he gave it a favorable turn. We did not want to shed any more blood but instead offered a proposition for a peaceful agreement, which was gladly accepted by all parties. Everybody then rode to the town of Cuero where the peace was signed. That was the big battle of Yorktown. The bandits gave their word to become peaceful citizens henceforth and they were pardoned. . . . The business here goes from bad to worse and appears

> headed for ruin. A competing railroad in eastern Texas, the so called Central Railroad is the cause of it. If our railroad does not find help and assistance soon, the entire trade in western Texas will die off, and that within a few months. Where I will go, I don't know yet. Either I'll go to the northern states or I will turn towards the Pacific Ocean, maybe I'll choose California. . . . "Life is a struggle" says Goethe, and the man is right. It is a constant hustle and bustle, and there is no end to it.[8]

With this colorful description, Hermann Paepcke actually told his relatives back home of his rather short participation in the longest and bloodiest frontier feud in Texas: the Sutton-Taylor feud in DeWitt County. This bitter quarrel lasted from 1867 until 1876 and was followed by twenty years of legal maneuvering to get a conviction for the outlaws. It had started as a dispute over longhorn cattle and horses, allegedly stolen, and turned into a bloody vendetta between the pioneer Taylor and the Sutton families with numerous fatalities on both sides. The farmer Thamilton whom Paepcke mentions, might have been the Sutton man Joe Tumlinson. One of the better known protagonists of this drama, which appears colorful and maybe even romantic only in retrospect (especially in movies like *The Lawless Breed* by Raoul Walsh, and *The Texas Rangers* by Phil Karlson) was the notorious gunman, outlaw, and in-law of the Taylors, John Wesley Hardin. Hardin shot down some of his foes in the streets of Cuero. The railroad that Paepcke is referring to, actually was the Houston and Texas Central Railway Company. It was a tough competitor for Morgan's Gulf, Western Texas, and Pacific Railroad when it reached Denison in 1873, thus establishing a connection to the Missouri, Kansas, and Texas Railway Company. This company gave Texas its first through-line to St. Louis. Morgan eventually sold G.W.T.&P. to C.P. Huntington in 1880, who acquired it for the Southern Pacific.[9]

Although it was a lot of work, business was not stable or predictable, and Hermann Paepcke was not sure if he had any future in this country, he always emphasized his positive feelings about the political situation in the United States: "You Germans, who for centuries have been used to dancing to the fiddle of a monarch installed by the grace of God, don't have the slightest idea what it means to live in a free country and to be free yourselves." The lawless times were not over for Cuero though. Despite the skirmish that Hermann witnessed, lawlessness prevailed and even worsened during 1873: "The wild, unorganized conditions of our town are beyond any imagination; after my return from Indianola, I found Cuero changed into a full-blown robber's nest. Two corps of regular bandits had seized the main buildings and faced each other clear for action, intending at any moment to open hostilities. It is still that way today, the property and even the life of every peaceful citizen is endangered and one makes preparations for self-defense, until the government throws militia into the town, which is expected to happen within a few days."[10] It was not the government that helped change this devastating situation. It was, in the end, the law-abiding citizens of Cuero themselves. During the first days of January 1874, Mayor O. L. Threlkeld called for a mass meeting at City Hall and there the Home Protection Club, a local militia, was founded. The seventy-four members of this militia had regular drills and were always ready to defend their young community. It is interesting to note that about half of the members were of German descent, like Gustav Schleicher, Rudolph Kleberg, the brothers Julius and Wilhelm (William) Gohmert, Georg Gerloff, Carl Staedtler, and Karl (Charles) Kleinecke. This military organization soon cleared the town of the most notorious bandits and made life in Cuero more or less safe. To bring law and order to the whole county, which was necessary to guarantee the safety of Cuero in the long run, the citizens of Cuero petitioned the Governor of Texas to send in the Rangers. Thus, in the summer of 1874, Captain L.H. McNelly arrived in DeWitt County with a full company of Rangers. He was quite successful in restoring law and order. When Jim Taylor and two of his friends were killed in a gunfight in the streets of Cuero on 27 December 1875, the feud died down at long last.[11]

Still, Hermann Paepcke went back to Europe a couple of times, once even for months, but only to return to Texas. He quit his job with the Heyck brothers and at the end of 1874 established his own business in Cuero: H. Paepcke, General Produce. He liked the simple way one could start a business in contrast to the rather complicated procedure in Germany: "A few references from respected firms are sufficient for the young beginner to procure funds and credits from banks. One simply appears one fine day, with these references in hand, at the location where one intends to fill ones empty pockets and rents an office in a nice part of town for $10 per month. One buys a desk, a chair and the necessary writing utensils and, above all, has a colossal sign made which one mounts above the door, informing every passerby of the grandious transactions that do not take place inside." It was not as humorous as he made it sound. He was mainly purchasing cotton firsthand and shipping it to New Orleans and even to New York. But that business was risky because of the unstable prices of cotton; and therefore, Hermann Paepcke was happy when R. Fromme offered him a partnership. Fromme was an old acquaintance of Paepcke, having been branch manager of Heyck and Brother first in Victoria and later in Cuero. When August Heyck retired in spring of 1874, Fromme took over the business. He dealt not only in cotton but kept the commission business the Heycks had established running. Business life was not so bad for Hermann Paepcke after all. But

> the social life one finds here falls far short of even my modest expectations. There is no social life here at all. At least, what little there is, is nothing in comparison to what you are used to. The citizenry of Cuero consists for the most part of remnants of old slaveholding families, a society which cannot get used to the equality of human rights and still lives in the memory of a nice, comfortable past, whose ladies rock themselves from morning until late in the evening in rocking chairs and whose gentlemen function for the most part as gamblers, whiskey peddlers and bad lawyers and medics and cannot bring themselves to take the plow into their own hands that for years their negroes willingly guided. No less in size than the American is the German population, which here in Cuero as well as in the rest of Texas makes up a large part of the population. Few of them, however, belong to the better classes, but mostly to the proletariat. There isn't a class of people I dislike more than these German-American proletarians. These people, who in Germany had lived only in servitude and who had been forced by floods, famine or other misfortunes to leave their homes and to go to America owning nothing but the shirts on their backs, did gain through undeniable diligence and persistence a certain level of wealth. But now they are more puffed up, in silly

> oblivion, than your German or Mecklenburgian aristocrats, and they attempt to act the fine republican, even though one can recognize the German Michel in them from twenty paces away. ["The German Michel" is an old nickname for a naive, unpolitical, law-abiding German citizen, usually drawn in caricatures as a stout man with a white nightcap.] Besides these Germans and Americans, we have some Englishmen, Frenchmen, and Spaniards, the rest of the population being made up of negroes. So, you can see that it is absolutely impossible to find a suitable acquaintance in this society.[12]

As exaggerated as this description might have been through personal disappointment, it nevertheless hints at two important social factors that formed the society of Cuero: as in the rest of DeWitt County, the German inhabitants amounted to twenty to thirty percent of the total population. The Ninth Federal Census of 1870 shows that 26.42 percent of the total population of that county was either German-born or first generation of German parentage. And second, the overwhelming majority of the Germans had been in favor of the Confederacy, many of them having served in various regiments of the South and considered themselves to be real Southerners.

Paepcke's partnership with Fromme did not last long and in April 1876, the two men liquidated their business, and Paepcke ran his own again. His former principal Valentine Heyck approached him offering him a partnership this time, which pleased Hermann Paepcke, as Heyck was wealthy and ran a well-known and respectable company. Before this could amount to anything, however, Valentine, and then his brother August Heyck, died. The job of liquidating the company Heyck & Bros. fell upon twenty-five-year-old Hermann Paepcke who then opened the successor company, H. Paepcke at Indianola. At the beginning of May 1877, the Heyck widows sold him the rather considerable business property of their deceased husbands. He came to this plagued city when a lot of businessmen had turned their backs on it after the disastrous hurricane in 1875. He was now running the business he had started in as a clerk and was engaged additionally in the ice business together with Louis Preisig. The name of their company was Indianola Ice House. Preisig was a well-known name in Indianola.

His Ice Cream Saloon, Confectionery and Fruit Store on Main Street had offered "Ice Cream and the usual summer beverages" already before the Civil War.[13] Alas, in the spring of 1878, the business of Hermann Paepcke was declining, and the restless young man again thought of selling it and moving back to Europe for good. Yet, suddenly his whole life changed.

Something that ran like a red thread through most of his correspondence was that he detested his life as a bachelor. This obviously was the main reason why he did not feel at home in Texas. Then he met Julius Wagner's daughter Paula. They fell in love right away and were married at the end of July 1878. Together with his young wife he made a tour through Germany, visiting his friends and family in the north and east of Germany, but there was no longer any thought of staying there. Now Hermann Paepcke saw his future in the United States, although not necessarily in Texas. In 1881 he visited several major cities in the West and East of the United States, giving a special preference to Boston and New York as he had friends and business connections in these cities. Instead, the Paepckes settled in Chicago where he knew nobody. The reason for this was very simple: Hermann Paepcke, himself a devoted family-man, did this for his young wife. In a long letter to his brother-in-law, Dr. Franz Eggert, Hermann explained that Karl Wagner, Wilhelm's oldest son, was living in Chicago with his family and that "he holds a significant and influential position in a large machine works."[14] Hermann also wrote Franz a couple of lines about the background and history of Wilhelm Wagner. Not only altruistic thoughts guided Hermann; he hoped that his new start would be helped by the circles he would be introduced to by his wife's relatives. Hermann sold his business in Indianola and together with Paula's sister Lina, who was to care for their children Sophie and Lydia, moved to Chicago at the beginning of September, 1881. From that moment on, the Paepcke history became a success story, the classic American "dishwasher-becomes-millionaire" story.

Well, Hermann Paepcke had never been a dishwasher, but once in Chicago he realized what the most lucrative businesses were lumber and packing. The lumber industry and Chicago as the world's leading lumber center actually were slowly declining after the Civil War for various reasons. With the emergence of the railroad as the leading means of transportation, the waterways, especially lakes like Lake Michigan, lost their importance, their predominance. Whereas in the Chicago of 1880, over ninety percent of the lumber arrived on Lake Michigan, at the turn of the century it was just a meager forty percent.[15] Hermann Paepcke did not confine himself simply to cutting wood and transporting it. In Chicago he first formed a partnership with a Mr. Wagner (not related to either Julius or Wilhelm). Within a few months he bought out his partner and ran the business, which consisted of a small planing mill and a box factory at the corner of Fifth Avenue and Harrison Street. After moving to North Carpenter Street, he incorporated his business under the name of Hermann Paepcke & Co. In 1885, Hermann Paecke founded the Chicago Packing Box Company. It was incorporated with a capital of $200,000 which was increased to $1,000,000 by 1902. From the end of the 1880s, Hermann Paepcke's star shone brighter and brighter. In 1892 he took over the Wolverine Lumber Company at Cairo, Illinois. He remodeled this plant and incorporated this new business under the name of Chicago Mill and Lumber Company. During that year, his father-in-law, Julius Wagner came to Chicago, along with his wife Emilie, his son Sigmund, and his daughter Sophie. Lina Wagner was still living in Chicago. Hermann gave his brother-in-law a chance by first making him assistant treasurer of the new company. Later Sigmund Wagner was in charge of the office end of the business at Cairo, where he died as a bachelor at the age of eighty-three.

In 1893, Hermann Paepcke received authorization to incorporate his old company Paepcke & Co. into the Paepcke-Leicht Lumber Company with himself president, William Wilms (who would become his son-in-law) as vice president, and Edward A. Leicht as treasurer. In 1905, Hermann Paepcke founded the American Box Company and bought many more mills and lumber businesses around the country. The great success Hermann Paepcke had with his boxes, wooden or paper, stemmed from the fact that Chicago after the disastrous fire of 1871 had emerged as the leading marketplace of the heartland and eventually became the capital of the nation's mail-order houses. It began with Aaron Montgomery Ward, who in 1872 founded the first general mail-order company in American history. Many more were to follow his example: Marshall Field in 1881, Carson Pirie Scott in 1891, Sears, Roebuck and Company in 1893, and Spiegel Home Furnishers in the same year.[16] They all needed boxes in which to pack their goods in order to send them to their customers safely. Hermann Paepcke had hit his ultimate gold mine.

The wealth of Hermann Paepcke not only showed itself in his homes in Chicago and Glencoe, Illinois, as well as Pasadena, California, but also in his affiliation to the Chicago Athletic Association, the Union Club League, the Mid-day Club, the South Shore Country Club, the Skokie Country Club, the Chicago Lincoln Club, the Chicago Historical Society and the Art Institute of Chicago. His membership in these institutions was not for idle entertainment but for the purpose of learning and preserving the cultural standards of the old German class of the *Gross Bürgertum* (the so-called high bourgeoisie). He detested idle diversions like golf or the free manners of American society of that time. For that reason he even forbade his children to bring home their friends to play. On 22 July 1922, he died.

Hermann Paepcke's wife Paula, the daughter of Julius Wagner, had already died in 1909. Her two sisters, Sophie and Lina Wagner, who had never married, lived at the Pearson Hotel on 190 E. Pearson Street (where the Ritz Hotel is today, south of the John Hancock Center) until their deaths in 1938 and 1933. The Pearson Hotel had been built in 1920 and served both as a residential and short-term hotel with a large, attractive dining room. From time to time, the unmarried Wagner sisters travelled to Texas, too, to visit their brothers Wilhelm (who called himself William) and Carl Friedrich Richard (who was called Richard) who both lived in Cuero, Texas.

When Sigmund Wagner returned to his parents at Indianola after his education in Germany in 1874, he had to fill the gap William had left. When he was twenty-one, William gave up his position as assistant postmaster and left home. It was not only that he wanted to earn more money and stand on his own feet; it seems that he had also in a way come to disdain his father. William never forgave his father for taking sides with the Union and fleeing to Mexico during the Civil War like a coward, as William saw it. The closest neighbors of the Wagners at the Coleto had been the von Roeders, the Klebergs, and the Schorres. It is not clear if the Schorres had owned slaves like Otto von Roeder, for instance, but all of them had felt it their duty to join the Confederate forces. Thus William grew up with children from families who were of a different opinion than his own parents. Very likely they all socialized: "Joachim [Rudolph von Roeder's son, who lived with the Klebergs after his father had died], as he was known, was the oldest member of a whole clan of cousins living near each other, and he, in all likelihood, was the leader of the pack in many a boyhood escapade."[17] Not only that, many of his friends and their fathers took up arms and fought for the cause of the South, which they believed to be a just and noble one. And one of them, Ludwig von Roeder, had even died for this cause. Julius Wagner simply had fled, as William saw it, and had brought shame on the family.[18]

Whether through a little help from his father or simply by his own, William found a job with his father's friend William Westhoff and became head of the William Westhoff Lumber Company branch at Victoria. He stayed there for two years until Westhoff opened an office at Cuero, and William took charge of that business. One year later, in 1875, he was employed by the George Seelingson & Company, a firm composed of George Seelingson and Otto Buchel (1849-1909). The Seelingson brothers, Henry and George, were very active and highly respected businessmen in Indianola.[19] When Morgan succeeded with his G.W.T.&P., and it became obvious that Cuero was the place to invest as it would become the main distributing point between Indianola and San Antonio, George Seeligson made his move. Like William Westhoff, his brother Henry, and others, he established a branch store at Cuero in December 1873 and made Otto Buchel his partner and at the same time manager of this store at Cuero. They dealt with cotton, wool, hides, and groceries. It was a fascinating time, the air smelling of business and adventure:

> Cuero soon became the shipping point of the entire West as far as the Rio Grande River, and even beyond into Mexico, and also a large part of Central Texas, extending to Austin and beyond. The transportation into the interior consisted in hauling freight by wagons and large Chihuaha trains from the West across the new Schleicher Bridge just finished over the Guadalupe River west of Cuero, a wooden structure built by Col. Schleicher in 1873. The wagon trains consisted of large prairie schooner wagons, drawn usually by twelve Mexican mules. The train generally consisted of ten to twelve wagon schooners in charge of a wagon master. All the eastern freight for San Antonio, which came by way of Indianola, was hauled in this manner. The streets of Cuero were crowded with these wagons and merchants and traders filled the town all day. At night the camp fires around the town glowed, and

> the soft songs of the Mexican teamsters accompanied with the thump of the guitar were heard in the distance; while the social revel of the frontiersmen and prosperous merchant was in evidence in the town, now and then interrupted by the sharp crack of a six shooter or a Winchester fired by a desperado or the city marshal, and the commercial growth of the town thus went on by leaps and bounds.[20]

As he himself had been "discovered" by George Seeligson, Otto Buchel grew fond of William Wagner and offered him a job as bookkeeper and handyman which William accepted. Two things changed the course of both men.

In 1881, William bought his own business from his brother-in-law Hermann Paepcke, who wrote: "I sold my business here in Indianola, including such items as safe, scale, office furniture, etc., for the sum of $600.00 to my brother-in-law, Willy Wagner, who for many years had been employed at a bank in Cuero. This means a loss of $900.00, since I paid $1,500.00 for this inventory, initially."[21] Hermann Paepcke mentioned that William worked in a bank. This is no contradiction with the aforesaid. When Otto Buchel became partner and manager of George Seeligson's store at Cuero in 1873, he was the first and only one to have a safe at his office:

> Next door to the store, on the site of the present bank, was a livery stable; across the street was a saloon. There was at this time a man near Cuero who came into town several times a year to sell his wares and produce, after which he would get drunk and tear up the saloon. He always paid for the expectant damages before they occurred. Otto Buchel saw him and felt sorry for him. He asked the drunk man when he was going to stop getting intoxicated. Otto also added that some night he could easily be knocked over the head and robbed. The other man said that he wished Buchel would put the money in the grocery safe until he was sober. Otto agreed. Soon he had other "banking" requests.[22]

That is how the Buchel National Bank began. Two years later, in 1875, Otto Buchel bought out the interests of George Seeligson and became the sole owner of the banking and exchange, wholesale and retail grocer's business. One year after William Wagner had bought his own business, Otto Buchel offered him a partnership which William accepted. The two men merged their businesses. The name now was: Otto Buchel and Company, Bankers, Wholesale and Retail Grocers and Commission Merchants. All ads, though, showed both their names. When the bank was incorporated in 1907 as Buchel International Bank, William was officially made one of its vice presidents.

The same year that William became the partner of Otto Buchel, he married Julia Sophia Schorre on 4 April 1882. Her parents had been close neighbors to the Wagners at the Coleto before the Civil War. William and Julia, therefore, had known each other since childhood. They built themselves a nice house on Hunt Street and raised five children there: Anna Julie, Emma Marie, Richard Julius, August Wilhelm, and Juanita Sophie. It was not his wife alone who linked William to his happy boyhood days at the Coleto. Two other of William's pals from good old times lived at Cuero, one even belonging to Cuero's founding fathers: the brothers Rudolph (1847-1924) and Robert J. Kleberg, Jr., (1853-1932).[23] William Wagner felt at home among these men, who at the same time must have deepened William's negative feelings towards his father. However Hermann Paepcke might have been biased, he had been quite correct at least in regard to the political opinion of the Germans of Cuero: whether it was Gustav Schleicher or the Kleberg brothers, most of them had served in the Confederate army, if their families had been in Texas at that time, and were very conservative.

William had found his place. From time to time, his sisters Sophie and Lina came down from Chicago to visit their brother's family and stay with them for a month or two. William's daughters, Anna Julia and Emma Marie, even visited their uncle Hermann and aunt Paula Paepcke in Chicago when they were young women. But these contacts grew less and less during the course of the years, as they must have felt the resentment William bore towards his siblings who lived off their rich and successful brother-in-law Hermann Paepcke. This tension might have been the reason, too, why William and his older brother Sigmund never again had any contact. In a way, Cairo and Cuero could have been located on distant planets light-years apart from each other. Nevertheless, he must have maintained some sort of contact with his father, who travelled down to Texas from Chicago twice to visit his children and old friends—the last time in 1901. William's youngest daughter Juanita remembered that "he just wanted to play the piano" when her grandfather came for a visit.[24]

William had to work hard to earn his money. In their partnership, Otto Buchel was the genius-type person and William the laborer: "Buchel had ideas and enthusiasm, which Mr. Wagner kept in line, and together they would reach a sound conclusion." Or, as William's daughter, Juanita, once described it: "The old Buchel only came into the store from time to time to talk to the customers and William practically ran the store, which was not always easy for him."[25] As he grew tired and planned to retire, William sold his interest in their business to his partner Otto Buchel in 1906. He stayed on as vice president of the Buchel National Bank, though, and made a little money dealing with cotton when the opportunity arose. All of this did not really satisfy him. When Judge Edward Koenig, Sr., who had served DeWitt County as county judge from 1892-1896, announced in 1915 that he would not run for the office of county treasurer again after having held that office for five years, William saw his chance. He announced his candidacy and was elected by a large majority in 1916. On Saturday, 29 April 1922, he suffered a great loss when his wife, Julia, died of cancer: "Although the deceased had been in poor health for the past several years, she was not taken ill until shortly after the noon hour Saturday. In company with members of her family she attended the Chautauqua Friday night."[26]

When William Wagner died in April 1926, shortly after announcing his upcoming retirement as county treasurer, *The Cuero Daily Record* announced his death on page one: "W. M. Wagner is dead at age of seventy-two years—one of Cuero's earliest pioneers succumbs to prolonged illness." The paper also printed a one-column-long obituary that listed all his memberships: "Mr. Wagner was a member of the old Home Guard and company of volunteers organized here in the early days to protect life and property during the Sutton-Taylor feud and other disturbances. He was a life member of the Cuero Fire Department, taking active part in its affairs during the Red Shirt and Helmet days. He was also a member of the W.O.W. lodge and the O.D.H.S." The paper also listed William's death in its editorial column, "Town Talk," on the front page as the first event: "The passing of another pioneer, splendid type of citizenship is mourned by Cuero and DeWitt county today in the death of William Wagner, one of the early settlers of this community, who as a young man was a prominent figure in the turbulent pioneer days of the community and has through his allotted span of years watched the growth of the community of his birth from a feud-torn village to a peaceful, prosperous and progressive town. Mr. Wagner's life was a glowing example of service."[27] Articles like these could not show how deeply Cuero respected its citizen William Wagner as adequately as their collective mourning, however. During the funeral services conducted by Reverend W. A. McLeod of the Presbyterian Church at the Wagners' home at 5:00, 23 April, all businesses and schools closed for one hour in tribute to his memory. No matter how much they might have been driven apart, Julius Wagner would have been proud of his son William. He would have been especially happy to know that William's grandson Michael, the son of August Wilhelm Wagner, became a lawyer, thus closing the circle. In what Julius Wagner had failed—and in what had brought him to Texas—his great-grandson succeeded when he graduated from St. Mary's law school in June 1954. And Michael's son Mark became a lawyer, too, in 1980.

There was still another son of Julius Wagner living in Cuero though: Carl Richard Wagner. When Julius moved to Chicago, his youngest son did not follow his family. Little is known about his life. His obituary mentioned that he lived in San Antonio until 1896 when he moved to Cuero. That would mean that he stayed there four years longer than his parents. What he did during these four years can no longer be determined. On 24 March 1892, he married Blanche Petty at San Antonio. According to the obituary, Carl Richard worked for Otto Buchel and was a faithful employee of that firm until a few months prior to his death.[28] His grandson Bob Wagner tells a different story. He recollects from accounts he heard in the family that Carl Richard worked at the cotton gin at the corner of Hutcheson & S.W. Railroad. Today this is the location of Allied Feeds Inc. First he worked as a freight hauler, then at the scales when the cotton came in. Thus he met with many people and, subsequently, he was able to speak four languages: German, English, Polish, and Spanish. With his knowledge and gentle, polite manners, he rose to become a bookkeeper at the Cuero Cotton Gin. As cotton was the dominant crop in DeWitt County, Cuero was proud to have five cotton gins, a cotton compress, a cotton oil mill, a cotton textile mill, and several cotton merchants. Cotton and turkeys were the predominant economic pillars on which this small community rested. From 1,333 inhabitants in 1880 it had grown to 2,442 in 1890, lost population between 1900 and 1910, had a population of 6,900 in 1972 and has a little over 7,000 today. The cotton industry has lost its importance for Cuero, and only a few turkeys are gobbling loud and healthy today; but the town is still celebrating its annual Turkeyfest. Back in 1972, Cuero saw something special: its second "Turkey Trot" (named after a popular dance at the beginning of the twentieth century). This "Cuero Centennial Turkey Trot" achieved national attention and drew crowds of visitors.[29]

By the time Carl Richard Wagner worked at the Cuero Cotton Gin, turkeys were only raised for private use and for individual sales at the Thanksgiving and Christmas markets. Like his brother William, he had to work hard although he never made as much money as William. Both brothers had two things in common: they hardly, if ever, spoke about their German past, that is, the past of their parents. And they followed their father's advice—they tried to give their children the best education possible. This was not that easy for Carl Richard, as he did not make enough money. He had six children: Sigmund Julius William, Emily Louisa, Blanche B., Carl Frederic Richard, Jr., Walter P., and Robert George. All the boys of Carl Richard Wagner went to high school, but with the exception of Robert, none of them had any further school or college training. In 1933, the youngest son of Julius Wagner, Carl, died.

7. Acculturation or Assimilation?

FOLLOWING THE HISTORY OF THE two Wagner brothers, the question of whether immigration is a process of acculturation or assimilation may be answered by analyzing when and how the Wagners became Americans, not in legal terms but in regards to their belief system and social behavior. Long before he emigrated to the United States, Wilhelm Wagner had developed the conviction that the United States was a desirable country to live in. Discussing the political situation in Germany with his relatives and friends as well as taking sides with the revolutionaries of 1848, he always envisioned America as the land of the free, as an alternative to the oppressive political system of his home country. In his letters he had expressed his belief that he belonged to a free country like the United States more than to Germany. Even though he missed his family and experienced a very hard time in the beginning on his farm on Skinner Creek, Wisconsin, in his first letter back home he nevertheless stated: "I realize more and more that such a future is now more likely to be found in America than in Germany . . . . Here in the land of freedom where no trace of police or military rule can be found, no bureaucracy, no nobles or such, where anyone can run a business undisturbed and give himself to a profession for which he feels strongly. . . where the father of a family can think without anxiety of the future of his children."[1] Wilhelm Wagner had fled Germany for political and not religious or economic reasons. Settling down in Freeport with its large German population he experienced the comfort of living among other German immigrants as well as the joy of living in a free country. As has been described, he was a married, educated man who tried to preserve the old standards of German culture—especially the *Bildungsideal*—as did many of the Forty-eighters. He knew a little English when he came to America and one can assume that his knowledge of the English language improved over the years, although he kept up his German. Writing in German for his German newspaper *Deutscher Anzeiger*, he nevertheless never stopped praising the liberties of America and emphasized the necessity for the German population in his area of becoming good Americans. He became a well-known and respected member of his community and served it in many functions. This acceptance, his rich family life, his successful business life as well as his personally satisfying service as a Protestant pastor were the dominant reasons that Wilhelm Wagner felt at home in the United States.[2] Nevertheless one has to concede that he belonged to a relatively small social group of German immigrants.

Analyzing Wilhelm Wagner in greater detail, one has to realize that he belonged to the comparatively small group of those middle-class Germans who came to America in the first half of the nineteenth century. They were not extremely rich nor completely poor; and they had university training. Although this highly educated middle-class elite was rather a minority, it had a considerable influence on the education system of the United States, on the press, and American politics towards Germany. The vast majority of German immigrants belonged to the lower and lower middle-classes: day laborers, peasants, small farmers, craftsmen, and a few artisans. During the first two-thirds of the nineteenth century most of the Germans came from the southwest: from the Palatinate, Baden, and Württemberg. It was not until the 1860s that this shifted towards the east, when more and more Germans from east of the river Elbe emigrated to the United States.[3] German immigration was not limited to the nineteenth century, of course. German settlers were among those Englishmen who founded Jamestown in 1607. Thirteen Quaker and Mennonite families from Krefeld on the lower Rhine were the first group of Germans who came to North America. Under the guidance of their minister, Francis Daniel Pastorius, they settled in the new colony established by William Penn and in 1683 founded what is today Germantown, Pennsylvania. Others followed, but the largest number of Germans arrived during the nineteenth century. In the 1880s a change set in. Prior to this time, the immigrants had come mainly from northwestern Europe. Up to World War I the eastern and southern Europeans then outnumbered the others three to one. Between 1901 and 1910, 4.2 percent of the immigrants came from Germany in contrast to 25.4 percent from Italy and 19.8 percent from Russia. Europe as a whole provided roughly ninety percent of all immigrants.[4]

Another aspect regarding the relative ease with which Wilhelm Wagner at the age of forty-eight adapted to his new environment might be seen in the fact that he came from a family "on the move." Migration ran through the family like a red thread. His grandfather Johann Christoph Wagner had moved from Ruhla, Thüringen, to Dürkheim, Palatinate, in 1743 as he had been given a new appointment as precentor and preceptor there. Wilhelm's father Peter had moved from one town to another in his search for the ideal position. His brother Karl became a mining engineer and emigrated to Austria where he became a highly decorated citizen. Wilhelm himself moved to Gersbach first and later to Brombach. In contrast to the von Roeders who, after the first mentioning of their family name in a sales document from 1218, had lived on their estates in Sachsen-Anhalt more or less for centuries, the Wagners had been migrants in one form or another throughout their history. From stories and personal experience they came to see emigration as a chance to improve their lives.

The first written account we have of an emigration can be found in the Bible. It is the Exodus of the Jewish people out of Egypt under the leadership of Moses. The Bible gives the number of 600,000 men (not counting the women and children) who left Egypt to follow Moses into the promised land (Exodus 12:37). This first mass emigration was due to political-religious oppression. Another strong motive for emigration throughout history has been overpopulation. Europe is the classical example with a rise from about 95 million inhabitants in 1600 to roughly 190 million in 1800 due to a fall in the death rate.[5]

Germans, like people from all other European nations, were constantly on the move throughout history. With their reputation of being hard-working and reliable, Germans had been called to settle in foreign countries quite often in history.[6] The eighteenth and nineteenth centuries had been the age of migration in Europe. Overpopulation, among many other things caused by increasingly better living conditions and steadily growing food supplies, was the reason people from the country moved into the cities. There were more job opportunities due to industrialization. Thus, the French *pauvres montagnards* (mountain farmers) moved into Paris, the Irish into London, and the small farmers and peasants from the Pyrenees into Madrid—and even further to where land was still available and would feed its owner.

The Wagners did not leave Germany because of overpopulation, however. All their many letters indicate that as much as they thought about emigration, their motivation for thinking about leaving Germany was primarily a political one. Being liberals, the Wagners saw no hope in staying in Germany. It was a clear decision for Wilhelm to leave his native country and try a new start . It was also clear for his wife Friedericke to follow him with their children. Very little is known about Friedericke Wagner and how she adapted to life in the United States. No letters from her have survived. In 1860, Wilhelm wrote his mother that his wife had become a true American:

> a busy house wife and a caring mother who isn't afraid of any work and very often does too much in the house and the garden. She doesn't care much about the English language because she has a perfect interpreter with whose help she can communicate easily with English speaking people whenever she has a chance to do so. This interpreter is Friedrich and much better than his sister Friederike.

She did not attend as many social activities as her husband but got along very well with her neighbors, according to Wilhelm.[7] Outspoken as Wilhelm was he would have admitted in his letters if his wife faced a hard time. If she ever did she obviously never showed it to her husband. Devoted as she seemed to have been, she knew that her husband loved his new homecountry and would never have spoiled this feeling, even if she had had any reason to. Wilhelm's love stemmed from political reasons. In a way he missed the German *Gemütlichkeit*, the German forms of socializing. He knew, though, that there was no way for him ever to return, since Germany—during his lifetime at least—never experienced democracy as he had found it in America. He was a real Forty-eighter and belonged to the group of German-Americans who felt like true citizens of the United States but, at the same time, belonged to a specific ethnic group. Thus, Wilhelm Wagner during his lifetime never assimilated completely. The German element as a form of personal identification was dominant with him throughout his life. At the same time it is important to realize that Wilhelm Wagner, like his brother Julius, lived on the frontier, in terms both of time and place. Without going into detail about the frontier debate one has to concede that both brothers began their lives in the United States in a society which was in the making. Therefore it might be difficult to talk about a dominant group in the societies where they lived. Both settled in areas with a strong German population. Wilhelm Wagner, for this reason, never had to assimilate totally in a dominant Anglo-American society as this society was beginning to form itself out of various elements, especially the Anglo-American and the German-American ones.

It is interesting to notice that every one of his seven surviving children married other German immigrants or children of German immigrants. This pattern only changed with the following generation which was born solely in the United States. The question when and how this branch of the Wagner family became Americans and lost their "hyphen-status" might be answered by looking at these next generations.

Wilhelm's son William followed in the footsteps of his father by joining the same German-American clubs and continuing the German paper *Deutscher Anzeiger*. It is of some significance that he also wrote the account of his father's life for the *Deutsch Amerikanische Geschichtsblätter* in German and not in English for a broader American readership. William's son Frederic, who took over the printing business, was not as successful a businessman as his father and grandfather had been. The new company might not have seen many prosperous years had it not been for Frederic's energetic wife, Emma Gund. Here it is important to take a closer look at her.

Emma Gund was the daughter of Abraham (1828-1883) and Emeline (nee Schottle) Gund (1837-1928). Abraham Gund belonged to the early settlers of Silver Creek who moved there in 1839. He was the first one of the Gund family to emigrate to the United States. His father Georg Michael Gund (1795-1850) and his mother Sophia Eder (1808-1850), together with their other eight children, came to the United States in 1848. The Gunds had been quite a wealthy family in Brühl, Germany, (the hometown of the recent German tennis star Steffi Graf), owners of the inn Zum Goldenen Ochsen and a lot of farmland. Georg Michael's father Johann Georg (1773-1819) had been the largest tax payer of Brühl. Abraham did not stay in Illinois all the time, though. After his family followed his call, he went to California in the gold rush of 1849. He was the most intellectual member of the family, fond of reading and conversation. All the gold he found, he sent back to the Freeport bank, only to learn on his return that the bank had gone bankrupt. Coming home, he also learned that his parents had died of cholera in 1850. His youngest brother Frederick (1846-1889) had married Josephine Hettinger (1849-1894), the sister of Matt Hettinger (founder and owner of the German bank and the German Insurance Company) who had married Abraham's sister Elizabeth (1837-1913). Abraham's daughter Emma spent her childhood days and adolescence on the family farm at Town Silver Creek.[8] On November 22, 1884, she married Frederic Wagner and moved to Freeport with him.

Frederic and his family lived in Silver Creek Township and ran a small fruit farm for twelve years after he suffered from a nervous breakdown at the press in 1910. He served as a member and secretary of the Silver Creek Township library board. When he moved back to Freeport after being named president of Wagner Printing in 1922, he became a member of the Freeport school board for four consecutive terms. He served on many local committees and was a vestryman of Grace Episcopal Church for many years. Frederic was never happy as president of Wagner Printing, however. He loved music and flowers. His greatest pride was his garden on his estate on 55 High Street, close to where his brothers Otto and Paul lived. All these years it was his wife Emma who ran the printing company.

After his death in 1928, Emma took over the business officially. Together with her twenty-four-year old son Paul, she ran the company through the Depression. Emma Gund Wagner was innovative. Her grandson Mark called her an early "women's libber." She had to borrow money, sometimes even from her own life insurance, in order to make payroll, but the company stayed in business. In 1936, three men bought out the micro switch production line from Burgess Battery Division of Clevite, one of Freeport's major industries, and formed the Micro Switch Corporation which had its production facilities on the third floor of the Wagner printing building on Spring Street. This proved to become a valuable asset for the Wagners during the second World War.

The United States entered World War II with the declaration of war on Japan on 8 December 1941. Already before the war, the Wagner Printing Company was producing thousands of forms for defense factories and instructions for use in training new employees. During the war, though, paper was not available for printing with the exception of military purposes.

These were hard times for many printing companies throughout the country and only those who could get military contracts survived. Pierre Cowan, who had come to Wagner Printing from Chicago in 1941 and soon became vice president, suddenly had the idea in 1942 that made the company survive through the war. Micro Switch Corporation had been producing switches for thermostats and other instruments of high precision. During the war these switches were needed in big numbers for use on tanks, radar equipment, antiaircraft guns, and ships. The government began subsidizing the Freeport company to develop better micro switches. These switches required assembly by hand, and Wagner Printing put in production lines for assembling switches in between the rows of the presses. Another deal was struck with Burgess Battery. Putting the little piece of setter on top of the carbon post was a manual process at that time. Wagner Printing bought the carbon posts from Burgess Battery, placed the setter on top and sold this unit back to the battery company. This work could not be done with the usual staff, especially since most men were off to war. Co-operating with the U.S. Employment Service in recruiting manpower and womanpower for war work, Wagner Printing employed more than one hundred women at the assembly lines, all of whom were very proud when they shared in an Army-Navy "E" pennant awarded to Micro Switch Inc. in September 1943. Emma's son Paul, who at that time was the company's secretary-treasurer and manager of the printing department, had done away with obsolete printing equipment and had even sold new machinery which was not needed at that time. The rest of the old office, bindery, pressroom, and composing room paraphernalia, including small, fast presses such as Kluges, Verticals, and a Simplex, were retained and squeezed into as small a space as possible. With these activities, Emma Gund Wagner, her son Paul, and Pierre Cowan did keep Wagner Printing alive during the war years. The company was doing even more though: it was planning already in 1944 for the time after the war. A two-color folder, mailed to clients and possible prospects asked: "Are you getting ready for tomorrow? One of these days a quiet hush is going to settle over the world. Never in history have such tremendous economic wants and desires for goods been so pent up. When that day comes, this business will go first to those concerns who have made the most effective use of sales promotion material and who have kept their names before dealers and the public."[9]

After the war, Emma Gund Wagner retired as president and her son Paul became her successor. In 1961, Emma Gund Wagner died at the age of eighty-eight. With her death, the Wagners had lost more than an affectionate mother and former president of the company. They had lost something that nobody bothered about at that time as it did not affect business. The Wagners had finally lost their German past, their consciousness of being German-American. This did not happen to the Wagners alone of course but to most Americans of German descent. The anti-German feelings in the wake of World War I had caused the deaths of many German-American papers like the Freeport *Deutscher Anzeiger*. "The effect of two world wars in a generation, along with the memory of Adolf Hitler, was devastating to German-American ethnic consciousness," as Leslie V. Tischauser put it. "After the second war, what with the new meaning the word 'German' had acquired, an ethnic consciousness appeared as something to consign to oblivion, and most German-Americans did just that.... Wounded in World War I, battered by the events of the interwar years, German-American ethnic consciousness ultimately became a casualty of World War II, one more victim—however inadvertently and ironically—of the forces which sought to create a 1000-year Reich enshrining their variant of Germanic culture."[10] This loss of their heritage did not happen overnight. Reflecting about their family's past, the generation of Emma's grandchildren suddenly realized that their grandmother had not told them very much about the German past of the Wagners. Therefore, only very little is known of the life and times of William's sons. Emma Gund Wagner took all this knowledge with her to her grave. And it was not this special knowledge about the past and the personal stories alone that vanished with her. The German language died out in the Wagner family too, as in most other German-American families, which became all-American families after 1917 following the political goal of "one country, one flag, one speech." The teaching of the German language at schools and universities was reduced if not totally abolished during and after World War I. Many Germans would not speak their original language in public any more, and the use of German was confined mainly to the house. With the slow dying of German as a spoken language, the newspapers printed in German died out too.[11] With the loss of the language, the German-American ethnic consciousness dissolved and, as a consequence, the German *Vereine*, the German *Theater* and of course the German *Schule* became extinct over the following decades.

The story of Emma Wagner is important in many aspects. For one thing she became a business executive at a time when it was not typical for women to be executives of a company.[12] It is not important that she inherited the company from her husband; it is important that she was able to keep the company alive during the Depression and World War II. When she hired Pierre Cowan in 1941 and made him vice president soon after, she broke with an old tradition of German immigrants taking only other German-Americans into a business partnership. Under the guidance of Emma Wagner, Wagner Printing became an American company and was not a German-American enterprise any more. The business's history reads like many other histories of American companies and, therefore, shows the change that took place under Emma's leadership.

The next Wagner generations were Americans and Wagner Printing today is still in business and family-owned with Wilhelm's great-great-grandson Mark Wagner as president. Despite the loss of the German language, the descendants of Wilhelm Wagner never completely lost the consciousness of having once come from Germany, however. Something else though had changed fundamentally: the family ties that had been so important for Wilhelm throughout his life had loosened, especially those to Germany. Only very few members of the various descendants of Wilhelm Wagner kept or established contact with relatives in Germany, although they all cherished the history of Wilhelm's flight to Switzerland and to the United States. One reason for the contact diminishing over the decades on the German side of the family was the inability of communicating in English, as it was not until the end of World War II that English was taught in schools. On the American side, the German language, as we have seen, was not used any more. When Mark's oldest daughter Martha May, now a professor of psychology, studied in Germany at the University of Freiburg i.Br. in 1987, she not only did a little research in the family history at Brombach, Wilhelm's last German place of work, but also established contact with Anneliese Ries there, the granddaughter of Wilhelm's sister Luise's fourth child: Karl Becker. Two branches of Wilhelm's descendants kept the contact alive for quite a long time. One was the family of Wilhelm's youngest son Friedrich, commonly called Fred. In the summer of 1912 he travelled to Germany together with his wife Emily Kupper[13] and his second son Archibald. They visited their cousin Anna (1846-1926), the daughter of Wilhelm's younger brother Karl. She had married Professor Johann Soellner (1837-1885), and the couple lived in Karlsruhe, Germany, together with their seven children. The contact between Fred's family and the Soellners survived the storms of time: Fred's granddaughter Pamela Ritter is still in close communication with Anna Soellner's great-grandson Hansjörg Soellner (b. 1930) and his family at Pforzheim. In a very special way, the Soellner family proved to be a cardinal point for keeping up transatlantic relations. Julius Wagner's oldest son Sigmund often visited Anna Soellner, to whom he was very close, at Karlsruhe during his education in Germany. One of the closest family ties existed between the Soellners and the Kleinpells.

Hans Otto Soellner (1899-1989), the grandson of Karl Wagner's daughter Anna Soellner cherished his friendship with his cousins, the well-known physician Dr. Henry Kleinpell from Flint, Michigan, and Henry's brother Julius who owned a lumber mill in Cassville, Wisconsin. Henry and Julius were two of the seven children of Carl Friedrich Kleinpell, brother of Heinrich W. and son of the immigrant Heinrich Kleinpell, who had married his cousin Luise, the daughter of Wilhelm Wagner, and lived as a harness maker, postmaster, and owner of a general store at Cassville, Wisconsin. The correspondence of their children, which spans over decades, not only tells a lot about various members of the Wagner, Soellner, and Kleinpell families but also about the liberal, antifacist attitude of the Soellners in the days before and during the Third Reich. The letters also reveal much about the economic situation in Germany before and after World War II as the Soellners, who owned (and still own) a jewelry manufacturing company in Pforzheim, talk a lot about production and working conditions.[14] The relationship between the cousins was not confined to writing alone. Henry, Julius, and their sister Frieda regularly visited the relatives in Germany before and after the wars. These contacts did not die with the deaths of Henry and Julius, who both had had no children, but were kept alive by Arthur Kleinpell, the son of Henry's and Julius' brother Carl who had been the editor of the German paper *Dakota Deutsche Zeitung* at Sioux Falls, Dakota Territory. Arthur and his brother Karl ran the Flint Lumber Company, Karl as president and Arthur as treasurer. Arthur was also president of the Michigan Retail Lumber Dealers Association for many years. Together with his wife and children, he travelled to Germany quite often and paid his visits to the Soellners and to Hildegard Kattermann (1909-1991), family historian of the Wagners and granddaughter of Wilhelm's sister Luise's fourth child, Karl Becker. Arthur, like his cousin Hildegard, was very fascinated by his family's history and tried to acquire as much information and as many documents as possible. This fascination stemmed from a positive image of the family, an image reaching back to their German past. This alone contradicts the idea mentioned in the introduction that the European immigrants wanted to forget their horrid past and hoped to form a new national character.[15] The example of this branch of the Wagner family shows that this idea is far too simplistic. Their German past melted into a new identity together with their experiences in the United States. Arthur Kleinpell also knew that there were still relatives in Texas, descendants of Julius Wagner, and tried to contact them, but without success. He seems to have been the only one who still knew that relatives existed somewhere in the south. But the knowledge that the Wagners in Ilinois, Iowa, and Wisconsin had cousins in Texas, and that Wilhelm had had a brother, had actually been lost by most of the Wilhelm Wagner descendants over the generations.

The migration story of Julius Wagner is quite different from that of his brother Wilhelm. He had joined a group of young radicals who wanted to fulfill their dreams of a communistic society in the United States. Julius was not driven out of Germany for political or religious reasons, nor was he forced to leave because of economic strains. There were and are various reasons for emigration. The British social scientist E. G. Ravenstein has described three main factors for emigration that he called "Laws of Migration." These three essential components are: the "push," the "pull," and the "means" factors. The push factor applies to situations outside of the emigrant that drive these particular persons out of their homeland, such as the infamous Irish potato famine or the Revolution of 1848, for example. The pull factor refers to either advertising or letters and reports by friends and family members that draw the emigrant to the new country. The means factor applies to the possibilities of the prospective emigrant of obtaining the papers and money necessary to migrate.[16] The most important point in emigration is the motivation of the person. It is the motivation to leave the old homeland and settle in the new one, to uproot one's life and one's family, and to begin life anew. Whereas Julius Wagner's motives can mainly be subsumed under the pull factor, Wilhelm Wagner's motives clearly belonged to the push factor group. And both had the means to emigrate to another country. Both Wagners therefore clearly fall into Ravenstein's catagories. The choice of both brothers to emigrate to America also reflects the image of this continent as the main land for immigration in the nineteenth century.

Looking at the early history of the United States, it becomes evident that this country always was an immigrant nation. The first men most likely came as hunters following the trails of the mammoth across the Bering Strait into the so-called Alaskan or Beringian Refuge between 25,000 B.C. and 17,000 B.C. The first permanent settlers came from England in the seventeenth century due to overpopulation as contemporaries saw it and the growing discontent between the Puritans and the Church of England. More than 60,000 Englishmen sought refuge in the New World during the first half of that century. By that time, the French, and most of all the Spaniards, had already set their feet on American soil. However, the members of those two nations had not come primarily as settlers. The French were mainly traders, and the Spanish saw South and Central America since its discovery in 1492, as a place to conquer, to exploit its riches for the Spanish crown, and to establish a new Jerusalem in America. Besides exploring the New World to find treasures for their monarchs, the Spaniards saw the unique chance to bring Christianity to the heathens, to mold the Indians into Christians. For the church, especially, it was a shining opportunity for spiritual conquest. None of the Spaniards originally came as settlers. One thing the Spaniards had in common with the first English settlers, however, was their crusade against the Indians, the "heathens."

The New England colonies that were formed by Puritanism have to been seen as the cradle of American culture, of American philosophy, and of American ideals. With the victory of the North over the South in the Civil War, it was not only the Union that was preserved, but also the predominance of Puritan thought. Inherent in Puritan thought is the belief of superiority over the Indians or any other pagans. The religions of the various Indian peoples in general see men as part of nature, unlike the Christians who face the task to subdue nature. The Christian settlers, therefore, had a mission; the nations they met with had none. This alone made the settlers stronger mentally. Even if one argues that it was not the Christian churches, but those frontiermen greedy for land and convinced that they were the soldiers of the Lord and "advance agents of civilization" who expelled the Indian nations from their land, it remains a fact that the Christian religion as a philosophy served as a basis to conquer the new continent.[17] This is only one reason, however, why America was unique as an immigrant nation. The other one was the geographical and climatic situation. In contrast to many other parts of the world, the area of the United States was and is best suited for settling and cultivating the land. It was neither easy to settle or cultivate in all cases, but it was mostly virgin land. It was not worn out through centuries of use as in Europe. And there was an abundance of untouched natural resources. The settlers on the frontier also did not meet resistance in a way that would have stopped their expansion. In the long run, the nomadic tribes and nations they met on the prairie could not stop the white men's advance. This "easy" advance fostered the feeling of superiority. At the same time the white man was superior in mechanics and technology. Among other things the Indian did not even have the wheel for example. This westward advance was also responsible for the myth that was and still is an essential part of American consciousness: the myth of the frontier. John F. Kennedy tried to revive this spirit with his New Frontier speech, for instance.

The importance of the frontier lay in its psychological influence on the people. The term "frontier" became synonymous with the westward movement although this westward extension of the United States simply was a geographical coincidence. If the American continents lay east of Europe we would speak of an eastward movement. This unrestrained expansion, which fed the feeling of superiority, was often fostered by events outside the influence of the Americans, like the sale of the Louisiana Territory by the French. One might speculate whether this territory would have become part of the United States sooner or later anyway; yet, it was this more or less easy spreading across a fast and seemingly open country that nurtured the feeling that became known as "Manifest Destiny." As every nation defines itself out of its history, the mixture of European thought and ideas and the challenge of the frontier created the American consciousness as a special nation.

The frontier, according to the historian Frederick Jackson Turner, was also essential in establishing the American democracy: "the democracy born of free land, strong in selfishness and individualism, intolerant of administrative experience and education, and pressing individual liberty beyond its proper bounds."[18] This image, whether true or not, was the one that appealed to Europeans and peoples from other continents so much that the United States became synonymous with the land of hope, the land of freedom, the land of opportunity for everyone. That included the chances for a better life in economic terms. Quite a number of immigrants came to find work, to make a better living than had been possible for them in their old home country. The economic aspect as the main reason for immigration would fall short of what emigration meant and means. It was not money and the prospects making a good living alone which brought immigrants to the shores of the United States. The autobiography of the northern Italian immigrant Rosa Cassettari, who published her accounts under the pen name Marie Hall Ets (*Rosa: The Life of an Italian Immigrant*) gives a clue to the true motives of millions of those who came to America: "The country where everyone could find work! Where wages were so high no one had to go hungry! Where all men were free and equal and where even the poor could own land!" It was just this combination: to be able to make good money in order to lead a decent life and to live in a free country, in a democracy.

To say that immigrants came largely for economic gain, as Roger Daniels did, also does not take into account the hardships and psychological barriers one had to overcome in order to take such a step.[19] This explanation might suffice for those Europeans who moved to the cities from the countryside in Europe. Those who emigrated though, left behind their friends, their accustomed surroundings and their way of living to a more radical extent than those who only went to the big cities. And those whose mother tongue was not English faced an even more uncertain future. Those who came to the United States as immigrants, that is with the desire to find a better place to live for good, gave up all their social securities, securities that stem from the familiarity with one's social environment. Those who came to the United States did hope for a better life, spiritually and physically. In return, this means that they experienced their lives in the Old World as unsatisfactory. Emigration was thus the manifesto of dissatisfaction. Julius Wagner and his friends are a good example of this attitude too. This may apply less to those who were forced to emigrate for political or religious reasons by their respective governments like the orthodox Jews coming from Russia and Poland, and yet it holds some significance even for this group as far as their desire to go to America in contrast to moving to other European states is concerned.

When the group of the Forty that Julius Wagner had immigrated with broke up, he did not return to Germany as a few others did. His reasons for this are not known. He settled down among other Germans and very much enjoyed the various forms of German socializing like the various singing societies he joined. How good his knowledge of the English language was is not known. He was a typical "Latin" farmer in Texas, hard-working and putting a lot of emphasis on education, following the same *Bildungsideal* as his brother Wilhelm did. In contrast to the family of his brother, we know more about the feelings and attitudes of his wife, Emilie, towards her new homeland than about Julius's ways of adapting to the country he had come to live in. She never liked her life in the New World; but according to her love and obedience to her husband and family, never returned to the country she came from and loved. The way Emilie Wagner decorated her home (as far as we know from her letters from Texas), was typical for those immigrants of the first generation who did not acclimate easily and tried to preserve at least a little bit of their home culture in their new homes.

One of the best descriptions in fiction of this phenomenon are the novels by Willa Cather: *My Ántonia* and *O Pioneers!* "The pleasantest rooms in the house are the kitchen . . . and the sitting-room, in which Alexandra has brought together the old homely furniture that the Bergsons used in their first log house, the family portraits, and the few things her mother brought from Sweden." This preservation of Old World relics was not confined to home decoration only. Willa Cather also describes how the characters cling to their mother tongue, how they love to plant flowers they know from Europe and how—at the same time—the next generation already dislikes these visible or audible connections to the lands of their forefathers.[20] At the same time Willa Cather's novels exemplify that the attempt of many first generation settlers to preserve certain things like language, various customs, and home decoration was not limited to one group of immigrants like the Germans. Especially those settlers from European nations whose language was not English, like the Scandinavians, the Germans, the Poles, and the Italians, tried to preserve some sort of cultural identity. Thus, the Wagners were and are typical for a vast number of first generation Americans. With her homesickness and the burden, never to have liked the country she had to live in, Emilie too is more typical of most women who immigrated than her sister-in-law Friederike was, as far as we can trust the accounts of her husband.[21] All we know about Julius Wagner and his wife indicates that they never became "real" Americans, never assimilated completely. As we have observed before, Julius, like his brother Wilhelm, began his life in the United States on the frontier. He settled among other Germans and was part of an immigrant group which established a fraction of the multi-cultural society pattern of Texas. In contrast to his brother Wilhelm though, he had to make a choice during the Civil War. He chose not to join the majority, but stick to his German principles. After this war therefore, Julius and his wife were in a different situation than at the time they had come to Texas. The society and its values had changed and they had not followed this change. During this second half of their lives in Texas, they did not assimilate to the post-war society of Texas as well as they had been able to before the war.

Looking at their children we see a twofold picture. Their second oldest daughter Paula had married the German immigrant Hermann Paepcke who became a highly successful businessman in Chicago. He was a member in various clubs and institutions, not for idle entertainment, but for the purpose of learning and preserving the cultural standards of the old German class of the *Gross Bürgertum* (the so-called high bourgeoisie). The story of his son Walter sheds an interesting light on the development of this branch of the family. Walter Paepcke, heir to a vast business empire, showed the same strong will, determination, and appetite for success as his father.

When Hermann Paepcke was laid to rest beside his wife, his mother-in-law and his father-in-law in Graceland Cemetery, Chicago, in July of 1922, Walter Paul Paepcke, twenty-six years old, had already been in charge of the company for one year. As the lumber business was declining, he had to nurture the company back to health first before he could make his decisive move: in June of 1926 he formed the Container Corporation of America (CCA) after having bought the Mid-West Box Company and the Philadelphia Paper Manufacturing Company. After early profits of over $1,000,000 in 1927, CCA got into some trouble during the Depression but recovered and grossed a profit of $1,287,000 in 1936. Business alone, however, did not comprise the personality of Julius Wagner's grandson. Having been introduced to the world of art by his father Hermann, Walter found a congenial partner and inspiration in his wife Elizabeth, the beautiful daughter of Hermann's friend William A. Nitze, chairman of the Romance Language Department of the University of Chicago. She was not only a legendary beauty of her times[22] but also the guiding spirit in one of the boldest and most successful business experiments in the history of American business: the introduction of modern art into company design.

At the suggestion of his wife, Walter Paepcke established an art department for his company and made the president of the Art Director's Club of Chicago, Egbert Jacobson, its head on 1 April 1935. The rest is legend. The first artist to work for CCA was the famous French poster artist A.M. Cassandre. Others like Toni Zepf, Man Ray, Henry Moore, Jean Carlu, Richard Lindner, Willem de Kooning, Herbert Bayer, Fernand Léger, and Miguel Covarrubias soon joined him. The unique advertising campaign these artists helped to create not only put CCA in the limelight but set standards for others too. Walter Paepcke did not stop there. When the famous painter and teacher at the *Bauhaus*, the Hungarian László Moholy-Nagy (1895-1946) came to Chicago in 1937, Walter Paepke was the essential force in creating the New Bauhaus in Chicago and making Moholy-Nagy its head.

The Bauhaus, founded in 1919 at Weimar by the architect Walter Gropius, was not just simply a school for designing crafts, architecture, and the arts but became the most influential and important institution for modern design in the twentieth century. Among its teachers were reknowned artists, like the architects Gropius himself and Ludwig Mies van der Rohe as well as such painters as Paul Klee, Oskar Schlemmer, Wassily Kandinsky, and Lyonel Feininger. In the somewhat typical German way of searching for a deeper truth behind simple looking things, Gropius had not just envisioned teaching modern industrial design, painting, and architecture in order to meet the practical ends of artists and industrialists. He wanted to give the universal, humanistic pretension of culture its clear, pure form: "Together let us desire, conceive, and create the new structure of the future which will embrace architecture and sculpture and painting in one unity which will one day rise toward heaven from the hands of a million workers like the crystal symbol of a new faith."[23] With its new, clear, functional style, the Bauhaus set standards in architecture and design around the world. The rise of the fascists had driven the Bauhaus and its members out of Germany. With the financial help of Walter Paepcke, they found a new home in Chicago. The Paepckes and the Moholy-Nagys became close friends; and in March of 1944, Walter Paepcke was one of the founding fathers of another cultural landmark of design: the Institute of Design at Chicago: "In this postwar era when practically every product is being redesigned, it seems particularly necessary to provide a complete education which encompasses artistry, technology and science. The well coordinated synthesis of these three educational fields is what the Institute of Design offers," he wrote in 1948.[24]

In a way, Walter Paepcke had spiritually become the true grandson of the "Latin" farmer Julius Wagner. When he brought Goethe to the Rocky Mountains, he went even further. The remote village of Aspen in Colorado had lain dormant since the silver mining boom had ended in 1893. Again it was Elizabeth Paepcke who set the eyes of her enterprising husband on an object that became the jewel in his crown. She had only seen an ideal area for America's newest popular sport: skiing. Riding the crest of his business triumphs, he saw more: a new cultural center, a center for music, literature, and philosophy. Buying most of the land in and around Aspen in 1945, he first began developing it into a modern ski resort with the longest ski lift in the world in order to create an economic base for his wider schemes: to establish a modern Weimar (the city Goethe lived in from 1775 until his death in 1832) in America together with his friend Walter Gropius. First came the annual Aspen Music Festival in the old, remodeled opera house, then a health center and finally his Institute for Humanistic Studies at Aspen in 1951. The climax of Walter Paepcke's cultural life and the fulfillment of his dreams, arrived in June of 1949, when his vision of the Goethe festival, the "Goethe Bicentennial Celebration" at Aspen, became reality.

Actually, Professor Giuseppe Antonio Borgese (1882-1952) had been the first one to formulate the idea to celebrate the bicentennial of Goethe's birth on his campus at the University of Chicago. He had suggested it to his colleague Robert H. Hutchins, and the latter talked it over with his colleague, Mortimer J. Adler, the American educator and philosopher. Adler and Hutchins were also initiators of the "Great Books" idea about adult education and the seminars at the University of Chicago of which Walter Paepcke was a trustee. Hutchins, Adler, and Paepcke also were close friends, tied together by the same *Bildungsideal*. Hutchins and Walter Paepcke had been students at Yale. The latter had studied German literature and economics and graduated in 1917, Phi Beta Kappa. It is very interesting to note that the Paepckes, in contrast to the other branches of the Wagner family, were always very proud of their German background and never ceased to speak the language of their forbears, even through both World Wars. Very likely their high position in society and their self-assuredness, fostered by wealth, education, and ties to artists and scientists, kept them immune from the waves of anti-German feelings and propaganda. On the contrary, Walter Paepcke wanted to show his fellow Americans that Germany had once meant more than the militaristic, fascist, and deadly spider, to which Hitler and the fascists had reduced it. But why celebrate Goethe? Johann Wolfgang von Goethe was chosen by these men from Chicago not only because he was the most famous German author, poet, playwright, and a universal genius, but also because he symbolized the manifestation of humanism. In his lecture on Goethe, Hutchins said: "In *Wilhelm Meister*, there is a speech which, it seems to me, is appropriately addressed to this assembly on this great occasion: 'Since we came together so miraculously, let us not lead a trivial life; let us together become active in a noble manner!'"

Hutchins and Borgese wrote a text for the opening of the festival which also became its testament: "If Goethe's particular time has any relevance to our difficulty, it is only that his time bridged the ancient and the modern worlds, enabling him to stand where he stood and comprehend them both. If his place has any relevance, it is only that Germany is the bloody battleground which we all feel, however vaguely, however variously, must be planted again if the difficulty of the human spirit is to be surmounted."[25] Dimitri Mitropolous conducted the Minneapolis Symphony Orchestra and the world-famous physician Albert Schweitzer was the guest of honor (it was the first and last time that Schweitzer came to the United States). The American playwright Thornton Wilder and the Spanish philosopher José Ortega y Gasset gave lectures, among many other illustrious guests from all sections of the arts. The list of the festival's guests, the notable lectures, the influence of the Aspen Institute on the arts and on American business in the 1950s would take more than a book on its own and shall not be discussed here. The importance of all this lies in the achievement of Walter Paepcke to have bridged the deadly and horrifying abyss of fascist Germany, not in order to forget the horrors of the Third Reich and to diminish German guilt for millions of innocent deaths but to remind the cultural world of what Germany had once stood for in the realm of the arts and that German humanism, though severely shattered, could still give meaning to the modern world. It was the old German *Bildungsideal* that was also propagandized by Mortimer J. Adler, editor of the *Great Books of the Western World* with its *Syntopicon* and leader of the Great Books movement. His Great Books seminar became the model for the Aspen Institute. In that sense, Walter Paepcke had thus finally fulfilled what men like Prince Solms-Braunfels had dreamt of 150 years before: to bring the best of the *Deutschtum* to other peoples. Julius Wagner would have loved what his grandson accomplished.[26]

The story of Walter Paepcke is not only interesting but even more important in comparison to the changes in the Wilhelm Wagner family branch brought about by Emma Wagner. Hermann Paepcke, like Wilhelm Wagner, was a real German-American. For the various executive offices of his many companies he only chose men of German descent. He always lived in Chicago's North Side amid a strong and predominant German neighborhood. His son Walter received a classical education at the Chicago Latin School before Yale, where he studied economics and German literature, thus reflecting his father's passions. Up to his old age, Walter was still able to recite by heart whole sections of Goethe's *Faust*. When he died, the photographer Ansel Adams wrote: "Walter was a truly great man." Walter Paepcke had been a highly successful, innovative, and aggressive American businessman as well as an extraodinary promoter of arts and sciences, "who did more for learning in this country than ten colleges and universities, and this simply by caring and doing. With twenty men of his caliber in the land, the cultural complexion of the United States would be unrecognizable."[27] Walter's strong ties to the German high culture and to the ideals of humanism can not be separated from his upbringing and his wealth. Both gave him the absolute independence to pursue his ideas without having to consider public opinion. Instead he was in a position to influence and shape public opinion. His ties to Germany existed on an intellectual level and not, as with many German-Americans, on the basis of personal feelings and an attachment to German forms of socializing. Thus being able to carry the *Bildungsideal* to an extreme, he, at the same time, marks the exception which proves the rule.

Things were quite different with his uncles, Julius's sons Wilhelm and Carl Friedrich Richard who lived in Texas. As has been described, both men tried to become good American citizens, leaving their past behind. They never spoke about their relatives or their German inheritance. A revealing story, illustrating this strong desire to assimilate, is told in the family of the Julius Wagner descendants. After Wilhelm Wagner was elected county treasurer in 1916, he encountered a man in the courthouse who spoke only a little English. Therefore, Wilhelm asked him what he wanted in German. As this happened just prior to World War I this was enough to indict Wilhelm for subversion. In court he defended himself without legal counsel in flawless English and was acquitted. This branch of the Wagner family had been Americans from the beginning. The story of Carl's son Walter reads like a typical Texas tale from days of old.

After Walter "Bully" Wagner left school in 1925 he bought a store on Main Street in Cuero. His brother, Carl, acquired a store across the street from his brother's and they opened two confectionaries: Wagner's No. 1, run by Carl, and Wagner's No. 2 run by "Bully." These stores not only grew famous for their five to six different handmade ice creams, but for their social importance. The Wagners sold soft drinks too, and the people of Cuero loved to spend a nickel or dime for a coke. Beer was not available, as Prohibition kept the United States dry and bootlegging profitable. Folks used to gather at the ice cream parlors and talk. Bully especially had a hand with people. They liked him; they loved him; they trusted him. And when they had problems, they came to his store and asked his advice. Upon his death decades later, the *Cuero Daily Record* published an obituary on page one: "Cuero Monday morning paid last tribute to Walter 'Bully' Wagner, prominent businessman and legendary figure in this little city's baseball history." It also commented on his death in its editorial "Town Talk," just as it had done when his uncle William had died:

> Oft-times a simple, sincere tribute to a man carries more weight than an eulogy. Such a tribute paid Sunday by a "man on the street" to the late Walter "Bully" Wagner, we would like to repeat today: "He was a good boy . . . he grew to be a good man. He was a devoted father. . . a devoted husband." Yes, Bully Wagner was a good man. He played the game of life as he played the game of baseball in his youth . . . hard . . . clean . . . fair. He was a true sportsman who took the bitter with the sweet without complaint. He was the type of man you like to deal with. He was the type of man you wanted for a neighbor.[28]

Thus they came to him, talking about everything they had on their minds, including their problems. And problems were quite common these days, as the Depression held the country in its firm grip. The Depression caused problems for the young Wagners, too, but they solved it their way. While Carl kept both stores going, Bully drove down to the Mexican border in his old Model T Ford to play "outlaw baseball," as it was called then. Already as a small boy, he had practiced by throwing stones up a hill close to where he grew up. He played for a Mexican team, mostly in Brownsville, as the Mexican wages were much higher than the American at that time. A homerun brought twenty-five to thirty dollars, quite a lot of money those days. And Bully made a lot of money. He was a good hitter, a good fielder, and an excellent shortstop. He had even made enough money to buy a farm of about 200 acres in 1939 from a man who was desperate to sell. Still, times were not easy, and Carl closed his store in 1938.

When the war came in 1941, Bully was forced to close up, too, as he could not get any sugar anymore. He was fortunate though. In 1939, when the United States had become aware of the fact that war was looming over the horizon after Germany's attack on Poland, they suddenly realized that they did not have enough trained aircraft pilots. In fact, they needed many more than could be trained at military fields alone. Therefore, a lot of privately owned training fields were established, one of them in Cuero. Veteran pilot Clyde E. Brayton, whose first license had been signed by Orville Wright, got the contract to run Cuero's pilot training field that was named after him: Brayton Flying Field. It had a staff of 550 civilians and one hundred military men and trained 6,611 students. Bully Wagner got a contract to operate the "saloon" on the premises, selling his famous ice cream, sodas, Coke, and candy. When he had sold his store on Main Street, the army had bought his equipment. That way he lost his store but stayed in business. He never was a supporter of President Roosevelt, but always a staunch Republican.

After the war, he looked for something else. His brother Carl had bought a jewelry store next to where the confectionary had been. In 1945 Bully Wagner's eyes fell on an old, run-down hardware store on Esplanade Street. This store had been founded in 1888 by R.C. Warn, and after his death was operated by his relatives, Hutchings and Bates. Bully Wagner bought this business. When he died in 1957, his wife Fay Lucille, who had come down to Texas as a schoolteacher from California, took over the Wagner Hardware & Machinery Co. She ran it with their son, Bob, who had just gotten his degree in finance from the University of Texas at Austin.

After he left high school in 1948, Bob had enrolled at Texas A&I with a major in agriculture. When the Korean War broke out, he signed up for four years in 1951, having just married Billie Leggett, and served first in the veterinarian service at San Antonio's Lackland Air Force Base and later in Austin. After three years, when the war ended, he was released from duty and went to the farm his father had acquired in 1939. There Bob wanted to put his agricultural training to the test. He started out with about thirty milk cows he had bought in Wisconsin. The day he and his wife Billie had arrived on the farm was the last day it rained for the next two years. The green pasture turned into a white, sandy desert. All the feed for the cattle had to be purchased, which made the venture a losing proposition. After these two years without any rain, he was forced to change his plans, and he gave up farming. His father had always wanted him to go to college and get a degree. Bully had only finished high school, and he wanted his son to have a better education. Now, Bob thought, his father might have been right, and so he went to the University of Texas at Austin to study finance. He was through with agriculture. Half the day he attended classes, the other half he worked at a lumberyard to earn the money for his tuition fees and to support his young family. The day of his final exam, his father Bully died of a heart attack. Bob's mother withheld this news from her son, in order to let him take his last test undisturbed, just as Bully would have wanted it. The hardware store had no management now, and thus Bob took his father's place. His training helped him a great deal to keep the hardware store running, despite all the competition from the big chain stores. He not only proved to be a good and clever businessman but also served his community when he won the 1960 election as city councilman with an overwhelming majority of votes. He served for four years and was commended by the council for his unselfish service when he left that body in 1964.[29] The hardware store is still in the possession of the family, run by Bob's son Reed and his wife Beverly. Bob's second son Walter Richard studied law. When he received his degree from St. Mary's at San Antonio on 12 May 1984, another descendant of Julius Wagner had achieved what his forebear had failed in, closing the circle once again.

And yet, no one of the Wagners in Texas knew anything about their German ancestors. Prior to my first visit to Cuero in 1988, they had only heard the story that their forefather Julius had come from Germany as a lawyer, which was not even true. Significantly, nobody of this vast family ever did any research into their family's past. Wilhelm and his brother must have conveyed the feeling of guilt and shame about their German past to their children. This must have hindered the descendants of Julius Wagner from searching for their roots. It is of significance when Carl Friedrich's grandson Robert Harrison Wagner, professor at the University of Austin, wrote: "I have the feeling that the Wagners were for some reason not proud of their German heritage."[30] Not only did no member of this branch of the Julius Wagner descendants search for their German past, but they had not known that many cousins of theirs lived in the United States too until I told them in 1988. In contrast, Paul Guenzel from Chicago, grandson of Julius Wagner's daughter Paula Paepcke, tried to find his relatives in Texas and succeeded in establishing contact with Wilhelm Wagner's daughter Juanita Sophie Dahme. This marks the difference between the various Wagner family branches. It is the difference between acculturation and assimilation.

The immigrant Wilhelm Wagner as well as Hermann Paepcke did not simply merge into a dominant Anglo-American society and receive a new identity, as the adherents of the melting pot theory would say. The Illinois branch of the Wagners as well as the Paepcke line, on the one hand, accepted their new home land and established themselves in a mostly Anglo-American society. On the other hand, they also contributed their social and ethnic background into this new society, thus changing it too. People with a German background or ethnic specification are often described with the terms: "hard-working" and "family-oriented." These are typical cliches about Germany and the Germans. These cliches still prevail among Americans when thinking about their different ethnic neighbors. Questioned about stereotypes that still exist, Americans tend to identify German-Americans as "hard-working," "drinking beer and eating fat food," "family oriented," "too serious," and even "very dour and sober." It is interesting to notice though that on closer examination most ethnic groups, like the Irish, the French, the Italians, and the Poles, label themselves as "hard-working" and "family oriented." Sociologists ascribe this form of labeling to the middle class which wants to see itself as hard-working and family oriented.[31] Both the Illinois Wagners as well as the Paepckes belonged to the middle class. An important element they brought to American society was their strong attachment to high German culture as well as the emphasis they put on education. Walter Paepcke can be seen as the most extreme example of blending German humanism and culture with Anglo-American culture. In this process of exchanging values and belief systems, these Wagners and Paepckes were part of an acculturation process, of an exchange in a multicultural society.

The history of the Wagners in Texas followed a different pattern. William Wagner as well as his brother Carl Friedrich grew up among Germans in Texas. Having experienced their German past and especially their father's behavior during the Civil War as shameful, they tried to merge into the dominant Anglo-American society and raise their children as Americans and not German-Americans. They blended in. They did not forget their past—although they did not tell their children much about it—but they did not share special German customs with their American-born neighbors. They actually contributed nothing German to American society. With their generation the assimilation process was complete. This comparison of family lines demonstrates that assimilation and acculturation are not contradictory or exclusive terms. They rather describe two ways of integrating. These examples, therefore, also show that we cannot look at American society and ask if it is a dominant one which forced the immigrant to assimilate or if it is a multicultural one which allowed acculturation. Various studies show that for one thing this was a question of how and where the immigrant settled down and how he and/or she wanted to merge in or share.[32]

The immigration history of the United States is one of both assimilation and acculturation. The history of the Wagner family also demonstrates that these different processes were not confined to the generation of the immigrants but were a development which took place over more than one generation. Here, Emma Gund Wagner, Walter Paepcke, and the Wagner brothers in Texas, William and Carl Friedrich, are specific persons in whom the transformation process is clearly visible. As I have described, the change from Germans to German-Americans and then to Americans for many was also sped up by the two World Wars. Due to the horrors of two devastating wars started by the two German Reichs, the positive consciousness of being German vanished. This also happened in the Wagner families in Texas and Illinois. During World War I, the parent generation of the Wagners ceased to speak German with their children and the children's generation of that time was the first Wagner generation unable to speak, read, and write German. Their parents had not wanted them to grow up with the stigma of still being German-Americans.[33] This specific situation made the German immigrants different from other immigrant groups as it gave their assimilation and acculturation process a special drive. Thus, apart from the assimilation and acculturation process, the second generation of Wagners born in the United States grew up to be real and only Americans.

Conclusion: Reflections on Immigration

ALL THAT HAS BEEN SAID so far should not conceal that not everyone who came to the United States wanted to stay permanently. Julius Wagner's granddaughter Sophie returned to Germany with her husband Alexander Pflüger. And not all of those immigrants who came to stay forever in order to begin a new life succeeded. They either failed to get a firm footing, failed in trying to lead a decent life, or failed in their efforts to make a good living for themselves and for their children. And then there were those who faced failure and returned home to Europe.[1] America had not fulfilled their hopes and dreams.

What made America so special? What made the United States the embodiment of hope? In 1883 Emma Lazarus wrote a poem: "The New Colossus," which rose to a very special prominence when it was inscribed in the base of one of the world's most famous statues, the Statue of Liberty. The best known lines are: "Give me your tired, your poor, your huddled masses yearning to breathe free, the wretched refuse of your teeming shore. Send these, the homeless, tempest-tost to me, I lift my lamp beside the golden door!"[2] Of course not only the poor, the wretched and the huddled masses came to the United States. The emphasis of this poem lies in the line: "I lift my lamp beside the golden door!" Behind this golden door, the immigrants, whether well-off or poor, expected a more prosperous life and freedom. The hope of the immigrants and the claim of the United States to give them a better future made this country the embodiment of an immigrant nation. It is not and was not the only one, but the most prominent. This claim was the reason Wilhelm Wagner emigrated to the United States.

And yet, not everyone who was dissatisfied with his or her life in the Old World emigrated to the United States. It is a well-known story how the first prominent German settler in Texas, Fritz Ernst, tried to persuade his friend Schwarz from Oldenburg to follow him to America.[3] Their social backgrounds, families, and their lives prior to 1831 are quite parallel. Although Fritz urged his friend to come over and join him in Texas, Schwarz never emigrated. Why? Talk about emigrating to the United States ran high in the Wagner family since the revolution in 1848-49. Julius' and Wilhelm's brother-in-law Carl Baumann thought about emigration as did old Peter Wagner and his wife. Times did not get worse for them but also not better. Yet, they never followed the example of the two Wagner brothers. One could argue that first the push-factor (when times got tough politically) and later the pull-factor (when Wilhelm urged his family to join him) just were not as strong with the rest of the Wagner family as they had been for the two emigrants. Still, others followed the example as we have heard—like Eduard Froböse having been lured to Texas by the stories of Georg Witting. The examples would be numerous and impossible to list here. Mary Paik in her autobiography: *Quiet Odyssey: A Pioneer Korean Woman in America* writes about her emigration from Korea in 1905 because of fear of the Japanese forces about to occupy her home country: "Many of our friends and neighbors came with us. Mother said that God must surely have been guiding us in the right direction."[4] She wrote that many of their friends and neighbors emigrated, but not all, although every one of them was in that same situation. This is the most important point, as it clearly shows that even in the same political, social, or economic situation, only some people take the step to leave everything behind in order to emigrate. It is the oldest and probably the most difficult question asked in the historiography of emigration: Why did people actually migrate? Why was it only Fritz Ernst, the von Roeders, Wilhelm and Julius Wagner and not the rest of their families and friends?

An answer might be found in the psychological structures of the immigrants. Psychological approaches to explain emigration have not been chosen too often, largely because of the still existing general distrust of mainstream historians towards psychology and their usual argument that we simply don't know enough about the persons or groups under discussion in order to come to a valid psychological assessment. This holds true for many cases, surely, but it does not exempt us from the duty to at least try to use every tool possible in order to find answers to the questions we pose. The historian Gert Raeithel has come up with an interesting interpretation based on the works of the psychoanalyst Michael Balint (1876-1970) who had already emphasized in 1935 that more attention should be given to the object-relationships of the individual. Object here refers to persons as well as things. There are personalities who are stronger and those who are weaker object-related. Raeithel argues that the predominant personality type of the immigrant was the weak object-related one. Being less bound to cling to persons, objects, or geographical surroundings, the emigrant found it easier to let go and move away, Raeithel says. This makes him conclude that the combination of this psychologal pattern and the sociocultural environment of the United States created a specific North American character with one predominant feature: a weak object-relationship.[5]

However brave the attempt may be to analyse all immigrants psychoanalytically, the question remains if this is possible at all—not to mention in what way the millions of family members who often had no choice but to follow fit into this weak object-relation pattern. To use psychoanalytical terms for describing migration motives is highly dangerous because of the small amount of detailed information we have about each one of those millions who came to America. It is doubtful, too, if psychoanalysis will get us far in terms of defining migration motivations anyway. Unlike a dream, emigration is a decisive act of a person in his or her environment. Migration always involves interpersonal behavior. Social psychologists have taken a look at motivations, emotions, and drives and have come up with various catagories as roots for social behavior, like biological needs, affiliation, dependency, sex, aggression, self-esteem, ego identity, and others.[6] No one will deny the existence of a personality, of a distinct biography which will generate a distinctive behavior in a specific situation. Many features of one person will affect his or her reactions in a definite situation. To act in a situation one finds unbearable and change this situation deliberately might well be based on a psychological disposition: the disposition to change things when one is not satisfied with them. How many people do we know who complain about their jobs, their marriages, their day-to-day lives? And how many of those find the strength to change what troubles them? There are not many.

If such a disposition really exists, if it is a psychological drive to act in times of personal dissatisfaction, then those who took their fates into their own hands and emigrated drained Europe of people with the ability to change a situation. What remained were those who could be pushed around and fall prey to demagogues and dictators. Therefore, without the United

States, World War I and World War II might not have happened. As oversimplifying such an approach might sound—with Europe's overpopulation during the nineteenh century, the question remains where all those people would have stayed if they had not migrated—historians have concurred that Europe had become too weak and exhausted to prevent these disastrous wars: "The Europe of old had lost its power and will to establish peace in its own system of states. Its self-laceration led to self-inflicted powerlessness."[7] According to the historian John Lukacs, even Winston Churchill believed that a strong union between Great Britain and the United States would have prevented the First and the Second World Wars.[8] These historians of course refer to political powers and not directly to national or even psychological characteristics. Political powers, however, grow on the abilities and characteristics of their peoples. In a democracy, the people with all their various beliefs and wishes elect a government according to a system of values that has developed out of their past, their beliefs, and their national characteristics. The government and representatives of this democracy thus represent this nation not only in a political sense; they also represent various national characteristics according to the prevailing spirit of the age. Visitors to the United States during the last century have often dwelt upon these national characteristics in the books they published later. The French lawyer and historian Alexis de Tocqueville for instance noticed in *Democracy in America*, that Americans were independent, free individuals and their equality had grown naturally, unlike in France where it had to be postulated by slogans and fought for. Such a democracy as grew in France could never produce independent individuals as the United States, whose citizens see any form of government as a potential threat to their liberties. This individual independence had also been noticed by the German Ernst Hohenwart who published his *Land und Leute in den Vereinigten Staaten* in 1886. He testifies, too, that this American individualism made the citizens of the United States independent and practical human beings, always ready for a change. The Wagner family showed this readiness from early times onwards when the grandfather of the immigrants, Christoph Wagner, moved from Thüringen to the Palatinate. This readiness to change their lives when it seemed appropriate and necessary had brought the immigrants to the United States in the first place, and it did not stop once they had arrived at the shores of the New World. The history of the overland migration and the settlement of the trans-Mississippi West between 1840 and 1860 is one dramatic example how that spirit lived on.[9] Its dramatic nature was greatly responsible for the creation of the western myth. In the same way, the belief that one can change a situation by moving to another place has become a myth which found its way into the arts, too.

From Herman Melville's *Moby Dick; or, The Whale* (1851), to Mark Twain's *The Adventures of Huckleberry Finn* (1884), and to Thornton Wilder's *Theophilus North* (1973), American authors have molded their key figures according to the American ideal, placing them in contrast and sometimes even in antagonism to American reality. John Steinbeck's *The Grapes of Wrath* (1939) harshly criticises the then prevailing economic conditions, but also endows the mother with so much energy and optimism, that this novel emphazises the will and ability to change things for the better. This becomes even more evident in the last lines spoken in the film version. Screenwriter Nunnally Johnson summed up the essence of the novel in a sentence he wrote for Ma Joad, played by Jane Darwell: "Rich fellows come up and they die; and their kids ain't no good and they die out; but we keep on coming. We are the people that live. They cannot wipe us out, they cannot lick us. We'll go on forever Pa, 'cause we're the people."

For those who grasped at the chance that was presented to them in the form of a country obviously waiting for them, the golden door became the symbol of hope. The golden door actually grew into a myth like the west and the frontier.[10] All those who immigrated to the United States had this dream of a better life, a life in freedom and prosperity, just as Wilhelm Wagner had described it in his letters. People would not come if this dream would not exist anymore. They do not come mainly from Europe today but from Asia and South America. With their arrival they continue to establish firmly the definition of the United States as an immigrant country. This is the official position of the government, too. In April 1997 Rosemary Jenks, Senior Fellow at the Center for Immigration Studies wrote in regards to the new immigration laws: "Immigrants who come to the United States legally and abide by U.S. laws will continue to be welcomed."[11] The American ideal, the myth of the immigrants constituting the melting pot, only holds good for about eighty-seven percent of the United States population, though. For a special group, the golden door must have seemed a mockery rather than an invitation: African Americans. The vast majority of the nearly thirteen percent of all United States citizens who are African Americans today are descendants of people who did not deliberately choose America as their new homeland. They were brought over to the New World by force and had to live as slaves.

A lot has changed since then and a black middle class has emerged. In Atlanta, Georgia, for instance, more than forty-five percent of all blacks belong to the middle class today. Still, quite a number of those who "made it," like the architect Max Bond from New York, believe that "many of the creative professions in America remain bastions of rascism."[12] The question is still whether they share in the American dream or not. For centuries they were only exploited and hardly had a chance to make a decent living on their own. How could they have harbored the same dreams and hopes as the immigrants? Obviously they did not come with these hopes, but they developed them over the centuries. As Dr. Martin Luther King said in his famous speech: "I have a dream that one day on the red hills of Georgia the sons of former slaves and the sons of former slaveowners will be able to sit down together at the table of brotherhood. . . . When we let freedom ring, when we let it ring from every village and every hamlet, from every state and every city, we will be able to speed up that day when all of God's children, black men and white men, Jews and Gentiles, Protestants and Catholics, will be able to join hands and sing in the words of the old Negro spiritual, 'Free at last! Free at Last! Thank God almighty, we are free at last!'"[13] With this speech, King transformed the descendants of former slaves into black immigrants, into just the same people who had arrived at Castle Garden and later at Ellis Island. With his words he also went farther than the founding fathers. Their belief system had established the white Anglo-Saxon Protestants as the dominant class of the United States. King said that there is no dominant class, that all men are equal.

As the founding fathers had not really meant all people to be equal, the golden door was not equally open for everybody all the time. Laws always restricted immigration. Forces trying to control immigration by keeping various groups out of the United States have been strong thoughout the centuries. From the Know-Nothing party (founded in 1854) to the racist forty-two volumes of the Dillingham report in 1911 which explained why immigrants from north and western Europe were superior to any others, the arguments of those who saw themselves as guardians of the American nation were based on two notions: labor and intolerance. With industrialization and the expanding economy during the second half of the nineteenth century, a cheap labor force was in high demand. Concentrating around the cities of the east and northeast, this urban economy needed large quantities of manual labor, and the millions of mostly unskilled workers from eastern and southern Europe filled this demand. The wage-conscious organized labor force, as well as the middle-class lobby, thus fought to minimize the flow of unskilled workers to protect and even increase wages.[14] During the first half of the twentieth century, another group of immigrants slowly but steadily took the place of the former immigrants from eastern and southern Europe. This group today comprises the second largest minority group in the United States: the Latino population.

Whereas 4,401,466 immigrants from Mexico, the West Indies, Central, and South America came to the United States between 1820 and 1940, there were 10,663,435 between 1941 and 1993. One can expect that the Latinos will grow to become the largest ethnical group by far between 2010 and 2045.[15] Besides the question of ethnicity, what does this change in immigration patterns mean? What does it mean, when the majority of immigrants does not come from Europe anymore but from Asia and, even more important, from Central and South America? One of the major issues is—as it was in the past—the labor market. Many fear the competition of skilled and unskilled workers just as they did a hundred years ago. At that time, workers, unskilled or skilled, were in high demand because the United States experienced an economic boom that lasted until the end of the 1920s. Industry grew rapidly, and work was available for most who sought it. The situation is different today. As we face another industrial revolution with the expansion of the computer market, the computer applications and computer controlled automatic production, the job market shrinks in general but most for unskilled workers.[16] As one result, black leaders and the African-American press have aimed some of their harshest criticism against Asian and Mexican immigrants. In a bitter irony of history, one minority lashes out against another for fear of displacement on the job market. This point of view is not a recent one though. Black leaders and journalists have always emphasized the opinion since the Civil War that black workers were only too readily displaced by immigrants, which makes it very difficult for blacks to rise from poverty. With Dr. Martin Luther King and his humanistic appeals, a certain change set in with many blacks. *A New York Times*/CBS poll from 1986 indicates interestingly enough that more blacks than whites are sympathetic to immigrants in general. It is a common fact that acceptance of immigration and immigrants tends to rise the higher the income and education of the questioned are. Yet, more blacks than whites believed that immigrants contribute to the United States and new immigrants would be welcomed in their specific neighborhoods.[17] This perhaps irrational and emotional attitude actually is supported by demographic data and analyses done by sociologists and historians. Based on the 1980 census, for instance, figures show clearly that in areas of a high immigrant concentration neither the wages nor the annual employment levels of native-born workers have decreased. This pattern did not change even in areas with a high percentage of unskilled legal or illegal immigrants. (More illegal immigrants belong to the unskilled work force than legal ones who tend to be professionals.) On the contrary, the various studies show that immigrant workers tend to have the effect of a rise in male wages and the creation of new jobs. At the same time, these studies emphasized that immigrant families are less likely to receive public assistance than comparative natives, another prejudice often heard. Most illegal immigrants are simply looking for work and do not come to receive a welfare check.[18]

The old argument that immigrants are dangerous competition for the American citizen on the job market does not live up to the facts. And yet, it is used repeatedly by conservative politicians trying to profit from prejudices. In 1995, Republican Representative Lamar Smith from Texas introduced bill number HR2202 which he called his immigration reform to curb legal and illegal immigration and to preserve jobs for American citizens. During the presidential election campaign in 1996, the Republican Pat Buchanan vowed to stop illegal immigration by building a fence along the Mexican border and declared he would initiate a moratorium on most legal immigration if elected president.[19]

With the labor market getting tighter and tighter and an increasing fight about labor distribution on the one hand and the prospect of a growing number of Asian and Latino citizens (estimates give a number for the Asian and Hispanic population of sixteen percent in the year 2020) changing the demographic picture of the United States on the other, it is easy to arouse fear among those United States citizens who are afraid of losing influence and status. All this generalizing, of course, holds the danger of oversimplifying. Much tension has arisen in those states of the United States that have to face the highest proportion of immigrants from Central and South America. And the population figures of 38.2 percent Latinos in New Mexico, 25.8 percent in California, 25.5 percent in Texas and 18.8 percent in Arizona do not include the illegal ones. In recent years, a development has set in that changes the old, known pattern of large Latino groups in the Southern States. Between 1980 and 1992, the Midwest States have seen a 45.5 percent increase in their Hispanic population. In consideration of the arguments about the job market, and the attitudes of blacks towards their Hispanic "competitors," it is interesting to note that the jobless rate of Midwestern Hispanics in 1992 ranged between that of white, non-Hispanics and blacks, with eleven percent jobless in contrast to five percent whites and nineteen percent blacks unemployed in that region. Their income was also higher in the Midwest, in general, than that of the black population.[20] This shows that the fears of many in the black community are not completely unfounded, although one has to be careful with quick generalizations. Acceptance of immigrants also is a twofold issue as not only the other, dominant groups in the United States have to develop more tolerance towards different ethnicities and a greater sense of sharing, but these immigrants have to show their willingness to share, too. One clear sign from the immigrant of wanting to contribute to American society is the application for United States citizenship. In 1988, 211,941 immigrants came from Latin America and the Caribbean, yet only 54,960 Latinos were granted American citizenship. Although rising, this figure is still rather low. For many, language is a problem, as—like in ancient Rome—a prospective citizen has to pass a language test.[21] This is only part of the problem though. The main question is whether the United States want to accept such a growing number of immigrants and prospective citizens from countries other than Europe.

Working on the reform of the McCarran-Walter Immigration and Nationality Act of 1952, young Senator John F. Kennedy began writing his little book *A Nation of Immigrants*. Probably because of his family's background, immigration was of immediate concern to him. In his book he summed up the essence of immigration:

> As we have seen, people migrated to the United States for a variety of reasons. But nearly all shared two great hopes: the hope for personal freedom and the hope for economic opportunity. In consequence, the impact of immigration has been broadly to confirm the impulses in American life demanding more political liberty and more economic growth. . . .Every ethnic minority, in seeking its own freedom, helped strengthen the fabric of liberty in American life. Similarly, every aspect of the American economy has profited from the contributions of immigrants.[22]

In his American University speech on 9 September 1997, President Bill Clinton not only evoked the Kennedy spirit, who had spoken there thirty-four years before, but also addressed the question of immigration in a multicultural society:

> In this century, we have absorbed wave after wave of immigrants, drawn here by our abundance and our ideals. This century has seen unparalleled racial progress as African Americans and other minorities join the American mainstream. . . . The age-old dilemma of racial inequality, racial prejudice, or just plain old fear and mistrust of people who are different from us is compounded by the new task of absorbing new immigrant groups into what is already the world's most diverse democracy. Within a decade our largest state, California, will have no majority race. Within just a few decades this entire country will have no majority race.[23]

At that time and place, Clinton did not want to say more about immigration. In his book Kennedy listed many names of industrialists, scientists, and inventors who had come as immigrants and have contributed enormously to America's growth. He also mentions that twenty-three percent of all painters, forty-six percent of all musicians and sixty-one percent of all actors in the eighteenth and nineteenth century had been immigrants. Interestingly enough, those artists came from Europe where the various cultural achievements had accumulated to specific signs of recognition for the power elite. Culture in Europe had become an expression of a hierarchy in power. In contrast to this, culture in America was obliged to popular sovereignty, establishing a different form of culture: popular culture. Movies and television are the most significant results of the creation of this popular culture. The market predominance of U.S. television shows and U.S. movies around the globe is definite proof for the consolidation of republican spirit mixed with a general distrust towards an implemented, bureaucratic central power. This is also evident in the dominance of U.S. movies on the world market which is due not so much because of an economic superiority but because of the narrative style of the so-called "Hollywood" movie. Deriving from popular entertainment, it is the classical representative of popular culture today—in contrast to many European movies and moviemakers who stand in the tradition of European culture, which was much more elitist. In consequence, European movies in the tradition of European culture and art are more epic and more dialog-orientated than American ones. Therefore, movies are not only America's foremost contribution to the world of arts in the twentieth century; the moving image has become the artistic expression of and for the twentieth century. Popular culture, as expression of a republican society, becomes visible also in one of America's most popular entertainment resorts: Disney World at Orlando, Florida. The EPCOT Center, which opened in 1982 as a new attraction in the form of a permanent world exibition, additionally pays tribute to one of the pillars of American society: to immigration. With the various "villages" from around the globe, Disney erected a monument for the many cultures, from which the immigrants came. At the same time, the EPCOT Center shows the danger of a one-sided presentation of history due to an uncritical market strategy.[24]

This was a rather late tribute though, considering that Walt Disney began with his parks in 1955 when he opened Disneyland at Anaheim, California. At that time, EPCOT was just a dream, and the first Disney park was divided into four catagories: Fantasyland, Adventureland, Frontierland, and Tomorrowland. These themes actually were chosen after the ones Disney used for his premiere television series: *Disneyland* from 1954 and which represented four familiar movie genres at the same time. In

Fantasyland he presented his cartoons and, in Frontierland, westerns. With the latter, he had choosen a genre that can be called the richest and longest lasting of Hollwood's repertoire. The first commercial narrative movie in history was a western: *The Great Train Robbery* by Edwin S. Porter from 1903. It is no coincidence that movies, and with them especially the genre of the western, emerged at a time when the frontier had been declared extinct by the Bureau of the Census only a few years earlier. The myth of the frontier was perpetuated by shows like Buffalo Bill's Wild West Show, and these shows, in return, were the first subjects of the film production, Thomas Alva Edison began in 1894. One of the first major successes for Disney's TV production was the three one-hour-long episodes of *Davy Crockett,* combining all this: western, frontier and myth. The western was instrumental in carrying the message of social Darwinism where the best man wins. Herbert Spencer's theories about social Darwinism found much greater acceptance in the United States than in their country of origin, England. And the western was essential in perpetuating the myth of the frontier. Immigrants have always been part of this myth. From the beginnning of the western, their stories and their characters have been connected with this film genre. James Cruze's *The Covered Wagon* (1923), Victor Seastrom's *The Wind* (1928), Joshua Logan's western musical *Paint Your Wagon* (1969), and Michael Cimino's *Heaven's Gate* (1980), are just a few examples of movies containing the combination of immigrants and myth of the frontier. The function of the western to transport the myth of the West is best and unforgettably expressed in the few sentences of a newspaperman in John Ford's, *The Man Who Shot Liberty Valance* (1961): "This is the West, Sir. When the legend becomes fact, print the legend."[25]

With the frontier gone, the United States began looking for a new self-definition. With an economy not growing as fast anymore, and the old definitions having become mostly invalid, many Americans see the United States in a deep crisis. This actually derives from a misunderstanding. It is a misunderstanding of what the frontier was and meant. Frederick Jackson Turner and the discussions about his thesis were mistaken by many in following the Bureau of the Census and its interpretation of the frontier as a geographic phenomenon. In fact—as William H. Goetzmann indicates in his book *Exploration and Empire*—the West and the frontier were not the cause for the development of American society but rather a stage on which the patterns of American society and culture developed. The frontier was the visible symptom of something that took place within the people. It was the strength within the settlers who tried to turn the American dream into reality. These people who pushed forward on the frontier had the strength to change their lives. They let go of their past and moved on because the frontier was within them. That means, also, that it was completely unimportant actually if someone lived on the frontier geographically or in the cities. The spirit was essential. The geographical line was just a visible expression of that spirit, like the western in the twentieth century. It is not the land that makes up the essence of the frontier: the frontier was and is within the people. Hermann Paepcke is a good example of the spirit of the inner frontier. First he moved to the geographical frontier and tried to establish himself as a businessman there. When he had the impression that he would not succeed there as much as he wanted, he moved to Chicago. Geographically he left the frontier, but the spirit was much alive in him and helped him to become a most successful businessman.

Reaching for an outer frontier, like space, is the feeble attempt to carry on in the old spirit that frontier has to be measured in geographical miles. Many have labeled space the last frontier. This would only be correct if the basic meaning of frontier is a geographical one. As the frontier is within the people, one has to look somewhere else. This basic spirit of the immigrants, their strength to rid themselves from unbearable situations is the strength the American people still possess today. It is the great potential they still have as long as they adhere to the principles of the founding fathers of freedom and liberty for all and to the spirit of tolerance evoked by Martin Luther King. It is the spirit of the inner frontier, the will to change what is bad, to strive for the better. This is the spirit Wilhelm Wagner showed when he came to the United States with the hope to live in a land "where the father of a family can think without anxiety on the future of his children."

However, for many this seems to be at risk. With the third industrial revolution brought about by the computer, not only blue-collar but also white-collar workers face what Louis Uchitelle and N.R. Kleinfield have called "the most acute job insecurity since the Depression of the 1930s." This spirit of general uncertainty and helplessness which began to grow among the middle-class since the beginning of the 1990s and is not confined to the working class or the poor any more is reflected in popular culture too. The title of the CD that rock musician Bruce Springsteen produced in 1995, is revealing in many ways: *The Ghost of Tom Joad*. Using the name of Steinbeck's main character from *The Grapes of Wrath*, Springsteen wrote a line: "Families sleepin' in their cars in the Southwest; No home no job no peace no rest."[26] With this song, the artist drew a parallel with the Great Depression of the 1930s. One of the differences to the thirties is, though, that since the Second World War, work in itself has become the most important criterion for the middle-class in judging and evaluating a person in the United States. This has always been a special trait in the Calvinistic American character.[27] The more you earn the better a person you are. The dangers of this attitude become evident now for more and more people who realize that they have not changed along with the labor market.

Better living conditions in terms of higher earnings in a way have always been a driving motive for many immigrants too, but, at the same time this has always been connected with the desire to live in a democracy like the United States. This was the dream of the immigrant: to have a good, decent life and to see that the next generation might have it even better. The Wagners, like most immigrants, saw their only chance in fulfilling this dream in guaranteeing their children a good education. They had had a good education themselves. They did not have to leave Europe for economic reasons as both brothers could have made a living in Germany. Yet, they did not see a future in staying in Europe. Julius Wagner and his friends saw the United States as a place where they did not only have an economical future but also a political one, where they could live their political vision. They belonged to those who even idealized the United States disproportionately as a place where they could find a better place to live. When they were faced with the hardships of the frontier their vision of a socialist society on American soil crumbled. They realized that the education they had received in Germany was of no use on the frontier. And although a few of them returned to their homeland, most of them stayed. Despite the trouble they might have had in the beginning to establish themselves on the frontier, the spirit of the inner frontier, the spirit that made them change their lives, was stronger than their homesickness. That does not mean that they gave up their political opinions altogether. During the

Civil War a considerable number of Germans —among them Julius Wagner—chose sides with the Union and went into exile. Wilhelm Wagner on the other hand had no utopian dream. Still, he too faced the hardships of the frontier. He knew though that there was no way back to Germany for him. Both Wagner brothers preserved German customs. Their English was poor and their lives on the frontier far from easy. They were typical examples of the first generation of immigrants. This already changed with their children. As well educated immigrants the Wagners nevertheless conveyed their beliefs to their children. These convictions included the faith in family ties, the faith in the democratic political system of the United States, the faith in one's own strength and the faith in a good education. With these convictions, the challenges of the frontier could be met. The first generation of the Wagners as well as Hermann Paepcke did not realize that they were able to endure the hardships of the geographical frontier only because the spirit of the inner frontier was alive in them.

The challenges of the inner frontier can only be met with a sound education. The citizens and the government (be it local or national) have to decide what they want to spend their money on and what is best for the future of the United States. In contrast to many other projects, money spent for education is never lost but will bear fruit. All of this is not easy to achieve, however. Especially in large cities one might question the validity of these statements. A student in Philadelphia in 1994 summed up all the doubts: "One society? No. We are white, black, rich, poor, each turning away in muted ignorance and contempt from those below us. Tolerance? Never . . . The American dream? Get real."[28] And yet, the teacher of this class, Michael Zuckerman, encountered a form of optimism and hope that brought him to believe that even the kids in the streets of our cities today not only see the problems which seem to be so overwhelming sometimes but face them with a willingness to cope with the challenges of our times. They seem to understand and face the inner frontier. As long as the people of the United States commit themselves to uphold this inner frontier, to meet the daily challenge of the pledges of the founding fathers, to keep the golden door open, this nation will be special and be home for more unsung heroes to come, as it had been for the Wagners in the nineteenth century.

Appendix A
Family Tree of Wilhelm Wagner

∞ = married * = born † = died

Wilhelm Wagner, 1803–1877
∞ Friederike Odenwald, 1812–1893
1. Karl, 1837–1838
2. Karl, 1839–1899
  ∞ 1.: Minnie, 1842–
    2.1. Henry, 1863–
    2.2. Charles, 1865–
    2.3. Lothe, 1868–
    2.4. Caroline, 1870–
    2.5. Matilde, 1873–
  ∞ 2.: Mathilde, 1854–
    2.6. Emma, 1878–
    2.7. Fredrick, 1880–
3. Luise, * + † 1840
4. Wilhelm, 1841–1910
  ∞ Wilhelmina Seyfarth, 1840–1922
    4.1. Albert F., 1861–1933
      ∞ Julia Junkunz, 1862–1932
        4.1.1.Aline
          ∞ Dudley Graw
            4.1.1.1. Marion
          ∞ Mr. Hannon
            4.1.1.2. Robert
        4.1.2. Louis, 1900–1911
    4.2. Otto, 1863–1934
      ∞ Mary Walz, 1863–1952
        4.2.1. Karl E.
          ∞ Ruby Walton
            4.2.1.1. John T.
        4.2.2. Margaret L., 1899–1990
    4.3. Herman, 1865–1935
      ∞ Lilly Kupper, 1867–1935
        4.3.1. Wilhelmina M., 1900–1993
          ∞ J. Stanley Dunlop, 1897–1959
            4.3.1.1. Stuart, * 1925
              ∞ Joan Dixon, * 1929
                4.3.1.1.1. Wilhelmina J., * 1951
                  ∞ Michael B. Healy
                4.3.1.1.2. Douglas D., * 1953
                  ∞ Janet
                4.3.1.1.3. Julia J., * 1956
                  ∞ Steve Weldon
                4.3.1.1.4. Victoria L., * 1958

4.3.1.2. Richard, *1929
∞ Florence Rice, * 1927
4.3.1.2.1. Bruce C., * 1951
∞ (1.) Laura (divorced)
∞ (2.) ?
4.3.1.2.2. Carole A., * 1952
∞ Michael Thomas, ?–1970
4.3.1.2.2.1. Adam M., 1970
4.3.1.2.3. Nancy L., *+† 1955
4.3.1.2.4. Susan L., * 1956
4.3.1.2.5. James C., 195?
4.4. Paul, 1867–1910
∞ Kate Kraft, 1868–1924
4.5. Oscar, 1869–1929
∞ Mary McCall, 1886–1931
4.6. Frederic, 1871–1928
∞ Emma Gund, 1873–1961
4.6.1.Elsa, 1900–1994
∞ Ray Nugent (were divorced around 1955)
4.6.1.1. Frederic T., * 1929
∞ 1.: Anne E. Madison
∞ 2.: Donna Van Wingeren
4.6.1.1.1. Margaret, * 1956
4.6.1.1.2. Thomas W., * 1958
4.6.1.1.3. Leslie A., * 1962
4.6.1.2. Thomas G., 1932–1986
∞ Harriet
4.6.1.2.1. Theodore
4.6.2. Paul, 1904–1975
∞ Margaret May, 1907–1997
4.6.2.1. Frederic N., * 1933
∞ Marline Lincoln
4.6.2.1.1. James
∞ Dana Leigh Martinez, *1971
4.6.2.1.2. Paul
4.6.2.2. Mark W., * 1937
∞ Susan Schneider, * 1939
4.6.2.2.1. William M., * 1963
∞ Elisabeth J. Bishop, *1957
4.6.2.2.1.1. William B., *1996
4.6.2.2.1.2. Margeurite T., *1999
4.6.2.2.2. Martha M., * 1964
∞ Petrit Alibali
4.6.2.2.3. Eric P., * 1966
∞ Eileen Renee Engel, *1970
4.6.2.2.3.1. Elise R., *1998
4.6.2.2.3.2. Charles E., *2000
4.6.2.2.4. Matthew M., * 1969
∞ Lisa Ann Kruto, *1967
4.6.2.2.34.1. Luke J., *2000

4.6.2.2.5. Amy A., * 1970
∞ Michael C. Makris, * 1953
4.6.2.2.5.1. Cassidy H., *1997
4.6.2.2.5.2. Courtney S., *1999
4.6.2.2.6. Molly M., *1972
4.6.2.2.7. Susan M., * 1977
4.6.2.2.8. Rebecca N., * 1978
4.6.2.2.9. Kurt W., * 1980
4.6.2.2.10. Kathryn R., * 1981
4.6.2.2.11. Claire A., 1983
4.7. William
∞ Jessie Wirts
4.7.1. Martin
5. Luise, 1843–1919
∞ Carl F. Kleinpell, 1838–1888
5.1. Carl, 1861–1890
∞ Henriette Schroeder, 1865–1904
5.1.1. Karl, 1887–1916
∞ Viola Behlmer, ?–1910
5.1.2. Arthur, 1889–1981
∞ Helen Davenport, 1897–1987
5.1.2.1. Peter, * 1927
∞ 1.: Joan Mitchell
5.1.2.1.1. Arthur II, * 1954
∞ Susan Stoner
5.1.2.1.1.1. Mary E., * 1980
5.1.2.1.1.2. Arthur III, * 1984
5.1.2.1.2. Katy, * 1957
∞ Mark B. Bollman III.
5.1.2.1.2.1. Laura, * 1983
5.1.2.1.2.2. Mark B. IV., * 1987
5.1.2.1.3. Virginia, * 1960
∞ John Sullivan
5.1.2.1.3.1. Sam M., * 1991
5.1.2.1.4. Peter D. , * 1967
∞ 2.: Nancy Pridmore
5.1.2.2. Henriette L, * 1933
∞ James G. Randolph
5.1.2.2.1. James E., * 1959
5.1.2.2.2. Charles F., * 1960
5.1.2.2.3. Glen T., * 1962
5.1.2.2.4. Marilyn H. , * 1968
∞ Frank Tobin
5.2. Julius, 1862–1954
5.3. William, 1864–1942
∞ (?)
5.3.1. Gela
5.3.2. Lulu
∞ Clarence Murphy

5.3.2.1. Lorna
5.3.2.2. Cathleen
5.3.2.3. Barbara (Moline)
5.4. Dr. Henry, 1869–1951
5.5. Walter, 1870–1915
∞ Carrie
5.5.1. Walter
∞ Gretchen
5.5.1.1. Julie
∞ Al Payleitner
5.5.2. Irma
∞ Dr. Clayton Townsend
5.5.2.1. Carol
5.5.2.2. daughter (?)
5.6. Frieda, 1872–1946
5.7. Reinhard, 1873–1932
∞ Grace
6. Hermann Ludwig, 1845–1902
∞ Maria M. Waldecker, 1845–1934
6.1. Wilhelm F., 1868–1926
∞ Christina Thoensen, 1869–1953
6.1.1. Arthur, 1893–1969
∞ Madge Curtis, 1895–1987
6.1.1.1. Curtis A., * 1922
∞ Margie Del Neal
6.1.1.1.1. (child)
6.1.1.1.2. (child)
6.1.1.1.3. (child)
6.1.1.1.4. (child)
6.1.1.2. Marjorie, * 1936
∞ David Irwin, * 1935
6.1.1.2.1. (child)
6.1.1.2.2. (child)
6.1.2. Karl H., 1897–1978
∞ Edith L. Cameron, * 1899
6.1.2.1. Edith L., * 1921
∞ Carl F. Meier, * 1919
6.1.2.1.1. Lorna C., * 1945
∞ Arlan K. Kay, * 1944
6.1.2.1.1.1. Heidi K., * 1967
∞ Daniel O. Amherdt
6.1.2.1.1.2. Erik A., * 1970
6.1.2.1.1.3. Kietra C., * 1973
6.1.2.1.2. Ellen B., * 1949
∞ 1.: James (?) †
∞ 2.: Stephen Nelmes
6.1.2.1.2.1. Andrew J., * 1981
6.1.2.1.2.2. Elizabeth C., *1989
6.1.2.1.3. Edith L., * 1951
∞ Pierce T. Marshall, * 1950

6.1.2.1.3.1. Travis F., * 1986
6.1.2.1.3.2. Christian C., *1993
6.1.2.1.4. Marian L., * 1953
∞ Wayne Kieffer, * 1946
6.1.2.1.4.1. Matthew C., * 1982
6.1.2.1.4.2. Alexandra L., * 1985
6.1.2.1.5. Carla J., * 1956
∞ H. Gaylon Barker, * 1954
6.1.2.2. Dr. Kenneth C., * 1922
∞ 1.: Grace Carson, * 1922
6.1.2.2.1. Judith J.
∞ Michael LaRue
6.1.2.2.1.1. Sara G.
6.1.2.2.2. Barbara C.,
∞ Marl Wulf
6.1.2.2.3. Merdeth L.
∞ Tracy Kuhn
∞ 2.: Rebecca McMichaels
6.1.2.3. Karl W., * 1926
∞ Thelma Smith, * 1927
6.1.2.3.1. Christine E.
6.1.2.3.2. Karl F.
6.1.2.4. Marian J., * 1931
∞ Charles D. Lindberg, * 1929
6.1.2.4.1.Christine M.
∞ John Molnar
6.1.2.4.2. John C.
∞ Susan E. Gordhammer
6.1.2.4.3. Breta H.
∞ Steve Magiera
6.1.2.4.4. Eric V.
6.1.2.5. Judith A., * 1937
∞ Armin Pavlovic, * 1935
6.1.2.5.1. Barbara Louise, * 1959
∞ Tom Wiedebeck, * 1958
6.1.2.5.1.1. Joy C., * 1981
6.1.2.5.1.2. Grace A., * 1984
6.1.2.5.1.3. Joshua J., * 1987
6.1.2.5.1.4. John T., * 1989
6.1.2.5.2. Jennifer Lynn, * 1969
∞ Jefrey Ambs
6.2 Ida T., 1870–1949
∞ Albert K. Fahrner, 1864–1950
6.3. Reinhart J., 1872–1945
∞ Josephine S. Stender, 1879–1959
6.3.1. Ernst H., 1906–1913
6.3.2. Julia J., 1913–1993
∞ Murrel E. Strickler, 1911–1995
6.3.2.1. Lietta M., * 1940
∞ Harold Milton, * 1937

6.3.2.1.1. Ami
6.3.2.1.2. Nathaniel
6.3.2.1.3. Neil
6.3.2.2. Jarold K., * 1943
∞ Phyllis
6.3.2.2.1. Virginia A., * 1982
6.3.2.2.2. Edward E., * 1984
6.3.2.2.3. Suzanne J., * 1987
6.3.2.3. Reinhard F., * 1945
∞ Elizabeth Anne, * 1949
6.3.2.4. Devra J., * 1947
∞ Doane Deems, * 1934
6.3.2.4.1. Derek
6.3.2.4.2. Darci
6.3.3. Ernestine M., 1915–1916
6.4. Julia, 1877–1879
7. Julius, 1848–?
∞ (?)
7.1. Julius A.
7.2. son
7.3. daughter
8. Friederike, 1851–?
∞ Carl Reineke
8.1. Mathilda
∞ Mr. Nessler
8.1.1. Elsa E.
∞ (?)
8.1.1.1. son
8.1.1.2. son
8.1.1.3. daughter
8.1.1.4. daughter
8.2 Charlie W.
8.3. Julius
9. Friedrich H., 1853–1927
∞ Emily Kupper, 1855–1948
9.1. Louis B., 1881–1951
∞ Ethellyn Ibberson, ?–1968
9.2. Archibald F., 1890–1969
∞ Dorothy Chadbourn, 1896–1981
9.2.1. Pamela A., * 1929
∞ John W. Ritter, Jr.
9.2.1.1. Carolyn C., * 1955
∞ Alan R. Butcher, * 1953 (div. 2000)
9.2.1.1.1. Laura Jean, * 1986
9.2.1.2. Patricia M., * 1957
∞ 1997 Glenn M. Schoolfield
9.2.1.3. Ellen M., * 1964
∞ Anson W. H. Taylor, III., *1961 (div. 1999)

Appendix B

Family Tree of Julius Wagner

∞ = married   * = born   † = died

- Julius Wagner, 1816–1903
  - ∞ Emilie M. Schneider, 1820–1896
    - 1. daughter, 1850
    - 2. Sigmund, 1851–1934
    - 3. Wilhelm, 1854–1926
      - ∞ Julie Schorre, 1861–1922
        - 3.1 Anna Julie, 1883–1977
        - 3.2 Emma Marie, 1884–1946
        - 3.3 Richard Julius, 1886–1939
          - ∞ Lena Kenyon
            - 3.3.1. Marian
        - 3.4 August Wilhelm, 1888–1978
          - ∞ Lucy Woods
            - 3.4.1. Ralph A., *1917
              - ∞ Margaret Ann Weiser, 1915–1990
                - 3.4.1.1. Margaret Frances, *1947
                - 3.4.1.2. Stephen Ralph, *1954
                  - ∞ Marsha Miller
                    - 3.4.1.2.1. Michael
                    - 3.4.1.2.2. Allison
            - 3.4.2. Ann Lucyle, 1919–1970
              - ∞ Julius J. Eccell, Sr. *1919
                - 3.4.2.1. Anne Marie, * 1951
                  - ∞ Mr. Saults (1.)
                  - ∞ Mr. (?) (2.)
                - 3.4.2.2. Julius J. , * 1957
                  - ∞ Cindy Deeds
                    - 3.4.2.2.1. Emily
                    - 3.4.2.2.2. Megan
            - 3.4.3. Michael W., * 1922
              - ∞ Evelyn Tabor
                - 3.4.3.1. Mark M. * 1954
                  - ∞ Deborah Padgett
            - 3.4.4. Mary, 1926–1983
              - ∞ James Little, *1924
                - 3.4.4.1. William Thomas, *1951
                  - ∞ Heidi F. Howell, ?–1994
                    - 3.4.4.1.1. Adrien
                    - 3.4.4.1.2. Mary
                - 3.4.4.2. Mary Lucyle, * 1952
                  - ∞ Gilbert Gonzales
                    - 3.4.4.2.1. Bryan
                - 3.4.4.3. Joseph, * 1955
                - 3.4.4.4. Mary Elizabeth, * 1959

3.5. Juanita Sophie, 1897–1993
∞ Leslie C. Dahme
4. Sophie, 1855–1936
5. Paula, 1857–1909
∞ Hermann L. Paepcke, 1850–1922
5.1. Sophie, 1879–1957
∞ Alexander W. Pflüger, 1869–1946
5.1.1. Marie Alice, 1902–1944
∞ Carl G. Siebel, 1903–1984
5.1.1.1. Carl Alexander, * 1935
∞ Carla–Margarethe Schiemann, * 1942
5.1.1.1.1. Karl A., * 1965
5.1.1.1.2. Andreas, * 1966
5.1.1.2. Walter G., * 1938
∞ Christa Rebell
5.1.2. Hertha, 1903–1985
∞ Karl Gelpcke, 1894–1941
5.1.2.1. Alice, * 1923
∞ Dr. Wolfgang Weber, 1923–1976
5.1.2.1.1. Klaus C., 1947–1978
5.1.2.1.2. Stefan, * 1954
5.1.2.2. Doris, * 14.7.1927, Bonn
∞ 1. Heinrich A. Flaig, * 1928 (div.)
5.1.2.2.1. Thomas A., * 1953
∞ ?
5.1.2.2.1.1. Lauren, * 1985
5.1.2.2.2. Ralph T., * 1957
∞ Sabine Schartmann
5.1.2.2.2.1. Maximilian, * 1993
∞ 2. Ronald Fairweather, 1912–1971
5.1.2.2.3. Lionel R. B., * 1964
∞ Cynthia Longo
5.1.2.3. Ingrid, * 1931
∞ Alan. Paterson, 1924–1989
5.1.2.3.1. Karl, * 1957
5.1.2.3.2. Alice, * 1958
∞ Peter Burgess, * 1953
5.1.2.3.2.1. Lindsay, * 1990
5.1.2.3.2.2. Hugh, * 1992
5.1.2.3.2.3. Keir, * 1994
5.1.2.3.3. Janet, * 1960
∞ David Maclean, * 1956
5.1.2.3.3.1. Guy, * 1988
5.1.2.3.3.2. Hannah, * 1989
5.1.2.3.3.3. Morwenna, * 1991
5.2. Lydia, 1881–1932
∞ William Wilms, 1868–1934
5.2.1. Hermann P., 1905–1976
∞ (1.) Ruth Spotswood White

∞ (2.) Vivian Kleman (no children)
5.2.1.1. Paula, * 1932
∞ Barr McCutcheon
5.2.1.1.1. Barr, III, * 1953
∞ (1.) Patricia Martin, (divorced 1982)
∞ (2.) Sue Griffith
5.2.1.1.1.1. Tara, * 1986
5.2.1.1.2. Lhotse P., 1954–1972
5.2.1.1.3. Paul Q., * 1955
∞ Margo Johnson
5.2.1.1.4. Marina C., * 1957
∞ David Cavalla
5.2.1.1.4.1. Alasdair S., * 1988
5.2.1.1.4.2. Anna M., * 1990
5.2.1.1.4.3. Evelyn P., * 1993
5.2.1.1.5. Ian A., * 1961
5.2.1.2. Hermann P. II., * 1934
∞ Barbara Godwin
5.2.1.2.1. Hermann P. III., * 1960
5.2.1.2.2. Allison G., * 1963
5.2.1.2.3. Erich G., * 1965
5.2.1.2.4. Grant G., * 1965
5.2.1.3. Welford W., *1939
∞ (1.) 1964 Barbara Clark (div.)
∞ (2.) 1982 Kirsten Falke (div., no children)
∞ (3.) 1988 Bridget Brewer (div., no children)
5.2.1.3.1. William, * 1967
∞ Yo Akino
5.2.1.3.1.1. Hana, * 1987
5.2.1.3.2. Thomas, * 1967
5.2.2. Paula E., 1906–1989
∞ Malcolm Henderson, 1905–1981
5.2.2.1. Lydia M. , * + † 1934
5.2.2.2. Ann, * 1936
∞ Ralph P. Youngren
5.2.2.2.1. Todd P., *1964
∞ Jeanmarie E. Morrill, * 1963
5.2.2.2.1.1. Madeline E., * 1995
5.2.2.2.2. Malcolm P., * 1966
∞ Margaret A. McGreal, * 1969
5.2.2.3. Jennifer, * 1938
∞ David Taggart, * 1937
5.2.2.3.1. Sean D., * 1965
∞ Astrid Leitner, * 1961
5.2.2.3.1.1. Christina L., * 1993
5.2.2.3.1.2. Alexander M., * 1994
5.2.2.3.2. Benjemin T., * 1967
∞ Ann Ruthren–Murray, * 1967
5.2.2.3.3. Rebecca M., * 1972

5.3. Emmy, 1883–1892
5.4. Alice, 1885–1978
∞ Louis F. Guenzel, 1860–1956
5.4.1. Paul W., 1910–1996
∞ Elizabeth C. Skinner, * 1917
5.4.1.1. Elizabeth A., * 1940
∞ David P. Carlin
5.4.1.1.1. Elizabeth P., *1965
5.4.1.1.2. Theodore W.*1970
5.4.1.2. William S., * 1946
∞ Penelope Child (divorced in 1994)
5.4.1.2.1. Louis C., * 1981
5.4.1.2.2. Phoebe A., * 1985
5.5. Walter P., 1896–1963
∞ Elizabeth H. Nitze, 1902–1994
5.5.1. Walter P., Jr., 1923–1926
5.5.2. Anina H., * 1926
∞ 1. Ian M. Hamilton, * 1922
5.5.2.1.Amanda R., * 1966
∞ 2. Leonoard Woods
5.5.2.2. Alexandra H.
5.5.3. Paula A., * 1928
∞ 1.: Allen McCrory Pargellis, * 1924 (div.)
5.5.3.1. Andrew N., * 1952
∞ Shanna Kleinhorsman (div.)
5.5.3.1.1. Sonia, * 1987
5.5.3.1.2. Amelia, * 1991
5.5.3.2. Christopher A., * 1954
∞ 2.: Victor K. Zurcher, 1919–1999
5.5.3.3.Antonia P., * 1958
5.5.3.4. Ariane A., * 1960
5.5.4. Alice A., * 1936
∞ Stephen M. DuBrul, Jr., * 1929
5.5.4.1. Nicholas P., * 1966
5.5.4.2. Jennifer E., * 1972
6. Carolina, 1859–1933
7. Karl Friedrich Richard,1861–.1933
∞ Blanche Petty, 1869–1955
7.1. Sigmund J., *1893
∞ Lois Spohr
7.1.1.Lois
∞ Mr. Young
7.1.2. Bertha
7.1.3. Blanche
∞ George (?)
7.2. Emily L., 1895–1944
∞ Harry M. Burger, 1904–1946
7.2.1. Harry M., * 1918
∞ Olga Holub, * 1930

7.2.1.1. Henry H., * 1963
∞ Lisa W. Albright, * 1962
7.2.1.1.1. Haley W., * 1995
7.2.1.2. Carl ., * 1964
7.3. Blanche B., 1897–?
∞ Fred Schaefer
7.3.1. Walter Carl (Dog), * 1924
∞ Jo Beth , * 1829
7.3.1.1. Sharon Lou, * 1950
∞ Terry L. Canipe
7.3.1.1.1. Kara, * 1973
7.3.1.1.2. Colin, * 1983
7.3.1.2. Linda Gayle, *1951
∞ Mr. Seals (divorced)
7.3.1.2.1. Carl Clayton, * 1977
7.3.1.2.2. Jo Allison, * 1981
7.3.1.3. Carla Jo, * 1952
∞ Mr. Stew (divorced)
7.3.1.3.1. Sarah B., * 1980
7.3.1.3.2. Samuel S., * 1982
7.3.2. Henry Fred, *1925
∞ Lillyan (divorced)
7.3.3. Gloria, Doris, * 1930
∞ Clinton H. Britsch, * 1924
7.3.3.1. Gerald H., * 1953
∞ Bobbye Jean Knieper
7.3.3.1.1. Justin, *1980
7.3.3.1.2. Travis, *1982
7.3.3.2. Roberta L., *1955
∞ Joe Carter
7.3.3.2.1. Christopher, *1984
7.3.3.2.2. Adam, *1986
7.3.3.2.3. Reed, *1991
7.3.4. Charles H., 1938–?
7.4. Carl F., 1901–1982
∞ Agatha Weber
7.5. Walter "Bully" P. , 1903–1957
∞ Faye Lucille Hisey, 1900–1991
7.5.1. Robert, *1930
∞ Billie Leggett, *1932
7.5.1.1. Robert R., *1954
∞ Beverly Vackar, *1957
7.5.1.1.1. Krista F., *1983
7.5.1.1.2. Robert C., *1986
7.5.1.2.Walter R., *1958
∞ Angelia Elaine Jefferies
7.5.1.2.1. Analiese E., *1999
7.5.1.3. Sandra F., *1963
∞ Thomas W. McCampbell, *1962

7.5.1.3.1. Sara C., *1986
7.5.1.3.2. Elizabeth J., *1990
7.5.1.3.3. Margaret K., *2001
7.5.2. Patricia K., *, † 1940
7.6. Robert G., 1909–1971
∞ Ruth Harrison, 1914–1988
7.6.1.Robert Harrison, *1937
∞ Roswitha Ehrhardt
7.6.1.1.Marcus, *1970
∞ Gambrill H. Hollister
7.6.1.2. Peter R., *1975
7.6.2. Virginia Ruth, *1941
∞ John Michael Davis, *1939
7.6.2.1.Robert Michael, *1962
7.6.2.2. John Matthew, *1964
7.6.2.3. Kathryn, *1972

Notes

Notes to Introduction

1. See for example the extensive bibliography in Thomas Dublin, ed., *Immigrant Voices, New Lives in America, 1773-1986* (Urbana: University of Illinois Press, 1993), and Kenneth L. Holmes, ed., *Covered Wagon Women: Diaries and Letters from the Western Trails, 1840-1849* (Lincoln: University of Nebraska Press, 1995). A short introduction on the historiography of immigration is given in Roger Daniels, "Going to America: Observations on the Historiography of Immigration," *Amerikastudien / American Studies* 42, no. 3 (1997): 333-43.

2. Theodore Roosevelt reportedly shouted across the theater to the author at the opening night of the play, "That's a great play, Mr. Zangwill!" thus making the term "melting pot" a popular phrase. See Joseph Leftwich, *Israel Zangwill* (London: Clarke, 1957), 252; and Neil L. Shumsky, "Zangwill's *The Melting Pot*: Ethnic Tensions on Stage," *American Quarterly* 27 (1975): 24-48. From Richard O'Connor, *The German-Americans: An Informal History* (Boston: Little, Brown, 1968), 469, to Winfried Becker, "Historische Aspekte der deutsch-amerikanischen Beziehungen," *Archiv für Kulturgeschichte* 71, no. 1 (1989): 201, this term is still used by historians today as an description of American society. Those critical of the term "melting pot" are more numerous, however, like Nathan Glazer and Daniel P. Moynihan, *Beyond the Melting Pot* (New York: M.I.T. Press, 1963); Philip Gleason, "Melting Pot: Symbol of Fusion or Confusion," *American Quarterly* 16 (1964): 20-46; Roger Daniels, *Coming to America: A History of Immigration and Ethnicity in American Life* (New York: Harper Perennial, 1991); and Michael D'Innocenzo and Josef P. Sirefman, eds., *Immigration and Ethnicity, American Society: "Melting Pot" or "Salad Bowl"?* (Westport, Connecticut: Greenwood Press, 1992).

3. For those critics arguing that American society is a dominant one that tries to establish Anglo-conformity rather than allowing a melting pot see, for instance, Milton Gordon, "Key Phrases in Assimilation and Integration," in William S. Bernard, ed., *Immigrants and Ethnicity* (New York: American Immigration and Citizenship Conference, 1972), 29. The definition of acculturation still valid today was given by Robert Redfield, Ralph Linton, and Melville J. Herskovits, "A Memorandum for the Study of Acculturation," *American Anthropologist* 38, no. 1 (January/March 1936): 149: "acculturation comprehends those phenomena which result when groups of individuals having different cultures come into continuous first-hand contact, with subsequent changes in the original cultural patterns of either or both groups." For questions concerning acculturation and assimilation see, for instance, Elliott A. Barkan, "Race, Religion, and Nationality in American Society: A Model of Ethnicity—From Contact to Assimilation," *Journal of American Ethnic History*, 14 (Winter 1995): 38-75; Ewa Morawska, "In Defense of the Assimilation Model," *Journal of American Ethnic History* 13 (Winter 1994): 76-87; Oliver Zunz, "American History and the Changing Meaning of Assimilation," *Journal of American Ethnic History* 4 (Winter 1984): 53-72; Milton Gordon, "Key Phrases in Assimilation and Integration," in Bernard, *Immigrants and Ethnicity*, 29; Alan Richardson, "A Theory and Method for the Psychological Study of Assimilation," *International Migration Review* 2, no. 1 (1967): 3-30; Russell Kazal, "Revisiting Assimilation: The Rise, Fall and Reappraisal of a Concept in American History," *American Historical Review* 100 (1995): 437-71; Milton M. Gordon, *Assimilation in American Life* (New York: Oxford University Press, 1964) (where the author presents a seven-phase model in which only the last, the cultural or behavioral assimilation is called acculturation) and the important study by Reinhard R. Doerries, *Iren und Deutsche in*

der Neuen Welt (Stuttgart: Franz Steiner Verlag Wiesbaden, 1986), with an extensive bibliography. For the ongoing controversy about immigration and the forming of a nation see the consecutive articles by Gary Gerstle, David A. Hollinger, and Donna R. Gabaccia: "Liberty, Coercion, and the Making of Americans," "National Solidarity at the End of the Twentieth Century: Reflections on the United States and Liberal Nationalism," and "Liberty, Coercion, and the Making of Immigration Historians" in *The Journal of American History* 84, no. 2 (1997): 524-75.

Although authors like Takenori Inoki in *Aspects of German Peasant Emigration to the United States 1815-1914* (New York: Arno Press, 1981), 13, deny the possibility of an analysis on the basis of case studies, authors like Klaus J. Bade clearly express the need for case studies to give the general fields of economic and social history more depth of field. See his: "Deutsche Überseeauswanderung und -einwanderung im 19. und frühen 20. Jahrhundert," *Archiv für Sozialgeschichte* 26 (1986): 487. Works like Walter D. Kamphoefner, *The Westfalians: From Germany to Missouri* (Princeton: Princeton University Press, 1987) have been groundbreaking and have refuted works like Oscar Handlin's *The Uprooted: The Epic Story of the Great Migrations That Made the American People* (Boston: Little, Brown, 1952) which claims that the process of assimilation always was a painful and forceful one. Major criticism against Handlin was expressed by Frank Thistlewaite, "Migration from Europe Overseas in the Nineteenth and Twentieth Centuries," *Rapports*, 5 (1960): 32-60; and Rudolph Vecoli, "Contadini in Chicago: A Critique of *The Uprooted*," *The Journal of American History* 51 (December 1963): 404-17.

4. Professor Kattermann is well-known for her studies about the Holocaust in Baden. See for example, *Das Ende einer jüdischen Landgemeinde. Nonnenweier in Baden, 1933-1945* (Freiburg i. Br.: Verlag Wolf Mersch, 1984).

5. Jane F. Healey, "Privately Published Autobiographies by Texans: Their Significance for Scholars," *SHQ* 95, no. 4 (April 1992): 498. See also, Virginia Yans-McLaughlin, "Metaphors of Self in History: Subjectivity, Oral Narrative, and Immigration Studies," in Virginia Yans-McLaughlin, ed., *Immigration Reconsidered* (New York: Oxford University Press, 1990), 254-90; Nancy Thym-Hochrein, "'Peter Left Because . . .'—A Comparative Study of Oral Family Histories," *Scandinavian Yearbook of Folklore* 37 (1981): 61-8; Wolfgang Helbich, "Problems of Editing and Interpreting Immigrant Letters," in Hieronim Kubiak, ed., *Emigration from Northern, Central and Southern Europe: Theoretical and Methodological Principles of Research*, International Symposium, Kroków, November 9-11, 1981, Zeszyty Naukowe Uniwersytetu Jagiellonskiego, DCCXXXII, Prace Polonijne* Z. 8, Krakow, 1983, and Brian Elliott, "Biography, Family History and the Analysis of Social Change," in Stephen Kendrick, Pat Straw, David McCrone, eds., *Interpreting the Past, Understanding the Present*, (London: MacMillan, 1990), 59-82.

6. The first quotation is from Hector St. John de Crèvecoeur, *Letters from an American Farmer* (New York: Fox, Duffield, 1904), 43, and the second by Arthur M. Schlesinger Jr., *The Disuniting of America: Reflections on a Multicultural Society* (Knoxville:Whittle Direct Books, 1991), 13.

7. See on the one hand Lawrence H. Fuchs, *The American Kaleidoscope: Race, Ethnicity, and the Civic Culture* (Hanover: Wesleyan UP, 1990) and Werner Sollors, *Beyond Ethnicity: Consent and Descent in American Culture* (New York: Oxford University Press, 1986); and on the other hand Gwendolyn Mink, *The Wages of Motherhood: Inequality in the Welfare State, 1917-1942* (Ithaca: Cornell University Press, 1996); Roy Rosenzweig, *Eight Hours for What We Will: Workers and Leisure in an Industrial City, 1870-1920* (New York: Cambridge University Press, 1983); Lizabeth Cohen, *Making a New Deal: Industrial Workers in Chicago, 1919-1939* (New York: Cambridge University Press, 1990); and Irving Howe, *World of Our Fathers: The Journey of the East European Jews to America and the Life They Found and Made* (New York:

Harcourt Brace Jovanovich, 1976).

8. See Michael Rogin's, "'Make My Day!': Spectacle as Amnesia in Imperial Politics," in H. Aram Veeser, ed., *The New Historicism Reader* (New York: Routledge, 1994), 229-54; and *Blackface, White Noise: Jewish Immigrants in the Hollywood Melting Pot* (Berkeley: University of California Press, 1996), and David R. Roediger, *The Wages of Whiteness: Race and the Making of the American Working Class* (London: Verso, 1991).

9. See Heinrich Rickert, *Science and History* (Princeton: Van Nostrand, 1962). For this debate see also: Cynthia Hay, "What is Sociological History?" in Kendrick, Straw, and McCrone, *Interpreting the Past, Understanding the Present*; and Frank R. Ankersmit, "Historicism: An Attempt At Synthesis," *History and Theory* 34 (1995): 143-61; as well as Georg G. Igger's answer: "Comments on F. R. Ankersmit's Paper, 'Historicism: An Attempt At Synthesis,'" in the same journal.

10. Eric Hobsbawm, "On History from Below," *On History* (London: Weidenfelf & Nicolson, 1997), 214. In regards to this approach see also Paul Ricœr, "History and Rhetoric," in François Bédarida, ed., *The Social Responsibility of the Historian* (Providence: Berghahn Books, 1994), 7-24.

11. For a detailed discussion of narrativity as a specific concept in historiography see Hayden White's, "Figuring the Nature of the Times Deceased: Literary Theory and Historical Writing," in Ralph Cohen, ed., *The Future of Literary Theory* (New York: Routledge, 1989), and his, "The Value of Narrativity in the Representation of Reality," in Joyce Appleby et. al., eds., *Knowledge and Postmodernism in Historical Perspective* (New York: Routledge, 1996), 395-407. See also Morton G. White, *Foundations of Historical Knowledge* (New York: Oxford University Press, 1965); Arthur C. Danto, *Analytical Philosophy of History* (Cambridge: Harvard University Press, 1965); and Jürgen Habermas, "Zum Thema: Geschichte und Evolution," *Zur Rekonstruktion des historischen Materialismus* (Frankfurt: Suhrkamp, 1977). The concept of micro- and macro-history is described by Charles Tilly, "Future History," in Kendrick, Straw, McCrone, *Interpreting the Past, Understanding the Present*. See also Eric Hobsbawm, "On the Revival of Narrative," *On History,* p. 190. For the discussion of Hempel's works see: Arthur C. Danto, "The Decline and Fall of the Analytical Philosophy of History," in Frank R. Ankersmit and Hans Kellner, eds., *A New Philosophy of History* (Chicago: University of Chicago Press, 1995), as well as Michel Foucault, "What is Enlightenment?" in Joyce Appleby et. al., eds., *Knowledge and Postmodernism in Historical Perspective* (New York: Routledge, 1996), 410-17.

12. Stephen Greenblatt, *Renaissance Self-Fashioning: From More to Shakespeare*, (Chicago: Illinois University Press, 1980), 119.

13. White defined his new historiographical approach: "By 'historicism' I shall mean the attempt to explain facts by reference to earlier facts; by 'cultural organism' I mean the attempt to find explanations and relevant material in social sciences other than the one which is primarily under investigation." See his *Social Thought in America: The Revolt Against Formalism* (New York: Viking, 1949), 12.

Notes to Chapter 1

1. Johann Christoph Wagner, in the service of the Duke of Leiningen, was cantor and preceptor at the boy's school in Leiningen. His father Johann Hartmann Wagner (born June 30, 1693, in Rhula, died February 14, 1771, in Rhula) was a cutler and musical instrument maker. See Hildegard Kattermann, ed., *Familienbriefe 1811-1871*, transcribed and photocopied, limited edition, Lahr 1977, p. Ch 27 and Bl 2, The Wagner Family Collection, The Center for American History, University of Texas at Austin. For the history of Dürkheim and the reign of the Dukes of Leiningen before the French Revolution see Eva Kell, *Das Fürstentum Leiningen, Umbruchserfahrungen einer Adelsherrschaft zur Zeit der Französischen Revolution*

(Kaiserslautern: Institut für Pfälzische Geschichte und Volkskunde,1993), 19-32.

2. See Caroline Valentin, *Theater und Musik am Leinigenschen Hofe* (Würzburg: Kabitzsch & Mönnich, 1921), and Kell, 31. The equivalence of one *Gulden/Florin* to forty cents is mentioned by Wilhelm Wagner in his letter to his family from America on 1 June 1851, in Kattermann, 123.

3. Petition of Peter Wagner and his colleague Walter to the Duke of Leiningen, cited after: Kattermann, p. Ch 30. For the various measurements see Harald Wiihöft, "Die Vereinheitlichung von Mass und Gewicht in Baden und Württemberg in Napoleonischer Zeit," *Baden und Württemberg im Zeitalter Napoleons,* vol. 2 (Stuttgart: Edition Cantz,1987), 233-53. For the situation in Amorbach see: Richard Krebs, *Amorbach im Odenwald—ein Heimatbuch* (Amorbach: Druck und Verlag der Gottlob Volkhardt'schen Druckerei, Gebr. Volkhardt, 1923), 110-14.

4. Hermann Schmid, "Die Säkularisation und Mediatisation in Baden und Württemberg," *Baden und Württemberg im Zeitalter Napoleons*, 135-55; and Volker Press, "Südwestdeutschland im Zeitalter der Französischen Revolution und Napoleons," ibid., 9-24.

5. Thus it is reported in the *Familienbuch* (Family book) by Johanna Krastel from Lahr, cited in Kattermann, *Familienbriefe,* p. Ch 31.

6. For statistics and early descriptions of Uiffingen see: Werner Blesch, *Uiffingen, Geschichte fränkischer Bauern und ihrer Dorfgemeinde* (Tauberbischofsheim: Fränkische Nachrichten Druck- und Verlags GmbH, 1985), 211, 284-9.

7. GLA 391/2153. Generallandesarchiv Karlsruhe.

8. Gustav Adolf Benrath, "Die Evangelische Kirche in Baden 1771-1821," *Baden und Württemberg im Zeitalter Napoleons*, 297-311. For more information on the reign of Margrave Karl Friedrich of Baden, see Loyd E. Lee, *The Politics of Harmony: Civil Service, Liberalism, and Social Reform in Baden, 1800-1850 (*Newark: University of Delaware Press, 1980).

9. For more information about the poverty in this region of Germany at that time see Helmut Neumaier, *Geschichte der Stadt Boxberg mit Beiträgen über ihre Stadtteile* (Boxberg: Stadt Boxberg,1987), 352-59.

10. See Demian, *Geographie und Statistik des Großerzogtums Baden*, 1820, File I, Chapter IV, p. 18., Generallandesarchiv Karlsruhe.

11 Dekan (Dean) Wittich wrote in 1820 that Wagner's sermons were very good, that his relationship to his parishioners was pleasing and that his work with the local youth was highly promising. GLA 435/27, Generallandesarchiv Karlsruhe.

12. In his letter to Carl Baumann, Wilhelm Wagner wrote on 10 October 1834: "Ich wünschte nur, mein Bruder Julius stünde mit dir so nahe am Eingang in das paradiesische Studentenleben, ermahne ihn zuweilen, wo es dir nötig erscheint, an Ausdauer und fröhliches Hoffen." (I wish my brother, Julius, would be as close to the paradise-like gates of student life as you are now; admonish him from time to time to be persistent, patient and full of hope, when you think it to be necessary.) Kattermann, *Familienbriefe,* 12.

13. The nickname "Icebear" is reported by Henriette Wagner in a letter to her brother Karl in Austria on 15 December 1837; in Kattermann, *Familienbriefe,* 28. For the matriculation of Julius see the letter of Dr. Weisert, archivist of the Ruprecht-Karls-University at Heidelberg to the author dated 4 August 1988, in The Wagner Family Collection, The Center for American History, University of Texas at Austin.

14. For more details on the history of the *Guestphalia-Corps* and others see Wilhelm Fabricius, *Die Deutschen Corps* (Berlin: Verlag Hans Ludwig Thilo, 1898), 319. For a description of the various festivities of the old German fraternities see ibid., 450 f.

15. See Werner Siebold, *Unser Fritzing—ein Lebensbild Fritz Reuters* (Gießen: Emil Roth Verlag, nd), 70-71.

16. Peter Wagner in a letter to Karl Wagner in Steiermark on 1 December 1842, in

Kattermann, *Familienbriefe,* 61.

17. GLA 234, No. 2998, Fasc. 298. Generallandesarchiv Karlsruhe.

18. See Peter Wagner to his son Karl in April 1846, in Kattermann, *Familienbriefe,* 76.

19. Adolf von Göler to Count Carl von Castell, Freiburg, 19 August 1845, in: Solms-Braunfels Archives (Originals in Fürst zu Solms-Braunfels'-sches Archiv in Braunfels, Lahn, Germany). Transcripts, Texas State Archives, Austin, Vol. X, p. 167-69, and same to same, Freiburg, 1 November 1845, ibid, Vol. XI, pp. 216-17.

20. See Christine Hansen: "Die deutsche Auswanderung im 19, Jahrhundert—ein Mittel zur Lösung sozialer und sozialpolitischer Probleme?" in Günter Moltmann, ed., *Deutsche Amerikaauswanderung im 19. Jahrhundert* (Stuttgart: Metzler, 1976), 9-61.

21. Rudolph Leopold Biesele, *The History of the German Settlements in Texas 1831-1861* (Austin: Von-Boeckman-Jones, 1930), 67. For the history of the *Adelsverein* see Stefan von Senger und Etterlin, *Neu-Deutschland in Nordamerika* (Baden-Baden: Nomos Verlagsgesellschaft, 1991), 221.

22. For a history of the *Adelsverein* see Glen E. Lich, *The German Texans* (San Antonio: Institute of Texan Cultures at San Antonio, 1981); Glen E. Lich, Günter Moltmann, and T. Michael Womack, "'New Crowns to Old Glory': Archives of the German Adelsverein," *The Yale University Library Gazette* 63, nos. 3-4 (April 1989): 145-57; Harald Winkel, "Der Texasverein—ein Beitrag zur Geschichte der deutschen Auswanderung im 19. Jahrhundert," *Vierteljahrschrift für Sozia—und Wirtschaftsgeschichte* 55 (1968): 348-72, Gilbert Giddings Benjamin, *The Germans in Texas: A Study in Immigration* (Austin: Jenkins, 1974), 30-54; Wolf-Heino Struck, *Die Auswanderung aus dem Herzogtum Nassau 1806-1866* (Wiesbaden: Franz Steiner Verlag, 1966); and Biesele. For a better understanding of the position of the Leiningens see Veit Valentin, *Fürst Karl Leiningen und das Deutsche Einheitsproblem* (Stuttgart: J.G. Cotta'sche Buchhandlung Nachfolger, 1910).

23. Louis Reinhardt, "The Communistic Colony of Bettina," *Quarterly of the Texas State Historical Association* 3, no.1 (January 1899): 33-34.

24. Ibid., 34.

25. For the biographical sketch on Dr. Grosse and the first meeting of Spiess and von Herff with the Count of Castell see Hartmut Heinemann: "'Wo der Stern im Blauen Felde eine Neue Welt verkündet'—die Auswanderung der Vierziger aus Darmstadt nach Texas im Jahre 1847 und ihre kommunistische Kolonie Bettina," *Archiv für hessische Geschichte und Altertumskunde* 52 (1994): 287-88.

26. For a detailed biography of John O. Meusebach (on his arrival in Texas in 1845, von Meusebach relinquished his title and called himself henceforth John O. Meusebach) see Irene Marshall King, *John O. Meusebach, German Colonizer in Texas* (Austin: University of Texas Press, 1967).

27. For a detailed biography of Ferdinand von Herff see Henry B. Dielmann, "Dr. Ferdinand Herff—Pioneer Physician and Surgeon," *Southwestern Historical Quarterly SHQ* 57, no. 3 (January 1954): 265-84.

28. See Camillus Wendeler, *Briefwechsel des Freiherrn Karl Hartwig Gregor von Meusebach mit Jacob und Wilhelm Grimm* (Heilbronn: Henninger,1880).

29. Although considered genuine at first, most of her letters to Goethe were probably fabricated by her. Hermann Grimm, *Goethes Briefwechsel mit einem Kinde* (Goethe's Correspondence with a Child), 3 Vols. (Berlin: Hertz, 1835). For the erotic moment in her work see Konstanze Bäumer, *"Bettine, Psyche, Mignon," Bettina von Arnim und Goethe* (Stuttgart: Hans-Dieter Heinz Akademischer Verlag, 1986).

30. See Manfred Görtemaker, *Deutschland im 19. Jahrhundert* (Opladen: Leske und Budrich, 1989), especially chapter 2, "Restauration und Revolution 1815-1848," 61-141.

31. Thus quoted in King, 27.

32. James R. Ozinga, *Communism, the Story of the Idea and its Implementation,* (Englewood Cliffs, New Jersey: Prentice-Hall, 1987), 1. For the citation of Cabet see Étienne Cabet, *Reise nach Ikarien*, reprint (Berlin: Kramer, 1979), 504. Translated by the author.

33. Robert Owen founded New Harmony on 1 May 1825, on the site of the second Rappite community in Harmony Township, Posey County, Indiana. His experiment failed in 1827, however. For more information on the New Harmony settlement as well as the general American attitude towards socialism and communism see Arthur Eugene Bestor, Jr., *Backwoods Utopia: The Sectarian and Owenite Phases of Communitarian Socialism in America: 1663-1829* (Philadelphia: University of Pennsylvania Press, 1950), 160; M. J. Heale, *American Anticommunism: Combating the Enemy Within, 1830-1970* (Baltimore: Johns Hopkins University Press, 1990); Ward Churchill, ed., *Das indigene Amerika und die marxistische Tradition: eine kontroverse Debatte über Kultur, Industrialusmus und Eurozentrismus* (Bremen: Agipa-Press, 1993); and Gert Raeithel, *Geschichte der Nordamerikanischen Kultur*, Vol. 1: *Vom Puritanismus bis zum Bürgerkrieg 1600-1860* (Frankfurt/Main: Zweitausendeins, 1995), 398-400.

34. Étienne Cabet, "Propagande communiste ou, Questions à discuter et à soutenir ou à écarter," originally published in Paris in 1842; here in translation, "Communist Propaganda: Debating Points to Support or Avoid," Paul E. Corcoran, ed., *Before Marx: Socialism and Communism in France, 1830-48* (London: Macmillan, 1983), 89.

35. Translated from an article in the weekly magazine *Der Deutsche Auswanderer* no. 24 (1847): 383-84.

36. Arnold Ruge in his critique of "Das Cajütenbuch oder nationale Charakteristiken," in *Deutsche Jahrbücher für Wissenschaft und Kunst*, no. 86 (October 9, 1841), 343 ff. Translation by author.

37. Charles Sealsfield, *The Making of an American: An Adaption of Memorable Tales by Charles Sealsfield,* trans. Ulrich S. Carrington (Dallas: Southern Methodist University Press, 1974), 117.

38. Translated by the author from the German original, Alexander Büchner, *Das "tolle" Jahr. Vor, während und nach 1848. Von einem, der nicht mehr toll ist. Erinnerungen v. Alex Büchner,* 2nd ed. Cited in Georg Wiesenthal, "Darmstädter Auswanderer aus dem Jahre 1847," *Der Odenwald*, no. 4 (1957): 81-83.

39. Letter from Dr. Ernst Grosse to Count von Castell, 25 December 1846, in Solms-Braunfels Archives. Transcripts, Austin, vol. 57, pp. 58, 73. Translated by the author.

40. Letter of Prince Solms-Braunfels to the Count von Castell dated 5 February 1847, in Solms-Braunfels Archives. Transcripts, Austin, vol. 61, pp. 115-17. Translated by the author.

41. See for example the critical article in *Allgemeine Auswanderungs-Zeitung*, no. 1 (September 29, 1846): 2-3.

42. For details on Spiess' paper see Heinemann, 289.

43. In his book *Deutsche Pioniere—zur Geschichte des Deutschtums in Texas* (San Antonio: Selbstverlag, 1894), Adolf Paul Weber falsely states on page 31, that the *Darmstädters* had to enlist 200 families to settle on their land in order to fulfill their contract. According to § 6 of the contract this was not the case. See copy of contract "Vertrag zwischen seiner Erlaucht dem Herrn Grafen Castell zu Wiesbaden, als Director des Vereins zum Schutze deutscher Einwanderer in Texas und den Herren Herrmann Spiess und Dr. med. Ferdinand von Herff zu Darmstadt," in Solms-Braunfels Archives. Transcripts, Austin, vol. 28, pp. 9-17.

44. See the article "Die Darmstädter Texas-Auswanderer" in the weekly magazine *Der deutsche Auswanderer—Zentralblatt der deutschen Auswanderung und Kolonisierung* (The German Emigrant—main publication of the German emigration and colonization), no. 10 (1847):

147-49, in Solms-Braunfels Archives. Transcripts, Austin, vol. 68, pp. 76-77.

45. For more about Dresel see his, *Gustav Dresel's Houston Journal: Adventures in North America and Texas, 1837-1841*, Max Freund, ed. (Austin: University of Texas Press, 1954). Hoffmann von Fallersleben's love for Elvira Détroit was not returned. But he and Elvira remained friends for life. She became a teacher in Warsaw later and married the university teacher Karl Elze in 1856. Hoffmann von Fallersleben, *Ausgewählte Werke in vier Bänden*, vol. 1, Hans Benzmann, ed., (Leipzig: Max Hesses Verlag, 1924), 40-41, 44-45. For more information on Fallersleben's poems on Texas see Winfred Lehmann, "Lone Star German," Joseph Wilson, ed., *Texas and Germany: Crosscurrents*, Rice University Studies 63, no. 3 (Summer 1977), 73-81. For the farewell party in Dresel's home see Hermann Haupt in his article: "Hessisch=Amerikanische Lebensbilder," *Volk und Scholle* 1 (July 1922): 6. Haupt gives more information about this party in his article, "Gustav Schleicher. Ingenieur und amerikanischer Staatsmann, 1823-1879," in Herman Haupt, ed., *Hessische Biographie*, vol. 2 (Darmstadt: Hessischer Staatsverlag, 1920), 9. The party and the poem are also mentioned by Fallersleben himself in his, *Mein Leben*, Vol. 4 (Rümpler: Hannover, 1868), 311-13. For more information about the diplomat von Bunsen see Stefan von Senger und Etterlin, *Neu-Deutschland in Nordamerika*, 137.

46. John O. Meusebach to Count von Castell on 28 July 1846 and same to same on 9 January 1847, in Solms-Braunfels Archives. Transcripts, Austin, Vol. 52 and 28, p. 219 and 182. For Spiess' relationship with the bank of Schuchardt and Gebhardt see Heinemann, "Wo der Stern," 290.

47. Count von Castell to Meusebach on 15 February and 17 February 1847, in Solms-Braunfels Archives. Transcripts, Austin, Vol. 52 , pp. 251-52. For more information about the *Nationalverein* see article "Der Nationalverein für deutsche Auswanderung und Colonisation," *Der Deutsche Auswanderer*, 10 (1847): 149-51, in Solms-Braunfels Archives. Transcripts, Austin, Vol. 68 , pp.77-78; and Stefan von Senger und Etterlin, *Neu-Deutschland in Nordamerika*, 97.

48. See "Der Texas Verein—Erklärung," *Der Deutsche Auswanderer*, no. 14 (1847): 219-21, in Solms-Braunfels Archives. Transcripts, Austin, Vol. 68, pp.112-13.

49. For Friedrich Schenk's poem and the paper regarding the Forty see Heinemann "Wo der Stern," 303-4. The five years that they had promised each other to work together are mentioned in a letter from Heinrich Backofen to his brother Franz in Darmstadt, Germany, January 22, 1848, in Wilhelm Welcker, *Bilder aus dem Leben der Familie Backofen*, page 113 of typescript copy, in Hessisches Staatsarchiv Darmstadt, O 61 Schuchardt-Osann No. 8/1.

50. See Reinhardt, 34. For the descriptions of the departure and the voyage see the published letter of one of the *Darmstädters* in "Die Darmstädter Texasauswanderer," *Der Deutsche Auswanderer*, no. 35 (1847): 553-54, in Solms-Braunfels Archives. Transcripts, Austin, Vol. 69, p. 117; *Allgemeine Auswanderungs-Zeitung*, no. 28 (April 13, 1847): 211; the *Darmstädter Zeitung*, no. 93 (April 3, 1847): 627; and "Verzeichnis der mit Adam Koeppel Auswandernden nach Texas," in Fritz Lauckhard, "Auswandererbriefe aus Texas 1848/49," *Volk und Scholle* 9 (1931): 95 f. For the exact date of the arrival of the *St. Pauli*—it was the only ship from Hamburg landing in Galveston in 1847—see Chester William Geue and Ethel Hander Geue, *A New Land Beckoned* (Waco: Texian Press, 1966), 168. For more information and descriptions about the sea-voyages of German emigrants in the 1840s see Lich, *The German Texans*, 28-30.

Notes to Chapter 2

1. For information on the William Tell Hotel see Charles W. Hayes, *Galveston: History of the Island and the City* (Austin: Jenkins Garrett Press, 1974), 309. For the other hotels in Galveston at that time see A. De Lono, *The Galveston Directory for 1856-57* (Galveston: News Book and Job Office, 1856), 7, 41; for more information on the Tremont House, see Gary

Cartwright, *Galveston, A History of the Island* (New York: Atheneum, 1991), 77, 306.

Brownson Malsch in his book *Indianola, the Mother of Western Texas*, states that Carlshafen and Indian Point or Indianola were one and the same place (Austin: State House Press, 1988, p. 11). Prince Carl von Solms-Braunfels had named this landing site after himself. This seems to be confirmed by the maps, the "Verein zum Schutze Deutscher Einwanderer in Texas" issued in 1851 (reprint: Berlin: Dietrich Reimer Verlag, 1983) and even by the diary of Prince Solms-Braunfels himself: Kurt Klotzbach, ed., *Die Solms-Papiere—Dokumente zur Deutschen Kolonisation von Texas* (Wyk auf Föhr: Verlag für Amerikanistik, 1990), 73, 75. Two settlers who probably cared more about these locations than the *Adelsverein* remembered this differently, however: "Karlshafen is situated a few miles from Indian Point, but it consists of only a few buildings. In other words, Indian Point and Karlshafen are not one and the same place, as Bracht states on page 147 [Viktor Bracht, *Texas im Jahre 1848*, Elberfeld und Iserlohn, 1849, translated by Charles Frank Schmidt under the title *Texas in 1848*, 1931]." W. Steinert's entry in his diary on 23 May 1849, in Gilbert J. Jordan, ed. and trans., "W. Steinert's View of Texas in 1849: May 22 to June 5," *SHQ* 80, no. 1 (1976): 64. Another account says: "J. G. Reininger landete mit einigen der ersten Einwanderern aus Deutschland im November 1844 in Galverston. Von dort wurden die Einwanderer mit ihren Familien und Habseligkeiten nach Powerderhorn Bayou gebracht, wo Prinz Karl seine erste Ansiedlung, genannt Karlshafen, unterhalb Indianola gegründet hatte. Von Karlshafen und Indianola ist jetzt nichts mehr übrig . . . ." Gus Reininger, "Erinnerungen aus dem Pionierleben eines Cowboys," *Jahrbuch der Neu-Braunfelser Zeitung für 1943*, Druck der Neu-Braunfelser Zeitung, 1943, 65. The way that Alwin Soergel uses the names of Karlshafen and Indian Point separately also indicates that they were different places at one time, Karlshafen dying out soon; see for example: W.M. Von-Maszewski, ed., *A Sojourn in Texas, 1846-47, Alwin H. Sörgel's Texas Writings* (San Marcos: Southwest Texas State Univesity, 1992), 6, 54, 80.

2. The first list of the group can be found in Friedrich Armand Strubberg Collection, WA S-1291, Box 25, Folder 196, Beinecke Rare Book and Mansucript Library, Yale University, New Haven, Connecticut. For the "original" list of the *Darmstädter* group see "Namensverzeichnis der Darmstädter Texasauswanderer," *Der Deutsche Auswanderer*, no. 15 (1847): 239-40; found in Solms-Braunfels Archives. Transcripts, Austin, Vol. 68, p.122. Adolf Weber's list is published in Adolf Paul Weber, ed., *Deutsche Pioniere - zur Geschichte des Deutschthums in Texas* (San Antonio: Selbstverlag, 1894), 26. For Reinhardt's account see 34-35. Louis Reinhardt, "The Communistic Colony of Bettina," *Quarterly of the Texas State Historical Association* 3, no.1 (January 1899): 34-35.

3. Chester William Geue and Ethel Hander Geue, *A New Land Beckoned, German Immigration to Texas, 1844 - 1847* (Waco: Texian Press, 1966), 76-164; and Ethel Hander Geue, *New Homes in a New Land, German Immigration to Texas, 1847-1861* (Waco: Texian Press, 1970), 48-151.

4. See for example the letter of Dr. Heinrich Kattmann to his mother dated 17 November 1847, published on 29 September 1849, in *Der Deutsche Auswanderer*, no. 38 (September 1849): 611 f.

5. For more information on the naturalist Lindheimer see Minetta Altgelt Goyne, *A Life among the Texas Flora* (College Station: Texas A&M UP, 1991, 9 ff, 228 ff. For information on Vogelsang and Blaudeck see the letter from Heinrich Kattmann to his mother dated 17 November 1847, in *Der Deutsche Auswanderer*, 1848, pp. 440 ff.

6. For the description of Galveston see the published letter of one of the *Darmstädter*s in the article "Die Darmstädter Texasauswanderer," *Der Deutsche Auswanderer*, no. 35 (1847): 553, translation by the author; found in Solms-Braunfels Archives. Transcripts, Austin, Vol. 69, p.117.

7. W. Steinert's entry in his diary on May 23, 1849, in G. Jordan. For the statistics on

Germans in Galveston see Terry G. Jordan, *German Seed in Texas Soil* (Austin: University of Texas Press, 1985), 53; and Gilbert Giddings Benjamin, *The Germans in Texas: A Study in Immigration* (Austin: Jenkins Publishing Company, 1974), 58. In his booklet, "Texas. Advice to Emigrants," Alwin H. Sörgel dwells on the splendor of Galveston too, mentioning the "roomy streets, the friendly homes, the pretty and elegant tropical gardens" but gives other population numbers for 1847: "About half of the 6,000-7,000 inhabitants are Germans." See: Von-Maszewski, 151.

8. Carl Baumann to his brother-in-law Friedrich Jacob Becker on August 21, 1847, in Hildegard Kattermann, ed., *Familienbriefe 1811-1871*, transcribed and photocopied, limited edition, Lahr 1977, The Wagner Family Collection, The Center for American History, University of Texas at Austin. p. 89.

9. For more information on the complicated history of the Mexican War see David M. Pletcher, *The Diplomacy of Annexation: Texas, Oregon and the Mexican War* (Columbia, MO: U of Missouri Press, 1973), 465-521.

10. Friedrich Schenck to his mother in his letter dated 11 November 1847, in Glen E. Lich, ed., "A Letter from Friedrich Schenck in Texas to His Mother in Germany, 1847," *SHQ*, 92, no. 1 (July 1988): 151. For the original German text see Friedrich Schenck Manuscripts, The Center for American History, University of Texas, Austin.

11. Reinhardt, 36.

12. Ibid.

13. For the wealth of some of the Forty see the letter of Adam Koeppel to his brother Wilhelm on 28 March 1847, in Fritz Lauckhard, "Auswandererbriefe aus Texas 1848/49," *Volk und Scholle* 9 (1931), 95. For the farm "Fürchtegott" see Weber, *Deutsche Pioniere*, 27. A very good analysis of the development of New Braunfels is given by Lauren Ann Kattner, "From Immigrant Settlement into Town: New Braunfels, Texas, 1845-1870," *Amerikastudien / American Studies* 36, no. 2 (1991): 155-77.

14. For an account of these negotiations see Irene Marshall King, *John O. Meusebach: German Colonizer in Texas* (Austin: Univerisity of Texas Press, 1967), 111-23; Glen Lich, *The German Texans*(San Antonio: The University of Texas Institute for Texan Cultures at San Antonio, 1981), 53-57; and Karl A. Hoerig, "The Relationship between German Immigrants and the Native Peoples in Western Texas," *SHQ* 97, no. 3, (January 1994): 429-33. In his recollection of Bettina's history, Louis Reinhardt states that he was present when the treaty was signed between Santana and Meusebach (36-37). Rudolph Biesele concludes from this that the Forty must have come earlier in 1847, probably in March 1847, in order to be present at the signing of the treaty on 9 May (see Biesele, *The History of the German Settlements in Texas 1831-1861* (Austin: Press of Von Boeckmann-Jones, 1930), 156 n. 51.). All other sources indicate strongly, however, that the dates Reinhardt gives, namely the arrival of the Forty in Galveston in July 1847 and their stay in New Braunfels in August, are correct. It is much more likely therefore that Reinhardt mixed up the signing of the peace treaty (which he undoubtedly had heard about) with visits of Santana and his Comanche delegation later that year.

15. Friedrich Schenck to his mother in his letter dated 11 November 1847, in Lich, "A Letter from Friedrich Schenck," 159.

16. Reinhardt, 37.

17. Friedrich Schenck to his mother in his letter from November 11, 1847, in Lich, "A Letter from Friedrich Schenck," 157. For an interesting analysis of the travel literature see Marilyn McAdams Sibley, *Travelers in Texas 1761-1860* (Austin: U Texas Press, 1967), 100.

18. Reinhardt, 38. The details of the Bettina settlement are compiled from Ibid, pp. 37-38; the letter of Friedrich Schenck to his mother on 11 November 1847, in Lich, "A Letter from Friedrich Schenck," 150; the letter by Wilhelm Hermes, "To the Emigration Company Land on

the Llano, Experiences of a German Immigrant in Texas," probably written around 1850, first published in the *Jahrbuch 1941* of the *Neu-Braunfelser Zeitung* and reprinted in Oscar Haas, *History of New Braunfels and Comal County, Texas 1844-1946* (Austin: Steck Co., 1968), 42; Ferdinand Lindheimer, "Kolonie der Darmstädter Communisten-Gesellschaft," *Allgemeine Auswanderungs-Zeitung* (1848), 778 ff; and the letter of the general agent of the *Adelsverein*, lieutenant Bene to the Count von Castell on November 25, 1847, in Solms-Braunfels Archives. Transcripts (Originals in Fürst zu Solms-Braunfels'-sches Archiv in Braunfels, Lahn, Germany), Texas State Archives, Austin, Vol. 63, p. 113. For the settlement of Castell, Leiningen, and Schönburg see Hartmut Heinemann, "'Wo der Stern in Blauen Felde eine Neue Welt verkündet'—die Auswanderung der Vierziger aus Darmstadt nach Texas in Jahre 1847 und ihre kommunistische Kolonie Bettina," *Archiv für hessische Geschischte und Altertumskunde*, vol. 52, 1994, 323.

19. For the various stories about the Comanches and the Germans see Weber, *Deutsche Pioniere*, 29; "Ein Deutsch-Texaner," *Darmstädter Zeitung* Mittwoch, (17 May 1893): 227, p. 1, in Jacob Kuechler Papers, The Center for American History, University of Texas at Austin; Henry B. Dielmann, "Dr. Ferdinand Herff—Pioneer Physician and Surgeon," *SHQ* 57, no. 3 (January 1954): 274.

20. Weber, *Deutsche Pioniere*, 31. The translation is by the author because the one by Rudolph Biesele in *The History of the German Settlements in Texas, 1831-1861*, on pages 156-57 is not correct.

21. Reinhardt, 39; and Wilhelm Hermes, "To the Emigration Company Land on the Llano," 42.

22. Friedrich Schenck to his mother in his letter on 11 November 1847, transcript made during the session 1940-1941 under the direction of Rudolph Leopold Biesele, from materials loaned by Mrs. J. M. Hadra, Dallas, Texas, in Friedrich Schenck Manuscripts, The Center for American History, University of Texas at Austin, p. 30. Translation by the author, because the translation by Glen E. Lich in "A Letter from Friedrich Schenck in Texas to His Mother in Germany, 1847," 163, is not fully correct here.

23. Dr. Heinrich Kattmann's letter from 17 November 1847, was published on September 29, 1849, *Der Deutsche Auswanderer*, no 38, p. 611 f. Translation by the author.

24. For the discussion in New Braunfels see the letter of Adam Koeppel to his father and siblings on 23 April 1848 in Lauckhard, 96; and the letter of Heinrich Backofen to his brother Franz from Galveston on 22 January 1848, in Wilhelm Welcker, *Bilder aus dem Leben der Familie Backofen*, Darmstadt, 1932 (typescript copy), pp. 112-116 and 105-107; also found in Hessisches Staatsarchiv Darmstadt, O 61 Schuchardt-Osann No. 8/1. For Backofen's quotation and his motivations see Ibid.

25. The other one of the two *Adelsverein* officials was Johann Jacob von Coll, who had been lieutenant in the Nassau army, before he joined the *Adelsverein*. According to rumors, Ludwig Bene (b. 1812 in Wetzlar) had killed someone in Trier and thus had to leave the army. In 1859 he committed suicide in New York. See Heinemann, 329, 350, nn. 170, 171.

26. See report and balancing of accounts by Lt. Bene from New Braunfels to the Count von Castell on 9 January in Solms-Braunfels Archives. Transcripts, Austin, Vol. 45, pp. 118-135 (here p. 121); letter from Bene to Castell on February 22, 1848, in ibid, Vol. 44, pp. 146-150 (here pp. 147-148); Bene to the *Adelsverein* without date, in ibid, Vol. 53, pp. 150-160 (here: 158/159); report from Bene to the committee of the *Adelsverein* on March 23, 1848, in ibid, Vol. 45, pp. 45-54 (here: p. 53); letter of Dr. Ludwig Martin to the Duke of Nassau on April 15th, 1852, in ibid, Vol. 60, pp. 58-79 (here: pp. 66-68). All translations by the author. For the exclusion of Schunk, the Neff brothers, Mördes, and Kappelhof see the descriptions in letter of Heinrich Kattmann to his mother on 17 November 1847, in *Der Deutsche Auswanderer*, no. 38 (29 September 1849): 440-42 and letter of Adam Koeppel to his brother Gottlieb from

10 May 1848, in Lauckhard, 99. For the letters of Adam Koeppel to his brother Wilhelm see ibid., pp. 95-101, and for the ones to his father and his brother Gottlieb, describing his anguish in Texas see ibid, pp. 96 and 99. For the report of Eberhard Ihrig see Karl Esselborn, ed., *Zwei Erbacher in Texas. Lebenserinnerungen von Ernst Dosch und Eberhard Ihrig* (Hessische Volksbücher, Darmstadt: H. L. Schlapp, 1937), 111 ff.

27. See the article by Hermann Spiess "Herrn K zur Antwort," *Neu-Braunfelser Zeitung*, 1, no. 37 (July 22,1853): 2, in Solms-Braunfels Archives. Transcripts, Austin, Vol. 70, p. 154. Translation by the author. The article by Lindheimer about the Forty was reprinted in *Allgemeine Auswanderungs-Zeitung*, (1848), 779. The letter from March 20, 1848, to the leadership of the *Adelsverein* was signed by thirty-five settlers from New Braunfels, in: Friedrich Armand Strubberg Collection, WA S-1316, Box 2, Folder 35, Beinecke Rare Book and Manuscript Library, Yale University, New Haven, Connecticut. The article in the *Wöchentlicher Anzeiger des Westens* from 4 August 1849 was reprinted in *Allgemeine Auswanderungs-Zeitung*, no. 79 (2 October 1849): 314.

28. Friedrich Kapp, *Aus und über Amerika: Tatsachen und Erlebnisse*, vol. 1 (Berlin: Julius Sprinter Verlag, 1876), 285.

29. See the letter from Heinrich Backofen to his brother Franz from Galveston, on 22 January 1848 in Wilhelm Welcker, *Bilder aus dem Leben der Familie Backofen*, typescript copy, Darmstadt 1932, pp. 114 f. in Hessisches Staatsarchiv Darmstadt, O 61 Schuchardt-Osann No. 8/1.

30. Adam Koeppel had complained about the bad soil on the Llano in the letter from April 23, 1848 to his father and siblings, in Lauckhard, 96. In an article that von Herff had written after his return to Germany for the *Darmstädter Zeitung* on 15 August 1849, he confessed: "All the members of our society, consisting of twenty-four persons still . . . are living at New Braunfels. Having founded a colony on the grant of the *Adelsverein*, our society gave up this settlement because that region proved to be too sparsely settled for our purposes in contrast to the rich and densely populated area of New Braunfels." Cited in Heinemann, 333.

31. For a history of these utopian communities and experiments in the United States see Arthur Eugene Bestor, *Backwoods Utopias: The Sectarian and Owenite Phases of Communitarian Socialism in America, 1663-1829* (Philadelphia: U Penn Press, 1950), especially the statistics on pages 235-43. For the history of Icaria and La Réunion see Gerry C. Cunnin, *French Communitive Socialist Experiments in Texas, 1846-1868*, M.A. thesis, Baylor University, Waco, Texas, 1964. For the settlement "Icaria" see Rondel V. Davidson, "Icarian Colony," in Ron Tyler, ed., *The New Handbook of Texas*, vol. 3 (Austin: Texas State Historical Association, 1996), 812; and for Cabet's life in the United States see Christopher E. Guthrie, "Cabet, Étienne," in ibid, vol. 1, 881.

32. See Ferdinand von Herff, *The Regulated Emigration of the German Proletariat with Special Reference to Texas,* trans. Arthur L. Finck (San Antonio: Trinity University Press, 1978), 20-25.

33. Unfortunately, Wilhelm Hermes doesn't say who the settler was who bought the remaining land of Bettina. See the letter of Wilhelm Hermes in Haas, 43. For more information on the biography of von Herff see Henry B. Dielmann, "Dr. Ferdinand Herff—Pioneer Physician and Surgeon," *SHQ* 57, no.3 (January 1954): 265-84; Kurt Lekisch, "Dr. Ferdinand von Herff, Idealistic Pioneer and Distinguished Texas Physician," *Texas Medicine*, vol. 82, (August 1986), 48-52; and Ferdinand Peter Herff, *The Doctors Herff: A Three-Generation Memoir*, Laura L. Barber, ed., 2 vols., (San Antonio: Trinity University Press, 1973). For biographical information on Schleicher see Zachary Taylor Fulmore, *The History and Geography of Texas – as Told in County Names* (Austin: Press of E. L. Steck, 1915), pp. 240 f, Vinton Lee James, *Frontier and Pioneer Recollections of Early Days in San Antonio and West Texas* (San Antonio: Artes Graficas,

1938), 130 f; and Frank W. Johnson, *A History of Texas and Texans* (Chicago: American Historical Society,1916), 1219-22. For a biographical sketch of Philipp Friedrich Karl Theodor Schenck see Lich, "A Letter from Friedrich Schenck," 164. For more information on Hermann Spiess and the last struggles of the *Adelsverein* see Eldon S. Branda, ed., *The Handbook of Texas: A Supplement* (Austin: Texas State Historical Association, 1876), 914 f; Louis E. Brister, ed., "William von Rosenberg's Kritik: A History of the Society for the Protection of German Immigrants to Texas," *SHQ* 85, no. 2-4, (October 1981 - April 1982): 161-186, 299-318, 409-422. (here: p. 315); and Kapp, vol. 1, 284.

34. Kapp, vol. 1, 287. Translation by the author. For more information about the "Latin" settlements see Lich, *The German Texans*, 64 ff; Ethel H. Geue, *New Homes*, 20.

35. For the life and times of Adam Koeppel, see Lauckhard, 95-101.

36. See Biesele, *The History of the German Settlements*, 172.

37. G. Jordan, "W. Steinert's View of Texas," 63.

38. For the deaths of Bub and Hahn see Heinemann, 338. Note his correction of the entries in Geue and Geue, *A New Land Beckoned*, 85, 98; in Heinemann, 351, n. 196. For the information about Otto Amelung, Wilhelm Friedrich, Heinrich Kattmann, Friedrich Louis, and Leopold Schulz see Geue and Geue, *A New Land Beckoned*, 76-164. Christian Hesse is mentioned by W. Steinert on June 20th, 1849 in G. Jordan, "W. Steinert's View of Texas," 284; and Jakob Obert is listed in the 1850 and 1860 Omal County Census, see Haas, 280. For the information on the year 1894 see Weber, *Deutsche Pioniere*, 34. For the biographical dates on Christoph Flach see Guido E. Ransleben, *A Hundred Years of Comfort in Texas: A Centennial History* (San Antonio: Naylor Company, 1954), 102, 127, 185, 194-96. For the death of Adam Koeppel see Lauckhard, 95. For the business activities of Theodore Schleuning see the correspondence with his friend Jacob Küchler in Jacob Küchler Papers, The Center for American History, the University of Texas at Austin.

39. Julius Wagner in a letter to his brother Wilhelm dated 24 August 1849, from Aglasterhausen, in Kattermann, *Familienbriefe*, 98. For the information about his early separation from the Forty see the letter by Peter Wagner and Emilie Wagner to Karl Wagner from 24 August 1849 in ibid., 97. For information about Steiner's settlement see Eichholz, "Die deutschen Ansiedlungen am Coletto," Albert Schütz, ed., *Schütze's Jahrbuch für Texas und Volkskalender für 1884*, 85; and Biesele, *The History of the German Settlements*, 58. On Carl Steiner's becoming a citizen of the United States see Probate Minutes, Victoria County, vol. A2, (Miss. Papers), p. 80, County Court, Victoria, Texas.

40. See the letter from Emilie Wagner to Karl Wagner dated 24 August 1849, in Kattermann, *Familienbriefe*, 97-98.

41. See the letter of Wilhelm Wagner to his brother Karl Wagner from Brombach on July 26, 1850, in Kattermann, *Familienbriefe*, 109. In Ethel Geue, *New Homes in a New Land*, the name Henkenius is misspelled as Hinkennis on page 83.

42. See the letter of Carl Baumann to his brother-in-law Karl Wagner in Steiermark, Austria, from Mannheim, on July 19, 1949, in Kattermann, *Familienbriefe*, 92.

43. For the figures of the German population in Texas see T. Jordan, 50.

44. Flora L. von Roeder, *These are the Generations* (Houston: Baylor College of Medicine, 1978), 23, 26.

45. The first quotation is from a biographical sketch of Rosa Kleberg, p. 2, in *Kleberg, Rudolph, Family Papers*, Box 2J54, Center for American Studies, The University of Texas at Austin. Translated by the author. And the second quotation is from Caroline von Hinueber, "Life of German Pioneers in Early Texas," *QTSHA* 2, no 3 (January 1899): 228.

46. For biographical dates about the Roeders and Klebergs see von Roeder, Glen E. Lich, *The German Texans*, 44, 110; the seven-page typescript biographical sketch of Rosa Kleberg in

Kleberg, Rudolph, Family Papers, Box 2J54, Center for American Studies, The University of Texas at Austin; the entries Kleberg, Robert Justus (No: F505) and Roeder, J. von (No: F782) in DeWitt County Historical Commission, *The History of DeWitt County, Texas* (Dallas: Curtis Media, 1991), 535, 695; and Cat Spring Agricultural Society, *The Cat Spring Story* (San Antonio: Lone Star Printing Company, 1956).

47. See Charles L. Wisseman, Sr., trans., *Fredericksburg, Texas . . . The first fifty years,* original in German published in 1896 (Fredericksburg: Fredericksburg Publishing Co., 1971), 26.

48. For the "Cart War" see J. Fred Rippy, "Border Troubles along the Rio Grande, 1848-1860," *SHQ* 23, no. 2 (October 1919): 91-111; Hedwig Krell Didear, "The Old Cart Road," chapter in *A History of Karnes County and Old Helena* (Austin: Jenkins Publishing Company, 1969), 16-21; and Charles Merritt Barnes, *Combats and Conquests of Immortal Heroes* (San Antonio: Guessaz and Ferlet Company, 1910), 125.

49. All the information and descriptions about the life of the Wagners on the Coleto as well as their relationship with their neighbors including all the quotations are from a twenty-eight-page letter from Emilie Wagner to her parents, written between April 22 and May 30, 1851, translation by the author, in The Wagner Family Collection, The Center for American History, University of Texas at Austin. The naturalization papers of Julius Wagner, Karl Wundt, and Julius Schorre are in District Clerks Records, Volume C, DeWitt County Courthouse, Cuero, Texas. For the biographical dates of the Schorre family, see Arlene Schorre Corner, "Schorre, Julius August Christian," (No. F823) in DeWitt County Historical Commission, *The History of DeWitt County, Texas*, 721.

50. The quotation is from Ottilie Fuchs Goeth, *Memoirs of a Texas Pioneer Grandmother; 1805-1915*, trans. by Irma Goeth Guenther (Austin: n.p., 1969), 23. For the life of Wilhelm von Roeder see von Roeder, 228-34.

51. For biographical dates about Eduard Froböse see Weber, *Deutsche Pioniere*, 27-37. The first history of "Steiner's Settlement" was published by W. T. Eichholz, "Die deutschen Ansiedlungen am Coletto" in Schütze, *Schütze's Jahrbuch*, 85. This account was used by Biesele, *The History of the German Settlements*, 58; and Craig H. Roell in his entry "Coletoville, Texas," in Ron Tyler, ed., *Handbook of Victoria County* (Austin: Texas State Historical Association, 1988), 10. For the settler's naming of this place (which they always wrote with a double *t*: Coletto) see Julius Schütze, "Meine Erlebnisse in Texas," *Texas Vorwärts*, (February 1, 1884): 2; and the letter from Julius Wagner to his mother and sister Henriette from Coletto on May 30, 1858, in Kattermann, *Familienbriefe*, 182. Most of the names that Biesele gives in his book as early settlers of Coletoville come from Julius Schütze's account, "Meine Erlebnisse in Texas." Schütze clearly mentions the Twelve-Mile Coleto which Biesele obviously mistook for the longer Coleto Creek that runs through Coletoville. The persons whom Schütze mentioned therefore lived closer to Cuero and Meyersville than to Coletoville.

52. Julius Schütze, "Meine Erlebnisse in Texas," 2, translation by the author.

53. For more information about German agriculture in Texas see Terry G. Jordan, *German Seed in Texas Soil*, 68-81. Carl Steiner's harvest is mentioned by Craig H. Roell in his entry "Coletoville, Texas," in Ron Tyler, *Handbook of Victoria County*, 10.

54. See the twenty-eight-page letter from Emilie Wagner to her parents, written between 22 April and 30 May 1851, 14-16. in The Wagner Family Collection, The Center for American History, University of Texas at Austin.

55. Marriage certificate of Karl Wundt, in: Rudolph Kleberg Family Papers, The Center for American History, University of Texas at Austin.

56. Julius Schütze, "Meine Erlebnisse in Texas," 2, translation by the author.

57. For the history of the first and second *Sängerfest* see Hermann Seele, *The Cypress and other Writings of a German Pioneer in Texas* (Austin: The University of Texas Press, 1979),

107f; Oscar Haas: "German Mansucript for a chronological History of the singers leagues in Texas, contemplated for publication in 1948 at the 57th Saengerfest," in Oscar Haas Papers, Box No.: 2N404, The Center for American History, University of Texas at Austin and Julius Schütze: "History of the German Texas Saengerbund," in program of the "Eighteenth Texas German Saengerfest, April 14, 15, 16, 17, 1891," Galveston, Texas, in: Oscar Haas Papers, "18th Saengerfest"-folder, Box No.: 2N404, The Center for American History, University of Texas at Austin. For a short history of the German singing societies in Texas see Lich, *The German Texans,* 145-52.

58. See for example the chapter "Robert Justus Kleberg" in John Henry Brown, *Indian Wars and Pioneers of Texas* (Austin: L. E. Daniell Publishers, 1890), 289.

59. The letter from Emilie Wagner to her parents, written between April 22 and May 30, 1851, p. 9 in The Wagner Family Collection, The Center for American History, University of Texas at Austin.

60. For a short history of Clinton see Frances Peyton, "Clinton" (T45) in DeWitt County Historical Commission, *The History of DeWitt County, Texas*, 85 f.

61. Letter from Julius Wagner to his mother and sister Henriette from 30 May 1858, in Kattermann, *Familienbriefe*, 182.

62. See letters of Carl Baumann to his brother-in-law Karl Wagner from Mannheim, on 17 October and 22 December 1858, as well as the letter from Julius Wagner to his mother and sister Henriette dated 30 May 1858 in Kattermann, *Familienbriefe*, 179-83.

63. Thus the ninety-one-year old Noah Smithwick in his memoirs, *The Evolution of a State; or, Recollections of Old Texas Days,* Nanna Donaldson, comp., (Austin: University of Texas Press, 1983), 5.

64. Ramsey Yelvington, ed., *Travels and Adventures in Texas in the 1820s being the Reminiscenses of Mary Crownover Rabb* (Waco: Texian Press, 1962), 14.

65. The first quotation is from Emilie Wagner's letter to her parents, written between 22 April and 30 May 1851, p. 18, in The Wagner Family Collection, The Center for American History, University of Texas at Austin. The second quotation is from Friedrich Schlecht, *Mein Ausflug nach Texas* (My Excursion to Texas) (Bunzlau: Voigt, 1851), 152-53, cited in Waltraud Bartscht, "'Da waren Deutsche auch dabei!' 'The Story of a Texas-German Family," in Joseph Wilson, ed., *Texas and Germany: Crosscurrents*, Rice University Studies, vol. 63, no. 3,(Summer 1977), 39.

66. For the piano of Rosa Kleberg see: Rosa Kleberg, "Some of my early experiences in Texas," *QTSHA* 1 (1898): 298. For the concerts of Adolf Douai see his reminiscences, "My Texas Adventure (1852-1856)," 105 f., transcripts in Douai Papers, The Center of American Studies, University of Texas at Austin; and for more information on German women in Texas see Crystal Sasse Ragsdale, "The German Woman in Frontier Texas," in Glen E. Lich and Dona B. Reeves, eds., *German Culture in Texas* (Boston: Twayne, 1980, pp. 144-156.

67. Alwin Sörgel to Professor Karl Biedermann, editor of the paper *Der Herold*, Leipzig, on 4 October 1846, in Von-Maszewski, 81.

68. The letter from Emilie Wagner to her parents, written between 22 April and 30 May 1851, p. 18, in The Wagner Family Collection, The Center for American History, University of Texas at Austin.

69. Family notes by Sophie and Carolina Wagner, written in German in Chicago, Illinois, in April 1926, p. 2, translated and transcribed by Malcolm Henderson and Paul W. Guenzel, The Wagner Family Collection, The Center for American History, University of Texas at Austin.

70. For the acquisition of the ninety-two acres see Caroline von Roeder deed to Julius Wagner, Deeds Records, Vol. K, p. 402/3, DeWitt County Courthouse, Cuero, Texas. For the

sale of some of Albrecht von Roeder's livestock see appraisement and list of sales, in The Wagner Family Collection, The Center for American History, University of Texas at Austin.

Notes to Chapter 3

1. See Armand Baumann's short biography of his uncle Wilhelm Wagner, in Hildegard Kattermann, ed., *Familienbriefe*, transcribed and photocopies, Lahr, 1977, pp. Ch 47-48. Wagner Family Collection, Center for American History, University of Texas, Austin.

2. See William H. Wagner, "Wilhelm Wagner, Gründer des Freeport 'Deutscher Anzeiger,'" *Deutsch-Amerikanische Geschichtsblätter* 4, no. 2 (April 1904): 6.

3. For the biographies of Paulus and Schlosser see *Allgemeine Deutsche Biographie*, vol. 25 (Leipzig: Duncker & Humblot, 1887), 287-295; and vol. 31 (Leipzig: Duncker & Humblot, 1890), 533-41.

4. Quoted after Armand Baumann's short biography of his uncle Wilhelm Wagner, citied in: Kattermann, *Familienbriefe*, p. Ch 42.

5. William H. Wagner, "Wilhelm Wagner," 7. Johann Peter Hebel was not only a well-known and respected poet but as *Prälat,* he was the head of the protestant *Landeskirche* (church) in Baden and had a considerable influence on the spiritual and cultural feelings of unification.

6. Wilhelm Wagner in a letter from Gersbach in 1841 to an unknown recipient, in: Kattermann, *Familienbriefe*, p. Ch 44. For his lifestyle see letter from Wilhelm Wagner to Carl Baumann from Gersbach on 17 August 1836, in ibid, pp. 23-24, and elsewhere in ibid.

7. Karl Odenwald, *Aus einer Familienchronik* (Karlsruhe: Aktiendruckerei, 1898), 3.

8. Wilhelm Wagner in a letter from Gersbach to Carl Baumann on 27 May 1839, in Kattermann, *Familienbriefe*, 36.

9. For more details on this part of Swiss history, see Peter Dürrenmatt, *Schweizer Geschichte* (Zürich: Schweizer Druck- und Verlagshaus AG, 1963), 201-6; Wolfgang von Wartburg, *Geschichte der Schweiz* (München: Verlag von R. Oldenbourg, 1951), 484; and Ernst Gagliardi, *Geschichte der Schweiz* (Zürich: Rascher & Co., Verlag, 1920), 386. For Wilhelm Wagner's excitement about Waller and Keller see his letter to Carl Baumann, in Kattermann, *Familienbriefe*, 47.

10. William H. Wagner, "Wilhelm Wagner," 8.

11. For more details on the situation in Baden at this time see Wolfgang Hug, *Geschichte Badens* (Stuttgart: Konrad Theiss Verlag, 1992), 216-25; and Gerd Hepp, Hans Schleuning and Gabriele Süsskind, eds., *Badische Geschichte—vom Großherzogtum bis zur Gegenwart* (Stuttgart: Konrad Theiss Verlag, 1979), 31-36.

12. For more details on the life of Friedrich Hecker see George S. Hecker, *Biographical Sketch of Friedrich Karl Franz Hecker and Family Tree* (St. Louis, 1991; Alice Reynolds Hecker, "Friedrich Hecker," *German-American Review* (April 1946): 4-7; and Roland Paul, "'Freie Erde und freies Vaterland' —Friedrich Hecker in den USA," in Alfred G. Fre, ed., *Friedrich Hecker in den USA*, (Konstanz: Stadter Verlagsgesellschaft mbH, 1993), 15-41.

13. For more information on the German revolution of 1848-49 and its impact on the history of Baden see, for instance Willy Real, *Die Revolution in Baden 1848/49* (Stuttgart: Verlag W. Kohlhammer, 1983); Horst Struke and Wilfried Forstmann, eds., *Die europäischen Revolutionen von 1848* (Königstein/Ts: Verlag Anton Hain Meisenheim, 1979), 62-69; Wolfram Fischer, "Staat und Gesellschaft Badens im Vormärz," in Werner Conze, ed., *Staat und Gesellschaft im deutschen Vormärz 1815-1848* (Stuttgart: Klett-Cotta, 1962), 143-72; Henri Brunschwig, "The Revolution of 1848," in Heinz Lubasz, ed., *Revolutions in Modern European History*, New York: Macmillan, 1966), 86-92; Theodore S. Hamerow, *Restoration, Revolution, Reaction: Economics and Politics in Germany 1815-71* (Princeton, N.J.: Princeton University Press, 1958); Robert W. Lougee, *Midcentury Revolution, 1848: Society and Revolution in France and Germany* (Lexington, Mass.: Heath, 1972).

14. See the letter by Peter Wagner to his son Karl from April 1846, in Kattermann, *Familienbriefe*, 75-79.

15. The anecdote is told by Alfred Caroli, "Ortsgeschichte Aglasterhausens," unpublished manuscript, Aglasterhausen 1970, p. 14. For the suspension from office see: GLA 391/2142. Generallandesarchiv Karlsruhe.

16. Quoted by Kattermann, *Familienbriefe*, p. Ch 37.

17. Odenwald, *Familienchronik*, 4.

18. Wilhelm Wagner in a letter to his brother Karl Wagner from Brombach on 26 July 1850, in Kattermann, *Familienbriefe*, 107-10. For the details on Wilhelm Wagner's trials see: ibid, p. Ch 46 and various of his letters, in ibid, 107-12.

19. See the letters from Wilhelm Wagner to Carl Baumann from 25 June and 29 June 1850, in Kattermann, *Familienbriefe*, 110-13.

20. This incident is reported by Wilhelm's son William H. Wagner, "Wilhelm Wagner," 9, and in Kattermann, *Familienbriefe*, p. Ch 48.

21. Wilhelm's statement of defence in Th. Scholz, *Revolutionäre. Der Aufstand des Jahres 1849*, as quoted in: Fritz Schülin, *Brombach* (Brombach: Druckerei Gebr. Weber, 1972), 192.

22. See the whole statement of the church committee in Kattermann, *Familienbriefe*, p. Ch 49. For the prices and social conditions of that time see Hug, *Geschichte Badens*, 216-22.

23. For more information on those who fled to the United States, see Real, 175-77.

24. The poltical activities of the Forty-eighters in the United States are best described by Jörg Nagler, "'Ubi libertas, ibi patria': Deutsche Demokraten im Exil," in Alfred G. Frei, ed., *Friedrich Hecker in den USA* (Konstanz: Stadler Verlagsgesellschaft, 1993), 61-71. See also Michel Cordillot, "Aux Origines du Socialisme Dans le Sud des Etats-Unis: Les Immigres Allemands Dans les Etats Esclavagistes, 1848-1865," *Mouvement Social* 139 (1987): 51-75.

25. Carl Baumann to his uncle von Steudel from Mannheim on 18 March 1851, in Kattermann, *Familienbriefe*, 120.

26. Quoted in William H. Wagner, "Wilhelm Wagner," 9-10.

27. The information on Wilhelm Wagner's journey to America sheds some light on a still unsolved problem in historiography: how exact were the passenger lists at that time? From a letter by Carl Baumann to his uncle von Steudel, on 18 March 1851, we know that Wilhelm had plans to go to Le Havre the other week. Wilhelm's first letter from the United States most likely was sent on 26 April 1851 as he hints himself in his first preserved letter from the United States to his family from 1 June 1851 (see this letter in Kattermann, *Familienbriefe*, 120, 121). In the biography of his father, William Wagner states that his father arrived on board the vessel *Zürich* on 2 September 1851 after a twenty-one-day journey (William H. Wagner, "Wilhelm Wagner," 10.). No ship from Le Havre arrived at New York on 2 September let alone a vessel named *Zürich*. The only *Zürich* from Le Havre arriving at New York between March and June was the one on 24 April and it was the only ship with the names Wagner and Früh on the passenger list. It lists a Joh. B. Früh, age forty-five, which is correct. As countries of departure for Früh and Wagner, Switzerland is given, which is correct also. The first name of the one Wagner on the list, though, is given as Joseph, whose age was forty-six. Wilhelm was forty-seven at that time. And no Anna Früh is mentioned on the list. This is not surprising, however, as no papers were required for entering the United States in 1851 and passenger lists must be seen more as freight papers. For the inaccuracy of the passenger lists see Markus Günther, Auswandererlisten und Passenger Lists 1855-1864 (M.A. thesis, Ruhr-Universität Bochum, 1992).

Notes to Chapter 4

1. For more information on this topic see Edward K. Spann, *The New Metropolis, New York City, 1840-1857* (New York: Columbia University Press, 1981), 25 ff. For a detailed study

of the Germans in New York see Stanley Nadel, *Little Germany: Ethnicity, Religion, and Class in New York City, 1845-80* (Urbana: University of Illinois Press, 1990). as well as the review of this book by Lizabeth Cohen, "Ethnicity and Class in Little Germany," *Reviews in American History* 19 , no. 3 (1991): 374-78; Michael Just, Agnes Bretting, and Hartmut Bickelmann, *Von Deutschland nach Amerika: Zur Sozialgeschichte der Auswanderung im 19. und 20. Jahrhundert* (Stuttgart: Steiner Verlag, 1992).

2. *New York Times*, 23 June 1853. For a detailed study of land agents awaiting immigrants see Ingrid Schöberl, *Amerikanische Einwandererwerbung in Deutschland, 1845-1914* (Stuttgart: Franz Steiner Verlag, 1990), especially pp. 19-37.

3. William Brown, *A Four Years Residence in the U.S. and Canada*, as quoted by Agnes Bretting, *Soziale Probleme deutscher Einwanderer in New York City 1800-1860* (Wiesbaden: Franz Steiner Verlag, 1981), 41.

4. For more information about Rischmüller and his company see Bretting, *Soziale Probleme*, 44 ff.

5. Quotation in Richard N. Current, *The History of Wisconsin*, volume 2, *The Civil War Era, 1848-1873* (Madison: State Historical Society of Wisconsin, 1976), 1.

6. For the early history of the State of Wisconsin and the various figures see Current, 42 ff, 53 ff, and 76 ff. For the letters sent back home to Germany also see: Richard H. Zeitlin, *Germans in Wisconsin* (Madison: The State Historical Society of Wisconsin, 1977), 9-12.

7. This anecdote is related in Robert W. Wells, *This is Milwaukee* (Milwaukee: Renaissance Books, 1970), 144. For the Forty-eighters coming to Wisconsin and the publications in Germany about Wisconsin see Wilhelm Hense-Jensen, *Wisconsin's Deutsch-Amerikaner bis zum Schluss des Neunzehnten Jahrhunderts*, 2 vols., Milwaukee: Im Verlage der Deutschen Gesellschaft, 1900-1902). Vol. 2, chapter two, "The Forty Eighters," translated by Joseph Schafer in 1939, in Joseph Schafer Papers, Box 6, Mss, 746, The State Historical Society of Wisconsin, Madison, Wis.

8. Thus Theodore Wettstein's son Carl remembered Market Square when he first saw it at the age of twelve. Quoted in John Goadby Gregory, *History of Milwaukee, Wisconsin*, vol. 2 (Chicago: The S.J. Clarke Publishing Co., 1931), 1284 f. For the history of Market Square and the German area in Milwaukee see Randy Garber, ed., *Built in Milwaukee: An Architectural View of the City* (Milwaukee: City of Milwaukee, 1983).

9. Quoted in "Wisonsin's German Element," collection of the State Historical Society, vol. 12, 1892, p. 316, transcribed by Lissack for the unfinished biography of Theodore Wettstein, in Field Notes for a Biographical Sketch of Wettstein, Theodore, 1812-1877. Wiss, Mss, MM, The State Historical Society of Wisconsin, Madison, Wis.

Born at Elberfeld on the valley of the Wupper on 5 January 1812, Wettstein was an intriguing and controversial figure in Milwaukee's public life. Having been an esteemed tradesman and highly respected citizen of his hometown, he grew very dissatisfied with Germany's economic and political situation in the 1840s. The manufacturing industry at the Wupper valley lost ground to increasing competition, wages went down, prices up. Many people contemplated emigrating to the United States and were encouraged by numerous reports and letters. Having four sons and three daughters, Wettstein regarded it as his responsibility to give his family the best start in life, and this he thought only possible in America. Together with 156 other emigrants from Elberfeld and Barmen he had recruited, he came to Milwaukee in 1848 on the same route as Wilhelm Wagner three years later. Forming a partnership with a Mr. Carline, Wettstein opened a store on Spring Street first, selling hardware, yard goods, and wines. One year after his arrival at Milwaukee, he became the talk of the town by arranging a subscription ball to bring together what he considered to be the German elite of the town. Admission to this ball was only allowed upon invitation, and all participants had to wear evening dress and suits. Up until that event, everyone had been free to attend social parties in heavy boots and Sunday coats. Many Germans protested at what they saw as bringing European customs and class rule to America. Wettstein nevertheless succeeded and arranged even more balls like that in the future. He also founded the *Schul Verein* (school society) to foster education in Milwaukee. He organized the *Musik Verein* (music society) with the Austrian Hans Balatka (a Forty-eighter himself) as director, and he was one of the organizers of the German Historical Society. The hotel Gasthof zum Deutschen Hause burnt down in 1855 but Wettstein reopened a new house in 1858 on Market Square, which he called the New Hotel Wettstein, and which became the St. Charles Hotel. For more biographical information on Theodore Wettstein see Rudolph H. Ross, *Milwaukee* (Milwaukee: Schnellpressen-Druck des "Herold," 1871), 272-416; Gregory, 619, 1284-89; Kate Everest Levi, "Geographical Origin of German Immigration to Wisconsin," *Wisconsin Historical Collections*, vol. 14 (Madison: The State Historical Society of Wisconsin, 1898), 373 f; Wilhelm Hense-Jensen, *Wisconsin's Deutsch-Amerikaner bis zum Schluß des neunzehnten Jahrhunderts*, vol. 1 (Milwaukee: Im Verlage der Deutschen Gesellschaft, 1900), 122-23, 134-35; and the Chronology of Theodore Wettstein's life as compiled by Zastrow for the unfinished biography of Theodore Wettstein, in Field Notes for a Biographical Sketch of Wettstein, Theodore, 1812-1877, WISS, Mss, MM, The State Historical Society of Wisconsin, Madison, Wis.

10. See Wilhelm's description of American food in his first letter from the United States on 1 June 1851, in Kattermann, *Familienbriefe 1811-1871*, transcribed and photocopied, limited edition, Lahr 1977, p. 122, The Wagner Family Collection, The Center for American History, University of Texas at Austin.. For the criticism of Wettstein's menu see A. C. Wheeler, *The Chronicles of Milwaukee: Being a narrative History of the Town from its earliest period to the present* (Milwaukee: Jermain & Brightman, Publishers, 1861), 284. The importance of food as a measurement of the standard of living in the United States for the German immigrants is described by Wolfgang Helbich in his article, "Die ''Englischen': German Immigrants Describe Nineteenth-Century American Society," *Amerikastudien / American Studies* 36, no. 4, (1991): 518.

11. Although Wilhelm Wagner's son William gives the name of the German farmer as Count Götz von Wrisberg (see William H. Wagner, "Wilhelm Wagner, Gründer des Freeport *Deutscher Anzeiger*," *Deutsch-Amerikanische Geschichtsblätter* 4, no. 2 [April 1904]: 10), the information of Wilhelm Wagner himself in his letter surely is more precise. See Wilhelm Wagner's first letter from the United States from June 1, 1851, in Kattermann, *Familienbriefe,* 122, The Wagner Family Collection, The Center for American History, University of Texas at Austin. For the information on Wriesberg see Hense-Jensen, 193; and N. N., *History of Green County, Wisconsin* (Springfield, Ill.: Union Publishing Company, 1884), 534, 774.

12. Born in Livermore, Maine, on April 22, 1818, Cadwallader Colden Washburn was the fourth of seven sons of Israel and Patty Washburn (who had eleven children in all) who were sure their sons would rise to fame in life, which they actually did. After studying law, Cadwallader moved west on the advice of his uncle Reuel Washburn and settled down at Mineral Point, Wisconsin, where he married Jeanette Garr from New York in 1849. In 1854 he was elected to the House of Representatives, where his brothers Elihu and Israel, Jr., already represented Illinois and Maine, and served for three terms.

It is interesting to note, however, why Cad Washburn came to Mineral Point in the first place, as this had to do less with land speculation than with another way of making a good profit. The first white men coming to what is now the state of Wisconsin were fur traders. Then they took advantage of the rich land and the abundance of trees. And although land remained the basic attraction of Wisconsin, for some time another industry played the dominant economic role in Wisconsin: lead mining. The first white man to discover that various Indian tribes had a century-long tradition of lead mining was the Frenchman Nicolas Perrot in 1690. More and more of his countrymen came, and the French began working the lead mines together with the Indians until Anglo-American prospectors ignored the old Indian rights and opened lead mines on their territory. In the beginning of the nineteenth century, miners from the Missouri and Galena mines in northern Illinois followed the call northward, and thus Elder William Roberts, Solomon Francis, and Christopher Law founded the settlement of Mineral Point in 1827. Like the price for lead, Mineral Point had its ups and downs until the end of the infamous Black Hawk War in 1832 when prices, profits, and population went up. That the Sauk and Fox Indians had been driven west of the Mississippi forever was the biggest national advertisement for this mining area. From then on, things developed rapidly. In 1834, Mineral Point not only got its post office but was also selected as the site of one of the two land offices for the Territory of Michigan—probably because it was the only county seat in the lead mining region. Its seems only natural, therefore, that two years later, when the Territory of Wisconsin was formed by dividing the Territory of Michigan, the formal ceremony of inauguration took place in Mineral Point. The city was booming. No wonder that an ambitious young lawyer like Cadwallader C. Washburn would choose this prosperous Western community for the beginning of his career. The gold rush to California and declining lead production led to the slow decline of Mineral Point, its economic importance, and population. When Cad Washburn sold the farm to Wilhelm and his friend, a little more than 2,000 people still lived at Mineral Point, some 700 having left for California the previous years.

For more information about the colorful and eventful life of Cadwallader C. Washburn and his family see Mary Hebberd, "Cadwalader [sic] Washburn—his gift to La Crosse was a library," *Coulee Gazette* (March 1976): 5; N.N., "The Washburn Triumvirate." *Wisconsin Then And Now* 7, no. 4,(November, 1960), 1, 8; Clare L. Marquette, The Business Activities of C. C. Washburn (Ph.D.diss., University of Wisconsin, 1940), 8; and Lilian Washburn, *My Seven Sons* (Portland, ME: Fairmont Publishing Company, 1940). For the history of Mineral Point and the lead mining industry in Wisconsin see George Fiedler, *Mineral Point: a History*, 3rd. ed.,(Mineral Point, Wisconsin: The Memorial Pendarvis Endowment Trust Fund, 1986); Joseph Schafer, *The Wisconsin Lead Region* (Madison: State Historical Society of Wisconsin, 1932) and Current, 8-9, 72, 102-3, 379-80.

13. See for instance the letter of Johann Fuss to the vicar Dohmen from Milwaukee, 20 February 1846: "But the climate in America where we live is a healthy region. In the summer the sun reaches the same height as in Germany and here it stands higher in winter than in Germany. Here in winter it is a trifle warmer, otherwise the climate is just like in Germany. . . . Here it is not as in Germany where one has to pay taxes and dues for everything one has earned in the sweat of his brow; here the farmer is his own master." Germans in the U.S., letters # 51-75, 1784-1933, Box 1, No. 201-433 (here No.: 294), WISS Mss HO., The State Historical Society of Wisconsin, Madison, Wis.; and the letter from Nikolaus Frett to a Mr. Marhöffer from Chicago, 30 August 1841: "When we had bought the land, we didn't know what to say when we saw the splendid fruit and the high grass. . . . Here one knows nothing about taxes. Here one does not need to worry about beggars as we do in Germany. Here a man works for himself. Here everybody is equal to everybody. Here nobody takes off one's hat for nobody. We no longer long for Germany. Every day we thank our dear LORD that he has brought us from slavery to paradise—so to speak." Germans in the U.S., letters # 51-75, 1784-1933, Box 1, No. 201-433 (here No.: 70), WISS Mss HO., The State Historical Society of Wisconsin, Madison, Wis. For German descriptions of the pioneer's life in Illinois see Raymond Jürgen Spahn, "German Accounts of Early Nineteenth-Century Life in Illinois," *Papers on Language and Literature* 14, no. 4 (Fall 1978): 473-88; and for an interesting example of an individual's life at the Illinois frontier see: Stephen J. Tonsor ed., "'I Am My Own Boss'—A German Immigrant Writes from Illinois," *Journal of the Illinois State Historical Society* 54, no. 4 (1961): 392-404.

14. William H. Wagner, "Wilhelm Wagner," 10. In contrast to this see: Wilhelm Wagner's first letter from the United States from 1 June 1851, in Kattermann, *Familienbriefe*, 123.

15. Wilhelm Wagner's first letter from the United States from 1 June 1851, in Kattermann, *Familienbriefe*, 124.

16. The first to arrive in that area had been John B. Skinner (the creek was named after him eventually) in 1829, not to settle down as a farmer but for the purpose of mining. More and more miners came over the years, followed by land speculators and farmers. Four men can be called the fathers of Monroe, as they owned the nucleus of the land on which Monroe grew: Joseph Payne, Jacob Andrick, Jarvis Rattan, and Jacob Lybrand. After some political fighting about whether the township of New Mexico should be made seat of justice for Green County as Andrick wanted it to be, or the township of Monroe, which actually made it at the ballot by a small majority of votes, the town was formally organized at a meeting in the courthouse on 3 April 1849. For the history of Monroe and Jordan see E.C. Hamilton, *The Story of Monroe . . . its Past and its Progress toward the Present* (Monroe, Wisconsin: The Print Shop, Monroe Public Schools, 1976); N.N., *History of Green County, Wisconsin*, 906-93, 890-905; Helen M. Bingham, *History of Green County, Wisconsin* (Milwaukee: Burdick & Armitage, Printers, 1877), 78-126, 202-10.

17. Michael Kachelhoffer was the fifth child of Henricus and Maria-Anna Pflugmacher Kachelhoffer and had immigrated to the United States in 1845, having been born in Schoenenbourg, Alsace, France, on 26 February 1826. The year he arrived in New York, his cousins Matthias and John Hettinger had started their business in the small and fairly new Yellow Creek settlement, The Yellow Creek Brewery, which became one of the most enterprising businesses of the area. Upon his arrival, Kachelhoffer first moved in with his cousins and opened his wagon manufacturing business right across the road from the brewery. The first people to come to that creek and stay there for good in 1836 were Henry C. Brown with his parents from Joliet, Illinois, S. J. Stebbins from Lebanon, New York, and Georg T. Lamm with his family from Baden, Germany. At the end of the 1830s, more settlers like John Bardel in 1839 from the various German countries including the Alsace arrived in Stephenson County and established their new home at the Yellow Creek. One of his daughters, Margaret, married one of the Kachelhoffers. Michael, who had married Catherine Mary Lamm, daughter of Georg and Gertrude Hausmann Lamm, on 2 September 1851—weeks before he met Wilhelm Wagner for the first time—was not the only Kachelhoffer in the Yellow Creek settlement. In 1852, his brother Joseph had arrived there too and became a partner of the Hettingers. Although small, Yellow Creek settlement was vastly populated by Germans.

For the history of Yellow Creek Settlement and the Kachelhoffers see Philip L. Keister and Mary X. Barrett, eds., *History of Stephenson County, 1970* (Freeport, Ill.,: County of Stephenson, 1972), 195; N.N., *The History of Stephenson County, Illinois* (Chicago: Western Historical Company, 1880), 678-83; and Helen K. Miner and Frances K. Halper, *The Kachelhoffer Families from Berne, Switzerland to Alsace, France and America,* typescript copy, n.p., 1980, in Freeport Public Library, Freeport, Illinois; and the *Freeport Weekly Bulletin*, 22 September 1904.

18. For the history of the railroad from Chicago to Galena see Howard Gary Brownson, "History of the Illinois Central Railroad to 1870," *University of Illinois Studies in the Social Sciences* 1 (1915), 68-69; William K. Ackerman, *Early Illinois Railroads*, Fergus Historical Series, No. 23, Chicago: np, 1884; and William Cronon, *Nature's Metropolis: Chicago and the Great West* (New York: W.W.Norton & Company, 1992), 65-70.

19. William H. Wagner, "Wilhelm Wagner," 11-12.

20. Michael Doll had moved to Freeport from Joliet, Illinois, in 1841 and worked as a butcher until 1849 when he opened the City Hotel, which he ran until 1853. Then he returned to

butchering. The hotel at the corner of Stephenson Street and Van Buren Avenue became the State Bank on August 1, 1891. That was forty years after the first bank had been established in Freeport. For more biographical information on Michael Doll and his family see N.N., *In the Foot-Prints of the Pioneers of Stephenson County, Illinois* (Freeport, Ill.: The Pioneer Publishing Co., 1900),151. For F. P. Koehler see: N.N., *The History of Stephenson County, Illinois,* 681.

Having been a courier in the Black Hawk War, William Baker did not want to only settle in the land of the Winnebago Indians (whose language by the way all the Bakers spoke fluently) but also to establish a town. Soon after the Bakers, the first Germans arrived in the area, including Michael Holler and his family from Alsace. For the history of Freeport see Keister and Barrett, 367.

21. For the history of St. Johns and Wilhelm Wagner's relationsship with it see: N.N., *In the Foot-Prints of the Pioneers*, 389; William H. Wagner, "Wilhelm Wagner," 12; and the Resolution of the Evangelical German United Lutheran & German Reformed Congregation from 13 March 1854, as well as the centennial church history from 1948 in Church Records of St. John United Church of Christ, 1010 South Park Boulevard, Freeport, Illinois. For the history of the St. Chrischona Pilgrim Mission in Basel, Switzerland, which had sent missionaries out into the world for about fifty years, see C. H. Rappard, *Die Pilgermission zu St. Chrischona, 1840-1908* (Basel: Schriften-Niederlage zu St. Chrischona, 1908).

22. See Wilhelm Wagner's letter to Carl Baumann and family from 22 March 1857, in Armand Baumann collection, pp. 49-52. in The Wagner Family Collection, The Center for American History, University of Texas at Austin. For the information on the Unitarian congregation that Wilhelm Wagner served until his death, see William H. Wagner, "Wilhelm Wagner," 12; and Emil Mannhardt, "Gemeinde-Chronologie - Chronologische Darstellung der äußeren Entwicklung des religiösen Lebens unter den Deutschen in Illinois," *Deutsch-Amerikanische Geschichtsblätter* 5, no. 4, (1905): 43. For the history of Ridott and Silver Creek Townships see Keister and Barrett, *History of Stephenson County*, 140-45, 190-94. Jakob Höbel was the brother of John Höbel who, in 1839 at the age of fourteen, had come to the United States alone to have a better start in life. One year later, his parents, along with his sister and his three brothers Jakob, Louis, and Philip, also came across the Atlantic and settled in Logansport, Indiana, for a short time. In August 1842 the Höbel family moved to Freeport. For more biographical information see: N.N., *Portrait and Biographical Album of Stephenson County, Ill.*, (Chicago: Chapman Brothers, 1888), 447.

23. For the history of the *Deutscher Anzeiger* see William H. Wagner: "Ein deutsches Zeitungs-Jubiläum in Illinois," *Deutsch-Amerikanische Geschichtsblätter* 4, no. 1 (January 1904): 60; and William H. Wagner: "50 Jahre!" *Deutscher Anzeiger*, fiftieth anniversary number, 14 October 1903, p. 3. For the land transactions see J.B. Früh & wife Anna to Johann Haesely, in Recorded Deeds, Vol. 10, p. 478, Green County records, Courthouse, Monroe, Wis.; Wilhelm Wagner & wife Frederike to Taylor & Daniel H. Morgan, in Recorded Deeds, Vol. 16, p. 514, ibid.; and Wilhelm Wagner & wife Frederike to Andrew Hansen, in Recorded Deeds, Vol. 36, p. 550, ibid. For details on Früh's business see *Deutscher Anzeiger,* 19 January 1855, p. 3, col. 4; and *Deutscher Anzeiger*, 8 January 1873, p. 1, col. 1.

24. Among those who wrote for and/or owned a newspaper were such prominent German writers and politicians as Carl Heinrich Schnauffer (founder of the *Baltimore Wecker*), Theodor Gülich (editor of the *Davenport Democrat*), August Thieme (editor of the *Wächter am Erie*), Oswald Ottendörfer (editor of the *New Yorker Staatszeitung*), Emil Preetorius (editor-in-chief of the *Westliche Post*), and Georg Schneider (editor of the *Illinois Staatszeitung*)—to name only a very few. See Carl Wittke, *Refugees of Revolution: the German Forty-Eighters in America* (Philadelphia: University of Pennsylvania Press, 1952), 262-79. Wittke even mentions Wilhelm Wagner, p. 269. For more information on Caspar Butz see Adolph E. Zucker, ed., *The Forty-*

Eighters: Political Refugees of the German Revolution of 1848 (New York: Russell and Russell, 1950), 61, 144, 148, 283; and Andrew Jacke Townsend, *The Germans of Chicago*, in *Jahrbuch der Deutsch-Amerikanischen Historischen Gesellschaft von Illinois* vol. 32 (Chicago: The University of Chicago Press, 1932), 21.

25. For the life and times of Dr. Adolf Douai see Carol Poore, "Changing Visions of the Future: Radical Forty-Eighters Encounter America," in Charlotte L. Brancaforte, ed., *The German Forty-Eighters in the United States* (New York: Peter Lang, 1989), 109-113; Lich, *The German Texans*, 136, 138; and Adolph Douai's unpublished, transcribed memoirs "My Texas Adventure (1852-1856)," 109, 114., in Adolph Douai Papers, The Center of American Studies, University of Texas at Austin.

26. For the founding of Freeport's *Sängerbund* and *Turnverein* see Robert F. Koenig, *Camera Studies of Freeport, Illinois* (Freeport, Ill.: Wagner Printing Co., 1954), 222; and William H. Wagner, "Wilhelm Wagner," 14. For the importance of the *Vereine* in the movement for a united democratic Germany, see for example Klaus Goebel and Manfred Wichelhaus, eds., *Aufstand der Bürger*, 3rd. ed. (Wuppertal: Peter Hammer Verlag, 1974), 232.

27. Biesele attributes the founding of singing societies only to the German's love for music and establishing societies. See Rudolph Biesele, *The History of the German Settlementsin Texas* (Austin: Press of von Boeckmann-Jones, 1930), 220-23. For Fritz Goldbeck and his poem "Ein Germane bin ich" see Hubert P. Heinen, "The Consciousness of Being German: Regional Literature in German Texas," in Theodore Gish and Richard Spuler, eds., *Eagle in the New World* (College Station: Texas A&M University Press, 1986), 138. For Hoffmann von Fallersleben's "Auswanderungslied," see Lutz Röhrich, "German Emigrant Songs," in Gish and Spuler, *Eagle in the New World*, 56. Wilhelm Wagner's poem on Robert Blum was printed in *Deutscher Anzeiger*, 10 November 1858, p. 1, col. 3-4. Singing societies as part of the *Deutschtum* are also mentioned by Francis Edward Abernethy, "Texas Folklore and German Culture," in Joseph Wilson, ed., *Texas and Germany: Crosscurrents*, Rice University Studies, vol. 63, no. 3 (Summer 1977): 91.

28. For the history and importance of the *Turner* societies see Augustus J. Prahl, "The Turner," in Zucker, ed., *The Forty-Eighters*, 79-110 (the quotation about the purpose of the Cincinnati-Turnverein is on p. 93); Hannes Neumann, *Die deutsche Turnbewegung in der Revolution 1848/49 und in der amerikanischen Emigration* (Stuttgart: Hofmann, 1968); Horst Überhorst, *Turner unter dem Sternenbanner* (München: Moos, 1978); Rolf Wagner, "Turner Societies and the Socialist Tradition," in Hartmut Keil, ed., *German Worker's Culture in the United States, 1850-1920* (Washington, D.C.: Smithsonian Institute, 1988), 221-39; C. Eugene Miller, "The Contributions of German Immigrants to the Union Cause in Kentucky," *Filson Club History Quarterly* 64, no. 4, (1990): 462-78; Mary Lou LeCompte, "German-American Turnvereins in Frontier Texas, 1851-1880," *Journal of the West* 26, no.1 (1987): 18-25; and Jörg Nagler, "Politisches Exil in den USA zur Zeit des Vormärz und der Revolution von 1848/49," in Michael Salewski and Jürgen Elvert, eds., *Deutschland und der Westen im 19. und 20. Jahrhundert*, Band 1, Historische Mitteilungen der Ranke Gesellschaft, Beiheft 7, (Stuttgart: Franz Steiner Verlag, 1993), 267-93 (here especially: 285-86). A case-study is described by La Vern J. Rippley, "Status versus Ethnicity: The Turners and Bohemians of New Ulm," in Brancaforte, *The German Forty-Eighters*, 257-78.

29. Gregory, *History of Milwaukee*, vol. II, p. 1288.

30. Lincoln's "House Divided Speech" as published in Henry Steele Commager, ed., *Documents of American History*, vol. 1, (Englewood Cliffs, N.J.: Prentice Hall, 1973), 345. The second quotation is from Allan Nevins, *The Emergence of Lincoln*, vol. 1 (London: Charles Scribner's Sons, 1950), 373.

31. For more details on the historical background of this and the other debates see for

instance Carl Sandburg, *Abraham Lincoln, The Prairie Years and the War Years* (New York: Harcourt Brace Jovanovich, 1974), 137-45; and Nevins, 374-99. For recollections of the Freeport debate see Robert J. Schmelzle, ed., *Freeport Debate Centennial* (Freeport, Ill.: Wagner Printing Company, 1958); and William T. Rawleigh, ed., *Freeport's Lincoln* (Freeport, Ill.: Wagner Printing Company, 1988, facsimile edition of the hardback book published by W. T. Rawleigh in 1930.)

32. The article on the arrival of the candidates and the topics of their speeches is printed under the heading, "Amerika—Die Volksversammlung in Freeport am 27. August," *Deutscher Anzeiger*, 2 September 1858, p. 2, col. 1 and 2. The evaluation of the speeches was given in the *Deutscher Anzeiger*, 8 September 1858, p. 2, col. 1 and 2. Translations by the author. In his articles, Wilhelm Wagner showed as much bias as all the other papers that reported about this event at that time. The *Freeport Bulletin* and the *Chicago Times* heavily campaigned for Douglas, whereas the *Freeport Journal* and the *Chicago Press and Tribune* were on Lincoln's side. And although the Democrats were strong in Freeport, the north of Illinois, including Stephenson County, brought forth a large majority for the Republicans. The south of Illinois voted mainly for Douglas, and the elections laws at that time favored the southern districts. The vote in the legislature—the people did not vote for the senators directly—was fifty-four for Douglas and forty-six for Lincoln.

33. Marvin Trask Grattan's recollections of the Freeport debate in Rawleigh, 140.

34. The first quotation about Wilhelm Wagner's campaign for Douglas is from *Deutscher Anzeiger*, 15 August 1860, p. 2, col. 1; and the second, putting the blame on Lincoln, is from *Deutscher Anzeiger*, 5 September 1860, p. 2, col. 1.

Wittke, in *Refugees of Revolutions*, still repeats the old legend that the Germans had been for Lincoln more or less unanimously (see 203-20) that originated in William E. Dodd's article, "The Fight for the Northwest, 1860," in *American Historical Review* 16, (July 1911): 774-88. For more critical and more recent research see James M. Bergquist, "The Forty-Eighters and the Republican Convention of 1860," in Brancaforte, *The German Forty-Eighters*, 141-56; Jörg Nagler, "The Lincoln-Fremont Debate and the Forty-Eighters," in ibid, 157-78; and Frederick Luebke, *Ethnic Voters and the Election of Lincoln* (Lincoln: University of Nebraska Press, 1971). A very good assessment of the German political attitude prior to the Civil War is given by Bruce Levine, *The Spirit of 1848: German Immigrants, Labor Conflict, and the Coming of the Civil War* (Urbana: University of Ilinois Press, 1992).

35. See the letter of Wilhelm Wagner to his mother Luise dated 25 March 1860, in Kattermann, *Familienbriefe*, 196; and William H. Wagner, "Wilhelm Wagner," 13. For the efforts of the Forty-eighters to establish their own schools see Bettina Goldberg, "The Forty-Eighters and the School System in America: The Theory and Practice of Reform," in Brancaforte, *The German Forty-Eighters*, 203-18.

36. Wilhelm Wagner in his letter to his family and friends in Germany dated 22 March 1857, in Kattermann, *Familienbriefe*, 163.

37. Thus Wilhelm Wagner in his letter to his mother Luise dated 25 March 1860, in Kattermann, *Familienbriefe,* 195.

38. Ibid.

39. Wilhelm Wagner to his sister Henriette Baumann 15 September 1870, in Armand Baumann collection, p. 54 in The Wagner Family Collection, The Center for American History, University of Texas at Austin. For Wilhelm Wagner's speech and his son's enlistments see N.N., *The History of Stephenson County, Illinois*, 308-41; and Military Records, Civil War, National Archives, Washington D.C. For German participation in the Civil War see for example the review of Bruce Levine's book *The Spirit of 184* by Hans L. Trefousse, "Class and Ethnicity: German Immigrants, Radicalism, and the Civil War," *Reviews in American History,* 21, no. 2

(1993): 213-17; Eugene C. Miller, "German Immigrants at Antietam," *Maryland Historical Magazine* 87, no. 3 (1992): 309-15; Edward G. Longacre, "A Young German Joins the Cavalry," *Manuscripts* 40, no. 4 (1988): 323-25; and Albert W. Haarmann, "Deutsche Regimenter in der Armee der Union," *Zeitschrift für Heereskunde* 52 (1988): 338-40.

39. In her letter to Julius Wagner from 5 January 1856, Luise Becker wrote that it was not very nice of him not to write anymore: "Have you forgotten us all completely, don't you think about those anymore who love you so dearly? . . . . We have no explanation for your not writing your mother even on our father's death. . . . Wilhelm complains about you. You have not answered his letters." She continues telling Julius about Wilhelm's family, his printing company, and the founding of the *Deutsche Anzeiger*, in Kattermann, *Familienbriefe* 148.

41. For the complete story of the lawsuit against Wilhelm Wagner see William H. Wagner, "50 Jahre!" *Deutscher Anzeiger*, fiftieth anniversary number, 14 October 1903, p. 3; and for the *Saengerfest*, *Deutscher Anzeiger*, 6 June 1877, p. 8, col. 2; 20 June 1877, p. 1, cols. 2-3 and June 27, 1877, page 1, cols. 2-6 and page 4, cols. 1-4. The following groups had come: ten people from the *Liederkranz* from La Crosse, Wisconsin; five people from the *Concordia* from Janesville, Wisconsin; seven from the Dubuque *Männerchor*; with twelve people from the *Germania Musiccorps*, the *Helvetia Männerchor*, Dubuque, Iowa; twenty from the *Gesangverein Germania*, Rockford, Illinois; twenty-three from the *Concordia*, Watertown, Wisconsin; twenty-nine from the *Gesang Sektion der freien Gemeinde*, Milwaukee; eleven from the *Germania Männerchor*, Sterling, Illinois; two from the *Germania Männerchor*, Waterloo, Iowa; two from the *Gesangsverein Teutonia*, Burlington, Wisconsin; two from the *Liedertafel*, Milwaukee; and two from the *Männerchor des Musikvereins,* Milwaukee.

42. N.N., *The History of Stephenson County, Illinois,* 423.

Notes to Chapter 5

1. Terry G. Jordan, *German Seed in Texas Soil* (Austin: University of Texas Press, 1985), 182-85; Rena Mazyck Andrews, "German Pioneers in Texas: Civil War Period," (M.A. thesis, University of Chicago, 1929), 29-34 and 46-54; Robert W. Shook, "The Battle of the Nueces, August 10, 1862," *SHQ* 66, no. 1 (July 1962): 31-42; Ella Lonn, *Foreigners in the Confederacy* (Chapel Hill: University of North Carolina Press, 1940), 311-13; James Marten, *Texas Divided - Loyalty and Dissent in the Lone Star State 1856-1874* (Lexington, Kentucky: The University Press of Kentucky, 1990), 113-21; and Glen E. Lich, *The German Texans* (San Antonio: The University of Texas Institute of Texan Cultures at San Antonio, 1981), 91-97. Many Germans in Texas opposed to secession were also closely associated with the Know-Nothing movement and nativism. See Walter L. Buenger, "Secession and the Texas German Community: Editor Lindheimer vs. Editor Flake," *SHQ* 82, no. 4 (April 1979): 379-402 and the same, *Secession and the Union in Texas* (Austin: University of Texas Press, 1984), 80-134.

2. These are the findings of Cornelia Küffner, "Texas-Germans' Attitudes Towards Slavery: Biedermeier Sentiments and Class Consciousness in Austin, Colorado and Fayette Counties," (M.A. thesis, University of Houston, 1994). The figure about Otto von Roeder's slaves is on page 136.

3. For Lindheimer's attitude see Selma Marie Metzenthin-Raunick, "One Hundred Years Neu Braunfelser Zeitung," *American-German Review* 19, no.6 (1953): 15-16; and Lich, *The German Texans*, 52. For new evidence regarding the German attitude towards the Confederacy and service in the army see Walter D. Kamphoefner, "Texas Germans and Civil War Issues: The Evidence from Immigrant Letters," *The Journal of the German-Texan Heritage Society* 13, no.1 (Spring 1991): 16-23.

4. This was actually quite a common attitude everywhere. This is confirmed already by the findings of Andrea Mehrländer in *In Dixieland I'll Take My Stand: The German Communities*

of Charleston, Richmond and New Orleans During the Civil War (Columbia: University of South Carolina Press, 2001) She concentrates her study on German behavior in Charleston, South Carolina; Richmond, Virginia; and New Orleans, Louisiana, stating that most Germans behaved very much like their Anglo-American neighbors.

5. "Family Notes" by Sophie and Lina Wagner, Chicago, Ill., April 1926, translated by Malcolm Henderson with explanations in brackets by Paul W. Guenzel, p. 2, in The Wagner Family Collection, The Center for American History, University of Texas at Austin. These "Family Notes" have to be used carefully as all the details about the early life of their father had been handed down to them by Julius Wagner himself or his wife Emilie. Therefore Julius very likely tried to extenuate his laziness at the university and his failure in exams by telling his children something different. Lina and Sophie wrote, "After leaving the university our father spent some years working as an 'Assessor' (assistant judge) in Baden." Ibid., 1. This implies that he had passed a final exam, which is in no way supported by the various examination files in the different German archives and in Kattermann, *Familienbriefe*.

6. Letter of Hermann von Roeder to his mother 16 April 1864 as quoted in Flora L. von Roeder, *These are the Generations* (Houston: Baylor College of Medicine, 1978), 156.

7. For more details about the battle of the Nueces see R. H. Williams and John W. Sansom, *The Massacre on the Nueces River* (Grand Prairie, Texas: Frontier Times Publishing House, n.d); Shook, 31-42; James Marten, *Texas Divided* (Lexington, Kentucky: University Press of Kentucky, 119-21; Robert H. Williams, *With the Border Ruffians: Memoirs of the Far West, 1852-1868* (London: John Murray, 1908), 235-50; Walter L. Buenger, *Secession and the Union in Texas* (Austin: The University of Texas Press, 1984), 80-86, 91-105; Guido E. Ransleben, *A Hundred Years of Comfort in Texas* (San Antonio: Naylor Company, 1954), 86-126; Claude Elliott, "Union Sentiment in Texas, 1861-1865," *SHQ* 50, no. 4 (April 1947), 463- 66; a very colorful description of the flight to Mexico is given by: N.N., Ein Deutsch-Texaner," *Darmstädter Zeitung* 17 May 1893, No. 227, p. 1 in Jacob Kuechler Papers, The Center for American History, University of Texas at Austin. (The author's sources spell the name with the umlaut, whereas the University of Texas Center spells it *Kuechler*. A distinction in spelling will be made in this book, depending on if the reference is to the collection or to the person Jacob Küchler.)

The colorful description of Küchler's escape also includes some gruesome stories like: "En route they [the group of Unionists who fled after the battle on the Nueces] learned that Duffs band had dragged a number of German women, loyal to the Union, out of bed in the middle of the night and hung them on the next trees available as a revenge for their lost fellow soldiers and because of the escape of those hated 'Dutch.'" Whether true or not, those Germans loyal to the Union faced hard times during the Civil War and often paid with their lives for this loyalty. The *Hängebund* (Hanging bands) and the atrocities performed by Captain J. P. Waldrip and his gang, like the killing of Julius Schütze's brother Louis in Fredericksburg, are only parts of the tragic story of the intra-German conflict from 1861 to 1865. For the cruel side of the War see especially Francis Edward Abernethy, "Texas Folklore and German Culture," in Joseph Wilson, ed., *Texas and Germany: Crosscurrents*, Rice University Studies, Vol. 63, No. 3, Summer 1977, pp. 87-89; Julius Schütze, "Meine Erlebnisse in Texas—die Ermordung der deutschen Unionisten in Fredericksburg, Texas, 1864," *Texas Vorwärts*, June 4, June 18, June 25 and July 2, 1886; Louis B. Engelke, "He got the Drop on Waltrip," *San Antonio Express Magazine*, 1 January 1954; Lich, *The German Texans*, 97; and Irene Marshall King, *John O. Meusebach: German Colonizer in Texas* (Austin: University of Texas Press, 1967),156-60. The quotation is from: N.N., "Ein Deutsch-Texaner," *Darmstädter Zeitung*, 17 May 1893, No. 227, p. 1 in Jacob Kuechler Papers, The Center for American History, University of Texas at Austin.

8. Charles Nagel, *A Boy's Civil War Story* (Saint Louis: Eden Publishing House, 1935), 236, 238.

9. See the transcribed copies of Jacob Küchler's letters to his wife from Parras, in: Jacob Kuechler Papers, The Center for American History, University of Texas at Austin. For another personal account about the attitude and decisions of the German-Texan community see August Siemering, "Texas, Her Past, Her Present, Her Future," manuscript trans. from *Texas Vorwärts*, 1984 as quoted in Lich, *The German Texans*, 97. Seba Bogart Brush, merchant from Austin, met a number of German-Texan traders during the Civil War. See Peyton O. Abbott, "Business Travel Out of Texas During the Civil War: The Travel Diary of S. B. Brush, Pioneer Austin Merchant," *SHQ* 96, no. 2, (October 1992): 259-71.

An interesting account of these business activities is given by Louis Sarasin from Butzbach (near Gießen in Hessen), for instance, who came to Texas at the age of twenty-two on board the ship *John Holland* from Antwerpen and arrived at Galveston on 27 November 1848. Together with his wife Josefine he settled down in Comal County. During the Civil War he joined the Confederacy, served in the Comal County 3rd Regiment of Infantry and rose to the rank of lieutenant. In May 1863 he wrote quite a long letter to his friend Heinrich Guenther, who together with Adolf Schlameus, had been the first teacher of New Braunfels' City School in 1853. Guenther also participated in the *Germania* singing society of New Braunfels, having been one of its early directors, and was elected president of the political mass meeting at the Vauxhall Garden on Alamo Street on the third day of the second Texas singing contest in May 1854. It was at this meeting that Siemering from Sisterdale and Louis Schütze, as well as Julius Wagner from Coletoville, were also present. Although Guenther had always been outspoken against slavery and secession, he remained on friendly terms with Sarasin who reported from Camp Luckett:

> To what extent the speculation and gambling spirit thrives on the other side of the river [Matamoros], you can surely picture, when I tell you that it is said there are over there those who induce our soldiers to go over to the Federals and at the same time furnish supplies for our army. They must be doing a tremendous business. . . . Many in Matamoros are conducting a vast business however the yellow fever soon will put a stop to that. And many who have gone there without funds will have to bite into the grass as it is not an easy matter to go from Matamoros into inner Mexico. In Matamoros one finds everything that below the 30th latitude has long been forgotten, the finest liquors, the finest cigars, in short everything, of course dear, and for specie only. . . Schlickum is in Matamoros and is doing a good business. Kuechler is in Saltillo and supposedly doing a good business. I saw Theodor Goldbeck in Matamoros, he had arrived from Parras.

Sarasin mentions other Germans who lived in Mexico and obviously made a good living there. For Heinrich Guenther see Rudolph L. Biesele, *The History of the German Settlements in Texas, 1831-1861* (Austin, Texas: Press of von Boeckmann-Jones, Co., 1930), 198, 212, 222. The quotation is from the letter of Louis Sarasin to Heinrich Guenther, 19 May 1863, translated from the German by Oscar Haas in March 1962, in: Oscar Haas Papers, Box 2N269, Center for American History, The University of Texas at Austin.

10. The quotation is from the "Report of Dr. Joseph Martin Reuss on the Yellow Fever Epidemic of 1867 at Indianola, Texas," cited in Brownson Malsch, *Indianola, the Mother of Western Texas* (Austin, Texas: State House Press, 1988), 272; and the information on the Wagners' sickness derives from a letter of Carl Baumann to his brother-in-law Karl Wagner, Mannheim, 31 December 1867, in Hildegard Kattermann, ed., *Familienbriefe*, transcribed and photocopied, Lahr, 1977, Wagner Family Collection, The Center for American History, University of Texas, Austin, 206. For the sale of Julius Wagner's farm at the Twelve-Mile Coleto see Julius Wagner & Wife Deed to Chas Lang, Deeds Records, Vol. K, DeWitt County Courthouse, Cuero, Texas.

11. For the consecutive appointments of Julius Wagner to the office of postmaster of Indianola from 5 April 1869, to 29 March 1882, always for four years, see Jim Wheat (compiler),

Postmasters and Post Offices of Texas, 1846-1930, in Jim Wheat Collection, MF No. # 3163, p. 737, Texas State Archives, Austin, Texas. For the appointment of Jacob Küchler see letter of J.K. McCreary to Jacob Küchler, Indianola, 15 May 1869, in Jacob Kuechler Papers, The Center for American History, University of Texas at Austin. For Reconstruction in Texas see Barry A. Crouch, "'Unmanacling' Texas Reconstruction: A Twenty-Year Perspective," *SHQ* 93, no. 3 (January 1990): 275-302; and Randolph B. Campbell, "Carpetbagger Rule in Reconstruction Texas: An Enduring Myth," *SHQ* 97, no. 4 (April 1994): 587-96.

12. See the letter of Peter Joseph Schneider to his daughter Emilie, Offenburg, 18 May 1871, in The Wagner Family Collection, The Center for American History, University of Texas at Austin. Translation by the author.

13. Emilie Wagner to Karl Baumann, from Indianola, 3 August 1871, in The Wagner Family Collection. Translation by author.

14. This might be deduced from an entry in *Indianola Scrap Book*, compiled and published by *The Victoria Advocate*, Victoria, Texas, 1936, reprinted by Calhoun County Historical Survey Committee, Port Lavaca, Texas, 1974, p. 34.

15. "A Flood—True Event, narrated by Sophie Wagner," Chicago, March 1895, from the German original translated by Malcolm Henderson, in The Wagner Family Collection. For more details on the hurricane that destroyed Indianola see Malsch, *Indianola*, 228-48.

16. Barrow was the administrator of the deceased John M. Brownson's estate, situated in Victoria County, originally granted to Maria Jesus de Leon, widow of Rafael Manchola. See "Julius Wagner to John M. Brownson. Administrator. Mortgage," Mortgage Records, Vol. 14, p. 201, Victoria County, Courthouse, Victoria, Texas.

17. All the information—including quotations from the 1879 *Postal Laws and Regulations*, the biennial *Official Register* and the microfilm *Register of Appointment of Postmasters 1832-1971* — are from the letter from Megaera Ausman, Historian of the Corporate Information Service, United States Postal Service, Washington, D.C., 2 November 1995, to the author.

18. For Julius Wagner borrowing money see "Julius Wagner to D. C. Proctor for use of D. Sullivan, Deed of Trust," Mortgage Records, Victoria County, Vol. 19, pp. 55-57, Courthouse, Victoria County, Texas. For the note that he paid back his debts, see "D. Sullivan to Julius Wagner, Release of Debt," Deed of Trust Records, Vol. 22, pp. 258-259, Victoria County Records, Courthouse, Victoria, Texas. The arrival of the Wagners at San Antonio even found its way into the local papers: "Mr. Julius Wagner, late postmaster of Indianola, is in the city and proposes to locate here," *The San Antonio Daily Express* 10 April 1883, page 1, col. 6. For the establishing of a grocery store see Morrison & Fourmy, comp., *Morrison & Fourmy's General Directory of the City of San Antonio 1887-1888* (Galveston: Morrison & Fourmy Publishers, 1888), 338. For the evaluation of Julius Wagner's property see Assessment of Property in Bexar County, owned by Residents and rendered for taxation by the owners or agents thereof for the year 1890, in Tax-Rolls, 1888-1892, Bexar County, Reel 101503-05, p. 269.

19. For the Eighteenth singing contest see "Concert Programme for the eighteenth Sängerfest of the Texas German Singer's League, held at Galveston, April 14th, 15th, 16th and 17th, 1891" in Oscar Haas Papers, Box 2N404, The Center for American History, University of Texas at Austin.

20. "Freundesworte am Sarge von Emilie Wagner," in The Wagner Family Collection, The Center for American History, University of Texas at Austin.

21. The quotation is from "Family Notes" by Sophie and Lina Wagner, Chicago, April 1926, translated by Malcolm Henderson with explanations in brackets by Paul W. Guenzel, p. 4, in The Wagner Family Collection. The information about the corps is from a letter by E. S. Schlange-Schöningen to the author dated 24 August 1988, in The Wagner Family Collection, The Center for American History, University of Texas at Austin.

22. For more on Lungkwitz and Petri and their lives in Texas see James Patrick McGuire, "Observations on German Artists in Texas," in Gish and Spuler, *Eagle in the New World* (College Station: Texas A&M University Press, 1986), 181-200. The importance a good dress had for those German woman is also emphasized in Emilie Wagner's letter to her parents on 22 April 1851, pp. 16, 17, in The Wagner Family Collection.

23. One author who mistakes the Romantic notions of the middle-class Germans for an expression of Biedermeier is Mack Walker, "Old Homeland and the New," in Glen E. Lich and Dona Reeves, *German Culture in Texas* (Boston: Twayne, 1980), 72-81. For a more detailed account of the art of Friedrich Petri see Sam DeShong Ratcliffe, *Painting Texas History to 1900* (Austin: University of Texas Press, 1992), 66. Typical of Petri's pictures are *The Pioneer Cowpen* and *Going Visiting*, both painted around 1853, and reproduced as Plates 33 and 34 in Ratcliffe. The *Biedermeier* household in Germany exemplified simplicity and was decorated with only very few paintings—just the opposite from the Wagner home as we have seen. See, for instance Eugen Kalkschmidt, *Biedermeiers Glück und Ende* (München: Verlag Georg D.W. Callwey, 1957), 34. For a good summary of the various epochs like Biedermeier and Romanticism in Germany see Wolfram Siemann, *Vom Staatenbund zum Nationalstaat—Deutschland 1806-187*, (München: C.H. Beck Verlag, 1995), 258-78. In his fascinating study of the German immigrant family Giesecke as a tale of merchants on the Texas frontier, Walter Struve in *Germans & Texans, Commerce, Migration, and Culture*, states that "existence near the American frontier and life in Biedermeier Germany were in many ways more similar than we might assume" (Austin: University of Texas Press, 1996; p. 9). For Struve, "the Germany Charles left, as well the Texas he settled in, were developing bourgeois societies" (9). These assumptions seem too far-fetched to me. Even if the German immigrants in Texas in the 1830s and 1840s preserved a lot from their old homeland, social development in Germany at that time was too different from that in Texas to draw a parallel or label the Germans, with their Romantic views, *Biedermeier*-Germans.

24. For more information on the German writings see Karin Ramspeck Sloan, Trading the Pen for the Spade: 19th-Century German Immigrant Literature in Texas, (Ph.D. diss., Texas A&I University, December 1990).

Notes to Chapter 6

1. *Deutscher Anzeiger*, 18 February 1903.

2. See the entry "William Henry Wagner," in Addison L. Fulwider, *History of Stephenson County, Illinois*, vol. 2 (Chicago: The S.J. Clarke Publishing Company, 1910), 136 f.

3. This shows that the propaganda against (and suppression of) the Japanese during World War II was not only based on racism, as Michael Rogin states in his essay "'Make My Day!': Spectacle as Amnesia in Imperial Politics," but was largely due to the creation of enemy images comparable to those which were established about the Germans during World War I. Rogin's essay is in H. Aram Veeser, ed., *The New Historicism Reader* (New York:Routledge, 1994), 242. See also Mark Ellis, "German-Americans in World War I," in Ragnhild Fiebig-von Hase and Ursula Lehmkuhl, *Enemy Images in American History* (Providence, RI: Berghahn Books, 1997), 183-208.

4. For the history of the *Freeport Banner* see: N.N., *In the Foot-Prints of the Pioneers of Stephenson County, Illinois* (Freeport, IL: Pioneer Publishing, 1900), 367. For the *Deutscher Anzeiger* see N.N., *History of Stephenson County, 1970* (Mount Morris, Illinois: Kable Printing Company, 1972), 464-65.

5. *Freeport Journal-Standard*, 30 January 1928, p. 1, c. 1 and p. 4, c. 8.

6. Malcolm Henderson, "Papers concerning the Wilms, Paepcke and Wagner Families," 1977, p. 6, in The Wagner Family Collection, The Center for American History, University of

Texas at Austin.

7. Rudolph Kleberg in a letter to Mrs. George J. Schleicher, describing the early history of Cuero, dated 12 July 1923, p. 2. in Rudolph Kleberg Papers, The Center for American History, University of Texas at Austin.

8. Letter by Hermann Paepcke to his mother from Cuero on 25 August 1873, translated by Otto Suchsland, in The Wagner Family Collection.

9. For the Sutton-Taylor Feud see: Wayne Gard, *Frontier Justice* (Norman, OK: University of Oklahoma Press, 1949), 40-46. For John Wesley Hardin see ibid. p. 42, Walter Clay Dixson, *Richland Crossing: A Portrait of Texas Pioneers* (Fort Worth: Peppermill Publishing, 1996); Leon Metz, *John Wesley Hardin: Dark Angel of Texas* (El Paso: Mangan, 1996); Jack Hays Day, *The Sutton-Taylor Feud* (San Antonio: Murray, 1937); and Charles Leland Sonnichsen, "Sutton-Taylor Feud," in Ron Tyler, ed., *The New Handbook of Texas*, vol. 6, pp. 162-63; and the same, *Ten Texas Feuds* (Albuquerque: University of New Mexico Press, 1957). For the various histories of the several railroads in Texas see St. Clair Griffin Reed, *A History of the Texas Railroads* (Houston: The St. Clair Publishing Company, 1941); and Ira G. Clark, *Then Came the Railroads: The Century from Steam to Diesel in the Southwest* (Norman, OK: University of Oklahoma Press, 1958).

10. First quotation from a letter by Hermann Paepcke to his brother-in-law Dr. Franz Eggert on 6 December 1873. The second quotation about the lawless conditions in Cuero from a letter by Hermann Paepcke to one of his sisters (which one could not be determined), 9 January 1874; both letters in The Wagner Family Collection, The Center for American History, University of Texas at Austin.

11. For the actions of the citizens of Cuero against the outlaws see Rudolph Kleberg in a letter to Mrs. George J. Schleicher dated 12 July 1923, pp. 5-8, in Rudolph Kleberg Papers, The Center for American History, University of Texas at Austin.

12. Both quotations are from the letter by Hermann Paepcke to his mother from Cuero on 28 March 1875, in The Wagner Family Collection, The Center for American History, University of Texas at Austin.

13. See Brownson Malsch, *Indianola: The Mother of Western Texas* (Austin: State House Press, 1988), 219; and Hermann Paepcke to his mother on 13 May and 3 August 1877, in The Wagner Family Collection, The Center for American History, University of Texas at Austin.

14. Hermann Paepcke to his brother-in-law Dr. Franz Eggert on 14 August 1881, in The Wagner Family Collection, The Center for American History, University of Texas at Austin.

15. See the anonymous article "Territorial Limitation in the Lumber Trade," *Northwestern Lumberman* 22 February 1890, p. 2; and William Cronon, *Nature's Metropolis: Chicago and the Great West* (New York: W.W. Norton & Company, 1992), 198.

16. For more information on the history of the mail-order houses see Cecil C. Hoge, Sr., *The First Hundred Years are the Toughest: What We can Learn from the Century of Competition between Sears and Wards* (Berkeley, CA: Ten Speed Press, 1988), and Rae Elizabeth Rips, "An Introductory Study of the Role of the Mail Order Business in American History, 1872-1914" (M.A. thesis, University of Chicago, 1938).

17. Flora von Roeder, *These are the Generations* (Houston: Baylor College of Medicine, 1978), 74.

18. William's attitude towards and opinion of his father is recollected in Juanita Sophie Dahme (William Wagner's daughter, 1897-1993) in a recorded interview with the author, 19 May 1988.

19. Henry Seeligson ran one of the principal hardware stores in town. His brother George was in the mercantile business. Henry had been one of the incorporators of the San Antonio and El Paso Railroad Company, established in April 1871 to fight Charles Morgan and surpass his

G.W.T.&P., a project that never materialized. Henry Seeligson also was a commissioner of the Indianola City Railroad Company that provided the coastal city with the first public transportation system. Engaging in the commission and forwarding business as well, Henry was active in all fields of transportation. For the details on Henry Seeligson see Malsch, *Indianola*, 209, 213, 220, 223, 225.

20. Rudolph Kleberg in a letter to Mrs. George J. Schleicher, describing the early history of Cuero, from 12 July 1923, p. 4., in Rudolph Kleberg Papers, The Center for American History, University of Texas at Austin.

Otto Buchel's father, Carl August, had come to Indianola, Texas, at the age of forty in 1845 from the state of Hesse in Germany together with his family and his younger brother August C. who rose to military prominence during the Civil War. His peace-loving brother Carl and his wife Juliane first made their home at Indianola where their second son Otto was born and in 1851 they settled at a farm in DeWitt County. There, Otto's father Carl soon died of an accident and subsequently, in 1860, the Buchel family joined a group of settlers who moved to Tampico, Mexico, where they hoped to establish a coffee plantation on the banks of the Rio Calabosa. This project failed, however, and the Buchels returned to Indianola in 1866. These were not easy times for them and seventeen-year-old Otto took up work where he could. His first job was that of a bark master where he had to check the barges and keep peace among the stevedores. That is where George Seeligson found him and took him on as a clerk. For the Buchel family history see Douglas Granberry, "Otto Buchel, Banker," *The Junior Historian* (Texas State Historical Association, nd), 11 and 28 in The Wagner Family Collection, The Center for American History, University of Texas at Austin; N.N., "Banking Institution is Honored With Official Historical Marker," *The Cuero Daily Record*, 8 October 1973, pp. 1 and 3; and Pamela Ater, "Buchel Family," DeWitt County Historical Commission, *The History of DeWitt County, Texas* (Dallas: Curtis Media Corporation, 1991), 322; and Lich, *The German Texans* (San Antonio: University of Texas Institute of Texan Cultures at San Antonio, 1981), 92-93.

21. Hermann Paepcke to his brother-in-law Dr. Franz Eggert, 14 August 1881, in The Wagner Family Collection, The Center for American History, University of Texas at Austin.

22. Granberry, "Otto Buchel, Banker," 11.

23. Robert Kleberg was just one year older than William Wagner and Rudolph six years older. Robert had received a scholarship from the Sack Foundation and studied law at the University of Virginia. When he earned his degree and was admitted to the bar one year later, he moved back to Cuero where he had already helped Gustav Schleicher survey the town with two men named Thompson and McBain. In 1881 he started practicing law in Cuero, if only for a short time, before he moved to Corpus Christi to work for the firm of Slayton and Wells. Defeating the impressive cattle baron Richard King in court proved to be Robert's luckiest hour, as the agile King hired the smart young lawyer right away. Five years later, Robert married King's daughter Alice Gertrudis. In the meantime, his older brother Rudolph left a more permanent mark on Cuero. Right after the founding of the city, he established its first newspaper, *The Cuero Star,* which he edited for four years. Serving his community in many ways on various committees, Rudolph Kleberg was elected county attorney of DeWitt County from 1876 (the year Cuero became the county seat) to 1880. In 1882, he was elected state senator and served two terms. Then, in 1885, President Grover Cleveland made him United States attorney for the Western District of Texas, in which capacity he served for eleven years until he was elected to the United States Congress where he stayed for seven years representing Texas. He was not the only one from Cuero though who had been elected to Congress. There was also the lawyer William Henry Crain (1848-1896) and Gustav Schleicher himself who served two terms. For more biographical details on Robert Justus Kleberg see Frank Goodwyn, *Life on the King*

Ranch (New York: Crowell, 1951), and "Kleberg, Robert Justus," DeWitt County Historical Commission, 535.

24. Thus Juanita is quoted in a letter by Wellford Wilms to Paul Guenzel on 7 July 1981, in The Wagner Family Collection. For Julius Wagner's visits to Cuero see the obituary in the *Deutsche Rundschau*, Cuero, 18 February 1903. Interestingly, the author of this obituary claims to have known Julius Wagner for forty years, and that he spent many a happy hour in his company. Unfortunately, the identity of the writer could not be established.

25. First quotation from Granberry, "Otto Buchel, Banker," 28; the second is from William's daughter Juanita from a recorded interview with the author, 19 May 1988.

26. *The Cuero Daily Record* 30 April 1922, p. 1, col. 3. For the biography of Judge Edward Koenig, Sr., see F. B. Burdine, "Koenig, Judge Edward, Jr.," DeWitt County Historical Commission, 548.

27. *The Cuero Daily Record*, 24 April 1926, p. 1, col. 2.

28. *The Cuero Daily Record*, 24 August 1933, p. 1, col. 5.

29. For the history of Cuero see Frank B. Sheppard, "Cuero," DeWitt County Historical Commission, 88- 93; and City of Cuero, Texas, *Historical Record Commemorating the 100th Anniversary of the Founding of Cuero* (Smithville, Texas: Tex-Print Corp., 1972), 6-8.

Notes to Chapter 7

1. Wilhelm Wagner to his family on 1 June 1851, in Hildegard Kattermann, ed., *Familienbriefe*, transcribed and photocopied, Lahr, 1977, Wagner Family Collection, The Center for American History, University of Texas, Austin, p. 123.

2. It is, of course, not easy to determine if Wilhelm Wagner craved the recognition, respect, and success he had. Such a strong desire to be accepted might betray constant insecurity, as has been pointed out by Wolfgang Helbich in his challenging article, "Die 'Englischen': German Immigrants Describe Nineteenth-Century American Society," *Amerikastudien / American Studies* 36, no. 4 (1991): 515-30, especially 528. For the importance of the role immigrant Lutheran pastors and other religious groups had in the history of immigration (an aspect that would lead too far to be discussed here in detail) see for instance, Martin Pörksen, "Schleswig-Holsteinische Pastoren für Nordamerika," *Zeitschrift der Gesellschaft für Kanada-Studien* 10, no. 2 (1990): 91-96; Royden Loewen, "New Themes in an Old Story: Transplanted Mennonites as Group Settlers in North America, 1874-1879," *Journal of American Ethnic History* 11, no. 2 (1992): 3-26; Anthony H. Richter, "A Heritage of Faith: Religion and the German Settlers of South Dakota," *South Dakota History* 21, no. 2 (1991): 155-72; Karl A. Lurix, "The Open Door," *Journal of the American Historical Society of Germans from Russia*, 11, no. 4 (1988): 15-20; Louise Buenger Robbert, "Lutheran Families in St. Louis and Perry County, Missouri, 1839-1870," *Missouri Historical Review* 82, no. 4 (1988): 424-38; Reinhard R. Doerries, "German Catholics in the New World: The Immigrants Struggle for Faith and Ethnic Identity," *In Their Own Words* 3, no. 2 (1986): 81-107; Albert T. Bostelmann, "Life and Ministry of Johann Wolter," *Concordia Historical Institute Quarterly* 61, no. 2 (1988): 61-73; and William A. Kramer, "The Saxons in Perry County," *Lutheran Quarterly* 3, no. 4 (1989): 357-72.

3. A good overview on German immigration is given in Walter D. Kamphoefner, Wolfgang Helbich, and Ulrike Sommer, eds., *News from the Land of Freedom: German Immigrants Write Home - 1830-1930*, trans. Susan Carter Vogel (Ithaca, New York: Cornell University Press, 1991), 9-35. See also Wolfgang von Hippel, *Auswanderung aus Südwestdeutschland; Studien zur württembergischen Auswanderung und Auswanderungspolitik im 18. und 19. Jahrhundert* (Stuttgart: Klett-Cotta, 1984). For migration of Germans from the area east of the river Elbe see, for instance, Uwe Reich, "Zur Sozialgeschichte der Auswanderung aus dem Regierungsbezirk Frankfurt/Oder im 19. Jahrhundert," *Jahrbuch für Wirtschaftsgeschichte* no.

2 (1992): 97-127.

4. Today this picture has changed completely. Almost eighty-five percent of those seeking a new home and a new future in the United States come from Asia and Latin America. For this change in immigration numbers see for example, Robert W. Tucker, "Immigration and Foreign Policy: General Considerations," in Robert W. Tucker, Charles B. Keely, and Linda Wrigley, eds., *Immigration and U.S. Foreign Policy* (Boulder: Westview Press, 1990), 1-14. Germans are still moving to the United States but in smaller numbers. Between 1820 and 1993, 7,085,324 German immigrants poured into the United States, making 11.67 percent of all immigrants. From these, more than six million came between 1820 and 1940. Between 1941 and 1950, 226,578 Germans came (21.89 percent), between 1951 and 1960 it was 477,765 (or 18.99 percent), between 1961 and 1970 it was 190,796 (5.74 percent), between 1971 and 1980 74,414 Germans immigrated (only 1.65 percent) and between 1981 and 1990 only 70,111 people from Germany migrated to the United States, which was only 0.9 percent of all immigrants. During this last decade, all immigrants from Asia in contrast made up more than twenty-eight percent of all immigrants. For these and more figures see N. N., *Information Please Almanac. Atlas and Yearbook. 1995*, 48th ed. (Boston: Houghton Mifflin Co., 1995), 832.

5. The death rate fell in Europe because of the increased food supply and also because of improvements in hygiene and medicine. A comparison with China (whose population rose from 150 million in 1600 to 300 million in 1800 due to a rise in the birthrate) shows, however, that the growth of population alone does not suffice as a reason for emigration. The correct term has to be overpopulation—meaning too many people for the resources of the land. During the nineteenth century, eighty-five percent of the European population left their homes and moved someplace else. Seventy percent, though, simply moved from the countryside into bigger cities. Only fifteen percent of those who left their homes emigrated from Europe. This might not sound like much, but it was about 51 million people who sought a new home on another continent during the last century and until the First World War. Roughly 45 million Europeans moved to the Americas, Australia, South Africa, and New Zealand; whereas 6 million chose the unpopulated areas of Russian Asia. For an overview of this epoch see Hagen Schulze, *Staat und Nation in der Europäischen Geschichte* (München: Verlag C.H. Beck, 1994), 152 ff. For the migration movements of the various European groups see the provocative paper by Dirk Hoerder, *People on the Move: Migration, Acculturation, and Ethnic Interaction in Europe and North America*, German Historical Institute Washington D.C. Annual Lecture Series No. 6 (Providence, R.I.: Berg Publishers, 1993), 5-46, especially 7-14.

6. When Konrad, Duke of Masovia, asked the *Deutschritterorden* (the Order of the German Knights) to help him fight back the Prussian tribes in 1224, he opened the door for German settlements on the river Weichsel, in Silesia, and other parts of Poland. After the Great Plague in 1349, mass pogroms forced German Jews to migrate eastwards. As the Jews were made scapegoats for the fury of the Black Death, they were expelled not only from Germany but also from France, Spain, Portugal and England. They could not live in peace in the realm of the czars though for ever, as restrictions of 1795 and 1835 confined them to live in ghettos, thus forming the now lost culture of the *shtetl*. Those who had expelled them had moved eastward before them. Sometimes there was a demand for immigrants. During the first half of the nineteenth century, the Brazilian Emperor Dom Pedro I (1798-1834) encouraged Germans to settle in Brazil in order to create a secure and settled zone in the south of the newly independent country. In 1763, more than 30,000 German emigrants followed the proclamation of Tsarina Katharina II to settle down at the river Volga and the area around Saratov in order to constitute some kind of bulwark against the nomadic peoples of the Steppe. The census of 1959 gave the number of 1,600,000 Germans living in the Soviet Union. Katharina II had invited Germans to Russia and Hungary did the same after the victory of the Turks in 1718 and the recapture of the

Banat region. More than 100,000 Germans thus settled in Hungary between 1740 and 1790. The Spanish king Philipp V asked Germans to come and cultivate the Sierra Morena which had been wasteland since the expulsion of the Moors. Thousands followed his call.

7. Wilhelm Wagner to his mother Luise Wagner on March 25, 1860, in Kattermann, *Familienbriefe,* 193.

8. "The Gunds were businessmen. The family fortunes were mostly made in banks and breweries. Louis Henry Gund and children were bankers. Frederick Gund was a successful man. John Gund was a brewer. His son Geo. Frederick Gund was president of a Gund Gold Company and owner of several mines—was a brewer in Cleveland and director of several banks. There have been 158 Gunds in the United States in the last eighty-three years. Of these all but eleven were born in this country. There have been of this number four brewers, ten schoolteachers, three officers in the U.S.A. army, one nurse, seven bankers, six farmers, one economist. The family is remarkably uninterested in the arts. I find no trace of any real musical or artistic taste in any of the Gunds. They are basically materialistic and of the type which lays the foundations for the prosperity of a community by marked instinct for business and for personal integrity and reliability." Family notes by May Gund, second daughter of Abraham's brother Henry and his wife Josephine Schottle, written in 1933, in The Wagner Family Collection, The Center for American History, University of Texas at Austin. For the history of the German Insurance Company—of which Frederick Gund became secretary for four years in 1867, while his brother-in-law Matt Hettinger was president—see N.N., *The History of Stephenson County, Illinois* (Chicago: Western Historical Co., 1880), 430. According to tales told in the family, the farm at Town Silver Creek where Emma grew up was close to Braun's Mill where Carrie Brown grew up. Carrie Brown later married John Edward Tracy. Their second son, Spencer B. Tracy, would become one of Hollywood's most famous stars. Emma Gund, through her lifelong friendship with Carrie Brown Tracy, also knew Spencer Tracy quite well.

9. This mailing piece is quoted by: N.N., "Versatility of Management," *Printing*, February 1944, p. 35.

10. Leslie Vincent Tischauser, "The Burden of Ethnicity: The German Question in Chicago, 1914-1941" (Ph.D. diss, University of Illinois at Chicago, 1981), 259-64.

11. A very good case study on this phenomenon is by Barbara Wiedemann-Citera, *Die Auswirkungen des Ersten Weltkrieges auf die Deutsch-Amerikaner im Spiegel der New Yorker Volkszeitung und der New York Times 1914-1926* (Frankfurt am Main: Peter Lang, 1993).

12. Between 1920 and 1940, only seven percent of all jobs were nonfarm executives, administrators, and managers. Only seven percent of these jobs were held by women in 1920 and elven percent in 1940. See Gary N. Powell, *Women and Men in Management* (Newbury Park, CA: Sage, 1988); Laurie Larwood and Marion M. Wood, *Women in Management* (Lexington, MA: Heath, 1977); and Ellen A. Fagenson, ed., *Women in Management: Trends, Issues, and Challenges in Managerial Diversity* (Newbury Park, CA: Sage, 1993).

13. Emily Kupper was the daughter of Jacob Kupper (1821-1901) who had come to America from St. Goar, Germany, in 1849 together with his first wife Anna Batcha. When Anna Batcha died in 1853, Jacob Kupper married Maria Morloch, the daughter of Johannes Morloch (1799-1854) and Maria Suszer (1807-1881). Their first daughter was Emily. Their seventh daughter Lilly (b. March 7, 1867, d. July 29, 1935) married William Wagner's son Herman twenty-five years after her sister had married Herman's uncle.

14. See the various letters of members of the Soellner family to Henry and Julius Kleinpell, in Henry Kleinpell Papers, Box 1—personal correspondence—WIS, MSS/38PB/Box 1, Wisconsin State Historical Society, Madison, Wisconsin.

15. See again for example, Arthur M. Schlesinger Jr., *The Disuniting of America* (Knoxville, TN: Whittle Direct Books, 1991), 13.

16. E.G. Ravenstein, "The Laws of Migration," *Journal of the Royal Statistical Society* (1889): 241-301. For an interesting new sociopolitical interpretation of migration see the model by N.D. Diamantides, *International Migration as a Dynamic Process*, MCB University Press, http://www.mcb.co.ul/services/articles/liblink/k/diamanti.htm.

17. Quotation from Henry Steele Commager, *The Empire of Reason* (Garden City, New York: Anchor Press/Doubleday, 1978), 101. The Indians were harassed, chased and expelled because they had something the white settler wanted and did not wish to share with them: their land. Tolerance was embedded in most religions of the Indians. It did not help them though. It was not until 1924 that they were granted civil rights under the Coolidge administration. Yet, the harassment continues even today and will continue as long as they reside on land that seems to bear profit for the white man. Like many others before them, the two Shoshone sisters Mary and Carrie Dan, for instance, fighting like the rest of their people to save the Western Shoshone's ancestral land in Nevada from seizure and nuclear destruction, were confronted with a legal system that doesn't exist to protect them but to move them if their land seems valuable enough for the white man. The combination of greed and intolerance was the ruin of the Indians.

Intolerance on racial and religious grounds had deep roots. "We in this country have been so imbued with the idea of democracy, or the equality of all men, that we have left out of consideration the matter of blood or natural born hereditary mental and moral differences. No man who breeds pedigreed plants and animals can afford to neglect this thing." "The Indians are so bigoted to their religion as the Mahometans are to their Koran, the Hindoos to their Shaster, the Chinese to Confucius, the Romans to their saints and angels, or the Jews to Moses and the Prophets. It is a principle of religion, at bottom, which inspires the Indians with such an invincible aversion both to civilization and Christianity." Two quotations, two men, two centuries and yet, the same intolerant and arrogant mind. The first one is from a congressman from the 1920s, and the second from a letter John Adams wrote to Judge Tudor in 1818. The first quotation is Joyce C. Vialet, *A Brief History of U.S. Immigration Policy* (Washington, D.C.: Congressional Research Service, 1991), 12; and the second is from a letter by John Adams to Judge Tudor on September 23, 1818, in Charles Francis Adams, ed., *The Works of John Adams*, vol. 10 (Boston: Little, Brown, and Company, 1856), 359-62. Both men showed the same intolerant mind towards other cultures, other religions. And they were not alone. Neither was John Adams the first one. The Pilgrim Fathers, the ones who settled Massachusetts, the Puritans were the first ones to bring intolerance to the shores of the New World. They fled from intolerance, and yet their strong belief in their own righteousness made them self-righteous. Puritanism in its purest form was intolerant and undemocratic. See for example John Winthrop's journal as quoted in Bert James Loewenberg, *American History in American Thought* (New York: Simon and Schuster, 1972), 106 f.

This has been branded by journalists, philosophers, historians, politicians, and artists alike, like Nathaniel Hawthorne in his novel *The Scarlet Letter*, published in 1850. From the witch trials at Salem in 1692 to the Scopes trial at Dayton, Tennessee, in 1925, religious fundamentalists have stained the coat of liberty and freedom throughout the centuries with their intolerance. Even political correctness can turn into the opposite and show an ugly face when it is used against works of art like Mark Twain's *The Adventures of Huckleberry Finn*. Those who do not understand that Twain was criticizing his times by using the word "nigger" in order to show the mind of the South during that epoch and, therefore, ban this book like many other classics from school and public libraries are just like the fundamentalists with their extreme arguments. These people not only fulfill what Ray Bradbury wrote in his novel *Fahrenheit 451* in 1953, but also turn political correctness into a mockery. Religious and racial intolerance turned against the immigrants, often in combination with the fear of competitors in the labor market. Still, even with this undercurrent of intolerance alive throughout the centuries in American thought and politics, the hopeful immigrant only saw or wanted to see the other side of the coin, the shining side, the promise, the golden door held open for him.

18. Frederick Jackson Turner, "The Significance of the Frontier in American History," in George Rogers Taylor, ed., *The Turner Thesis* (Lexington, MA: D.C. Heath and Company, 1972), 24.

19. Roger Daniels, *Coming to America; a History of Immigration and Ethinicity in American Life* (New York: Harper Perennial, 1991), 184. The account of Rosa Cassettari is quoted in Thomas Dublin, ed., *Immigrant Voices: New Lives in America, 1773-1986* (Urbana: University of Illinois Press, 1993), 113.

20. The quotation is from Willa Cather, *O Pioneers!* (Boston: Houghton Mifflin Company, 1941), 84. For a thorough annalysis of Willa Cather's novel *My Antonia* as far as immigration is concerned see Christopher Sten, "Against the Grain: Willa Cather and the Myths of Immigration in *My Antonia*," in Michael D'Innocenzo and Josef P. Sirefman, eds., *Immigration and Ethnicity: American Society— "Melting Pot" or "Salad Bowl"?* (London: Greenwood Press, 1992), 155-62.

21. For research on the role of women as immigrants see for instance Agnes Bretting, "Frauen als Einwanderer in der Neuen Welt: Überlegungen anhand einiger Selbstzeugnisse deutscher Auswanderinnen," *Amerikastudien / American Studies* 33, no. 3 (1988), 319-27; Carol Berkin, *First Generations: Women in Colonial America* (New York: Hill and Wang, 1996); Paula A. Treckel, *To Comfort the Heart: Women in Seventeenth-Century America* (New York: Twayne, 1996); Linda S. Pickle, "Stereotypes and Reality: Nineteenth-Century German Women in Missouri," *Missouri Historical Review* 79, no. 3 (1985): 291-312; and same, "Rural German-Speaking Women in Early Nebraska and Kansas: Ethnicity as a Factor in Frontier Adaptation," *Great Plains Quarterly* 9, no. 4 (1989): 239-51.

22. Rudolf A. Hofmeister, *The Germans of Chicago* (Champaign: Stipes Publishing Company, 1976), 133.

23. Walter Gropius, "Program of the Staatliche Bauhaus in Weimar," in Hans M. Wingler, *The Bauhaus: Weimar, Dessau, Berlin, Chicago,* trans. Wolfgang Jabs and Basil Gilbert, ed. by Joseph Stein (Cambridge, MA: MIT Press, 1969), 31. See also Walter Gropius, *The New Architecture and The Bauhaus*, trans. P. Morton Shand, (Cambridge, MA: MIT Press, 1965); and Gillian Naylor, *The Bauhaus* (London: Studio Vista/Dutton Pictureback, 1968).

24. From a statement by Walter Paepcke for the advertisement leaflet of the institute of design in 1948, in Wingler, *The Bauhaus,* 209.

25. This text quoted in Sidney Hyman, *The Aspen Idea* (Norman, Oklahoma: University of Oklahoma Press, 1975), 81. The short quotation from Hutchins' speech on *Wilhelm Meister* is in ibid., 86.

26. For a precise evaluation of the life and times of Walter P. Paepcke see James Sloan Allen, *The Romance of Commerce and Culture* (Chicago: The University of Chicago Press, 1983); and Marquis W. Childs, "The World of Walter Paepcke," *Horizon* (Sept. 1958): 96-103, 133-34. A fascinating facet of this romance between commerce and the arts is the biography and work of the artist Herbert Bayer (1900-1985) who moved to Aspen in 1946. Strong ties bound him to Walter Paepcke. Bayer was adviser to the design department of the Container Corporation of America, member of the planning group of the city of Aspen and architect of many buildings at Aspen like the Aspen Institute for Humanistic Studies, the Walter Paepcke Memorial Building, and the Wheeler Opera House. For more information see Herbert Bayer, *Herbert Bayer: Painter, Designer, Architect* (New York: Reinhold Publishing Corporation, 1967).

With Walter Paepcke's death in April 1963, however, things began to change. The Aspen Institute modified its program slowly, moving away from the purely humanistic concept to "more specific economic, social and political problems of American society," as stated in a letter to Mortimer J. Adler from August 29, 1962, as quoted in: Allen, 285. New programs, organizations, and seminars, like the Aspen Film Conference and the Aspen Center for Theoretical Physics were established. This expansion at the same time diminished Aspen's role as a center for humanistic studies. Today the institute sees itself as an international organization "whose programs are designed to enhance the ability of leaders of business, government, the nonprofit sector, academia, and the media to understand and act upon the issues that challenge the national and international community," according to the brochure, *The Aspen Institute*, "The Mission and Method of the Aspen Institute," Queenstown, Maryland: The Aspen Institute, March 1994, p. 2 and also the interview with Joseph E. Slater, president emeritus of the Aspen Institute, in Dana H. Allin, ed., *Twenty Years Aspen Institute Berlin* (Berlin: Aspen Institute Berlin, 1994). A dominant focus of the institute lay on east-west relations. In 1974, Aspen Institute Berlin was founded, in 1984 the Aspen Institute France and in the same year the Aspen Institute Italy. The more the institution grew, the more it lost its clear shape as once conceived by Robert Hutchins, Walter Paepcke, and Mortimer Adler. At the end of the sixties the recreational aspect of the city of Aspen had outgrown the cultural one, and skiing—what Elizabeth Paepcke had had in mind originally—became the most important economic and social factor for this town. At the same time Aspen grew into a fashionable resort for the political and financial jet set as well as for Hollywood stars, and the prices went up astronomically. In 1978 the Aspen Skiing Corporation was sold to Twentieth Century Fox for $40 million. Had Gary Cooper been proud once to be host to Ortega y Gasset on occasion of the Goethe festival at Aspen, today the tourist feels thrilled when catching a glimpse of Sylvester Stallone.

Walter Paepcke's Container Corporation of America expanded after his death until it finally became a minor subsidiary of the gigantic Mobil Oil Corporation in 1974. This was not the end of CCA, but its uniqueness was gone forever.

27. Jacques Barzun on Walter Paepcke's death as quoted in Allen, 283. For Walter Paepcke's education see Hyman, 22. For a detailed analysis of Chicago's German North Side see Christiane Harzig, "Chicago's German North Side, 1880-1900: The Structure of a Gilded Age Ethnic Neighborhood," in Hartmut Keil and John B. Jentz, eds., *German Workers in Industrial Chicago, 1850-1910: A Comparative Perspective* (DeKalb, Illinois: Northern Illinois University Press, 1983), 127-44.

28. *Cuero Daily Record* 16 July 1957, p. 1, col. 1 and 2.

29. The stories about Walter "Bully" and his son Bob Wagner are from Bob Wagner's recorded interview with Andreas Reichstein, 19 May 1988, and a second interview on 14 May 1995. For Robert's election to the city council see *The Cuero Record*, 6 April 1960, pp. 1 and 8 and 21 April 1964, p. 1.

30. E-mail to the author, 4 October 1995.

31. For a sociological study that covers stereotypes about German-Americans see Mary C. Waters, "The Construction of a Symbolic Ethnicity: Suburban White Ethnics in the 1980s," in D'Innocenzo and Sirefman, 75-90.

32. See, for example, Carolyn A. Heald, "The Irish Palatines in Ontario: Religion, Ethnicity and Rural Migration," *Canadian Papers in Rural History* 9 (1994): 17-185; Milo Kearney and Harriett Denise Joseph, "Brownsville's French and German Distant Reflection of Their Interaction," *Journal of the American Studies Association of Texas* 23 (1992): 61-76; Gabriele Lunte, "The German Bohemian Culture and Heritage of the Catholic Bucovinians in Ellis, Kansas," *Heritage of the Great Plains* 27, no. 2 (1994): 51-64; Wilma B.N. Tilby, "Jakob Brand's Register of Dutchtown, German Mining Colony," *Utah Historical Quarterly* 61, no. 1 (1994): 53-70; Daniel L. Boxberger, "The Germans from Russia and the 1911 Report of the U.S. Immigration Commission," *Journal of the American Historical Society of Germans from Russia* 14, no.4 (1991): 23-25; David A. Gerber, "'You see I speak very well Englisch': Literacy and the Transformed

Self as Reflected in Immigrant Personal Correspondence," *Journal of American Ethnic History* 12, no. 2 (1993): 56-62; Carol J. Halverson, "Volga German-Russians in Minnesota," *Journal of the American Historical Society of Germans from Russia* 14, no. 2 (1991): 15-23; Winfried Becker, "Historische Aspekte der Deutsch-Amerikanischen Beziehungen," *Archiv für Kulturgeschichte* 71, no. 1 (1989): 177-208; Linda Schelbitzki Pickle, "Rural German-Speaking Women in Early Nebraska and Kansas: Ethnicity as a Factor in Frontier Adaptation," *Great Plains Quarterly* 9, no.4 (1989): 239-251; Glen E. Lich, "Survival and Succession: Immigrant Autobiography as Cultural Legacy," *Yearbook of German-American Studies* 24 (1989): 59-72; Barbara Lang, "Immigration in German-American Literature," *Yearbook of German American Studies* 22 (1987): 39-57; Ruth Ann Alexander, "Nature, Ethnics, and Land: the Making of a South Dakota Novel," *South Dakota History* 18, no.3 (1988) 152-72; Theodore Mueller, "Milwaukee's German Cultural Heritage," *Milwaukee History* 10, no. 3 (1987): 95-108; Berndt Ostendorf, "'America is a Mistake, a Gigantic Mistake': Patterns of Ethnocentrism in German Attitudes Towards America," *In Their Own Words* 3, no. 2 (1986): 19-47; Dianna Everett and Cathy Kelly, "First, You Work: Germans from Russia to Texas," *Panhandle-Plains Historical Review* 56 (1983): 65-83; and Andrew P. Yox, "Bonds of Community: Buffalo's German Element," *New York History* 66, no.2 (1985): 140-63; Linda Schelbitzki Pickle, "A German Immigrant in Postbellum Fulton," *Missouri Historical Review* 86, no.2 (1992): 149-63; Theodore Stempfel, *Fifty Years of Unrelenting German Aspirations in Indianapolis, 1848-1898* (Indianapolis: German-American Center and Indiana German Heritage Society, 1991); Karin Ramspeck Sloan, "Trading the Pen for the Spade: 19th-Century German Immigrant Literature in Texas" (Ph.D. diss., Texas A&I University ,1990); Barbara Handy-Marchello, "Assimilation of German-Russian and Norwegian Immigrants: A Comparison of North Dakota Pioneers," *Heritage Review* 17, no. 2 (1987): 29-32; Gordon L. Iseminger, "The Mcintosh County German-Russians: The First Fifty Years," *North Dakota History* 51, no.3 (1984): 4-23; Robert P. Swierenga, "The Settlement of the Old Northwest: Ethnic Pluralism in a Featureless Plain," *Journal of the Early Republic* 9, no.1 (1989): 73-105; and Peter Winkel, "Skepticism Turns to Enthusiasm: Seventeen Letters Written by a German Immigrant in New Jersey to His Father in Hesse-Darmstadt Between 1852 and 1859," *Yearbook of German-American Studies* 24 (1989): 41-58. For an interesting discussion of the cultural exchange between German immigrants and Indians see Timothy J. Kloberdanz, "In the Land of Inyan Wosleta: Plains Indian Influences on Reservation Whites," *Great Plains Quarterly* 7, no. 2 (1987): 69-82.

33. For the change in German-American consciousness see also the book by John A. Hawgood, *The Tragedy of German-America* (New York: G.P. Putnam's Sons, 1940), especially chapter 10, "The Dissolution of the Hyphen and the American Germans of Today," and Peter Bodo Gawenda, *The Use of the German Language in the Schools of San Antonio, Texas, from 1880-1910*, Dissertation, University of Houston, 1986.

Notes to Conclusion

1. See for instance the article by Günter Moltmann, "American-German Return Migration in the Nineteenth and Early Twentieth Centuries," in George E. Pozzetta, ed., *Emigration & Immigration; The Old World Confronts the New* (New York: Garland Publishing, Inc., 1991), 470-84.

2. Poem quoted from: Maldwyn A. Jones, *Destination America* (London: Weidenfeld and Nicolson, 1976), 10. However, this door was not open all the time for everybody. The Immigration Act of 1882 marked the beginning of federal regulations for immigration. The same year, the United States began to control immigration with restrictions. The first one was the Chinese Exclusion Act prohibiting the further entry of Chinese laborers to the United States. The initiative for this regulation actually came from the Irishman Dennis Kearney, who was bitter that the Chinese were cheap competitors on the job market. Although the Chinese—who had come in considerable numbers after the completion of the Union Pacific Railroad in 1869—made up

only nine percent of California's population, they compressed the wage scale for all. A law in 1917 banned Asian immigrants altogether. Other regulations followed. With the Immigration Act of 1921 (Johnson Act), national quotas for immigration were introduced for the first time. Only 150,000 persons were allowed to enter the United States annually and at least 100 persons from each nation were permitted to immigrate. The percentage of the various groups from all the different nations was based on the population figures from 1910. In 1924 this law was tightened by the Johnson-Reed Act. Now the national quotas were based on the census of 1890, only allowing three percent of every group existing at that time to enter the United States. This regulation was directly aimed at eastern and southern Europeans who had started immigrating in considerable numbers after 1890. The strict exclusion of Asian immigrants was loosened up a bit in 1943 (allowing 105 Chinese annually into the country). It was not until the Immigration and Nationality Act of 1952 that the tight laws which had closed the golden door to a large extent were loosened up a bit by allowing Asians into the United States according to a certain quota. The restrictions were dropped altogether in 1965 with the introduction of a new law. Other laws liberating immigration followed. For the various restrictions and laws concerning immigration see Herbert Dittgen, "Die Reformen in der Einwanderungs- und Flüchtlingspolitik in den achtziger Jahren," *Amerikastudien/American Studies* 40, no. 3, (1995): 345-66; and Lucy E. Salyer, *Laws Harsh as Tigers: Chinese Immigrants and the Shaping of Modern Immigration Law* (Chapel Hill: University of North Carolina Press, 1995). For the special period of 1920-1925 see: Charles B. Keely, "Immigration in the Interwar Period," in Robert W. Tucker, Charles B. Keely, and Linda Wrigley, eds., *Immigration and U.S. Foreign Policy* (Boulder: Westview Press, 1990), 43-70.

A large number of Chinese came to the United States after 1849 as laborers. Like many Italians at the beginning of this century, however, a lot of them did not come with the intention to stay. Thus, they were not immigrants. They did not want to settle down in the United States but to earn enough money to go back to China and buy a decent home there. Although about 300,000 Chinese arrived in America between 1849 and 1882, only some 105,000 were counted in the census of 1880—seventy percent of these living in California. For a detailed analysis of Asian immigrants see Roger Daniels, "Asian Americans: The Transformation of a Pariah Minority," *Amerikastudien/ American Studies* 40, no. 3 (1995): 469-83.

Four decades after the first Chinese had set foot on American soil, the first Japanese came. As in the case with the Chinese, return migration was very high. This Asian labor competition was not greeted with enthusiasm, and the already mentioned restrictions on immigration were enforced. Between 1951 and 1990, 557,433 Chinese and 179,261 Japanese and in 1993 alone, 79,907 Chinese and 6,908 Japanese immigrated into the United States adding up to a total of 1,645,472 Chinese and 847,562 Japanese living in the United States according to the U.S. Census data of 1990. The second largest Asian American group, after the Chinese, are the Filipinos with 1,406,770 members. The census of 1990 showed that nearly three percent of all American citizens were of Asian origin, and this figure might move up to about five percent by the next census. They are a growing number, but although the neo-conservative sociologist William Petersen labeled the Asian Americans—as diverse as the various groups are—as "model minorities" (*Japanese Americans: Oppression and Success* [New York: Random House, 1971].) they, nevertheless, face continuous discrimination.

3. For Fritz Ernst's famous letter see Detlev Dunt, *Reise nach Texas* (Bremen: Carl Wilhelm Wiehe, 1834), 4-16. For the story of Fritz Ernst, who was born in 1796 as Christian Friedrich Dirks, see Hugh E. Meredith, "Ernst, Johann Friedrich," *The New Handbook of Texas*, vol. 2, p. 884; Glen E. Lich, *The German Texans*(San Antonio: University of Texas Institute of Texan Cultures at San Antonio, 1981), 38-46; and Rudolph Leopold Biesele, "The First German Settlement in Texas," *SHQ*, 34 (1931): 334-39.

4. Mary Paik's account is quoted in Thomas Dublin, ed., *Immigrant Voices: New Lives in America, 1773-1986* (Urbana: University of Illinois Press, 1993), 175. For other accounts of groups and individuals migrating to the United States see, for instance, Antonio Donno, "Il Mito dell' America nell' Ebraismo Tedesco Dell' Ottocento," *Clio*, 28, no.1 (1992): 47-60; Sophie A. Welisch, "Bukovina-German Pioneers in Urban America," *Journal of the American Historical Society of Germans from Russia* 12, no. 1 (1989): 19-26; George R. Nielsen, *In Search of a Home: Nineteenth-Century Wendish Immigration* (College Station: Texas A&M University Press, 1989).

5. Gert Raeithel, *"Go West" : Ein psychohistorischer Versuch über die Amerikaner,* 2nd ed. (Hamburg: Europäische Verlagsanstalt, 1993).

6. For an introduction see Michael Argyle, *The Psychology of Interpersonal Behaviour,* 4th ed. (London: Penguin Books, 1990), 20-29.

7. Erwin Hölzle, *Die Selbstentmachtung Europas* (Göttingen: Musterschmidt, 1975), 593. Trans. by the author.

8. John Lukacs, *The Last European War* (New York: Anchor/ Doubleday, 1976), 385.

9. For the history of this westward movement see for example John D. Unruh, Jr., *The Plains Across: The Overland Emigrants and the Trans-Mississippi West, 1840-60* (Urbana/ Chicago: University of Illinois Press, 1982).

10. For a critical evaluation see, for example, Mark Gibney, "United States Immigration Policy and the 'Huddled Masses' Myth," *Georgetown Immigration Law Journal* 3 (1989): 361-386.

11. Rosemary Jenks, "Byliner: Rhetoric versus reality - the new U.S. immigration law," *U.S. Information and Texts*, Z 12481 B, No. 017, April 30, 1997, p. 17. Also see the figures for legal immigrants during 1996: "I.N.S. on legal immigration figures for FY-1996," in ibid., p. 18. For the ongoing discussion as to what constitutes the United States as a nation see Gary Gerstle, "The Power of Nations," *The Journal of American History* 84, no. 2 (1997): 576-80.

12. Gary Pergl, ed., *Generation of Change: The Civil Rights Movement in America* (Washington, D.C.: United States Information Agency, 1989), 52.

13. This speech is quoted in Stephen B. Oates, *Let the Trumpet Sound: The Life of Martin Luther King, Jr.* (New York: Mentor Books, 1985), 254.

14. For the historiography of the influence of labor on immigration see Ewa Morawska, "The Sociology and Historiography of Immigration," in Virginia Yans-McLaughlin, ed., *Immigration Reconsidered* New York: Oxford University Press, 1990), especially 196-212; and Jeffrey G. Williamson, "Migration to the New World: Long Term Influences and Impact," *Explorations in Economic History* 11, no. 4 (Summer 1974), especially 386.

15. These figures are from Felicity Barringer, "Minorities on the Move, Often Unpredictably," *New York Times*, 6 June 1993, p. E4, as quoted in Uwe Wenzel, "Auf dem Weg zur Integration? Probleme und Perspektiven politischer Partizipation von Latinos in den USA," *Amerikastudien/ American Studies* 40, no. 3 (1995): 443-68.

16. Today we see only the beginning of what many have already labeled the "Third Industrial Revolution." Digitalisation and automatic production modes have started to change our world of labor dramatically. John M. Keynes, in "General Theory of Employment, Money, and Interest," was prophetic when he wrote about technological unemployment (*Collected Writings of John Maynard Keynes,* vol. 5, London: Macmillan, 1973). For the changing world of employment today see for example Jeremy Rifkin, *The End of Work: The Decline of the Global Labor Force and the Dawn of the Post-Market Era* (New York: Putnam, 1995); and William Bridges, *Job Shift. How to Prosper in a Workplace without Jobs* (Reading, MA.: Addison Wesley, 1994).

17. For the numbers cited and the question of black attitudes towards immigrants see Lawrence H. Fuchs, "The Reaction of Black Americans to Immigration," in Yans-McLaughlin,

especially p. 309.

18. See for example: Gregory DeFreitas, "Economic Effects of Recent Immigration to the United States," in Michael D'Innocenzo and Josef P. Sirefman, eds., *Immigration and Ethnicity: American Society –"Melting Pot" or "Salad Bowl"?* (London: Greenwood, 1992), 309-331; and Philip L. Martin and Leon F. Bouvier, "Immigration and the American Future," in ibid, 297-308.

19. "Candidates on the Issues," Associated Press, February 29, 1996

20. Figures in states like Minnesota have sometimes even doubled—from 32,123 Hispanics there in 1980 to 62,316 in 1992, an increase of 93.9 percent. For these figures see Debbie Howlett, "Midwest New Hub for Hispanics," *USA Today* International Edition,18 December 1995, p. 3A.

21. For the estimates about the United States population in the year 2020 see: Robert W. Tucker, Charles B. Keely, and Linda Wrigley, eds., *Immigration and U.S. Foreign Policy* (Boulder: Westview, 1990), 10; for the figures about citizenship among Latinos see Wenzel, 454; and for the general questions about Mexican migration see: Alejandro Portes, "From South of the Border: Hispanic Minorities in the United States," in Yans-McLaughlin, 160-184; and Arthur F. Corwin, "Causes of Mexican Emigration to the United States: A Summary View," *Perspectives in American History* 7 (1973): 555-635.

22. John F. Kennedy, *A Nation of Immigrants* (New York: Perennial Library/Harper & Row. Publishers, 1986), 64.

23. Clinton American University Speech on Upcoming Agenda, in *U.S. Information and Texts*, Z 12481 B, Nr. 017, April 30, 1997, EUR205 09/09/97, p. 15.

24. See the critical essay by Mike Wallace, "Mickey Mouse History: Portraying the Past at Disney World," *Mickey Mouse History and Other Essays in American Memory* (Philadelphia: Temple University Press, 1996), 133-57.

25. For the various messages and motives of the Western see for example: Lee Clark Mitchell, *Westerns: Making the Man in Fiction and Film*, (Chicago: University of Chicago Press, 1996); and Thomas Schatz, *Hollywood Genres: Formulas, Filmmaking, and the Studio System* (New York: Random House, 1981), 45-80. For the television concept of Walt Disney and that of Disneyland see Christopher Anderson, *Hollywood TV: The Studio System in the Fifties* (Austin: University of Texas Press, 1994), 133-55.

26. Louis Uchitelle and N.R. Kleinfield, "The Downsizing of America: Paying the Price in People," *Herald Tribune*, 6 March 1996, pp. 1 and 6.

27. For the dominant influence of Calvinism on the history of the United States see for example, James A. Henretta, "The Protestant Ethic and the Reality of Capitalism in Colonial America," in Hartmut Lehmann and Günther Roth, eds., *Weber's Protestant Ethic: Origins, Evidence, Contexts* (Washington, D.C.: Cambridge University Press, 1993), 327-46; and Douglas F. Kelly, *The Emergence of Liberty in the Modern World* (Phillipsburg: Presbyterian and Reformed Publishing, 1992).

28. As quoted in: Michael Zuckerman, "The Turnerian Frontier: A New Approach to the Study of American Character," *OAH Newsletter* 23, no. 4 (November 1995): 7.

Bibliography

Archival Sources

Caroli, Alfred. "Ortsgeschichte Aglasterhausens." Unpublished manuscript. Aglasterhausen 1970.

Deed of Trust Records. Victoria County Court House. Victoria, Texas.

Deeds Records. Vol. K. DeWitt County Courthouse. Cuero, Texas.

District Clerks Records. DeWitt County Courthouse. Cuero, Texas.

Douai, Adolph, Papers. The Center for American History. University of Texas at Austin.

Haas, Oscar, Papers. The Center for American History. University of Texas at Austin.

Kattermann, Hildegard, ed. *Familienbriefe 1811-1871*. transcribed, and photocopied, Lahr, 1977. Wagner Family Collection. The Center for American History. University of Texas at Austin.

Kleberg, Rudolph, Family Papers. Center for American History. The University of Texas at Austin.

Kleinpell, Henry, Papers. Box 1-5, WIS, MSS/38PB. Wisconsin State Historical Society. Madison, Wisconsin.

Kuechler, Jacob, Papers. The Center for American History. The University of Texas at Austin.

Military Records. Civil War. National Archives. Washington, D.C.

Miner, Helen K. and Frances K. Halper. "The Kachelhoffer Families from Berne, Switzerland to Alsace, France and America." typescript copy, n.p., 1980. in Freeport Public Library, Freeport, Illinois.

Mortgage Records. Victoria County Courthouse. Victoria, Texas.

Probate Minutes. Victoria County. County Court. Victoria,Texas.

Recorded Deeds. Green County Records. Courthouse. Monroe, WI.

Schafer, Joseph, Papers. Mss, 746. The State Historical Society of Wisconsin. Madison, Wisconsin.

Schenck, Friedrich, Manuscripts. The Center for American History. University of Texas at Austin.

Solms-Braunfels Archives. Transcripts. (Originals in Fürst zu Solms-Braunfels'-sches Archiv in Braunfels, Lahn, Germany) Texas State Archives. Austin, Vol. 1 – 70.

St. John United Church of Christ, 1010 South Park Boulevard, Freeport, Illinois. Church Records.

Strubberg, Friedrich Armand, Collection. Beinecke Rare Book and Mansucript Library. Yale University.

Tax-Rolls, 1888-1892. Bexar County, Texas. Reel No.101503-05.

Wagner Family Collection. The Center for American History. University of Texas at Austin.

Welcker, Wilhelm. "Bilder aus dem Leben der Familie Backofen." Darmstadt, 1932. (typescript-copy) Hessisches Staatsarchiv Darmstadt, O 61 Schuchardt-Osann No. 8/1.

Wettstein, Theodore, Field Notes for a Biographical Sketch of, 1812-1877. Wiss, Mss, MM. The State Historical Society of Wisconsin. Madison, Wisconsin.

Wheat, Jim, Collection. Texas State Archives. Austin, Texas.

Newspapers

Abendblatt, Chicago, Illinois
Allgemeine Auswanderungs-Zeitung
Chicagoer neue Freie Presse, Chicago, Illinois
Chicago Press and Tribune
Chicago Times
The Cuero Daily Record, Cuero, Texas
The Daily Times, Davenport, Iowa
Dallas Herald, Dallas, Texas
Darmstädter Zeitung, Darmstadt
Deutsche Rundschau, Cuero, Texas
Deutscher Anzeiger, Freeport, Illinois
Der deutsche Auswanderer—Zentralblatt der deutschen Auswanderung und Kolonisierung
Freeport Journal, Freeport, Ill.
Freeport (Ill.) Journal Standard
Freeport Weekly Bulletin, Freeport, Ill.
Freie Presse und Daheim, Chicago, Illinois
International Herald Tribune, Frankfurt
New York Times
San Antonio Daily Express
San Antonio Express
San Antonio Light
Texas Vorwärts, Austin, Texas
USA Today

Primary Published Sources

Adams, Charles Francis, ed. *The Works of John Adams*, Vol. 10. Boston: Little, Brown, and Company, 1856.

Bracht, Victor. *Texas in 1848*. Elberfeld: Julius Baedeker, 1849.

Brister, Louis E., ed. "William von Rosenberg's Kritik: A History of the Society for the Protection of German Immigrants to Texas." *SHQ* 85, nos. 2-4 (October 1981 - April 1982), 161-186, 299-318, 409-422.

Cabet, Étienne. *Propagande communiste ou, Questions à discuter et à soutenir ou à écarter*. Paris: np, 1842.

———. *Reise nach Ikarien*. reprint. Berlin: Kramer, 1979.

Cather, Willa. *My Ántonia*. Boston: Houghton Mifflin Company, 1946.

———. *O Pioneers!* Boston: Houghton Mifflin Company, 1941.

Commager, Henry Steele, ed. *Documents of American History*. 9th ed. Vol. 1. Englewood Cliffs, N.J.: Prentice Hall, Inc., 1973.

De Lono, A. *The Galveston Directory for 1856-57*. Galveston: News Book and Job Office, 1856.

Demian. *Geographie und Statistik des Großerzogtums Baden*. 1820. Ordner I, Kap. IV, p. 18.

Dresel, Gustav. *Gustav Dresel's Houston Journal: Adventures in North America and Texas, 1837-1841*. ed. Max Freund. Austin: University of Texas Press, 1954.

Dublin, Thomas, ed. *Immigrant Voices: New Lives in America, 1773-1986*. Urbana: University of Illinois Press, 1993.

Dunt, Detlev. *Reise nach Texas, nebst Nachrichten von diesem Lande für Deutsche, welche nach Texas zu gehen beabsichtigen*. Bremen: Carl Wilhelm Wiehe, 1834.

Esselborn, Karl, ed. *Zwei Erbacher in Texas, Lebenserinnerungen von Ernst Dosch und Eberhard Ihrig*. Hessische Volksbücher, Darmstadt: H. L. Schlapp, 1937.

Goeth, Ottilie Fuchs. *Memoirs of a Texas Pioneer Grandmother; 1805-1915*. trans. Irma Goeth Guenther. Austin: n.p., 1969.

Goyne, Minetta Altgelt. *Lone Star and Double Eagle: Civil War Letters of a German-Texas Family*. Ft. Worth: Texas Christian University Press, 1982.

Grimm, Hermann, *Goethes Briefwechsel mit einem Kinde*. Vols. 1-3. Berlin: Hertz, 1835.

Helbich, Wolfgang, Walter D. Kamphoefner, and Ulrike Sommer. *Briefe aus Amerika: Deutsche Auswanderer schreiben aus der Neuen Welt 1830-1930*. München: Verlag C.H. Beck, 1988.

Hense-Jensen, Wilhelm. *Wisconsin's Deutsch-Amerikaner bis zum Schluß des neunzehnten Jahrhunderts*. Vols. 1-2. Milwaukee: Im Verlage der Deutschen Gesellschaft, 1900-1902.

Hoffmann von Fallersleben, August Heinrich. *Ausgewählte Werke in vier Bänden*. ed. Hans Benzmann. Vols. 1-4. Leipzig: Max Hesses Verlag, 1924.

———. *Gedichte und Lieder*. eds. Hermann Wendebourg and Anneliese Gerbert. Hamburg: Hoffmann und Campe, 1974.

———. *Mein Leben*. Vols. 1-4, Hannover: Rümpler, 1868.

Holmes, Kenneth L., ed. *Covered Wagon Women: Diaries and Letters from the Western Trails, 1840-1849*. Lincoln: University of Nebraska Press, 1995.

James, Vinton Lee. *Frontier and Pioneer Recollections of Early Days in San Antonio and West Texas*. San Antonio: Artes Graficas, 1938.

Jordan, Gilbert J., ed. "W. Steinert's View of Texas in 1849: May 22 to June 5." *SHQ* 80, no. 1 (July 1976): 57-78; no. 2 (October 1976): 177-200; no. 3 (January 1977).

Kamphoefner, Walter D., Wolfgang Helbich, and Ulrike Sommer, eds. *News from the Land of Freedom: German Immigrants Write Home - 1830-1930*. trans. Susan Carter Vogel. Ithaca, New York: Cornell University Press, 1991.

Kapp, Friedrich. *Aus und über Amerika: Tatsachen und Erlebnisse*. Vols. 1-2. Berlin: Julius Springer Verlag, 1876.

Kleberg, Rosa, "Some of my early experiences in Texas." *Quarterly of the Texas State Historical Association* 1 (1898): 297-302.

Klotzbach, Kurt, ed. *Die Solms-Papiere - Dokumente zur Deutschen Kolonisation von Texas*. Wyk auf Föhr: Verlag für Amerikanistik, 1990.

Lauckhard, Fritz. "Auswandererbriefe aus Texas 1848/49." *Volk und Scholle* 9 (1931): 95-101.

Lich, Glen E., ed. "A Letter from Friedrich Schenck in Texas to His Mother in Germany, 1847." *SHQ* 92, no. 1 (July 1988): 144–65.

Lindheimer, Ferdinand. "Kolonie der Darmstädter Communisten-Gesellschaft." *Allgemeine Auswanderungs-Zeitung* (1848): 776 ff.

MacLean, John. *One Hundred Years in Illinois (1818-1918)*. Chicago: Peterson Linotyping Company, 1919.

Mannhardt, Emil. "Gemeinde-Chronologie - Chronologische Darstellung der äußeren Entwicklung des religiösen Lebens unter den Deutschen in Illinois." *Deutsch-Amerikanische Geschichtsblätter* 5, no. 4 (1905): 1-43.

Morrison and Fourmy, comps. *Morrison & Fourmy's General Directory of the City of San Antonio 1887-1888* Galveston: Morrison & Fourmy Publishers, 1888.

N.N. *Indianola Scrap Book*. comp. and published *The Victoria Advocate,* Victoria, Texas, 1936; reprinted by Calhoun County Historical Survey Committee, Port Lavaca, Texas, 1974.

———. "Versatility of Management." *Printing*. February 1944, p. 35.

Nagel, Charles. *A Boy's Civil War Story*. Saint Louis, MO: Eden Publishing House, 1935.

Odenwald, Karl. *Aus einer Familienchronik*. Karlsruhe: Aktiendruckerei, 1898.

Olmsted, Frederick Law. *A Journey through Texas: or, A Saddle-Trip on the Southwestern Frontier*. New York: Dix, Edward & Co., 1857.

Ragsdale, Crystal Sasse, ed. *The Golden Free Land: The Reminiscences and Letters of Women on an American Frontier*. Austin: Landmark Press, 1976.

Rawleigh, William T., ed. *Freeport's Lincoln*. Freeport, Ill.: Wagner Printing Company, 1988. Facsimile edition of the hardback book published by W. T. Rawleigh in 1930.

Regenbrecht, Adalbert. "The German Settlers of Millheim (Texas) before the Civil War." *SHQ* 20 (1916): 28-34.

Reinhardt, Louis. "The Communistic Colony of Bettina." *Quarterly of the Texas State Historical Association* 3, no. 1 (Jan 1899): 33-40.

Reininger, Gus. "Erinnerungen aus dem Pionierleben eines Cowboys." *Jahrbuch der Neu-Braunfelser Zeitung für 1943*. Druck der Neu-Braunfelser Zeitung, 1943, 65-71.

Schlecht, Friedrich. *Mein Ausflug nach Texas* Bunzlau: Voigt, 1851.

Sealsfield, Charles. *The Making of an American: An Adaption of Memorable Tales by Charles Sealsfield*. trans. Ulrich S. Carrington. Dallas: Southern Methodist University Press, 1974.

Seele, Hermann. *The Cypress and Other Writings of a German Pioneer in Texas*. Austin: The University of Texas Press, 1979.

Smithwick, Noah. *The Evolution of a State; or, Recollections of Old Texas Days*. comp. Nanna Smithwick Donaldson. Austin: University of Texas Press, 1983.

Tonsor, Stephen J., ed. "'I Am My Own Boss'—A German Immigrant Writes from Illinois." *Journal of the Illinois State Historical Society* 54, no. 4 (1961): 392-404.

von Herff, Ferdinand. *The Regulated Emigration of the German Proletariat with Special Reference to Texas*. trans. Arthur L. Finck. San Antonio: Trinity University Press, 1978.

von Hinueber, Caroline. "Life of German Pioneers in Early Texas." *Quarterly of the Texas State Historical Association* 2, no. 3 (January 1899): 227-32.

Von-Maszewski, W. M., ed. *A Sojourn in Texas, 1846-47, Alwin H. Sörgel's Texas Writings*. San Marcos, Texas: German-Texan Heritage Society, Southwest Texas State University, 1992.

von Wrede, Friedrich W. *Sketches of Life in The United States of North America and Texas*. comp. Emil Drescher. trans. Chester W. Geue. Waco: Texian Press, 1970.

Wagner, William H. "Wilhelm Wagner, Gründer des Freeport *Deutscher Anzeiger*." *Deutsch-Amerikanische Geschichtsblätter* 4, no. 2 (April 1904): 5-19.

Wendeler, Camillus. *Briefwechsel des Freiherrn Karl Hartwig Gregor von Meusebach mit Jacob und Wilhelm Grimm*. Heilbronn: Henninger, 1880.

Wettstein, Theodore. *Der Nordamerikanische Freistaat Wisconsin*. Elberfeld, 1851.

Wheeler, A. C. *The Chronicles of Milwaukee: Being a Narrative History of the Town from its Earliest Period to the Present*. Milwaukee: Jermain & Brightman, 1861.

Williams, Robert H. and John W. Sansom. *The Massacre on the Nueces River*. Grand Prairie, Texas: Frontier Times Publishing House, n.d.

Williams, Robert H. *With the Border Ruffians: Memoirs of the Far West, 1852-1868*. London: John Murray, 1908.

Yelvington, Ramsey, ed. *Travels and Adventures in Texas in the 1820's being the Reminiscences of Mary Crownover Rabb*. Waco: Texian Press, 1962.

Secondary Works

Abbott, Peyton O. "Business Travel Out of Texas During the Civil War: The Travel Diary of S. B. Brush, Pioneer Austin Merchant." *SHQ* 96, no. 2 (October 1992): 259-71.

Abernethy, Francis Edward. "Texas Folklore and German Culture." in Joseph Wilson, ed. *Texas and Germany: Crosscurrents*. Rice University Studies 63, no. 3 (Summer 1977): 83-99.

Ackerman, William K. *Early Illinois Railroads*. Fergus Historical Series, no. 23. Chicago: np, 1884.

Adshead, S.A.M. *China in World History*. 2nd. ed. London: Macmillan, 1995.

Alexander, Ruth Ann. "Nature, Ethnics, and Land: the Making of a South Dakota Novel." *South Dakota History* 18, no. 3 (1988): 152-72.

Allan, Howard W. "Isolationism and German-Americans." *Journal of the Illinois State Historical Society* 56 (Summer 1964): 143-49.

Allen, James Sloan. *The Romance of Commerce and Culture*. Chicago: The University of Chicago Press, 1983.

Allin, Dana H., ed. *Twenty Years Aspen Institute Berlin*. Berlin: Aspen Institute Berlin, 1994.

Anderson, Christopher. *Hollywood TV: The Studio System in the Fifties*. Austin: University of Texas Press, 1994.

Andrews, Rena Mazyck. "German Pioneers in Texas: Civil War Period." M.A. thesis. University of Chicago, 1929.

Ankersmit, Frank R. "Historicism: An Attempt At Synthesis." *History and Theory* 34 (1995): 143-61.

———. *History and Tropology: The Rise and Fall of Metaphor*. Berkeley: University of California Press, 1994.

———. ed. *Knowing and Telling History: the Anglo-Saxon Debate*. Middletown, Conn.: Wesleyan University Press, 1986

Ankersmit, Frank R. and Hans Kellner, eds. *A New Philosophy of History*. Chicago, Ill.: University of Chicago Press, 1995.

Argyle, Michael. *The Psychology of Interpersonal Behaviour*. 4th ed. London: Penguin Books, 1990.

Ater, Pamela. "Buchel Family." in DeWitt County Historical Commission. *The History of DeWitt County, Texas*. Dallas: Curtis Media Corporation, 1991, p. 322.

Bade, Klaus J. *Europa in Bewegung; Migration vom späten 18. Jahrhundert bis zur Gegenwart*. München: C.H. Beck, 2000.

———. "Deutsche Überseeauswanderung und -Einwanderung im 19. und frühen 20. Jahrhundert." *Archiv für Sozialgeschichte* 26 (1986): 480-87.

Barkan, Elliott A. "Race, Religion, and Nationality in American Society: A Model of Ethnicity—From Contact to Assimilation." *Journal of American Ethnic History* 14 (Winter 1995): 38-75.

Barnes, Charles Merritt. *Combats and Conquests of Immortal Heroes*. San Antonio: Guessaz and Ferlet Company, 1910.

Bartscht, Waltraud. "'Da waren Deutsche auch dabei!' The Story of a Texas-German Family." in Joseph Wilson, ed. *Texas and Germany: Crosscurrents*. Rice University Studies 63, no. 3 (Summer 1977): 35-46.

Bäumer, Konstanze. *"Bettine, Psyche, Mignon" : Bettina von Arnim und Goethe*. Stuttgart: Hans-Dieter Heinz Akademischer Verlag, 1986.

Bayer, Herbert. *Herbert Bayer: Painter, Designer, Architect*. New York: Reinhold Publishing Corporation, 1967.

Beck, Earl. "The German Discovery of American Education." *History of Education Quarterly* 5 (1965): 3-13.

Becker, Winfried. "Historische Aspekte der Deutsch-Amerikanischen Beziehungen." *Archiv für Kulturgeschichte* 71, no. 1 (1989): 177-208.

Benjamin, Gilbert Giddings. *The Germans in Texas: A Study in Immigration*. Austin: Jenkins, 1974.

Benrath, Gustav Adolf. "Die Evangelische Kirche in Baden 1771-1821." *Baden und Württemberg im Zeitalter Napoleons*. Vol 2. Stuttgart: Edition Cantz, 1987.

Berkin, Carol. *First Generations: Women in Colonial America* New York: Hill and Wang, 1996.

Bernard, William S. ed. *Immigrants and Ethnicity*. New York: American Immigration and Citizenship Conference, 1972.

Bestor, Arthur Eugene, Jr. *Backwoods Utopias: The Sectarian and Owenite Phases of Communitarian Socialism in America: 1663-1829*. Philadelphia: University of Pennsylvania Press, 1950.

Biesele, Rudolph Leopold. "The First German Settlement in Texas." *SHQ* 34 (1931): 334-39.

———. *The History of the German Settlements in Texas 1831-1861*. Austin: Press of von Boeckmann-Jones Co., 1930.

Billigmeier, Robert W. *Americans from Germany: A Study in Cultural Diversity*. Belmont, CA: Wadsworth Publishing Company, 1974.

Bingham, Helen M. *History of Green County, Wisconsin*. Milwaukee: Burdick & Armitage, Printers, 1877.

Blesch, Werner. *Uiffingen. Geschichte fränkischer Bauern und ihrer Dorfgemeinde*. Tauberbischofsheim: Fränkische Nachrichten Druck-und Verlags GmbH., 1985.

Borjas, George J. *Heaven's Door: Immigration Policy and the American Economy*. Princeton: Princeton University Press, 1999.

Bostelmann, Albert T. "Life and Ministry of Johann Wolter." *Concordia Historical Institute Quarterly* 61, no. 2 (1988): 61-73.

Bowman, Shearer Davis. "Antebellum Planters and Vormärz Junkers in Comparative Perspective." *American Historical Review* 85 (1980): 779-808.

———. *Masters & Lords: Mid-19th-Century U.S. Planters and Prussian Junkers*. New York: Oxford University Press, 1993.

Boxberger, Daniel L. "The Germans from Russia and the 1911 Report of the U.S. Immigration Commission." *Journal of the American Historical Society of Germans from Russia* 14, no. 4 (1991): 23-25.

Brancaforte, Charlotte L., ed. *The German Forty-Eighters in the United States*. New York: Peter Lang, 1989.

Bree, T.H. and Stephen Foster. "Moving to the New World: The Character of Early Massachusetts Immigration." *William and Mary Quarterly* 30, no. 2, Third Series, Vol. 30, No. 2, April 1973, p. 189-222

Bretting, Agnes. "Frauen als Einwanderer in der Neuen Welt: Überlegungen anhand einiger Selbstzeugnisse deutscher Auswanderinnen." *Amerikastudien / American Studies* 33, no. 3 (1988): 319-27.

———. *Soziale Probleme deutscher Einwanderer in New York City 1800-1860*. Wiesbaden: Franz Steiner Verlag, 1981.

Bridges, William. *Job Shift. How to Prosper in a Workplace without Jobs*. Reading, MA.: Addison Wesley, 1994.

Brimelow, Peter. *Alien Nation: Common Sense About America's Immigration Disaster*. New York: Random House, 1995.

Brown, John Henry. *Indian Wars and Pioneers of Texas*. Austin: L. E. Daniell Publishers, 1890.

Brownson, Howard Gary. "History of the Illinois Central Railroad to 1870." *University of Illinois Studies in the Social Sciences* 1 (1915): 1-182.

Brubaker, William Rogers. "Citizenship and Naturalization: Policies and Politics," in William Rogers Brubaker, ed. *Immigration and the Politics of Citizenship in Europe and North America*. Lanham: University Press of America, 1989.

Brunschwig, Henri. "The Revolution of 1848," in Heinz Lubasz, ed. *Revolutions in Modern European History*. New York: Macmillan, 1966. 86-92.

Buenger, Walter L. *Secession and the Union in Texas*. Austin: The University of Texas Press, 1984.

———. "Secession and the Texas German Community: Editor Lindheimer vs. Editor Flake." *SHQ* 82, no. 4 (April 1979): 379-402.

Buley, R. Carlyle. *The Old Northwest: Pioneer Period, 1815-1840*. Bloomington, IN: Indiana University Press, 1950.

Campbell, Randolph B. "Carpetbagger Rule in Reconstruction Texas: An Enduring Myth." *SHQ* 97, no. 4 (April 1994): 587-96.

Carrier, Lois A. *Illinois: Crossroads of a Continent*. Urbana: University of Illinois Press, 1993.

Cartwright, Gary. *Galveston, A History of the Island*. New York: Atheneum, 1991.

Cat Spring Agricultural Society. *The Cat Spring Story*. San Antonio: Lone Star Printing Company, 1956.

Childs, Marquis W. "The World of Walter Paepcke." *Horizon*. (Sept. 1958): 96-103, 133-34.

Churchill, Ward, ed. *Das indigene Amerika und die marxistische Tradition: eine kontroverse Debatte über Kultur, Industrialusmus und Eurozentrismus*. Bremen: Agipa-Press, 1993.

Clark, Ira G. *Then Came the Railroads: The Century from Steam to Diesel in the Southwest*. Norman, OK: University of Oklahoma Press, 1958.

Cohen, Lizabeth. "Ethnicity and Class in Little Germany." *Reviews in American History* 19, no. 3 (1991): 374-78.

———. *Making a New Deal: Industrial Workers in Chicago, 1919-1939*. New York: Cambridge University Press, 1990.

Commager, Henry Steele. *The Empire of Reason*. Garden City, NY: Anchor Press-Doubleday, 1978.

Conners, Michael. "Development of Germanophobia." *Social Justice Review* 53 (January 1961): 328-31.

Conzen, Kathleen Neils. "German-Americans and the Invention of Ethnicity." Frank Trommler and Joseph McVeigh, eds. *America and the Germans*. Vol. 1. Philadelphia: University of Pennsylvania Press, 1985; 131-47.

———. *Immigrant Milwaukee, 1836-1860: Accommodation and Community in a Frontier City*. Cambridge: Harvard University Press, 1976.

Corcoran, Paul E., ed. *Before Marx: Socialism and Communism in France, 1830-48*. London: Macmillan, 1983.

Cordillot, Michel. "Aux Origines du Socialisme Dans le Sud des Etats-Unis: Les Immigres Allemands Dans les Etats Esclavagistes, 1848-1865." *Mouvement Social* 139 (1987): 51-75.

Corwin, Arthur F. "Causes of Mexican Emigration to the United States: A Summary View." *Perspectives in American History* 7 (1973): 555-635.

Crawford, Ann Fears and Crystal Sasse Ragsdale. *Women in Texas: Their Lives, Their Experiences, Their Accomplishments*. Burnet, TX: Eakin Press, 1982.

Crèvecoeur, Hector St. John de. *Letters from an American Farmer*. New York: Fox, Duffield, 1904.

Cronon, William. *Nature's Metropolis: Chicago and the Great West*, New York: W.W.Norton, 1992.

Crouch, Barry A. "'Unmanacling' Texas Reconstruction: A Twenty-Year Perspective." *SHQ* 93, no. 3 (January 1990): 275-302.

Cuero, Texas, City of. *Historical Record Commemorating the 100th Anniversary of the Founding of Cuero*. Smithville, Texas: Tex-Print Corp., 1972.

Current, Richard N. *The History of Wisconsin*. Vol. 2: *The Civil War Era, 1848-1873*. Madison: State Historical Society of Wisconsin, 1976.

Danto, Arthur C. *Analytical Philosophy of History* Cambridge, MA.: Harvard University Press, 1965.

Daniels, Roger. "Asian Americans: The Transformation of a Pariah Minority." *Amerikastudien/ American Studies* 40, no. 3 (1995): 469-83.

———. *Coming to America: A History of Immigration and Ethnicity in American Life*. New York: Harper Perennial, 1991.

———. "Going to America: Observations on the Historiography of Immigration." *Amerikastudien / American Studies* 42, no. 3 (1997) 333-43.

Danquah, Nana-Ama, ed. *Becoming American: Personal Essays by First Generation Immigrant Women*. New York: Hyperion, 2000.

Day, Jack Hays. *The Sutton-Taylor Feud*. San Antonio: Murray, 1937.

DeWitt County Historical Commission. *The History of DeWitt County, Texas*. Dallas: Curtis Media, 1991.

Diamantides, N.D. *International Migration as a Dynamic Process*. MCB University Press. http://www.mcb.co.ul/services/articles/liblink/k/ diamanti.htm.

Didear, Hedwig Krell. *A History of Karnes County and Old Helena*. Austin: Jenkins Publishing Company, 1969.

Dielmann, Henry B. "Dr. Ferdinand Herff: Pioneer Physician and Surgeon." *Southwestern Historical Quarterly* 57, no. 3 (Jan 1954): 265-84.

D'Innocenzo, Michael and Josef P. Sirefman, eds. *Immigration and Ethnicity: American Society - "Melting Pot" or "Salad Bowl"?* Westport, CT: Greenwood Press, 1992.

Dittgen, Herbert. "Die Reformen in der Einwanderungs- und Flüchtlingspolitik in den achtziger Jahren." *Amerikastudien/American Studies* 40, no. 3 (1995): 345-66.

Dixson, Walter Clay. *Richland Crossing: A Portrait of Texas Pioneers*. Fort Worth: Peppermill Publishing Company, 1996.

Dobbert, Guido A. "German-Americans Between New and Old Fatherland, 1870-1914." *American Quarterly* 19 (Winter 1967): 663-80.

Dodd, William E. "The Fight for the Northwest, 1860." *American Historical Review* 16 (July 1911): 774-88.

Doerries, Reinhard R. "German Catholics in the New World: The Immigrants Struggle for Faith and Ethnic Identity." *In Their Own Words* 3, no.2 (1986): 81-107.

———. "German Emigration to the United States: A Review Essay on Recent West German Publications." *Journal of American Ethnic History* 6, no.1 (1986): 71-83.

———. *Iren und Deutsche in der Neuen Welt: Akkulturationsprozesse in der Amerikanischen Gesellschaft im Späten Neunzehnten Jahrhundert*. Stuttgart: Franz Steiner Verlag Wiesbaden, 1986.

Donno, Antonio. "Il Mito dell' America nell' Ebraismo Tedesco Dell' Ottocento." *Clio* 28, no. 1 (1992): 47-60.

Doughty, Robin W. *At Home in Texas: Early Views of the Land*. College Station, TX.: Texas

A&M University Press, 1987.

Dreher, Martin N. *Kirche und Deutschtum in der Entwicklung der Evangelischen Kirche Lutherischen Bekenntnisses in Brasilien.* Göttingen: Vandenhoeck & Ruprecht, 1978.

Dürrenmatt, Peter. *Schweizer Geschichte.* Zürich: Schweizer Druck- und Verlagshaus AG, 1963.

Duleep, Harriet Orcutt and Phanindra V. Wunnava *Immigrants and Immigration Policy: Individual Skills, Family Ties, and Group Identities.* Greenwich, CT: JAI Press, 1996.

Elliott, Brian. "Biography, Family History and the Analysis of Social Change." in Stephen Kendrick, Pat Straw, David McCrone, eds. *Interpreting the Past, Understanding the Present.* London: MacMillan, 1990. 59-82.

Elliott, Claude. "Union Sentiment in Texas, 1861-1865." *SHQ* 50, no. 4 (April 1947): 449-77.

Ellis, Mark. "German-Americans in World War I," in Ragnhild Fiebig-von Hase and Ursula Lehmkuhl, eds. *Enemy Images in American History.* Providence, RI: Berghahn Books, 1997. 183-208.

Ellis, Tuffly L. "Maritime Commerce on the Far Western Gulf, 1861-1865." *SHQ* 72, no. 2 (Oct 1973): 167-226.

Everett, Dianna and Cathy Kelly. "First, You Work: Germans from Russia to Texas." *Panhandle-Plains Historical Review* 56 (1983): 65-83.

Fabricius, Wilhelm. *Die Deutschen Corps.* Berlin: Verlag Hans Ludwig Thilo, 1898.

Fagenson, Ellen A., ed. *Women in Management: Trends, Issues, and Challenges in Managerial Diversity.* Women and Work Series, Vol. 4. Newbury Park, CA: Sage Pub., 1993.

Faust, Albert B., *German Element in the United States,* 2 Vols., New York: Steuben Society, rev.ed., 1927

Ferrie, Joseph P. *Yankeys Now: Immigrants in the Antebellum United States, 1840-1860.* Oxford: Oxford University Press, 1999.

Fiedler, George. *Mineral Point: A History.* 3rd. ed. Mineral Point, WI: The Memorial Pendarvis Endowment Trust Fund, 1986.

Fischer, Wolfram. "Staat und Gesellschaft Badens im Vormärz," in Werner Conze, ed. *Staat und Gesellschaft im deutschen Vormärz 1815-1848.* Stuttgart: Klett-Cotta, 1962. 143-172.

Foik, Paul Joseph. *Early Plans for the German Catholic Colonization in Texas, 1820-1860.* Austin: Texas Catholic Historical Society, 1934.

Foucault, Michel. *The Order of Things.* New York: Vintage, 1970.

———. "What is Enlightenment?" in Joyce Appleby , et. al., eds. *Knowledge and Postmodernism in Historical Perspective.* New York: Routledge, 1996,. 410-17.

Fouquet, Carlos. *Der Deutsche Einwanderer und seine Nachkommen in Brasilien: 1808-1824-1974.* Sao Paulo: Inst. Hans Staden, 1974.

Frank, Gerald David. *A German Organbuilder on the Texas Frontier: The Life and Work of Johann Traugott Wandke.* Harrisville, N.H.: Boston Organ Club Chapter of the Organ Historical Society, 1990.

Frantz, Joe B. "Remembering Walter Prescott Webb." *SHQ* 92, no. 1 (July 1988): 17-30.

Frost, Alan. *Botany Bay Mirages: Illusions of Australia's Convict Beginnings.* Carlton, Victoria: Melbourne University Press, 1994.

Fuchs, Lawrence H. *The American Kaleidoscope: Race, Ethnicity, and the Civic Culture.* Hanover: Wesleyan University Press, 1990.

———. "The Reaction of Black Americans to Immigration", in: Virginia Yans-McLaughlin, ed. *Immigration Reconsidered.* New York: Oxford University Press, 1990. 293-314.

Fulmore, Zachary Taylor. *The History and Geography of Texas - as told in county names*. Austin: np, 1915.

Fulwider, Addison L. *History of Stephenson County, Illinois*. Vol. 2. Chicago: The S.J. Clarke Publishing Company, 1910.

Gabaccia, Donna R. "Liberty, Coercion, and the Making of Immigration Historians." *The Journal of American History* 84, no. 2 (1997): 570-75.

Gagliardi, Ernst. *Geschichte der Schweiz*. Zürich: Rascher & Co. Verlag: 1920.

Garber, Randy, ed. *Built in Milwaukee: An Architectural View of the City*. 2nd. ed. Milwaukee: City of Milwaukee, 1983.

Gard, Wayne. *Frontier Justice*. Norman: University of Oklahoma Press, 1949.

Gawenda, Peter Bodo. "The Use of the German Language in the Schools of San Antonio, Texas, from 1880-1910." Ph.D. dissertation, University of Houston, 1986.

Geertz, Clifford. *The Interpretation of Cultures*. New York: Basic Books, 1973.

Geitz, Henry, ed. *The German-American Press*. Madison: Max Kade Institute at the University of Wisconsin, 1992.

Gerber, David A. "'You see I speak very well Englisch': Literacy and the Transformed Self as Reflected in Immigrant Personal Correspondence." *Journal of American Ethnic History* 12, no. 2 (1993): 56-62.

Gerstle, Gary. "Liberty, Coercion, and the Making of Americans" and "The Power of Nations." *The Journal of American History* 84, no. 2 (1997): 524-58, 576-80.

Geue, Chester William and Ethel Hander Geue. *A New Land Beckoned: German Immigration to Texas, 1844-1847*. Waco: Texian Press, 1966.

Geue, Ethel Hander. *New Homes in a New Land: German Immigration to Texas, 1847-1861*. Waco: Texian Press, 1970

Gibney, Mark. "United States Immigration Policy and the 'Huddled Masses' Myth." *Georgetown Immigration Law Journal* 3 (1989): 361-86.

Glazer, Nathan and Daniel P. Moynihan. *Beyond the Melting Pot*. New York: MIT Press, 1963.

Gleason, Philip. "Melting Pot: Symbol of Fusion or Confusion." *American Quarterly* 16 (1964): 20-46.

Goebel, Klaus and Manfred Wichelhaus, eds. *Aufstand der Bürger*. 3rd. ed.. Wuppertal: Peter Hammer Verlag, 1974.

Goodwyn, Frank. *Life on the King Ranch*. New York: Crowell, 1951.

Gordon, Milton M. *Assimilation in American Life*. New York: Oxford University Press, 1971.

Görtemaker, Manfred. "Restauration und Revolution 1815-1848." *Deutschland im 19. Jahrhundert*. Opladen: Leske und Budrich, 1989. 61-141.

Goyne, Minetta Altgelt. *A Life among the Texas Flora*. College Station: Texas A&M University Press, 1991.

Grabbe, Hans-Jürgen. "Before the Great Tidal Waves: Patterns of Transatlantic Migration at the Beginning of the Nineteenth Century." *Amerikastudien / American Studies* 42, no. 3 (1997): 377-89..

Graham, Richard. *Patronage and Politics in Nineteenth-Century Brazil*. Stanford, CA.: Stanford University Press, 1990

Granberry, Douglas. "Otto Buchel, Banker." *The Junior Historian*. Texas State Historical Association, nd, p. 11 and 28.

Greenblatt, Stephen. *Renaissance Self-Fashioning: From More to Shakespeare*. Chicago: University of Illinois Press, 1980.

Gregory, John Goadby. *History of Milwaukee, Wisconsin*. Vol. 2, Chicago: The S.J. Clarke Publishing Co., 1931.

Gropius, Walter. *The New Architecture and The Bauhaus*. trans. P. Morton Shand. Cambridge, MA: MIT Press, 1965.

Gunnin, Gerry C. "French Communitive Socialist Experiments in Texas, 1846-1868." M.A. thesis, Baylor University, 1964.

Günther, Markus. "Auswandererlisten und Passenger Lists 1855-1864 - Eine vergleichende Quellenkritik als methodischer Beitrag zur Auswanderungs-forschung." M.A. thesis Ruhr-Universität Bochum, 1992.

Gutmann, Myron P. and Christie G. Sample. "Land, Climate, and Settlement on the Texas Frontier." *SHQ* 99, no. 2 (Oct 1995): 137-72.

Haarmann, Albert W. "Deutsche Regimenter in der Armee der Union." *Zeitschrift für Heereskunde* 52 (1988): 338-40.

Haas, Oscar. *History of New Braunfels and Comal County, Texas 1844 – 1946*. Austin: Steck, 1968.

Habermas, Jürgen. *The Philosophical Discourse of Modernity*. Cambridge, MA: MIT Press, 1993.

———. "Zum Thema: Geschichte und Evolution." *Zur Rekonstruktion des historischen Materialismus*. Frankfurt: Suhrkamp, 1977.

Häderle, Irene. "Einwanderinnen und ihre Töchter: Deutsche kirchliche Frauenvereine und ihre Akkulturation in Ann Arbor, Michigan, 1870-1930." *Periplus 1997*. Jahrbuch für aussereuropäische Geschichte. Münster: Lit Verlag, 1997. 59-70.

Hagwood, John A. *The Tragedy of German-America: The Germans in the United States of America during the 19th Century and After*. New York: Putnam, 1940.

Halverson, Carol J. "Volga German-Russians in Minnesota." *Journal of the American Historical Society of Germans from Russia* 14, no. 2 (1991): 15-23.

Hamerow, Theodore S. *Restoration, Revolution, Reaction: Economics and Politics in Germany 1815-71*. Princeton, NJ: Princeton University Press, 1958.

Hamilton, E.C. *The Story of Monroe. . . its Past and its Progress toward the Present*. Monroe, WI: The Print Shop, Monroe Public Schools, 1976.

Handlin, Oscar. *The Uprooted: The Epic Story of the Great Migrations the Made the American People* Boston: Little, Brown, 1952.

Handy-Marchello, Barbara. "Assimilation of German-Russian and Norwegian Immigrants: A Comparison of North Dakota Pioneers." *Heritage Review* 17, no. 2 (1987): 29-32.

Hansen, Christine. "Die deutsche Auswanderung im 19, Jahrhundert - ein Mittel zur Lösung sozialer und sozialpolitischer Probleme?" in Günter Moltmann, ed. *Deutsche Amerikaauswanderung im 19. Jahrhundert*. Stuttgart: Metzler, 1976.

Hansen, Marcus Lee. "The History of American Immigration as a Field for Research." *The American Historical Review* 32, no. 3 (April, 1927): 500-18.

———. *The Immigrant in American History*. Cambridge, MA: Harvard University Press, 1940.

Harzig, Christiane. "Chicago's German North Side, 1880-1900: The Structure of a Gilded Age Ethnic Neighborhood," in Hartmut Keil and John B. Jentz, eds. *German Workers in Industrial Chicago, 1850-1910: A Comparative Perspective*. DeKalb: Northern Illinois University Press, 1983. 127-44.

——. *Familie, Arbeit und Weibliche Öffentlichkeit in einer Einwanderungsstadt: Deutschamerikanerinnen in Chicago um die Jahrhundertwende*. St. Katharinen: Scripta Mercaturae, 1991.

Hatton, Timothy J. *Migration and the International Labor Market, 1850-1939*. London: Routledge, 1994.

Haupt, Herman. "Hessisch-Amerikanische Lebensbilder. Der Verein der Vierziger und

Gustav Schleicher." *Volk und Scholle, Heimatblätter für beide Hessen, Nassau und Franfurt a.M.* Heft 1 (Juli 1922): 5-8.

———. "Gustav Schleicher: Ingenieur und amerikanischer Staatsmann, 1823-1879," and "Johann Jakob Küchler. Ingenieur und amerikanischer Politiker, 1823-1893." *Hessische Biographien.* Vol. 2. Darmstadt: Hessischer Staatsvertrag, 1920, 7-10, 112-14.

Hawgood, John A. *The Tragedy of German-America.* New York: G.P. Putnam's Sons, 1940.

Hay, Cynthia. "What is Sociological History?" in Stephen Kendrick, Pat Straw, and David McCrone, eds. *Interpreting the Past, Understanding the Present.* London: Macmillan, 1990, p. 20-37.

Hayes, Charles W. *Galveston: History of the Island and the City.* Vols 1-2. Austin: Jenkins Garrett Press, 1974.

Heald, Carolyn A. "The Irish Palatines in Ontario: Religion, Ethnicity and Rural Migration." *Canadian Papers in Rural History* 9 (1994): 17-185.

Heale, M. J. *American Anticommunism: Combating the Enemy Within, 1830-1970.* Baltimore: John Hopkins University Press, 1990

Healey, Jane F. "Privately Published Autobiographies by Texans: Their Significance for Scholars." *SHQ* 95, no. 4 (April 1992): 497-508.

Hebberd, Mary. "Cadwalader Washburn - his gift to La Crosse was a library." *Coulee Gazette* March 1976, p. 5.

Hecker, Alice Reynolds. "Friedrich Hecker." *German-American Review* (April 1946): 4-7.

Hecker, George S. *Biographical Scetch of Friedrich Karl Franz Hecker and Family Tree*, St. Louis: np, 1991.

Heinemann, Hartmut . "'Wo der Stern im Blauen Felde eine Neue Welt verkündet': die Auswanderung der Vierziger aus Darmstadt nach Texas im Jahre 1847 und ihre kommunistische Kolonie Bettina." *Archiv für hessische Geschichte und Altertumskunde* 52 (1994): 283-352.

Heinen, Hubert P. "The Consciousness of Being German: Regional Literature in German Texas." in Theodore Gish and Richard Spuler, eds. *Eagle in the New World.* College Station: Texas A&M University Press, 1986. 132-58.

Helbich, Wolfgang. "Deutsche Auswanderer in den USA im 19. Jahrhundert: Asylbewerber, Gastarbeiter, Wirtschaftsflüchtlinge." *Periplus 1997.* Jahrbuch für aussereuropäische Geschichte, Münster: LIT, 1997, 14-32.

———. "Die 'Englischen': German Immigrants Describe Nineteenth-Century American Society." *Amerikastudien / American Studies* 36, no. 4 (1991): 515-30.

———. "Immigrant Adaptation at the Individual Level: The Evidence of Ninetenth-Century German-American Letters." *Amerikastudien / American Studies* 42, no. 3 (1997): 407-18.

———. "The Letters They Sent Home: The Subjective Perspective of German Immigrants in the Nineteenth Century." *Yearbook of German-American Studies* 22 (1987): 1-20.

———. "Problems of Editing and Interpreting Immigrant Letters," in Hieronim Kubiak ed. *Emigration from Northern, Central and Southern Europe: Theoretical and Methodological Principles of Research.* International Symposium, Kroków, November 9-11, 1981, Zeszyty Naukowe Uniwersytetu Jagiellonskiego, DCCXXXII, Prace Polonijne* Z. 8, Krakow, 1984.

Henretta, James A. "The Protestant Ethic and the Reality of Capitalism in Colonial America," in Hartmut Lehmann and Günther Roth, eds. *Weber's Protestant Ethic - Origins, Evidence, Contexts.* Washington, D.C.: Cambridge University Press, 1993, 327-46.

Hense-Jensen, Wilhelm. *Wisconsin's Deutsch-Amerikaner bis zum Schluss des Neunzehnten Jahrhunderts.* Vols. 1-2. Milwaukee: Im Verlage der Deutschen Gesellschaft, 1900-

1902. Vol. 2, chapter two, "The Forty Eighters," translated by Joseph Schafer in 1939, in Joseph Schafer Papers, Box 6, Mss, 746, The State Historical Society of Wisconsin, Madison, Wis.

Hepp, Gerd, Hans Schleuning, and Gabriele Süsskind, eds. *Badische Geschichte - vom Großherzogtum bis zur Gegenwart*. Stuttgart: Konrad Theiss Verlag, 1979.

Herff, Ferdinand Peter. *The Doctors Herff: A Three-Generation Memoir*. Vols 1-2. San Antonio: Trinity University Press, 1973.

Hobsbawm, Eric. "On History from Below" and "On the Revival of Narrative." *On History*. London: Weidenfeld&Nicolson 1997, 201-16, 186-91.

Hofmeister, Rudolf A. *The Germans of Chicago*. Champaign, IL: Stipes Publishing Company, 1976.

Hoerder, Dirk. *People on the Move: Migration, Acculturation, and Ethnic Interaction in Europe and North America*. German Historical Institute Washington, D.C., Annual Lecture Series No. 6. Providence, RI: Berg Publishers, 1993.

Hoerder, Dirk and Nagler, Jörg, eds. *People in Transit: German Migrations in Comparative Perspective, 1820-1930*. New York: Cambridge University Press, 1995.

Hoerder, Dirk and Horst Rössler, eds. *Distant Magnets: Expectations and Realities in the Immigrant Experience*. New York: Cambridge University Press, 1993.

Hoerig, Karl A. "The Relationship between German Immigrants and the Native Peoples in Western Texas." *SHQ* 97, no. 3 (Jan 1994): 423-51.

Hoerner, Ludwig. *Das photographische Gewerbe in Deutschland*. 1839-1914, Düsseldorf: GFW-Verlag, 1989

Hofstadter, Richard. *The Paranoid Style in American Politics and Other Essays*. New York: Alfred A. Knopf, 1965.

Hoge, Cecil C., Sr. *The First Hundred Years are the Toughest: What We can Learn from the Century of Competition between Sears and Wards*. Berkeley, CA: Ten Speed Press, 1988.

Hollinger, David A. "National Solidarity at the End of the Twentieth Century: Reflections on the United States and Liberal Nationalism." *The Journal of American History* 84, no. 2 (1997): 559-69.

Hölzle, Erwin. *Die Selbstentmachtung Europas*. Göttingen: Musterschmidt, 1975.

Höppner, Joachim und Waltraud. *Von Babeuf bis Blanqui - Französischer Sozialismus und Kommunismus vor Marx*. Vols. 1-2. Leipzig: Verlag Philipp Reclam jun., 1975.

Holtmann, Antonius. "Vom 'finstern Winkel Deutschlands' nach Amerika." *Genealogie* 46 (1997): 449-62.

Howe, Irving. *World of Our Fathers: The Journey of the East European Jews to America and the Life They Found and Made*. New York: Harcourt Brace Jovanovich, 1976.

Howard, Robert P. *Illinois: A History of the Prairie State*. Grand Rapids: William B. Eerdmans, 1972.

Hug, Wolfgang. *Geschichte Badens*. Stuttgart: Konrad Theiss Verlag, 1992.

Hutchinson, Edward P. *Immigrants and their Children*. New York: Oxford University Press, 1956.

Hyman, Sidney. *The Aspen Idea*. Norman, OK: University of Oklahoma Press, 1975.

Igger, Georg G. "Comments on F. R. Ankersmit's Paper, 'Historicism: An Attempt At Synthesis.'" *History and Theory* 34 (1995): 162-67.

Inoki, Takenori. *Aspects of German Peasant Emigration to the United States 1815-1914*. New York: Arno Press, 1981.

Iseminger, Gordon L. "The Mcintosh County German-Russians: The First Fifty Years." *North Dakota History* 51, no. 3 (1984): 4-23.

Jenks, Rosemary. "Byliner: Rhetoric versus reality - the new U.S. immigration law," *U.S. Information and Texts*, Z 12481 B, No. 017, April 30, 1997, p. 17

Jensen, Richard J. *Illinois: A Bicentennial History*. New York: W.W.Norton & Company, Inc., 1978.

Johannsen, Robert *Stephen A. Douglas*. New York: Oxford University Press, 1973.

Johnson, Frank W. *A History of Texas and Texans*. Vol. 3. Chicago: The American Historical Society, 1916.

Johnson, Hildegarde B. "The Location of German Immigrants in the Middlewest." *Annals of the Association of American Geographers* 41 (March 1951): 1-51.

Jones, Maldwyn A. *Destination America*. London: Weidenfeld and Nicolson, 1976.

Jordan, Gilbert. *German Texana*. Austin: Eakin Press, 1980.

Jordan, Terry G. *German Seed in Texas Soil*. Austin: University of Texas Press, 1985.

———. "The German Settlement of Texas after 1865." *SHQ* 73, no. 2 (Oct. 1969): 193-212.

Just, Michael, Agnes Bretting, and Hartmut Bickelmann. *Von Deutschland nach Amerika: Zur Sozialgeschichte der Auswanderung im 19. und 20. Jahrhundert*. Stuttgart: Steiner Verlag, 1992.

Kalkschmidt, Eugen. *Biedermeiers Glück und Ende*. München: Verlag Georg D.W. Callwey, 1957.

Kamphoefner, Walter D. "Texas Germans and Civil War Issues: The Evidence from Immigrant Letters." *The Journal of the German-Texan Heritage Society* 13, no.1 (Spring 1991): 16-23.

- *The Westfalians: From Germany to Missouri*. Princeton: Princeton University Press, 1987.

Kattermann, Hildegard. *Das Ende einer jüdischen Landgemeinde. Nonnenweier in Baden, 1933-1945*. Freiburg i. Br.: Verlag Wolf Mersch, 1984.

Kattner, Lauren Ann. "From Immigrant Settlement into Town: New Braunfels, Texas, 1845-1870." *Amerikastudien / American Studies* 36, no. 2 (1991): 155-77.

Kazal, Russell. "Revisiting Assimilation: The Rise, Fall and Reappraisal of a Concept in American History." *American Historical Review* 100 (1995): 437-71.

Kearney, Milo and Harriett Denise Joseph. "Brownsville's French and German Distant Reflection of Their Interaction." *Journal of the American Studies Association of Texas* 23 (1992): 61-76.

Keil, Hartmut. "Einwandererviertel und Amerikanische Gesellschaft: Zur Integration Deutscher Einwanderer in die Amerikanische städtisch-industrielle Umwelt des ausgehenden 19. Jahrhunderts am Beispiel Chicagos." *Archiv für Sozialgeschichte* 24 (1984): 47-89.

Keister, Philip L. and Mary X. Barrett, Mary X., eds. *History of Stephenson County, 1970*. Freeport, IL: The County of Stephenson, 1972.

Kell, Eva. *Das Fürstentum Leiningen, Umbruchserfahrungen einer Adelsherrschaft zur Zeit der Französischen Revolution*. Kaiserslautern: Institut für Pfälzische Geschichte und Volkskunde, 1993.

Keller, Phyllis. *States of Belonging: German-American Intellectuals and the First World War*. Cambridge, MA: Harvard University Press, 1979.

Kelly, Douglas F. *The Emergence of Liberty in the Modern World*. Phillipsburg: Presbyterian and Reformed Publishing Company, 1992.

Kennedy, David M. "Can we still afford to be a Nation of Immigrants?" *The Atlantic Monthly* 278, no. 5 (Nov 1996): 52-68.

Kennedy, John F. *A Nation of Immigrants*. New York: Perennial Library/Harper & Row. Publishers, 1986.

Keynes, John Maynard. "General Theory of Employment, Money, and Interest." *Collected Writings of John Maynard Keynes*. Vol. 5. London: Macmillan, 1973.

King, Irene Marschall. *John O. Meusebach: German Colonizer in Texas*. Austin: University of Texas Press, 1967.

Kloberdanz, Timothy J. "In the Land of Inyan Wosleta: Plains Indian Influences on Reservation Whites." *Great Plains Quarterly* 7, no. 2 (1987): 69-82.

Klotzbach, Kurt. "Ernst Kapp, der Gründer der 'Lateinischen Kolonie' Sisterdale." *Mindener Geschichtsverein* 54 (1982): 21-51.

Koch, Fred C. *The Volga Germans: In Russia & The Americas, 1763 to the Present*. University Park, PA.: Pennsylvania State University Press, 1977.

Koenig, Robert F. *Camera Studies of Freeport, Illinois*. Freeport, IL: Wagner Printing Co., 1954.

Konecny, Lawrence H. and Clinton Machann. "German and Czech Immigration to Texas: The Bremen to Galveston Route, 1880-1886." *Nebraska History* 74 ,no. 3 (1993): 136-41.

Kramer, William A. "The Saxons in Perry County." *Lutheran Quarterly* 3, no.4 (1989): 357-72.

Krebs, Richard. *Amorbach im Odenwald: ein Heimatbuch*. Amorbach: Druck und Verlag der Gottlob Volkhardt'schen Druckerei, Gebr. Volkhardt, 1923.

Küffner, Cornelia. "Texas-Germans' Attitudes Towards Slavery: Biedermeier Sentiments and Class-Consciousness in Austin, Colorado and Fayette Counties." M.A. thesis, University of Houston, 1994.

Kuyper, Susan Jean. "The Americanization of German Immigrants: Language, Religion and Schools in Nineteenth Century Rural Wisconsin." Ph.D. dissertation. University of Wisconsin at Madison, 1980.

Lang, Barbara. "Immigration in German-American Literature." *Yearbook of German American Studies* 22 (1987): 39-57.

Larwood, Laurie and Marion M. Wood. *Women in Management*. Lexington, MA.: Heath, 1977.

LeCompte, Mary Lou. "German-American Turnvereins in Frontier Texas, 1851-1880." *Journal of the West* 26, no. 1 (1987): 18-25.

Lee, Loyd E. *The Politics of Harmony; Civil Service, Liberalism, and Social Reform in Baden, 1800-1850*. Newark: University of Delaware Press, 1980

Leftwich, Joseph. *Israel Zangwill*. London: Clarke, 1957.

Lehmann, Hartmut and Hermann Wellenreuther, eds. *In Search of Peace and Prosperity: New German Settlements in Eighteenth-Century Europe and America*. University Park, PA: Pennsylvania State University Press, 1999.

Lehmann, Winfred. "Lone Star German."in Joseph Wilson, ed. *Texas and Germany: Crosscurrents*. Rice University Studies 63, no. 3 (Summer 1977): 73-81.

Lekisch, Kurt. "Dr. Ferdinand von Herff: Idealistic Pioneer and Distinguished Texas Physician." *Texas Medicine* 82 (August 1986): 48-52.

Levi, Kate Everest. "Geographical Origin of German Immigration to Wisconsin." *Wisconsin Historical Collections*.Vol. 14. Madison, WI: The State Historical Society of Wisconsin, 1898. 341-93.

Levine, Bruce. *The Spirit of 1848: German Immigrants, Labor Conflict, and the Coming of the Civil War*. Urbana: University of Illinois Press, 1992.

Lich, Glen E. *The German Texans*. San Antonio: The University of Texas Institute of Texan Cultures at San Antonio, 1981.

———. "Survival and Succession: Immigrant Autobiography as Cultural Legacy." *Yearbook of German-American Studies* 24 (1989): 59-72.

Lich, Glen E., Günter Moltmann, and T. Michael Womack. "'New Crowns to Old Glory': Archives of the German Adelsverein." *The Yale University Library Gazette* 63, nos. 3-4 (April 1989): 145-57.

Lich, Glen E. and Dona B. Reeves. *German Culture in Texas.* Boston: Twayne, 1980.

Loewen, Royden. "New Themes in an Old Story: Transplanted Mennonites as Group Settlers in North America, 1874-1879." *Journal of American Ethnic History* 11, no. 2 (1992): 3-26.

Loewenberg, Bert James. *American History in American Thought* New York: Simon and Schuster, 1972.

Longacre, Edward G. "A Young German Joins the Cavalry." *Manuscripts* 40, no. 4 (1988): 323-25.

Lonn, Ella. *Desertion during the Civil War.* New York: Century Co., 1928.

———. *Foreigners in the Confederacy*. Chapel Hill: University of North Carolina Press, 1940.

Lougee, Robert W. *Midcentury Revolution, 1848: Society and Revolution in France and Germany*. Lexington, MA: Heath, 1972.

Luebke, Frederick C. *Ethnic Voters and the Election of Lincoln.* Lincoln, NE: University of Nebraska Press, 1971.

———. *Germans in the New World: Essays in the History of Immigration.* Urbana: University of Illioins Press, 1990.

———. "The Germans," in John Higham, ed. *Ethnic Leadership in America.* Baltimore: John Hopkins University Press, 1978, 64-90.

Lukacs, John. *The Last European War.* New York: Anchor Press/ Doubleday, 1976.

Lunte, Gabriele. "The German Bohemian Culture and Heritage of the Catholic Bucovinians in Ellis, Kansas." *Heritage of the Great Plains* 27, no. 2 (1994): 51-64.

Lurix, Karl A. "The Open Door." *Journal of the American Historical Society of Germans from Russia* 11, no. 4 (1988): 15-20.

McComb, David G. *Galveston: A History*. Austin: University of Texas Press, 1986.

McGuire, James Patrick. *Hermann Lungkwitz: Romantic Landscapist on the Texas Frontier*. Austin: University of Texas Press, 1983.

———. "Observations on German Artists in Texas," Theodore Gish and Richard Spuler, eds. *Eagle in the New World.* College Station: Texas A&M University Press, 1986. 181-200.

McKay, Seth S. *Texas Politics, 1906-1944: With Special Reference to German Counties.* Lubbock, Texas: Texas Tech. University Press, 1952

McWilliams, Carey. *Ill Fares the Land: Migrants and Migratory Labor in the United States.* Boston: Little, Brown & Company, 1942

Malsch, Brownson. *Indianola, the Mother of Western Texas.* Austin: State House Press, 1988.

Marquette, Clare L. "The Business Activities of C.C. Washburn," Ph.D. dissertation, University of Wisconsin, 1940.

Marten, James. *Texas Divided: Loyalty and Dissent in the Lone Star State 1856-1874.* Lexington, Kentucky: The University Press of Kentucky, 1990.

Maurer, Heinrich H. "The Lutheran Community and American Society: A Study in Religion as a Condition of Social Accomodation." *American Journal of Sociology* 34 (Sept 1928): 282-95.

Mehländer, Andrea. *"In Dixieland I'll Take My Stand" : The German Communities of Charleston, Richmond and New Orleans During the Civil War.* Columbia, SC: University of South Carolina Press, 2001.

Meredith, Hugh E. "Ernst, Johann Friedrich." *The New Handbook of Texas*. Vol. 2. Austin: The Texas State Historical Association, 1996, 884.

Metz, Leon. *John Wesley Hardin: Dark Angel of Texas*. El Paso: Mangan Books, 1996.

Metzenthin-Raunick, Selma Marie. "One Hundred Years *Neu Braunfesler Zeitung*." *American-German Review* 19, no. 6 (1953): 15-16.

Miller, Eugene C. "The Contributions of German Immigrants to the Union Cause in Kentucky." *Filson Club History Quarterly* 64, no. 4 (1990): 462-78.

———. "German Immigrants at Antietam." *Maryland Historical Magazine* 87, no.3 (1992): 309-15.

Mink, Gwendolyn. *The Wages of Motherhood: Inequality in the Welfare State, 1917-1942*. Ithaca: Cornell University Press, 1996.

Mitchell, Lee Clark. *Westerns: Making the Man in Fiction and Film*. Chicago: University of Chicago Press, 1996.

Moltmann, Günter. *Germans to America: 300 Years of Immigration, 1683-1983*. Stuttgart: Institute for Foreign Cultural Relations, 1982.

———. "American-German Return Migration in the Nineteenth and Early Twentieth Centuries," in George E. Pozzetta. *Emigration & Immigration: The Old World Confronts the New*. New York: Garland Publishing, 1991, 470-84.

———. "Roots in Germany: Immigration and Acculturation of German-Americans," in Theodore Gish and Richard Spuler, eds. *Eagle in the New World: German Immigration to Texas and America*. College Station: Texas A&M University Press, 1986, 3-25.

Morawska, Ewa, "In Defense of the Assimilation Model." *Journal of American Ethnic History* 13 (Winter 1994): 76-87.

- "The Sociology and Historiography of Immigration," in Virginia Yans-McLaughlin, ed. *Immigration Reconsidered*. New York: Oxford University Press, 1990, 187- 238.

Mostert, Noël. *Frontiers: The Epic of South Africa's Creation and the Tragedy of the Xhosa People*. New York: Alfred A. Knopf, 1992.

Mueller, Theodore. "Milwaukee's German Cultural Heritage." *Milwaukee History* 10, no. 3) (1987): 95-108.

Murphree, Nellie and Robert W. Shook. *A History of DeWitt County*,.Victoria, np, 1962.

N.N., *Allgemeine Deutsche Biographie*. Vols. 25 and 31. Leipzig: Duncker & Humblot, 1887.

———. *History of Green County, Wisconsin*. Springfield, IL: Union Publishing Company, 1884.

———. *The History of Stephenson County, Illinois*. Chicago: Western Historical Company, 1880.

———. *History of Stephenson County, 1970*. Mount Morris, IL: Kable Printing Company, 1972.

———. *Information Please Almanac. Atlas and Yearbook. 1995*, 48th ed. Boston: Houghton Mifflin, 1995.

———. *In the Foot-Prints of the Pioneers of Stephenson County, Illinois*. Freeport, IL: The Pioneer Publishing Co., 1900.

———. "The Mission and Method of the Aspen Institute." *The Aspen Institute*. Queenstown, MD: The Aspen Institute, 1994.

———. *Portrait and Biographical Album of Stephenson County, Ill*. Chicago: Chapman Brothers, 1888.

———. "The Washburn Triumvirate." *Wisconsin Then And Now* 7, no. 4 (Nov 1960): 1, 8.

———. "Territorial Limitation in the Lumber Trade," *Northwestern Lumberman* 22 (February 1890): 2.

Nadel, Stanley. *Little Germany: Ethnicity, Religion, and Class in New York City, 1845-80.* Urbana: University of Illinois Press, 1990.

Nagler, Jörg. "Politisches Exil in den USA zur Zeit des Vormärz und der Revolution von 1848/49," Michael Salewski and Jürgen Elvert, eds. *Deutschland und der Westen im 19. und 20. Jahrhundert.* Band 1, Historische Mitteilungen der Ranke Gesellschaft, Beiheft 7, Stuttgart: Franz Steiner Verlag, 1993, 267-93.

———. "'Ubi libertas, ibi patria': Deutsche Demokraten im Exil," in Alfred G. Frei, ed. *Friedrich Hecker in den USA.* Konstanz: Stadler Verlagsgesellschaft, 1993. 61-71.

Naylor, Gillian. *The Bauhaus.* London: Studio Vista/Dutton Pictureback, 1968.

Neumaier, Helmut. *Geschichte der Stadt Boxberg mit Beiträgen über ihre Stadtteile.* Boxberg: Stadt Boxberg, 1987.

Neumann, Hannes. *Die deutsche Turnbewegung in der Revolution 1848/49 und in der amerikanischen Emigration.* Stuttgart: Hofmann, 1968.

Nevins, Allan. *The Emergence of Lincoln.*Vol. 1-2. London: Charles Scribner's Sons, 1950.

Newcomb, William W. and Mary S. Carnahan. *German Artist on the Texas Frontier: Friedrich Richard Petri.* Austin: University of Texas Press, 1978.

Nielsen, George R. *In Search of a Home: Nineteenth-Century Wendish Immigration.* College Station: Texas A&M University Press, 1989.

Nugent, Walter. "Four New-World Migration Targets: Some Comparisons." *Amerikastudien / American Studies* 42, no. 3 (1997): 391-406.

Oates, Stephen B. *Let the Trumpet Sound; the life of Martin Luther King, Jr.* New York: Mentor Books, 1985.

O'Connor, Richard. *The German-Americans: An Informal History.* Boston: Little, Brown, 1968.

Ostendorf, Berndt. "'America is a Mistake, a Gigantic Mistake': Patterns of Ethnocentrism in German Attitudes Towards America." *In Their Own Words* 3, no. 2 (1986): 19-47.

Ostendorf, Berndt. ed. *Multikulturelle Gesellschaft: Modell Amerika?* München: Fink Verlag, 1994.

Ozinga, James R. *Communism: The Story of the Idea and its Implementation.* Englewood Cliffs, NJ: Prentice-Hall, 1987.

Pakenham, Thomas. *The Scramble for Africa.* London: George Weidenfeld & Nicolson, 1991.

Paul, Roland. "'Freie Erde und freies Vaterland'—Friedrich Hecker in den USA," in Alfred G. Frei, ed. *Friedrich Hecker in den USA.* Konstanz: Stadler Verlagsgesellschaft mbH, 1993. 15-41.

Pergl, Gary, ed. *Generation of Change: The Civil Rights Movement in America.* Washington, D.C.: United States Information Agency, 1989.

Petersen, William. *Japanese Americans: Oppression and Success.* New York: Random House, 1971.

Pickle, Linda Schelbitzki. "A German Immigrant in Postbellum Fulton." *Missouri Historical Review* 86, no. 2 (1992): 149-63.

———. "Rural German-Speaking Women in Early Nebraska and Kansas: Ethnicity as a Factor in Frontier Adaptation." *Great Plains Quarterly* 9, no. 4 (1989) 239-51.

———. "Stereotypes and Reality: Nineteenth-Century German Women in Missouri." *Missouri Historical Review* 79, no. 3 (1985): 291-312.

Pickrell, Annie Doom. ed. *Pioneer Women in Texas.* Austin: Jenkins Publishers, 1970.

Pletcher, David M. *The Diplomacy of Annexation: Texas, Oregon and the Mexican War.* Columbia, MO: University of Missouri Press, 1973.

Pochmann, Henry A. *Bibliography of German Culture in America to 1940.* Madison: State Historical Society of Wisconsin, 1953.

Pörksen, Martin. "Schleswig-Holsteinische Pastoren für Nordamerika." *Zeitschrift der Gesellschaft für Kanada-Studien*. Vol. 10, no.2 (1990): 91-96.
Portes, Alejandro. "From South of the Border: Hispanic Minorities in the United States," in Virginia Yans-McLaughlin. *Immigration Reconsidered*. New York: Oxford University Press, 1990, 160-84.
Powell, Gary N. *Women and Men in Management*. Newbury Park, CA: Sage Pub., 1988.
Pozzetta, George E. *Emigration and Immigration: The Old World Confronts the New*. New York: Garland, 1991.
Press, Volker. "Südwestdeutschland im Zeitalter der Französischen Revolution und Napoleons." *Baden und Württemberg im Zeitalter Napoleons*. Vol 2. Stuttgart: Edition Cantz, 1987.
Raeithel, Gert. *Geschichte der Nordamerikanischen Kultur*. Vols 1-3. Frankfurt/Main: Zweitausendeins, 1995.
———. *"Go West" : Ein psychohistorischer Versuch über die Amerikaner*. 2nd. ed. Hamburg: Europäische Verlagsanstalt, 1993.
Ransleben, Guido E. *A Hundred Years of Comfort in Texas, A Centennial History*. San Antonio: Naylor, 1954.
Rappard, C. H. *Die Pilgermission zu St. Chrischona, 1840-1908*. Basel: Schriften-Niederlage zu St. Chrischona, 1908.
Ratcliffe, Sam DeShong. *Painting Texas History to 1900*. Austin: University of Texas Press, 1992.
Ravenstein, E.G. "The Laws of Migration." *Journal of the Royal Statistical Society* (1889): 241-301.
Real, Willy. *Die Revolution in Baden 1848/49*. Stuttgart: Verlag W. Kohlhammer, 1983.
Redfield, Robert, Ralph Linton, and Melville J. Herskovits. "A Memorandum for the Study of Acculturation." *American Anthropologist* 38, no. 1 (Jan-Mar 1936)
Reed, St. Clair Griffin. *A History of the Texas Railroads*. Houston: The St. Clair Publishing Company, 1941.
Reich, Uwe. "Zur Sozialgeschichte der Auswanderung aus dem Regierungsbezirk Frankfurt/Oder im 19. Jahrhundert." *Jahrbuch für Wirtschaftsgeschichte* no. 2 (1992): 97-127.
Reimers, David M. *Unwelcome Strangers: American Identity and the Turn against Immigration* New York: Columbia University Press, 1999.
Rese, Beate. *Texas, Ziel deutscher Auswanderung im 19. Jahrhundert*. Pfaffenweiler: Centaurus Verlag, 1996.
Richardson, Alan. "A Theory and Method for the Psychological Study of Assimilation." *International Migration Review* 2, no. 1 (1967): 3-30.
Richter, Anthony H. "A Heritage of Faith: Religion and the German Settlers of South Dakota." *South Dakota History* 21,no. 2 (1991): 155-72.
Rickert, Heinrich. *Science and History*. Princeton: Van Nostrand, 1962.
Ricœr, Paul. "History and Rhetoric," in François Bédarida, ed. *The Social Responsability of the Historian*. Providence/Oxford: Berghahn Books, 1994, p. 7-24.
Rifkin, Jeremy. *The End of Work. The Decline of the Global Labor Force and the Dawn of the Post-Market Era*. New York: Putnam's Sons, 1995.
Rippy, J. Fred. "Border Troubles along the Rio Grande, 1848-1860." *SHQ* 23, no. 2 (Oct 1919): 91-111.
Rips, Rae Elizabeth. "An Introductory Study of the Role of the Mail Order Business in American History, 1872-1914." M.A. thesis, University of Chicago, 1938.
Robbert, Louise Buenger. "Lutheran Families in St. Louis and Perry County, Missouri, 1839-1870." *Missouri Historical Review* 82. no. 4 (1988): 424-38.

Roeber, A. Gregg. "'Troublesome Riches': Protestant and Catholic Stewardship of a Capitalist World, 1698-1815." *Amerikastudien / American Studies* 42, no.3 (1997): 357-75.

Roediger, David R. *The Wages of Whiteness: Race and the Making of the American Working Class*. London: Verso, 1991.

Röhrich, Lutz. "German Emigrant Songs," in Theodore Gish and Richard Spuler, eds. *Eagle in the New World*. College Station: Texas A&M University Press, 1986. 47-84.

Rogers, Andrei, ed. *Migration and Settlement: A Multiregional Comparative Study*. Dordrecht: Reidel, 1986.

Rogers, Theresa F. and Nathalie S. Friedman. *Printers Face Automation*. Lexington MA: D. C. Heath and Company, 1980.

Rogin, Michael. *Blackface, White Noise: Jewish Immigrants in the Hollywood Melting Pot*. Berkeley: University of California Press, 1996.

———. "'Make My Day!': Spectacle as Amnesia in Imperial Politics," in H. Aram Veeser, ed. *The New Historicism Reader*. New York: Routledge, 1994, 229-54.

Rosenzweig, Roy. *Eight Hours for What We Will: Workers and Leisure in an Industrial City, 1870-1920*. New York: Cambridge University Press, 1983.

Ross, Rudolph H. *Milwaukee*. Milwaukee, WI: Schnellpressen-Druck des "Herold," 1871.

Rudnick, Adalbert. *Die Kommunistische Idee: Geschichte und Darstellung*. München: Günter Olzog Verlag, 1972.

Salyer, Lucy E. *Laws Harsh as Tigers: Chinese Immigrants and the Shaping of Modern Immigration Law*. Chapel Hill: University of North Carolina Press, 1995.

Sandburg, Carl. *Abraham Lincoln, The Prairie Years and the War Years*. New York: Harcourt Brace Jovanovich, 1974.

Schafer, Joseph. *The Wisconsin Lead Region*. Madison: State Historical Society of Wisconsin, 1932.

Schatz, Thomas. *Hollywood Genres: Formulas, Filmmaking, and the Studio System*. New York: Random House, 1981.

Schenk, Trudy and Ruth Froelke. *The Wuerttemberg Emigration Index*. Vol. 2. Salt Lake City, Ancestry Publishing, 1986.

Schieber, Clara E. *The Transformation of American Sentiment Toward Germany, 1870-1914*. Boston: Cornhill Publishing, 1923.

Schlesinger, Arthur M., Jr. *The Disuniting of America: Reflections on a Multicultural Society*. Knoxville, TN: Whittle Direct Books, 1991.

Schmelzle, Robert J., ed. *Freeport Debate Centennial*. Freeport, IL: Wagner Printing Company, 1958.

Schmid, Hermann. "Die Säkularisation und Mediatisation in Baden und Württemberg." *Baden und Württemberg im Zeitalter Napoleons*. Vol 2. Stuttgart: Edition Cantz, 1987.

Schöberl, Ingrid. *Amerikanische Einwandererwerbung in Deutschland, 1845-1914*. Stuttgart: Franz Steiner Verlag, 1990.

Schuck, Peter H. *Citizens, Strangers, and In-Betweens: Essays on Immigration and Citizenship*. Boulder, CO: Westview Press, 1998.

Schuck, Peter H. and Rainer Munz, eds. *Paths to Inclusion*. Providence, RI: Berghahn Books, 1998.

Schülin, Fritz. *Brombach*. Brombach: Druckerei Gebr. Weber, 1972.

Schulze, Hagen. *Staat und Nation in der Europäischen Geschichte*. München: Verlag C.H. Beck, 1994

Senger und Etterlin, Stefan von. *Neu-Deutschland in Nordamerika*. Baden-Baden: Nomos Verlagsgesellschaft, 1991.

Shook, Robert W. "The Battle of the Nueces, August 10, 1862." *SHQ* 66, no. 1 (July 1962): 31-42.

Shumsky, Neil L. "Zangwill's *The Melting Pot*: Ethinc Tensions on Stage." *American Quarterly* 27 (1975): 24-48.

Sibley, Marilyn McAdams. *Travelers in Texas 1761-1860*. Austin: University of Texas Press, 1967.

Siebold, Werner. *Unser Fritzing - ein Lebensbild Fritz Reuters*. Gießen: Emil Roth Verlag, n.d.

Siemann, Wolfram. *Vom Staatenbund zum Nationalstaat - Deutschland 1806-1871*. München: C.H. Beck Verlag, 1995.

Sloan, Karin Ramspeck. "Trading the Pen for the Spade: 19th-Century German Immigrant Literature in Texas." Ph.D. dissertation, Texas A&I University, 1990.

Sollors, Werner. *Beyond Ethnicity: Consent and Descent in American Culture*. New York: Oxford University Press, 1986.

Sonnichsen, Charles Leland. *Ten Texas Feuds*. Albuquerque: University of New Mexico Press, 1957.

Spahn, Raymond Jürgen. "German Accounts of Early Nineteenth-Century Life in Illinois." *Papers on Language and Literature* 14, no. 4 (Fall 1978): 473-88.

Spann, Edward K. *The New Metropolis, New York City, 1840-1857*. New York: Columbia University Press, 1981.

Stempfel, Theodore. *Fifty Years of Unrelenting German Aspirations in Indianapolis, 1848-1898*. Indianapolis: German-American Center and Indiana German Heritage Society, 1991.

Stephenson, George M. *A History of American Immigration*. New York: Russell & Russell, 1964.

Stöhr, Louise. "Die erste deutsche Frau in Texas." *Der deutsche Pionier* 16 (1884): 372-75.

Stratton, Joanna L. *Pioneer Women*. New York: Simon and Schuster, 1981.

Struck, Wolf-Heino. *Die Auswanderung aus dem Herzogtum Nassau 1806-1866: Ein Kapitel der modernen politischen und sozialen Entwicklung*. Wiesbaden: Franz Steiner Verlag, 1966.

Struke, Horst and Wilfried Forstmann, eds. *Die europäischen Revolutionen von 1848*. Königstein/Ts.: Verlag Anton Hain Meisenheim, 1979.

Struve, Walter. *Germans and Texans: Commerce, Migration, and Culture in the Days of the Lone Star Republic*. Austin: University of Texas Press, 1996.

———. *Die Republik Texas, Bremen und das Hildesheimische*, Hildesheim: Verlag August Lax, 1983.

———. "German Merchants, German Artisans, and Texas During the 1830s and 1840s." *Yearbook of German-American Studies* 23 (1988): 91-103.

Swierenga, Robert P. "The Settlement of the Old Northwest: Ethnic Pluralism in a Featureless Plain." *Journal of the Early Republic* 9, no. 1 (1989): 73-105.

Sudhaus, Fritz. *Deutschland und die Auswanderung nach Brasilien im 19. Jahrhundert*. Hamburg: Christians Verlag, 1940.

Thistlewaite, Frank. "Migration from Europe Overseas in the Nineteenth and Twentieth Centuries." *Rapports* 5: *Histoire Contemporaine*, XIe Congrès International des Sciences Historiques. Stockholm: Almquist&Wiksell, 1960, 32-60.

Tilby, Wilma B.N. "Jakob Brand's Register of Dutchtown, German Mining Colony." *Utah Historical Quarterly* 61, no. 1 (1994): 53-70.

Tilly, Charles. "Future Histor," in Stephen Kendrick, Pat Straw, David McCrone, eds. *Interpreting the Past, Understanding the Present*. London: The Macmillan Press, 1990, 9-19.

Tischauser, Leslie Vincent. "The Burden of Ethnicity: The German Question in Chicago, 1914-1941." Ph.D. dissertation, University of Illinois at Chicago, 1981.

Thym-Hochrein, Nancy. "'Peter Left Because . . .': A Comparative Study of Oral Family Histories." *Scandinavian Yearbook of Folklore* 37 (1981): 61-68.

Tolzmann, Don Heinrich. *German-Americana: A Bibliography*. Metuchen, NJ: Scarecrow Press, 1975.

———. *Germany and America (1450-1700): Julius Friedrich Sachse's History of the German Role in the Discovery, Exploration, and Settlement of the New World*. Bowie, MD: Heritage Books, 1991.

Townsend, Andrew Jacke. *The Germans of Chicago. Jahrbuch der Deutsch-Amerikanischen Historischen Gesellschaft von Illinois* 32. Chicago: The University of Chicago Press, 1932.

Treckel, Paula A. *To Comfort the Heart: Women in Seventeenth-Century America*. New York: Twayne, 1996.

Trefousse, Hans L. "Class and Ethnicity: German Immigrants, Radicalism, and the Civil War." *Reviews in American History* 21, no.2 (1993): 213-17.

Trommler, Frank and Joseph McVeigh, eds. *America and the Germans: An Assessment of a Three-Hundred-Year History*. Vols. 1-2. Philadelphia: University of Pennsylvania Press, 1985.

Tucker, Robert W. "Immigration and Foreign Policy: General Considerations," in Robert W. Tucker, Charles B. Keely, and Linda Wrigley, eds. *Immigration and U.S. Foreign Policy*. Boulder: Westview Press, 1990, 1-1

Turner, Frederick Jackson. "The Significance of the Frontier in American History," in George Rogers Taylor, ed. *The Turner Thesis*. Lexington, MA: D.C. Heath and Company, 1972, 3-28.

Tyler, Ron, ed. *The New Handbook of Texas*. Vols. 1-6. Austin: Texas State Historical Association, 1996.

Überhorst, Horst. *Turner unter dem Sternenbanner: Der Kampf der deutsch-amerikanischen Turner für Einheit, Freiheit und soziale Gerechtigkeit*. München: Moos, 1978.

Ulam, B. Adam. *The Unfinished Revolution, an Essay on the Sources of Influence of Marxism and Communism*. New York: Random House, 1960.

Unruh, John D., Jr. *The Plains Across: The Overland Emigrants and the Trans-Mississippi West, 1840-60*. Urbana: University of Illinois Press, 1982.

Valentin, Caroline. *Theater und Musik am Leinigenschen Hofe*. Würzburg: Kabitzsch und Mönnich, 1921.

Valentin, Veit. *Fürst Karl Leiningen und das Deutsche Einheitsproblem*. Stuttgart: J. G. Cotta'sche Buchhandlung Nachfolger, 1910.

Vecoli, Rudolph. "Contadini in Chicago: A Critique of *The Uprooted*." *The Journal of American History* 51 (Dec 1963): 404-17.

Venable, Charles L. "Texas Biedermeier Furniture." *Magazine Antiques* 127, no. 5 (1985): 1166-71.

Vialet, Joyce C. *A Brief History of U.S. Immigration Policy*. Washington, D.C.: Congressional Research Service, 1991.

von Hippel, Wolfgang. *Auswanderung aus Südwestdeutschland: Studien zur württembergischen Auswanderung und Auswanderungspolitik im 18. und 19. Jahrhundert*. Stuttgart: Klett-Cotta, 1984.

von Roeder, Flora L. *These are the Generations*. Houston: Baylor College of Medicine, 1978.

Wagner, Rolf. "Turner Societies and the Socialist Tradition," in Hartmut Keil, ed. *German Worker's Culture in the United States, 1850-1920*. Washington, D.C.: Smithonian

Institute, 1988, 221-39.

Wagner, William H. "Ein deutsches Zeitungs-Jubiläum in Illinois." *Deutsch-Amerikanische Geschichtsblätter* 4, no. 1 (January 1904): 60.

Walker, Mack. *Germany and the Emigration*. Cambridge, MA: Harvard University Press, 1964.

Wallace, Mike. "Mickey Mouse History: Portraying the Past at Disney World." *Mickey Mouse History and Other Essays in American Memory*. Philadelphia: Temple University Press, 1996, 133-57.

Wartburg, Wolfgang von. *Geschichte der Schweiz*. München: Verlag von R. Oldenbourg, 1951.

Washburn, Lilian. *My Seven Sons*. Portland, ME: Fairmont Publishing Company, 1940.

Weber, Adolf Paul, ed. *Deutsche Pioniere - zur Geschichte des Deutschtums in Texas*. Vols. 1-2. San Antonio: Selbstverlag, 1894.

Welisch, Sophie A. ""Bukovina-German Pioneers in Urban America." *Journal of the American Historical Society of Germans from Russia* 12, no. 1 (1989): 19-26.

Wells, Robert W. *This is Milwaukee*. Milwaukee, WI: Renaissance Books, 1970.

Welsch, Johann. *Arbeiten in der Informationsgesellschaft*. Studie für den Arbeitskreis "Arbeit-Betrieb-Politik" der Friedrich-Ebert-Stiftung, Bonn 1997.

Wenzel, Uwe. "Auf dem Weg zur Integration? Probleme und Perspektiven politischer Partizipation von Latinos in den USA." *Amerikastudien/ American Studies* 40, no. 3 (1995): 443-68.

White, Hayden. *The Content of the Form: Narrative Discourse and Historical Representation*. Baltimore: John Hopkins University Press, 1987.

———. "Figuring the Nature of the Times Deceased: Literary Theory and Historical Writing," in Ralph Cohen, ed. *The Future of Literary Theory*. New York: Routledge, 1989.

———. "The Value of Narrativity in the Representation of Reality," in Joyce Appleby et.al., eds. *Knowldege and Postmodernism in Historical Perspective*. New York: Routledge, 1996, 395-407

White, Morton G. *Foundations of Historical Knowledge*. New York: Oxford University Press, 1965.

———. *Social Thought in America: The Revolt Against Formalism*. New York: Viking, 1949.

Wiedemann-Citera, Barbara. *Die Auswirkungen des Ersten Weltkrieges auf die Deutsch-Amerikaner im Spiegel der New Yorker Volkszeitung und der New York Times 1914-1926*. Frankfurt am Main: Peter Lang, 1993.

Wiesenthal, Georg. "Darmstädter Auswanderer aus dem Jahre 1847." *Der Odenwald* no. 4 (1957).

Wiihöft, Harald. "Die Vereinheitlichung von Mass und Gewicht in Baden und Württemberg in Napoleonischer Zeit." *Baden und Württemberg im Zeitalter Napoleons*. Vol 2. Stuttgart: Edition Cantz, 1987.

Williamson, Jeffrey G. "Migration to the New World: Long Term Influences and Impact." *Explorations in Economic History* 11, no. 4 (Summer 1974): 357-89.

Wills, Garry. *Inventing America: Jefferson's Declaration of Independence*. New York: Vintage Books, 1979.

Wingler, Hans M. *The Bauhaus: Weimar, Dessau, Berlin, Chicago*. trans. Wolfgang Jabs and Basil Gilbert. ed. Joseph Stein. Cambridge, MA: MIT Press, 1969.

Winkel, Harald. "Der Texasverein : ein Beitrag zur Geschichte der deutschen Auswanderung im 19. Jahrhundert." *Vierteljahrschrift für Sozial- und Wirtschaftsgeschichte* 55 (1968): 348-72.

Winkel, Peter. "Skepticism Turns to Enthusiasm: Seventeen Letters Written by a German Immigrant in New Jersey to His Father in Hesse-Darmstadt Between 1852 and 1859." *Yearbook of German-American Studies* 24 (1989): 41-58.

Wisseman, Sr., Charles L., trans. *Fredericksburg, Texas. . . The First Fifty Years*. German original published 1896. Fredericksburg: Fredericksburg Publishing, 1971.

Wittke, Carl. *The German Language Press in America*. Lexington, KY: University of Kentucky Press, 1957.

———. *Refugees of Revolutions: The German Forty Eighters in America*. Philadelphia: The University of Pennsylvania Press, 1952.

———. *We Who Built America: The Saga of the Immigrant*. n.p.: The Press of Western Reserve University, 1964.

———. "American Germans in Two World Wars." *Wisconsin Magazine of History* 27 (Spring 1943): 6-16.

Yans-McLaughlin, Virginia. "Metaphors of Self in History: Subjectivity, Oral Narrative, and Immigration Studies." *Immigration Reconsidered*. New York: Oxford University Press, 1990, 254-90.

Yox, Andrew P. "Bonds of Community: Buffalo's German Element." *New York History* 66, no. 2 (1985): 140-63.

Zeitlin, Richard H. *Germans in Wisconsin*. Madison: The State Historical Society of Wisconsin, 1977.

Zimmermann, Wendy and Michael Fix. "Immigrant Policy in the States: A Wavering Welcome." *Amerikastudien/American Studies* 40, no. 3 (1995): 367-88.

Zucker, Adolph E., ed. *The Forty-Eighters: Political Refugees of the German Revolution of 1848*. New York: Russell and Russell 1950.

Zuckerman, Michael. "The Turnerian Frontier: A New Approach to the Study of American Character." *OAH Newsletter* 23, no. 4 (Nov 1995): 1, 4, 7.

Zunz, Oliver. "American History and the Changing Meaning of Assimilation." *Journal of American Ethnic History* 4 (Winter 1984): 53-72.

Index

Y

Z